PERCHANCE TO DREAM

T0285278

Perchance to DREAM

A Legal and Political History of the
DREAM Act and DACA

Michael A. Olivas

With a Foreword by Bill Richardson

NEW YORK UNIVERSITY PRESS
New York

NEW YORK UNIVERSITY PRESS
New York
www.nyupress.org

© 2020 by New York University
Paperback edition published 2024
All rights reserved

References to Internet websites (URLs) were accurate at the time of writing. Neither the author nor New York University Press is responsible for URLs that may have expired or changed since the manuscript was prepared.

Library of Congress Cataloging-in-Publication Data
Names: Olivas, Michael A., author. | Richardson, Bill, 1947 November 15—writer of
    foreword.
Title: Perchance to DREAM : a legal and political history of the DREAM act and DACA /
    Michael A. Olivas ; foreword by Bill Richardson
Description: New York : New York University Press, 2020. | Includes bibliographical
    references and index.
Identifiers: LCCN 2019033383 | ISBN 9781479878284 (cloth) | ISBN 9781479830992 (paper-
    back) | ISBN 9781479868766 (ebook) | ISBN 9781479851225 (ebook)
Subjects: LCSH: Children of illegal aliens—Legal status, laws, etc.—United States. | United
    States. Congress. Development, Relief, and Education for Alien Minors Act (Dream Act)
Classification: LCC KF4800.O45 2020 | DDC 342.7308/3—dc23
LC record available at https://lccn.loc.gov/2019033383

New York University Press books are printed on acid-free paper, and their binding materials are chosen for strength and durability. We strive to use environmentally responsible suppliers and materials to the greatest extent possible in publishing our books.

Manufactured in the United States of America

10 9 8 7 6 5 4 3 2

Also available as an ebook

Dedicated to the many thousands of undocumented and DACAmented immigrants for whom and with whom I have worked over these many years. As my own life trajectory shifts into retirement, I will never quit until you are all able to participate in this, the country you are helping forge. You have my respect and affection, on this holiest of Holy Days. Easter Sunday, 2019

CONTENTS

BILL RICHARDSON

I wish I could write a very different prologue for my dear friend's book. I wish that Dr. Michael A. Olivas and I could reflect on the advancement of immigration reform since we worked tirelessly together in New Mexico, where I served as governor from 2003 to 2011. We knew we were ahead of our time when we passed the most progressive residency law for undocumented students in the United States. We just didn't know how far ahead we were. Despite being a headline issue for the 2016 presidential campaign, it feels as if we are further away than ever before from passing comprehensive and effective immigration reform. Rather, today's dialogue is one of combativeness, not negotiation, and it is being driven by fearmongers, racial stereotypes, and misinformation.

Michael's book sets the record straight. It is an exhaustive and honest examination of where we have gone wrong and where we can still go right. If only *Perchance to DREAM* could be required reading for every member of Congress and elected official in the United States.

I first met Michael after his father, Sabino Olivas III, a prominent Albuquerque accountant, agreed to serve as the treasurer for my first congressional campaign. Later as governor I would often turn to Michael for advice. In 2005, at his urging, New Mexico passed one of the most progressive residency and scholarship laws in the country. Undocumented immigrants were eligible for state residency after twelve months and then immediately eligible for Lottery Scholarships, which gave them reduced tuition at our colleges and universities. This occurred when our neighbor Arizona was passing some of the strictest anti-immigrant

Bill Richardson served as Governor of New Mexico (2003–11), US Secretary of Energy (1998–2001), US Ambassador to the United Nations (1997–98), and US Congressman from New Mexico's Third District (1983–97).

laws in the country that denied undocumented immigrants—including children—basic social services and made all Latinos subject to humiliating searches at the whim of any law enforcement officer.

In 2005 in New Mexico, like in the country today, we were at a crossroads. There was escalating violence at our borders, and many were fleeing in search of a better life here. We could choose to pass laws that helped integrate and support our immigrant community or laws that hindered and hurt them. I have always felt that there is a decided positive in biculturalism and living and working together, so that is where I, with Michael's help, directed my legislative energy. In addition to the residency law, as governor I also signed legislation to make undocumented immigrants eligible for driver's licenses and to expand their access to health care.

Those legislative battles were not easy. Immigration was a divisive issue, one that never was popular, even in a predominantly Hispanic state like New Mexico. Those fights with Michael were well fought, but they wouldn't have been necessary at all had Congress ever stepped up to the plate to pass immigration reform. And we are still waiting. That's why Michael's book is critical reading at this time in our nation's history. The Hispanic population has been the principal driver of US population growth since 2000. Yet it still feels like our voices are not being heard in the political and social realm. Democrats—my party—often rely on Latino votes, though once elected they seem all too willing to use DREAMers as political pawns. The path to citizenship becomes a bargaining chip on the negotiation table.

Michael was in the immigration law field before it was a field. He is not only one of our nation's leading experts in immigration law and history but also one of the first. He approaches this book, which compiles decades of work, not as an advocate or activist but as an observer and historian who has witnessed and documented the lengthy and roundabout efforts of DREAMers to become citizens of the country that they have called home since childhood. He eloquently and expertly details the trials and tribulations of the Deferred Action for Childhood Arrivals (DACA) program. Contrary to the divisive rhetoric in the media, DACA remains enormously popular with Americans. Only a scholar with his depth and experience could give us such a clear and concise narrative on this complicated issue. Michael recounts his own late conversion to

DACA and the dismay and disappointment at watching the promising and generous program be pushed to the brink of elimination by a barrage of angry sound bites and tweets.

Most important, this book is an homage and tribute to the thousands of DREAMers who have shared their stories with Michael. DACA only came into existence thanks to the brave young people who began a campaign of sit-ins and marches to bring attention to the plight of immigrant youth in this country. Many of these outspoken youngsters risked deportation and separation from their families to come forward and fight for a more secure existence.

Their story, no matter how it ends, deserves to be on the shelves along with other Americans' history. I only hope that one day we can coax Michael out of retirement so that he may write the final chapter on DACA. I still believe that chapter could end with DREAMers becoming legal citizens of the country they call home.

March 2019
Santa Fe, New Mexico

1

College Residency, Race, and Reaction

Before 1996

Beginning this inquiry with residency requirements may seem an unsexy and drab way to set the larger stage. However, from early on, the major issues for undocumented college students have been their ability to pay for school, because as they were ineligible for federal and most state financial assistance—hence the emphasis on lower resident tuition—and their inability to work legally, which precluded many from campus employment, even extending in some jurisdictions to being residence assistants in dorms or other such cooperative arrangements. The ability of colleges to set residency policies and tuition rates is well established, with court cases dating back to 1882 clearly holding not only that states can charge tuition differentials[1] but also that they may decide which students are entitled to be classified as residents and which are not.[2] However it is conceived, any serious examination of undocumented college students starts with residency, both in the litigation dimensions and in the governance or legislative sense.

In most situations, this procedure works well enough because state institutions carefully spell out the basic residency requirements and students seem to understand the rules. Officials in most states have realized that a mix of in-state and out-of-state students is desirable and therefore have made it possible in most cases for students to migrate to public colleges as long as the higher tuition costs "equalize" the tax burden on residents.[3] The balance properly favors the children of resident taxpayers, yet it does not usually fence out those nonresidents who wish to attend schools in that state. This arrangement acts as an incentive for states to establish strong public postsecondary sectors and to prevent a mass migration to states with lower tuition. The practice also engenders loyalties, both political and academic, to those state institutions. In addition, by means of compacts and consortia agreements, states can also distribute scarce placements in highly specialized and expensive curricula, such as optometry, pharmacy, and veterinary medicine, where not all states offer such programs.[4]

The practical application of residency policies, however, lacks the elegance of its theoretical premises. In a surprisingly large number of situations, applicants or students have presented increasingly sophisticated residency claims that were not anticipated by the state legislatures, resulting in inconsistencies in the way the rules are applied. Since there are a comparable number of factual permutations when it comes to immigration issues, even more problems arise with respect to undocumented college students.

By employing several approaches, this chapter reviews the law, theory, and administration of residency requirements and their centrality to issues of undocumented college students. First, I outline basic operational definitions of the legal and fiscal issues, including the vexing problem of defining "domicile" versus "residence." Second, I categorize the different governance structures of the states according to their formality and level of decision-making, including a comparison of the various state practices through an analysis of their residence requirements. Third, I discuss the extensive system of exemptions, exceptions, and waivers to the residency rules. One commentator has noted that this elaborate set of rules and regulations is a patchwork which has resulted in a dissimilarity of treatment that has given rise not only to inconvenience to the participants but also to injustice, concluding that "this heterogeneity is neither in the interest of the students, of the states, nor of the nation."[5] Additionally, I discuss the problems with institutional practice, as there is considerable administrative discretion at the institutional level in the indices and criteria of residential intent, the burden of persuasion, the evidentiary requirements, and the weight accorded the various criteria.

In many respects, these requirements are troubling: the residency statutes, regulations, and practices are often confusing and illogical; potential students "forum shop" among colleges and exploit technical loopholes; and many statement-of-intent criteria are difficult to administer or verify. Such flaws in the system invite circumvention and dishonesty. Moreover, these complex technicalities very often work against immigrants, who do not always have the requisite paperwork or documents for establishing their residence, which is often a matter of delineating permanence or length of time, requiring extensive documentation. In addition, the immigration categories themselves are often a bramble-bush of conflicting definitions and technical distinctions. The ebb and flow of federal and state nativism is a palimpsest for public policy.

Persons who have lived in a single state for many years are tradition-ally easily defined as residents. Conversely, a student who moves from State A to State B solely for the purpose of attending State B College is clearly a nonresident, at least at first, before meeting any durational requirements. The wide space between these two situations, however, is the rub. As a general rule, states will allow a person who moves to a state to become reclassified as a resident after a specified period of time. This time period ranges from ninety days to twelve months, the period used by nearly all the states.[6]

Absent other exceptions or complications, when the specified time passes, states with a simple durational requirement (usually twelve months before enrollment) will allow a citizen student to pay the lower tuition as a resident; in most states, beginning as a nonresident will re-quire you to remain a nonresident, ineligible for resident status until the student "stops-out" for the required twelve months. This is usually an objective standard with certain proofs about continuous presence required for the reclassification. To be sure, this objective standard is subject to measurement problems, because as even the seemingly sim-ple standard of counting a particular number of days can become com-plicated: Do holidays away from the state count? Does the clock begin when the person moves to the state? What proofs can be tendered as evidence of residence or presence?

As difficult as this so-called objective measurement becomes, most states have complicated matters by requiring more than mere duration: these states also require that residents establish domicile, which entails forming the legal intention of making that state their "true, perma-nent, and fixed abode."[7] This is a very complicated requirement, both conceptually and operationally. Instead of merely counting days in the requisite waiting period (already noted as deceptively complicated), states that employ the domicile element may require a legal declaration and evidence to prove that such residents consider the state their sole principal establishment. Confusion frequently arises because the terms "residence" and "domicile" are often used interchangeably; sometimes "residence" is measured with language denoting intentionality, which is generally not required for mere residence.[8] As a point of law, "domicile" includes "residence" but has a more specific meaning than does "residence."[9]

To establish a domicile, students must prove two elements: (1) residence and (2) an intention to make that residence their permanent home. Persons may maintain more than one residence but only one domicile.[10] For example, many students can plausibly maintain several residences, some simultaneously (summer state, mother's and father's state, the state in which they live and vote). Incidentally, the place where students vote is not necessarily their domicile, as mere residence and brief waiting periods are the requirements to register for voting in local or federal elections. As difficult as the concept of domicile is for US citizens or permanent residents, it is even more difficult in the immigration context. Surprisingly to most observers, this very issue has been litigated dozens of times, most recently where there is a pattern of states suppressing student voter registration.[11]

Given the high degree of confusion in ascertaining student intentions, why do states employ domicile as a determinant of residence? The likely logic is threefold: (1) to ensure, as effectively as possible, that students establish and maintain genuine ties to the state; (2) to ensure that students do not forum-shop among several states where they can manufacture or allege contacts; and (3) to make the declaration of residence more meaningful and seriously considered than mere presence requires. Taken individually, these intentions do not always advance state interests, except through the attendant complexity that discourages (to a limited extent) frivolous claims and thereby protects the states' fiscal resources. This unarticulated premise appears to be a strong driving force behind several residency policies and practices.[12]

Upon closer examination, however, the rationales for the widespread practice of exacting declarations of intention fail to advance any substantial guarantees for establishment of domicile beyond those provided by mere durational requirements. The cost of administering intentions is high, both in dollar terms and in the considerable ill will it often can exact. None of the three ostensible reasons for domiciliary requirements truly guarantees loyalty or, more to the point, tax contributions, either by a would-be student or her parents.

In fact, none of the three rationales for strict domiciliary requirements assures states that the newly arrived nonresidents have been transformed into genuine residents, a situation as true for citizens as it is for undocumented immigrants.[13] First, the fact that students establish a legitimate principal home and abode does not guarantee that they will remain in the state beyond commencement or contribute to the tax system while they are enrolled in school. In all likelihood, students will move wherever employment is available or the quality of life, family considerations, and circumstances allow. Through the use of domicile requirements, states may achieve the second goal of preventing forum shopping because students cannot maintain more than one domicile. However, a variety of permutations is possible for some students, as they can maintain more than one legal residence, which can give sufficient evidence for them to meet residency requirements in more than one state.[14] A more common problem is the possibility that students may have to relinquish residence or domicile in their home state to establish sufficient contacts in the new state. This has led, in many instances, to students having no single state in which they can successfully claim a domicile for tuition purposes.[15] The third rationale—making declarations more meaningful—is only exhortatory and unlikely to prove efficacious in determining domicile because there is no legal means to force students to remain in the state after they consume the postsecondary resources.

Despite the demonstrable defects of domiciliary requirements, particularly those that also include waiting periods, states and institutions persist in requiring them. More than lower resident tuition lies in the balance. Many other benefits may accrue to state residents in public or private colleges, such as preferential admissions, scholarship or loan assistance, inclusion in special programs, eligibility for consortia or exchange programs, and participation in specialized programs negotiated among states in legislative compacts.[16] It is these stakes, not merely the tuition differentials (which, in certain instances for citizens and permanent residents, can be "equalized" by federal need-based aid formulas), that have contributed to the overall rise in residency litigation.

To complicate matters, there is an extraordinary number of exemptions, exceptions, and waivers to state residency practices.[17] The most common factors singled out for special treatment include whether individuals are a dependent or minor, what their marital status is, whether they are military personnel, and, for many years but especially since 1996, what their alienage or immigration status is. These four areas receive some type of special consideration in nearly all states; in addition, states employ special treatment for a wide range of categories, resulting in thousands of exceptions to residency requirements. Other groups frequently singled out for special treatment include university employees, financially needy students, and senior citizens. As complicated as these practices are, any comprehensive listing would significantly understate the exemptions, owing to the different ways the legislatures confer exemptions and ways these rules are applied. For example, states may use fiscal riders, revenue bills, or appropriations language to enact exceptions (for one year or several), and these or other quasi-legislative means could not be discovered in a statute search or by most applicants.[18]

The most striking feature among these patterns is how rarely exemptions or special treatment have anything to do with the fundamental concepts of duration or intention, the two fulcrums on which domicile and residency rest. In some instances, the exceptions are aimed at classes of persons who are mobile, such as military or migrant workers, or for whom domicile is difficult to determine, as with minor children or Native Americans.[19] However, the largest class is those for whom residency (or a tuition waiver) is a conferred benefit, without reference to duration or intent. Some states are truly spectacular in their legerdemain around strict requirements. For example, Texas offers more than eighteen categories of exceptions or special treatment to a strict domiciliary requirement with a one-year waiting period, including graduate assistants, recipients of "merit" scholarships, and certain border nonresidents.[20] In nearly every instance, such benefits are conferred to reward a desirable characteristic or a favored class of persons, such as graduate students (as an employment perquisite), meritorious students, certain fortunate employees, or residents of certain adjoining states or even a foreign nation.[21] Ironically, in other respects, the Texas legislature has for many years sought to make state residency even more difficult to achieve, especially for undocumented aliens residing within its borders.[22]

Some of these exemptions may not pose bad results as such, but they are for the most part unprincipled, except when they ease the evidentiary burden on groups for whom duration or domicile genuinely poses a particular problem. Graduate students are rarely paid well and certainly provide important instructional or research services to institutions. Paying their tuition seems like a modest benefit and one well worth preserving, but using the residency mechanism to deem the students "residents" is a curious bookkeeping maneuver that undermines the actual residency determination system. Particularly troubling are the many discretionary means to confer residency upon the advantaged, as when the state confers residency exceptions to its employees or to children of employees of choice industries.[23] The growth of such arbitrary and unprincipled exceptions, exemptions, and waivers undermines the already weak scheme erected to regulate the migration of out-of-state students.

On the one hand, it is understandable that exceptions would occur and desirable that some flexibility is available for the institutions that must administer these strict residency requirements; play in the joints is always useful for large organizations, and reasonable accommodations seem to be a social good. On the other hand, the extensive and unprincipled exemptions in this area have gone far beyond their original purpose. They suggest that the basic residency requirements are so outmoded or wrongheaded that only irregular institutionalized circumvention can make the system work.[24] This Goldbergian scheme is neither rational nor reasonable, and institutional practices (discussed next) only add to the confusion.

The first step in understanding these discretionary practices is an examination of the indices and criteria used to implement residency requirements.[25] As already noted, domiciliary requirements entail subjective as well as objective measures of evidence. In the purest sense, one who has never left a state and never intends to leave incontestably meets all the presence, duration, and intent criteria. At the other end of the spectrum, someone who has never been in a state and never intends to go there is just as clearly not its domiciliary. Between these two points, however, there is much room for judgment. In most instances, the first inquiry is: Do the circumstances indicate any presence in the state? If so, was it for a sufficient time to meet the durational requirement? As simple as this appears to be, merely counting the time periods frequently poses problems: When does the clock start? When does it stop? Do absences from the state count? If so, how long can I be out of the state and still establish it as my domicile? A review of admissions practices reveals that nearly half the sampled institutions require that applicants for residence status reside in the state for the appropriate period, as counted backward from the date of application, on the theory that events could change between that time and the time of enrollment; the other states permit students to run the clock until enrollment, a practice that can substantially shorten the waiting period.[26]

The measurement of intent is even more inexact than is the measurement of duration, and many states with domiciliary requirements predictably employ a wide range of criteria to determine the concept.[27] Often, other measures of long-term residence and community ties are used: for example, voter registration is widely used by institutions to indicate students' intent. In truth, it is a poor proxy because durational residency requirements for voting are required by law to be of short duration, usually between ninety days to six months, and are rarely probative of long-term intent.[28] People may regularly vote in their domicile, but they need not do so, as revealed by the extensive use of absentee ballots and other such mechanisms.[29] Conversely, not being registered to vote in a new state is likely to be interpreted as not having established domicile. In any event, the extensive litigation in student voting rights cases suggests the great degree of difficulty in measuring intentionality for meeting voting residency requirements.[30] However, virtually every state either allows or requires voter registration as a substantial criterion of domiciliary intent for adults.

The problems of evidence and burden of proof are important for determining both objective facts (for example, how long have students resided in the state) and subjective intent (where is their true, permanent, and fixed abode), but those states that hold students to durational standards appear to exact the same evidentiary requirements as those states where domicile must be proven. Therefore, even where subjective intent is not required, similar proof—including items that measure intentionality—is exacted.[31] This curious finding suggests that even nondomiciliary states are employing domiciliary criteria and evidence, creating higher standards than the technical requirements of the statutes or regulations, but not explicitly saying so.

The kinds of evidence allowed to prove residence or domicile show a remarkable consistency, for nearly every state requires or allows the following as evidence: Internal Revenue Service (IRS) returns; automobile registration or other tax records; property ownership; voter registration card; paycheck stubs; affidavits from landlords, employers, or others; students' sworn statements; transcripts; and other documents, testimony, or proof of residence. Of course, some of these prerequisites are unavailable to immigrants, particularly undocumented immigrants, who are called "undocumented" for a reason.[32]

Many states grant wide latitude in the evidence required to prove residence, but it is the patterns of the evidence that administrators rely on to make their determination. For instance, a student holding all the documentation required for State A, but voting in State B, will likely be classified a nonresident in B; even if the student registered to vote in the new state, many registrars would likely start the clock at the point of reregistration. The burden of proof is always on the student in classification cases, and courts will likely uphold such a state practice unless it includes an irrebuttable presumption (that is, that students, once classified nonresidents, can never become residents)[33] or an unconstitutional provision, which attempts to do what only the federal government can do, such as regulate immigration.[34] Thus, to overcome the burden of proof, many students will not only be required to show that they are residents or domiciliaries of the state; they must also show they are *not* domiciliaries or residents of any other state. These are heavy burdens to overcome, and although the requirements for duration are less stringent than those for domicile, the evidence deemed necessary for one is in many cases no less than that required for the other.

There are also occasions where institutions reinterpret state legislation or regulations, as in one state where a virtually unenforceable provision of dubious constitutionality was ignored by the state institutions in an unspoken compact.[35] As one example, following a 2012 presidential policy to allow certain undocumented students to receive Deferred Action for Childhood Arrivals (DACA)—a formal status that acts as a temporary reprieve and stays deportations—state laws regarding these students had not been brought into conformity with the law prevailing over postsecondary residency decisions, and one public college in the state was advised by legal counsel to ignore the formal state requirements and abide by the tenets of the earlier decision and collateral case law.[36] The state attorney general actually brought suit against the public institution for its broader accommodationist approach (jump forward to Appendix 3, which reveals the extensive litigation history triggered by DACA).

The fluctuations of enrollments, institutional priorities, and legal criteria all contribute to the accordion-like tightening and loosening of the evidentiary requirements, burdens of proof, legal standards, and discretionary factors in residency determination. Like the multiple exemptions found in nearly all states, the wide swings evident in the administration of residency suggest the deterioration of the system into one that does not always protect either the institutions' interest or the students' rights. As troubling as the system is for citizens simply moving to a new state, the calculus for aliens, particularly undocumented aliens, is even more complex.

The 1982 case *Plyler v. Doe*[37] remains at the apex of immigrants' rights in the United States. With this decision, the United States Supreme Court (SCOTUS) struck down Texas's attempt to deny free public education to undocumented children.[38] The Texas statute denied state funds to school districts enrolling children who were not "citizens of the United States or legally admitted aliens."[39] Justice Brennan, in his majority opinion striking down the statute, characterized the Texas argument for charging tuition as "nothing more than an assertion that illegal entry, without more, prevents a person from becoming a resident for purposes of enrolling his children in the public schools."[40] He employed an equal protection analysis to find that a state could not enact a discriminatory classification "merely by defining a disfavored group as nonresident."[41] He then considered and dismissed arguments proffered by Texas in support of the challenged statute.

Later in 1982, the Supreme Court also decided *Toll v. Moreno*.[42] *Toll* was the first postsecondary residency case to be decided by the Supreme Court construing a state statute affecting nonimmigrants and aliens with permission to remain only temporarily in the United States.[43] Justice Brennan also wrote the majority opinion in *Toll*. After reviewing the confusing history of the case,[44] the Court, on Supremacy Clause grounds, struck down the University of Maryland's policy of denying domiciled treaty organization individuals, or "G-4" aliens, the opportunity to pay reduced, in-state tuition.[45] The Court therefore did not reach the questions of due process or equal protection, which had been considered by both the district[46] and appellate courts.[47] The Supreme Court based its opinion on the premise that the federal government is preeminent in matters of immigration policy and that states may not enact alienage classifications except in limited cases of political and government functions.[48]

In 1976, when the *Toll* case was first brought, the district court held that the original policy denying residency was a violation of due process and constituted an irrebuttable presumption.[49] In reviewing that case, the Supreme Court noted that it had previously held in 1978 that G-4 visa holders could be US domiciliaries[50] and had certified a question to the Maryland Court of Appeals to determine whether G-4 aliens and dependents could be Maryland domiciliaries.[51] On remand, the Maryland court determined that these individuals were capable of acquiring domicile,[52] thus rendering the university's previous reliance upon inability to establish domicile incorrect. However, before the Supreme Court could render its opinion on this interpretation, the university's Board of Regents issued a "Reaffirmation of In-State Policy."[53] That statement actually constituted a substantial retreat from its previous position, although it still did not allow residency tuition for plaintiff Moreno.[54] The Supreme Court, noting that the university's action had "fundamentally altered" the domicile issue, remanded the case to the federal district court.[55]

On this second remand, the university lost again. The district court held that, while domicile was no longer of "paramount consideration," the revised policy was defective on Equal Protection and Supremacy Clause grounds.[56] In the lower court's view, the "revised" policy concerning alienage (which made domicile only one of several criteria) could not survive strict scrutiny,[57] and further the policy impermissibly encroached on federal immigration prerogatives.[58] The federal appellate court affirmed on the same grounds.[59]

In *Toll*, Justice Brennan reviewed the precedents in *Takahashi*,[60] *Graham*,[61] and *De Canas*,[62] reading them for the principle that "state regulation[,] not congressionally sanctioned that discriminates against aliens lawfully admitted to the country[,] is impermissible if it imposes additional burdens not contemplated by Congress."[63] He found that Congress had allowed G-4 visa holders to establish domicile in the United States[64] and also had conferred tax exemptions upon G-4 aliens "as an inducement for these [international] organizations to locate significant operations in the United States."[65] Therefore, Justice Brennan reasoned, it was clearly the congressional intent that G-4 visa holders not bear the "additional burdens" Maryland sought to impose: "The State may not recoup indirectly from respondents' parents the taxes that the Federal Government has expressly barred the State from collecting."[66]

On the merits of the case, Brennan mustered a seven-to-two vote, with Justice O'Connor concurring in the result.[67] Justice Blackmun's concurring opinion[68] was aimed at rebutting the dissent by Justice Rehnquist that argued at length that treaty organization aliens should not be strictly scrutinized, as they were an advantaged group, not the disadvantaged aliens envisioned as requiring protection in *Graham v. Richardson*.[69] Additionally, Justice Rehnquist found the majority's preemption analysis flawed: "First, the Federal Government has not barred the States from collecting taxes from many, if not most, G-4 visa holders. Second, as to those G-4 nonimmigrants who are immune from state income taxes by treaty, Maryland's tuition policy cannot fairly be said to conflict with those treaties in a manner requiring its preemption."[70]

Justice Rehnquist's dissent does not help clarify the problems that had been finessed over in the majority opinions. First, it is not disadvantage per se that provokes the need for strictly scrutinizing alienage statutes but rather aliens' conceded powerlessness in political disputes.[71] Treaty organization aliens, like all other nonimmigrant classes, cannot vote or participate in the electoral process. However wealthy or advantaged World Bank employees may be (and these plaintiffs surely could not invoke the same moral claims as did undocumented alien children)[72], the university's additional charges for nonresidents clearly constituted a burdensome extra cost that the university was ultimately required to refund.[73] Moreover, in attempting to suggest that the Maryland tuition policy was not in conflict with the state's tax exemption,[74] Rehnquist was simply wrong. Not only did the university concede openly that the surcharges were calculated in an attempt at "granting a higher subsidy" and "achieving equalization,"[75] both of which are tax terms; in its brief the university also noted that the nonresident tuition differential was "roughly equivalent to the amount of state income tax [a G-4 alien] is spared by [the state] treasury each year."[76]

What Rehnquist might have more usefully queried was the extent to which public universities may appropriately regulate their admissions policies concerning residence, particularly policies concerning foreign nationals following *Toll*. A significant number of states had residency requirements that were identical to or functionally resembled Maryland's practice. Not all have granted G-4 alienage tax exemptions. Given the complexity of administration in foreign student affairs, it is likely that many administrators in public and private universities frequently do not understand their legal responsibilities to foreign nationals who apply for admission, in-state tuition, and state financial assistance.[77] Therefore, the majority's broad language[78] was unhelpful to guide admissions officers in drafting acceptable guidelines. For example, how can a state university track relevant federal immigration statutes in admissions and financial aid so as to meet the requirements of the preemption doctrine? How may states regulate tuition charges for other similarly situated nonimmigrants who are not G-4 aliens, a large and variegated category that runs from the letter A to V?[79] Should the categories be different for the primary (G-I) nonimmigrants than for their dependent children (G-4)?

Read with *Plyler*, *Toll* raises several important questions concerning the "residency clock" for undocumented adults: Does the proper determination for establishing domicile begin when they enter the country? When they apply for a formal status? When they receive formal, adjusted status?[80] What happens if the state has no common law on immigrant domicile? Although *Toll* may have resolved the narrow issue of domiciled G-4 aliens in states that grant tax exemptions, it is clear its significance lies beyond this narrow setting.[81]

Soon after *Plyler* and *Toll* were decided, their postsecondary applications were tested in a 1985 California case, *Leticia "A" v. Board of Regents of the University of California* (*Leticia "A" I*).[82] Five undocumented students who had been admitted into the University of California (UC) for the 1984 fall term were notified by the university that they were required to pay nonresident tuition and fees because they were not entitled to California in-state resident status.[83] The five plaintiffs had graduated from California high schools and had resided continuously in California for an average of seven years each, ranging from three years to eleven years. All were brought to the United States as children by their parents, leading to a postsecondary-*Plyler* fact pattern.[84]

In 1983, California's state legislature had revised the residency statute, including an amended reference to aliens: "[A]n alien, including an unmarried minor alien, may establish his or her residence, unless precluded by the Immigration and Nationality Act (INA; this is a state law that adopts federal law and is commonly known as the Education Code)[85] from establishing domicile in the United States."[86] UC read this statute as precluding undocumented aliens from establishing California residence. The California statute defined a "resident" for purposes of in-state tuition as "a student who has a residence, pursuant to Article 5 (commencing with Section 68060) of the Chapter in the state for more than one year immediately preceding the residency determination date."[87] A nonresident, under the California statute, was a person who does not meet this code definition.

The statutes, although employing the term "residence," actually exacted the traditional criteria for establishing a "domicile." For example, a resident could only maintain "one residence,"[88] and "residency [could] be changed only by the union of act and intent."[89] Section 68061 stated that "every person who is married or 18 years of age, or older, and under no legal disability to do so, may establish residence."[90] UC argued that the undocumented students were "under such a legal disability" and therefore could not establish the requisite intent.

The university's position was buttressed by a California Attorney General's Opinion stating that the university could deny resident status to the students because, in adopting Section 68062(h), the legislature had intended only to make the statute conform to *Toll*—that is, to nonimmigrants—and had not intended to grant residency to undocumented immigrants.[91] However, the California Superior Court judge in *Leticia "A,"* Ken Kawaichi, was not persuaded by the university's argument or the attorney general's opinion. Instead, he held that UC's policy of "precluding undocumented alien students . . . from establishing California residency in the same manner and on the same term as United States citizens" invalid under the California constitution.[92] He quickly dismissed the state's "clean hands" argument,[93] noting that the plaintiffs had been brought into California as children.[94] The United

States Supreme Court had similarly dismissed this line of reasoning in *Plyler*,[95] in the same fashion as did Judge Kawaichi.

As the Supreme Court had in *Plyler*,[96] Judge Kawaichi found education to be more than a minimal interest requiring a mere rational relationship.[97] Noting the "importance of [public] higher education in California,"[98] he stated that heightened scrutiny was the appropriate standard.[99] The judge, however, did not find it necessary to apply the elevated standard because he found that the policy did not serve any rational government basis whatsoever.[100] Unlike the attorney general's opinion, which did not even attempt to mount a constitutional justification for its result,[101] Judge Kawaichi showed a sophisticated grasp of immigration law relative to student residency issues. He discerned that not all undocumented aliens are similarly situated and that such status is fluid. For example, during the trial, one of the plaintiffs was in the process of becoming a permanent resident.[102] Indeed, several of the undocumented students became eligible to apply for permanent resident status and were not subject to deportation.[103]

Judge Kawaichi pointed to the difficulty in employing federal immigration residency laws as criteria for determining students' domiciles:

> The policies underlying the immigration laws and regulations are vastly different from those relating to residency for student fee purposes. The two systems are totally unrelated for purposes of administration, enforcement and legal analysis. The use of unrelated policies, statutes, regulations or case law from one system to govern portions of the other is irrational. The incorporation of policies governing adjustment of status of un-documented aliens into regulations and administration of a system for determining residence for student fee purposes is neither logical nor rational. . . . Under this reasoning, it would be a difficult legislative task for a state to track federal immigration law for purposes of student residency requirements, without violating principles of Equal Protection or Preemption.[104]

Plyler, *Toll*, and *Leticia "A"* all seemed to erode states' ability to employ federal immigration criteria irrebuttably to their postsecondary residency determinations. However, in an unusual resuscitation of the issue in California, an employee of the University of California, Los Angeles

(UCLA) refused to administer the residency policy, claiming it was encouraging illegal immigration, and then filed a taxpayer whistleblower suit challenging the position in *Bradford v. Board of Regents of the University of California* (*Bradford I*) (1990).[105] Bradford, one of the original plaintiffs, asserted that the California attorney general's opinion overruled in *Leticia "A"* was correct and that the Education Code residency provision struck down by *Leticia "A"* should be considered valid.[106] To do so would restore the state provision that had provoked the *Leticia "A"* case and would make it impossible for undocumented students to be considered California residents for tuition purposes.

By this time, California's higher education officials had become converts to Judge Kawaichi's ruling. The state and its universities had not appealed his 1985 ruling and had since decided that some of the undocumented students deserved to be considered as residents, provided they met all the other tests for in-state status.[107] For one thing, many of the undocumented students at state institutions did quite well in school. Further, allowing the undocumented to declare residency had not loosed the floodgates: in a public postsecondary education system of more than two hundred thousand students, UC and California State University (CSU) officials estimated that fewer than a thousand students in the two systems were undocumented when admitted, fewer than one-half of 1 percent of the total enrollment.[108] One study of San Diego, the city closest to the US-Mexico border, estimated that fewer than a hundred of the 35,000 students at the CSU–San Diego campus, and only one student at the new CSU–San Marcos campus, were undocumented.[109] Even the open-door community college system estimated that fewer than 1 percent of 1.5 million students were undocumented.[110]

Even so, on May 30, 1990, the Los Angeles County Superior Court ruled against UCLA and in favor of Bradford.[111] The court ruled that the original Education Code provisions (pre–*Leticia "A"*) were constitutional and that the state was required to charge the aliens nonresident tuition because they did not have the legal capacity to establish domicile, as required by the code.[112]

With this ruling, the public colleges attempted a new approach, seeking to dismiss the action or to have it transferred to Alameda County, where Judge Kawaichi sat, in effect, to consolidate it with *Leticia "A."*[113]

Judge David Yaffe denied both the motion to dismiss and to transfer the case and scolded the university for its tactics:

> You have this action pending in this court. You litigate it through to a decision against you, and then, at that point, you claim that the court should yield its jurisdiction because there's another action that is still pending, in essence, up in Alameda County. . . . It doesn't seem to me that there is any sound rule of judicial policy that would permit a litigant to do that.[114]

At that point, the university was in for a penny, in for a pound. It had brought in outside counsel to assist in an attempt to reverse Judge Yaffe's original ruling that found for Bradford and his subsequent denial of the motions to dismiss and transfer.[115] The appellate court upheld the trial judge's opinion, finding that he had not abused his discretion in refusing to transfer and consolidate *Bradford* with *Leticia "A"* in Alameda County.[116] In addition, the state appellate court held that the original section 68062(h) properly excluded undocumented students from becoming in-state residents for tuition purposes and that the statute was constitutional.[117]

In the meantime, Judge Kawaichi was petitioned by the original *Leticia "A"* plaintiffs to reconsider his decision and order in light of the competing *Bradford* Superior Court decision.[118] He issued a modified holding, retaining jurisdiction and affirming his original decision striking down section 68062(h).[119] Despite Judge Kawaichi's ruling,[120] however, both parties found themselves mousetrapped: because the original defendant (the university) had not appealed the judge's 1985 decision, neither party had an appellate decision on which to rely. By this time, the institutions had come to see the issue as one where they could accommodate the wishes of the original undocumented plaintiffs. However, with the ostensibly competing decisions, the state institutions did not wish to be whipsawed on this issue, especially when they were being criticized for management practices and were bracing for financial cutbacks.[121]

The conflict between the two cases was finally addressed by a collateral taxpayer case, *American Association of Women (AAW) v. California State University*.[122] The Federation for American Immigration Reform (FAIR), an immigration restrictionist group, brought the suit to force the state's hand on this issue.[123] In *AAW*, Judge Robert O'Brien of the Los Angeles County Superior Court considered the discrepancies between *Leticia "A"* (as clarified) and *Bradford* and decided that there were no conflicts.[124] He held that Judge Kawaichi's "clarification" actually constituted a substantive shift in the holding:

> Unlike the original injunction the *Leticia "A"* clarification no longer requires CSU automatically to treat undocumented students the same as U.S. citizens. Thus, although the trial court does not specifically follow the law established by *Bradford*, it has tempered its original holding so that it in effect gives credence to *Bradford*, as well as the process required by Section 68062(h).[125]

By creating a distinction without a difference, Judge O'Brien found that the modified *Leticia "A"* decision was already tried and determined on its merits (res judicata) and that there was no "substantial identity of parties or those who are in privity with a party."[126] Judge O'Brien held that *Bradford* was "the only relevant California appellate court decision, [and as such] controls this case on the legal issues involved."[127] Finally, he enjoined the CSU system "from violating Education Code sections 68050 and 68062(h) or from treating undocumented aliens as residents, for purposes of tuition, without first establishing them as such in accordance with Education Code section 68062(h)."[128]

At this point UC considered itself bound by *Bradford*,[129] but the CSU system appealed *Leticia "A" I* as modified in order to have an appellate court resolution of the conflict.[130] Thus, in summer 1994, undocumented students were able to establish residency for CSU purposes, but not for UC or the 110 public community colleges. Of course, given the legal transfer policies and mobility among the three state systems, this straddle could not be sustained.

Leticia "A" was quintessentially a residency dispute, as it turned on factual findings of *intent*: *Bradford* and *AAW* held that the undocumented cannot establish the requisite intent,[131] whereas *Leticia "A"* held that they were not prevented from establishing residence.[132] Judge Kawaichi's holding in *Leticia "A"* with its clarification was clearly the more correct of the two competing versions for two reasons: First, *Bradford* and *AAW* misrepresented the elements of domicile and residence; second, neither

opinion carefully distinguished among the different types of undocumented alienage, including those who had able to establish domicile in
the state.

For example, the *Bradford* appellate court inverts the Education
Code's statutory language by requiring undocumented aliens to prove
they *are permitted* to adjust their status.[133] The court deftly reversed the
burden set out under the statute, which affirms aliens' rights to establish
residence unless they are specifically not allowed to do so.[134] To slip this
knot, the *Bradford* court mocked the university's argument as "Daeda-
lian but unpersuasive" and as "senseless."[135] Further, by equating the acts
of "not precluding" and eliding with "authorizing," the court ignored the
precedent of *Toll*, where the US Supreme Court had certified the question of whether Maryland state law enabled long-term nonimmigrant
employees' children to establish domicile for postsecondary tuition purposes.[136] By requiring the state court to answer this technical question,
it is clear that the Supreme Court envisioned the acquisition of postsecondary residency at the time as a matter of *state* law, not federal statute.
If, as in California, the controlling state statute incorporated a federal
classification ("unless precluded by the INA"), a state court cannot in-
vert the statute's presumption so as to defeat an alien's ability to establish
domicile under state law.[137]

This error then enabled the *Bradford* court to misapply California law
concerning residency. In *Cabral v. State Board of Control*,[138] a California
appellate court had held that undocumented aliens are state "residents"
for purposes of establishing standing (the litigant's recognized ability to
bring a claim) for state benefits. The *Bradford* court held that *Cabral* was
not controlling because it "arose under a statute which contain[ed] no
definition of the term 'resident.'"[139] However, the court misapplied the
Toll test for interpreting California's Education Code section 68062(h)[140]
by acting as if federal law controlled for one purpose (i.e., finding that
congressional language was "unremarkable" but controlling)[141] while
state law controlled for another (i.e., the existence of a state residence
statute distinguished what would have otherwise been a controlling construction of state domicile).[142]

Moreover, even if federal law were controlling for determination of
domicile purposes, the *Bradford* and *AAW* courts mischaracterized the
extent to which the INA enables and in some cases requires domicile

in the United States for long-term undocumented aliens who eventually apply for the various forms of relief from deportation available at the time. First, under the immigration regime then in place, once aliens *entered* the United States, either surreptitiously or through actions that rendered them out of legal status, they could be removed only through an elaborate proceeding of deportation wherein the government had the burden of proof by "clear, unequivocal, and convincing evidence that the facts alleged as grounds for deportation are true."[143] The Supreme Court had further held that this standard "applies to all deportation cases, regardless of the length of time the alien has resided in this country."[144] Additionally, several statutory means of gaining legal status at the time were available only to long-term undocumented residents, as was an array of discretionary reliefs from deportation. For example, suspension of deportation, the relief provision at issue in *Immigration and Naturalization Service v. Chadha*,[145] required "a continuous period of not less than seven years immediately preceding the date of such application,"[146] whereas registry provisions are still available only to undocumented persons who entered the United States before January 1, 1972, and have resided in the United States "continuously since such entry."[147] In both of these situations, statutes and practice have evolved to ensure that the immigrants had established residence in the United States and had not maintained domicile elsewhere or even physically left the country for more than brief periods of time.[148] Federal immigration law contemplates relief for long-term residents—but only for those who remain in the country in uninterrupted fashion.[149] Thus, *Bradford* and *AAW* misconstrued federal law concerning undocumented domicile as well as California state law determining residence. The final ace was that the *Plyler* decision itself had held that the undocumented could establish domicile under traditional intentional tests.[150]

In a subsequent undocumented student case, *Martinez v. Bynum*,[151] the US Supreme Court affirmed *Plyler*, upholding a post-*Plyler* Texas statute[152] as applied, in which undocumented Mexican parents could establish residence if the family were intact or if bona fide guardians lived in the district.[153]

In order for the undocumented students in *Leticia "A"* to be denied residency under the *Martinez* rationale, they would have had to enter surreptitiously in order to attend college or, in the alternative, would have had to have nonimmigrant status as students and then done something in violation of their visa requirements (such as holding unauthorized employment while in student status).[154] The record makes it clear that the plaintiff students in *Leticia "A"* were long-term residents who had graduated from California high schools, a number of whom had become permanent residents during the course of the trial.[155] Furthermore, there was no indication that higher education was a factor in attracting illegal entry to the country and every indication that they intended to reside in the United States.[156] This intention, combined with actual presence, constituted residence and domicile in California at that time.

The fact that federal law does not preclude the undocumented from establishing domicile is clear from careful readings of *Plyer* and *Martinez* as well as the INA provisions.[157] Even *Toll* appeared to rule out such arbitrary residency requirements with regard to nonimmigrants: "[W]e cannot conclude that Congress ever contemplated that a State, in the operation of a university, might impose discriminating tuition charges and fees solely on account of the federal immigration classification."[158]

As a final piece to this puzzle, the treatment of legalization benefits—derived from the federal Immigration and Reform and Control Act of 1986 (IRCA)—also suggested that federal law did not preclude aliens from establishing domicile under state laws that incorporate the INA. The *Bradford* appellate court attempted to trump the *Leticia "A"* analysis by arguing that even the generous amnesty to legalize the undocumented status of some aliens under IRCA's provisions did not contemplate generosity toward the undocumented:

> Federal law, too, discriminates against undocumented aliens in the most basic way: it forbids their entry into the country and authorizes their arrest and deportation. Even undocumented aliens given preferred status under federal law—those authorized under the Immigration Reform and Control Act of 1986 to become lawful temporary residents and thereafter permanent residents—are disqualified for five years from most federal programs of financial assistance to the needy. If federal financial assistance may be withheld from newly legalized aliens who, under the 1986 amnesty law, 'are to be welcomed as full and productive members of our nation,' surely the state is not constitutionally required to subsidize the university education of other aliens who have never legalized their status.[159]

But the *Bradford* court, in its pell-mell rush to close every door, got it wrong: IRCA did allow legalizing students to receive its benefits. The only public benefits that legalizing aliens were entitled to during their probationary status were those considered most essential, and these specifically included access to the various college student financial aid provisions of the federal Higher Education Act of 1965. Moreover, the Immigration and Naturalization Service (INS) had promulgated 1994 guidelines, noting that no federal legislation had ever been enacted "that would permit states or state-owned institutions to refuse admission to undocumented aliens or to disclose their records" to the INS.[160] Financial aid eligibility was available to these "welcomed" aliens. In its attempt to show otherwise, the appellate court misread the very benefits statute it was using to buttress its argument that federal law did not reference undocumented aliens.[161] In this light, it was not "senseless" but sensible and possible to interpret the California Education Code provision literally and to find that undocumented aliens were not precluded from establishing residence. This decision ended the ability of undocumented California high school graduates to enter the state's public institutions as resident students, requiring them to pay the higher non-resident tuition. It also did not allow them to receive state financial aid.

Just when undocumented students in the country's most populous state thought that things couldn't get worse for them, lightning struck with the passage of California's Proposition 187, a 1994 ballot initiative designed to eliminate virtually all state benefits to undocumented immigrants.[162] This draconian measure, passed overwhelmingly by the state's electorate, would have stripped undocumented immigrants of all but the most essential health and emergency medical services; would have overruled *Plyler* and denied educational benefits to these children; and would have required public officials to report undocumented immigrants' status to police and security authorities.[163] Almost immediately, declaratory and injunctive relief preventing Proposition 187's enforcement was granted by federal courts, and ultimately almost all of its provisions were struck down. The bar on postsecondary residency, however, was upheld.[164] As this chapter amply demonstrates, by the mid-1990s a number of states had also challenged what they considered failed federal immigration enforcement policy, just a decade after IRCA's legalization and comprehensive reform, seeking additional federal resources.[165] Six of the major receiver states brought such suits; all were eventually unsuccessful, but the full nativist flares were in the atmosphere.[166] Given the rapid change in California to become the most liberal of all the states, it is almost hard to appreciate how recent and pervasive the fears were.

At the same time, Representative Elton Gallegly (R-CA) introduced federal legislation to overturn *Plyler*, and while the "Gallegly Amendment" was unsuccessful,[167] the new Republican-controlled Congress in 1995 resulted in two major 1996 laws restricting immigration and the status of immigrants: the Personal Responsibility and Work Opportunity Reconciliation Act of 1996 (PRWORA) and the Illegal Immigration Reform and Immigrant Responsibility Act of 1996 (IIRIRA).[168] These omnibus laws dramatically changed the landscape, affecting federal benefits in many areas of health and welfare, including the requirement that, if a state wished to accord resident tuition to the undocumented, it must do so "only through the enactment of a State law after August 22, 1996, which affirmatively provides for such eligibility." These were done so no state could "grandfather in" their undocumented.[169] The enactment of these federal statutes led the judge in the challenge to Proposition 187[170] to determine that the federal government preempted similar state actions expressing the "intention of Congress to occupy the field of regulation of government benefits to aliens."[171] When the state of California appealed this decision, the newly elected Democratic governor, Gray Davis, invoked the federal Ninth Circuit's special arbitration and mediation provision, which resulted in a July 1999 settlement.[172]

In 2001, Texas passed the first statute to accord the state resident tuition allowed by IIRIRA and PRWORA, affirmatively providing resident status to immigrant students.[173] The same year, on September 11, the world fundamentally changed, and any immediate hopes for immigration reform were dashed by the onset of overwhelming national security concerns.[174] Even so, federal legislation was introduced in 2001, giving the DREAM Act its acronym.[175]

2001–2010 State DREAM Acts and Litigation

The DREAM Act (for Development, Relief, and Education for Alien Minors) was introduced in the United States Senate in 2001. The original and subsequent bills never passed Congress, yet the effects on undocumented college students have been prominent in the news media and on federal and state legislative agendas to this day.[1] Presidential candidates in 2008, 2012, and 2016 would debate the DREAM Act and the issues it addressed. Especially coming on the heels of a near-miss passage in 2007, when the bill almost gained approval in the Senate, the issue of undocumented college residency has all the earmarks of an agenda-building subject, situated in the complex and treacherous context of modern policy debate, especially comprehensive immigration reform. Given that the DREAM Act's subset of larger immigration, higher education, and tuition policies commands our attention, its politics are a useful bellwether for astute observers of domestic politics in the twenty-first century.

This chapter examines the general topic of undocumented college residency, played out in state DREAM Acts, and to a great extent reveals the difficulty inherent in conducting research on pending legislation, especially legislation that is so fluid and so embedded in a larger, systemic regime, and includes the background for the DREAM Act, at the state and federal level. I review the extensive litigation and legal developments, as well as the several state DREAM Acts and other issues concerning college residency and tuition. Chapter 3 reviews the federal DREAM Act and its failure to gain traction during votes in the US House and Senate. I consider the politics of immigration reform that are the backdrop for these developments, and the conclusion assesses the prospects for enactment of the legislation, either as a standalone statute or, more likely, as one of many components in the larger comprehensive immigration reform efforts. Considering how small this undocumented college student population is in the larger scheme of things (never more than 50,000 or 60,000 each year by any estimates),[2] extensive state and national legislative history reveals a surprising degree of attention in the polity and within US legislative arenas. It stood on its own legs, and the odds have grown longer against its eventual enactment as a separate legislative program.

Chapter 1 chronicled the pre-1996 developments of residency tuition and the application to undocumented college students. It highlighted the federal role in the governance of immigration-relation status, benefits, and categories of students and the current architecture of residency requirements that was established. The first version of what is known now as the DREAM Act was introduced in Congress in 2001, and many observers thought it would be easily enacted into law. But it did not enter the world naked. Prior to its proposed enactment, several news stories were written about successful college students whose parents had brought them to the United States as children, who either entered without inspection or entered legally and then overstayed a visa, or did one of the many things that can render a family out of status.[3] These children stayed in school by virtue of *Plyler v. Doe*, the 1982 Supreme Court case that struck down restrictive Texas laws that would have allowed school districts to charge tuition or to ban unauthorized students outright from the public school.[4] Over the many years since *Plyler*, school districts have accommodated the children, who against all odds were graduating from high school and applying to colleges and universities.[5]

When their numbers began to grow and attracted attention, some public higher education institutions and states began to impose residency restrictions. Such restrictions precluded undocumented students from achieving domiciliary-based residency tuition (effectively creating a reprise of *Plyler* in postsecondary guise) or charged them tuition rates as if they were international students without visas.[6] Other states and institutions allowed students to establish residency and to pay the lower, in-state tuition; private institutions, which traditionally do not charge tuition based on state residency criteria, either allowed them to enroll or held that they could not do so, often on the grounds that to do so would implicate their standing to issue I-20 visa documents, such as those employed by traditional F-1 or M-1 international students.[7] Given their many educational disadvantages, their ineligibility to receive most state aid and any federal financial assistance, and their inability to work while in school, only a small number of undocumented students were actually affected by state and postsecondary educational institutions' reactions to *Plyler*.[8]

Then, lightning struck with the passage of Proposition 187, California's 1994 ballot initiative designed to eliminate virtually all state benefits to undocumented immigrants.[9] This draconian measure, passed overwhelmingly by the state's electorate, would have stripped undocumented aliens of all but the most essential health and emergency medical services, would have overruled *Plyler* and denied educational benefits to these children, and would have required public officials to report undocumented aliens' suspected status to police and security authorities.[10] Almost immediately, declaratory and injunctive relief was granted by federal courts, and ultimately almost all of Proposition 1 87's provisions were struck down. The bar on postsecondary residency, however, was upheld.[11] By the mid-1990s, a number of states had also challenged what they considered failed federal immigration enforcement policy, seeking additional federal resources.[12] Six of the major receiver states brought such suits; all were eventually unsuccessful.[13]

At approximately the same time, Representative Elton Gallegly (R-CA) introduced federal legislation to overturn *Plyler*, and while the "Gallegly Amendment" was unsuccessful,[14] the Republican-controlled Congress in 1995 enacted two major 1996 laws restricting immigration and the status of immigrants: the Personal Responsibility and Work Opportunity Reconciliation Act of 1996 and the Illegal Immigration Reform and Immigrant Responsibility Act of 1996 —both signed into law by President Bill Clinton.[15] These omnibus laws dramatically changed the landscape, affecting federal benefits in many areas of health and welfare, including the requirement that, if a state wished to accord resident tuition status and eligibility to the undocumented, it must do so "only through the enactment of a State law after August 22, 1996, which affirmatively provides for such eligibility."[16] The enactment of these federal statutes led the judge in the challenge to Proposition 187[17] to determine that the federal government preempted similar state actions expressing the "intention of Congress to occupy the field of regulation of government benefits to aliens."[18] When the state of California appealed this decision, the newly elected governor, Gray Davis, invoked the Ninth Circuit's special arbitration and mediation provision, which resulted in a July 1999 settlement.[19] Thus, the case was never appealed to the Supreme Court, and for several years efforts at residency tuition legislation were stalled, that is until June 2001, when Texas passed the first statute to accord the state resident tuition allowed by IIRIRA and PRWORA, affirmatively providing resident status to immigrant students.[20] The same year, on September 11, the world fundamentally changed, and any immediate hopes for immigration reform were dashed by the onset of overwhelming national security concerns and the war on terrorism.[21] Even so, federal legislation was introduced in 2001, giving the DREAM Act its acronym.[22]

Other states followed Texas's lead, and through 2019 nearly two dozen states allowed undocumented students to establish residency and pay in-state tuition: one state (Oklahoma) had granted this status and then rescinded its financial aid provisions, while Wisconsin rescinded its tuition statute after two years, with very few students having invoked its benefits.[23] South Carolina voted to ban the undocumented from attending its public colleges.[24] The other states allowed them to enroll but charged them nonresident tuition.[25] Given undocumented students' ineligibility to secure lawful employment, these students did not qualify for jobs in college or after graduation, and no one saw DACA as an alternative in the making.[26] Depending on the jurisdiction and occupation, they may or may not be licensed or gain authorization for skilled professions such as teaching, law, or the medical professions.[27] As is evident from the narratives that follow, this is highly contested terrain, especially considering how few such students exist in the context of more than 18 million college students. At the time, no estimates exceeded 50,000–60,000 students nationally each year,[28] which would constitute the enrollment at the main Columbus campus of The Ohio State University. In order to clear up the confusion on the issue, and to provide a path to legalization for the affected students after their graduation, the DREAM Act was introduced in 2001, in essentially its present form.[29]

In 2005, the Washington Legal Foundation (WLF) filed a complaint with the Department of Homeland Security (DHS) to challenge the Texas and New York statutes regarding undocumented students, although it is not entirely clear why this agency would have jurisdiction over these sections of IIRIRA.[30] As of spring 2014, a decade later, no action had been taken on this matter by DHS, and discussions with attorneys and officials involved indicated that there would be no action forthcoming.[31] Indeed, the answer was issued in a response to a different question, one posed by North Carolina officials about their own admissions policies.[32] In July 2008, DHS had indicated that any determinations of tuition residency or admissions policy by states were state matters, not in the federal domain:

> [T]he individual states must decide for themselves whether or not to admit illegal aliens into their public post-secondary institutions. States may bar or admit illegal aliens from enrolling in public post-secondary institutions either as a matter of public policy or through legislation. Please note, however, that any state policy or legislation on this issue must use federal immigration status standards to identify which applicants are illegal aliens. In the absence of any state policy or legislation addressing this issue, it is up to the schools to decide whether or not to enroll illegal aliens, and the schools must similarly use federal immigration status standards to identify illegal alien [sic] applicants.[33]

This would also be the appropriate response to the 2005 WLF complaint to the DHS as well, for state tuition and admissions policies have always been state issues, and it is surprising that a state entity would pose such a question, implicitly suggesting that the determination of a state status might turn on a federal determination; one wonders what the North Carolina response would have been had the federal department responded that the federal government actually would assert jurisdiction over the matter. The DHS response to the North Carolina query occurred during the final stages of the appellate decision being rendered in *Martinez v. Regents of the University of California*,[34] but the court did not take notice of the letter.

In *Day v. Sibelius*, lawyers challenged the Kansas statute allowing undocumented college students to establish residency status for tuition.[35] The judge ruled for the state, finding that the plaintiffs did not have standing to bring suit.[36] The Federation for American Immigration Reform filed an appeal to the federal court of appeals, and on August 30, 2007, the Tenth Circuit affirmed the trial court decision in the case.[37] The United State Supreme Court denied the petition for certiorari, thereby upholding the statute.[38]

In December 2005, the same groups that filed the Kansas matter filed in California state court challenging AB 540,[39] the California residency statute, on a parallel track, hoping to prevent the practice at both the federal and state levels.[40] In October 2006, FAIR's attempt to bring a case similar to the Kansas federal case in California state court lost when the trial judge ruled against them.[41] However, in fall 2008, an appellate court overturned the decision, ordered the matter back to trial, and found against the state.[42] The University of California announced that it would be appealing the AB 540 appellate court ruling to the state supreme court and, just as important for students in the short term, would continue to award AB 540 tuition exemptions during the appeal process.[43] Thus, in the country's largest state, with the largest number of undocumented students and largest number of college students, the entire program was clouded by the possibility that the California Supreme Court could uphold the plaintiffs and render the program a violation of federal law. This did not happen, as *Martinez v. UC Regents* unanimously reversed the appeals court in late 2010 and found for the state and the students.[44]

In another higher education immigration/residency case that occurred in California during this period, a number of immigrant organizations filed suit in November 2006 to challenge California's postsecondary residency and financial aid provisions[45] in *Student Advocates for Higher Education et al v. Trustees, California State University et al.*[46] Citizen students with undocumented parents were being prevented from receiving the tuition and financial aid benefits due to them, at least in part because the California statute was not precisely drawn (or was being imperfectly administered, in several instances). The challenge highlighted several overlapping policies: immigration, financial aid independence/dependence upon parents, and the age of majority/domicile.[47] The state agreed to discontinue the practice and entered into a consent decree resolving the matter in the plaintiffs' favor.[48] The order overturned CSU's unusual take on undocumented college student residency—that a citizen, majority-age college student with undocumented parents was not able to take advantage of the California statute according the undocumented in-state residence, even if the student were otherwise eligible.[49] In a similar fashion, the Virginia attorney general and the Colorado attorney general also ruled that US citizen children could establish tuition residency status on a case-by-case basis, even if their parents were undocumented.[50] These rulings made a virtue of necessity, inasmuch as citizen children who reach the age of majority by operation of law establish their own domicile: their parents' undocumented status is (or should be) irrelevant to the ability of the children to establish residency or eligibility for other postsecondary benefits or status on the basis of citizenship status. Flash forward to 2010, the time of the final *Martinez* decision, and two more states were also found to have similar criteria: New Jersey in its awards of state financial aid,[51] and Florida in its even more fundamental residency requirement.[52]

In 2005, the state of Texas enacted several modifications to its postsecondary residency statutes (Senate Bill 1528) and the implementing Texas Coordinating Board regulations, some of which affected undocumented students.[53] These revisions made it slightly easier for students to avail themselves of in-state tuition and ended the anomalous situation where international students (required to maintain foreign domiciles in F-1 visa status) took advantage of the original statute and regulations. In an interesting twist, following the California appellate decision, a restrictionist Texas state legislator requested an attorney general opinion, seeking to apply the intermediate appellate decision in the California *Martinez* case. In response, on July 23, 2009, the Texas attorney general waffled, concluding that the Texas tuition law would "not likely" violate the Equal Protection Clause of the Fourteenth Amendment, but refused to issue an opinion on whether the in-state tuition law would be preempted by federal law.[54] Texas governor Rick Perry, who in 2001 had signed the original legislation establishing House Bill 1403, said he would not accept or sign any changes to the state law.[55]

In a related development, the same Texas attorney general issued an opinion saying that the phrase "citizen of Texas" in the state's Hazlewood Act (a military scholarship program) should be interpreted as a person who lives in the state and is a US citizen.[56] Prior to this opinion, Texas public colleges and universities gave the Hazlewood benefit to all qualifying military veterans, regardless of whether they were US citizens or lawful permanent residents when they entered the military. In 2007, two Mexican American permanent resident veterans were rendered ineligible under this revised criterion; they brought suit, which was resolved in 2008, when the state attorney general reversed his position.[57]

Following the lead of Texas, New Mexico in January 2005 became the first state to enact residency tuition for the undocumented who graduated from the state's high schools and met the other residency requirements; it also extended resident tuition to the undocumented and altered its residency statutes for some American Indians and for Texans from border counties.[58] In doing so, it became among the most generous program, extending financial aid and lottery scholarship eligibility as well as resident tuition, with only a twelve-month durational requirement.

Many state-level developments took place in 2006. In January, the Utah attorney general issued an opinion, determining that the Utah statute granting tuition status to the state's undocumented college students was constitutional.[59] Although the state enacted considerably tighter legislation in 2008, barring the undocumented from many benefits, the move to repeal this tuition provision failed.[60] A safe harbor was created, and the state's senior US senator, widely regarded as a conservative legislator, continued his advocacy for passing federal immigration legislation that would grant legalization to college students.[61]

Also in January 2006, the Massachusetts legislature voted down a measure that would have accorded in-state tuition to the undocumented.[62] In 2007, the governor proposed to abolish tuition at the state's community colleges, but the proposal did not gain traction due to financial difficulties.[63] In 2008, another false start occurred when the governor decided not to pursue extending resident tuition to the students in any public college sector, citing the economic downturn.[64]

Early in 2007, legislation was introduced in Minnesota,[65] both to broaden residency and to restrict it. At the end of a complicated session, on May 30, 2007, Minnesota governor Tim Pawlenty signed into law an interesting partial victory for in-state/residency tuition advocates.[66] Under the Minnesota bill, a number of the state college system institutions eliminated nonresident rates altogether, allowing anyone, apparently regardless of state of residence or immigration status, to qualify for the flat (formerly in-district) rate. The press coverage on this never fully sussed the entire legislation, which was complex and originally included a specific DREAM Act provision that was ultimately stripped.[67] While the legislation somewhat finessed the larger issue (and contained a 2009 sunset provision), this approach had a nimble aspect to it, removing the immigration dimension.[68] It was an intriguing approach, as many

DREAM Act students are likely to attend two-year colleges.[69] In Texas, even before HB 1403 passed, several large community college districts had moved to this practice of in-district tuition, led by the Houston and Dallas community college systems, which were the real precursors of this practice in Texas.[70] Many of these students enroll in transfer curricula; however, partly due to the rising costs, other administrative and paperwork requirements, and their inability to work for pay, these students rarely ended up transferring to senior colleges.[71] Given the declining state appropriation support for higher education and the difficult economy, eliminating tuition seems an unlikely scenario for any college sector, especially the burgeoning two-year universe, which has been inundated with overflow enrollments from strapped senior institutions.[72] In addition, it is not clear in all states how state law affects local two-year college tuition policies, which are often district or county determinations based on "attendance zone districts" or substate line-drawing cartography.

On January 23, 2006, the Colorado attorney general issued an opinion on whether the state coordinating board had the authority to grant in-state residency status; he held that the Colorado Commission on Higher Education did not have such authority.[73] However, in 2007, he determined that state residency law did allow citizen students of undocumented parents to establish residency if they otherwise met the durational requirements.[74] In this decision, he opined: "[B]ecause it is the student, rather than the parents, who is the legal beneficiary of in-state tuition status, the fact that the parents may be in the country illegally is not a bar to the student's receipt of that benefit."[75] At the same time, Colorado newspapers reported on undocumented Colorado students who, through a reciprocal arrangement with New Mexico colleges, were allowed to attend New Mexico public colleges and to pay resident tuition. In addition, a single state college acted on its own before the state mooted the point in 2012, when it enacted a statute.[76]

On April 14, 2006, Nebraska became the tenth state to provide in-state tuition to undocumented immigrant students who had attended and graduated from Nebraska high schools. It did so in dramatic fashion, overriding Governor Dave Heineman's veto. The bill passed by a 26–19 margin but needed thirty votes for an override; supporters managed to change exactly four votes to reach the necessary thirty.[77]

During this period in the spring of 2006, very large crowds of immigrants and their supporters held widely publicized rallies, called "*marchas*," drawing substantial attention in the media.[78] By one estimate, more than half a million persons marched in Los Angeles alone, even risking apprehension by police and immigration authorities.[79] These were the first national, substantial public displays of support on behalf of immigrants, and they energized supporters and opponents alike.[80]

On September 30, 2006, California governor Arnold Schwarzenegger declined to sign S.B. 160, vetoing a bill that would have allowed undocumented students in California, already eligible for in-state tuition, to participate in the state's financial aid grant programs.[81] The state's budget crisis was beginning to become evident, and higher education suffered a large cut in support, including closing programs, limiting enrollments in many institutions, and even furloughing faculty and staff.[82] Several other states enacted legislation affecting international students, though these did not implicate in-state tuition status for the undocumented students who remained ineligible. Virginia extended tuition status to political refugees,[83] while Wyoming enacted state scholarship programs valuable only to residents who are lawful permanent residents (LPRs) or citizens.[84] During 2006, additional states considered but did not enact resident tuition statutes.[85]

The pace did not slow in 2007. The Oklahoma Taxpayer and Citizen Protection Act of 2007 repealed the 2003 financial aid provision that accorded residency tuition and grants to eligible undocumented students (although the actual language of the bill, signed into law in May 2007, continued residency exceptions and grandfathered in those students already eligible and enrolled.)[86] In January 2008, Oklahoma's Board of Regents issued a memo outlining the new policies.[87] Even so, restrictionists prevailed in the repeal action, making Oklahoma the only state to have extended this status and aid and then to have rescinded the state grant eligibility.

In spring 2007, Connecticut's legislature passed and sent a bill to Governor Jodi Rell for her signature, which would have granted alien students who graduated from the state's high schools the opportunity to qualify for resident tuition.[88] She vetoed the bill on June 26, 2007, and wrote: "I understand these students are not responsible for their undocumented status, having come to the United States with their parents. The fact remains, however, that these students and their parents are here illegally and neither sympathy nor good intentions can ameliorate that fact."[89]

In fall 2007, uncertainties arose over what the more restrictionist state statutes from Georgia and Arizona would mean for this issue, and things were in flux in these two states. Georgia held public hearings in April 2007 to obtain public input as to how it should proceed, but the behind-the-scenes waiver system, which allowed each public college to use waivers for up to 2 percent of their headcount, changed.[90] The statute took effect on July 1, 2007.[91] At the start of the spring 2007 semester, Arizona officials were confused about what to do with the statute's new requirements.[92] However, they decided that they would not enroll these students any longer, and by summer 2007 they reported that nearly 5,000 students had been removed from the state's institutions and adult basic education classes. In response, Arizona State University awarded students private money to help with financial aid needs.[93] The funds (contested by the same political opponents who enacted the restriction-ist legislation) ran out in spring 2008; the overall fiscal crisis in the state has continued, causing furloughs of regular faculty and severe cutbacks in college services.[94]

Following the lead in Missouri, which in 2007 saw the introduction of a death-penalty provision that would have banned undocumented students from enrolling in any fashion in its public colleges, Virginia legislators introduced a similar bill in the legislature in August 2007. The legislation died.[95]

The Missouri Senate Committee on Pensions, Veterans' Affairs, and General Laws heard testimony on March 14, 2007, on five proposed bills, including the Missouri Omnibus Immigration Act and a bill to ban undocumented students from enrolling in public institutions.[96] The Missouri legislation was not enacted in 2007.[97] In 2008, the Missouri legislature considered two separate bills addressing the undocumented college student tuition issue, one in the state house and one in the state senate: HB 1463 would have prohibited state institutions of higher educa-tion from admitting undocumented individuals. It was not enacted, as the legislature ran out of time in May 2008.[98] However, House Bill 1549 was enacted into law and incorporated by reference the federal provisions of sections 1621 and 1623; Missouri public and private colleges have acted as if the legislation prohibits them from enrolling students without legal status after January 1, 2009.[99] By restating the 1621 and 1623 provisions, the Missouri statutory scheme parses federal law ("public benefits") in a fashion not dictated by the language. The *Martinez*[100] state court litigation in California also turned on this crucial statutory construction, already construed by the federal decisions in *Merten*[101] and *Sibelius*.[102] If the legislative language simply incorporated the federal language, there was no need for the Missouri statute to have been enacted, especially if the IIRIRA and PWORA provisions require a state to take a formal action before according resident tuition to these students. If they are ineligible for the tuition status, as they were prior to the enactment, then no legislative action was required for determining or denying college resident status. This confusing set of events, especially in light of the clear July 2008 DHS apportionment of state authority to establish state policy, is most likely explained as a punitive measure to stake out political ground and to force immigrant supporters to go on record so that the vote—even on an unnecessary and superfluous matter—can be used in future elections as a signal of conservative political correctness.

The year 2008 started out with a bang, including ongoing national electoral politics over tuition benefits. In Virginia, citizen applicants of undocumented parents were the subject of an attorney general memo; the memo advised its client colleges to deal with these students on a case-by-case basis for residency tuition purposes.[103] In Utah, although a comprehensive restrictionist state law was enacted in 2008, it exempted undocumented college students from its coverage, so they remained eligible for resident tuition.[104]

In North Carolina, an odd and twisted scenario occurred in 2008. Early in the year, the state's community colleges indicated that they would enroll undocumented students and charge them in-district tuition.[105] In May, the attorney general's office issued a letter (which is less binding than an attorney general opinion), indicating that the state's colleges were not allowed even to enroll the undocumented, much less accord them resident tuition, citing DHS policy.[106] When the state officials sought actual guidance from DHS, the department indicated that, to the contrary, states were able to determine their own policy in accord with sections 1621 and 1623.[107] After receiving this guidance, state college officials indicated that they would not enroll the students at in-state tuition rates.[108]

A similarly confused reading of federal law occurred in Arkansas, where schools had silently enrolled students until it became publicly known and the state higher education agency and governor ended the practice; an Arkansas attorney general opinion ruled that Arkansas law allowed the undocumented to attend state institutions, although not at resident tuition rates.[109] In September 2008, Alabama's two-year college board also moved to ban their attendance.[110] In 2008 and 2009, resident tuition legislation was considered but not enacted in Maryland, Colorado, Virginia, Nebraska, Ohio, and New Jersey.[111]

In June 2008, South Carolina became the first state to enact state legislation that banned undocumented students from even attending public colleges; a decade later made it impossible for DACA students to gain resident tuition eligibility; and also played hardball for what should have been an easy call: residency tuition for US citizen children of undocumented parents. But after prevailing on the issue at the Fourth Circuit, it agreed to rewrite their regulations and accord them resident tuition.[112] Charging non-resident tuition in the other states has allowed few such students to enroll; the prohibitions on federal financial assistance make it virtually impossible for undocumented students to attend colleges and pay nonresident rates.[113] Even in Texas, the first state to enact a law broadening its tuition status and the state with the longest border adjoining Mexico, official figures for 2007 revealed there to be only 9,062 undocumented enrollees out of the total public college enrollment of 1,102,572 full-time students, or fewer than 1 percent.[114] In Washington, of the 427 students applying for and receiving "WA 1079" status in 2007–08, only 314 were presumed to be undocumented.[115] California's data were not widely available, but reports revealed that nearly two-thirds of the beneficiaries of AB 540 were citizens who had either moved away from the state or who were able to claim the in-state status because of the statutory language that grandfathered in former high school graduates as "residents."[116] In June 2009, Wisconsin became the eleventh state to offer the tuition provision, although later events led to its rescission.[117] As late as 2010, action was under way in New Jersey and Rhode Island to enact law extending resident tuition status to the undocumented, while in Texas and Nebraska, efforts were undertaken to rescind earlier statutes, both by litigation and legislation.[118]

These complex events are examined in detail in Chapters 4 (state developments after 2010). As it would be characterized in Texas, the DREAM Act had become "all-hat-and-no cattle," a disappointing set of affairs. But as bleak as these developments had appeared in the years leading up to 2010, there was a small but certain sense of momentum, as more and more undocumented students, buoyed by *Plyler* and positive legislation in California, Texas, and the smaller states. It had also become more obvious that it would have to be the various state laboratories, to paraphrase Justice Louis Brandeis, that would accord the enhanced educational civil rights to undocumented immigrants, envisioned by him as "novel social and economic experiments"[119] that the Supreme Court should make possible.

3

The DREAM Act in Congress and Federal Developments

Thus far, the chapters have focused on the broad and deep state efforts, which showed on balance an accommodationist bent more so than a restrictionist series of actions. Almost all the major immigrant feeder states—those with the largest populations of noncitizens—had made special provisions to accept and fund college students who had benefitted from *Plyler*'s permission to attend public K–12 schools. If Arizona had been more accommodating, all the Southwest border states, as well as more than a dozen other states across the country, would have been in the positive column. Public discursive narratives were largely positive, and the small pockets of nativist resistance were still in play as repeated efforts were undertaken in statehouses, in the normal way of all legislation, where it often took many efforts to effectuate statutory change—especially true in areas of contentious public debate and disagreement such as immigration integration.

The federal stage had also been active following the introduction of the DREAM Act in 2001,[1] but this is a tale of legislative failure, reprised with different stories and the same unsatisfying conclusion. To analogize, it was rather like an English parlor-murder mystery, with different murders and casts of characters, yet all frustratingly unsolved. In effect, neither Hercule Poirot nor Miss Marple nor Jane Tennison nor Inspector Morse could determine who had killed the starlet in the library and why she had been killed. In both 2003 and in 2005, the DREAM Act was reintroduced in Congress, even with 2004 Senate Judiciary Committee hearings, but it languished there until comprehensive immigration reform efforts failed in the summer of 2007.[2] In July 2007, the Senate tried a different legislative approach by developing plans to attach the DREAM Act legislation to the Department of Defense (DoD) authorization bill,[3] but it was pulled from the floor when an amendment on an Iraq timetable failed; the Senate never got to the DREAM vote.[4] The DoD authorization bill was scheduled to return to the Senate floor in September 2007, but by late fall 2007 there had been no additional movement. The House Judiciary Committee held a DREAM Act hearing on May 18, 2007.[5] On September 6, 2007, the House held subcommittee hearings on the STRIVE Act, the comprehensive House immigration legislation that contained, among other provisions, postsecondary tuition and the other features of the DREAM Act.[6] In a late attempt to enact legislation to address the status of the college students, on October 24, 2007, the Senate considered and voted down the standalone DREAM Act, 44–52, on the cloture motion.[7] This was the first actual congressional vote on the subject.

In addition, there were developments in other related immigration categories, such as college developments for victims of human trafficking ("T" nonimmigrant visas).[8] As noted, DHS in 2008 acted to situate the responsibility for state status as a state court decision.[9] On balance, this was a fertile period, with many legislative feints and initiatives, none of which ever sprouted into actual law or policy.

Even as the DREAM Act languished in Congress, dozens of national news stories, several books on the subject, and many national studies, including reports by the Heritage Foundation, in support of the restrictionist law professor Kris Kobach's California state court litigation on in-state tuition residency.[10] The Congressional Research Service published studies on the subject.[11] National professional associations, such as the National Association of College Admissions Counselors, were drawn to this issue, making the DREAM Act an organization priority.[12] The College Board also made it a priority, and in 2009 the Board released a comprehensive report that drew press attention.[13] The national and trade press regularly covered the subject.[14]

Another national barometer of interest in this larger issue is the scorecard of how many legislatures were considering legislation on immigration-related issues.[15] At the time, the National Conference of State Legislatures (NCSL) issued a report detailing all forms of state-level immigration legislation in the first six months of 2009: "more than 1,400 bills were considered in all fifty states.[16] No fewer than 144 laws and 115 resolutions [had] been enacted in 44 states, with bills sent to governors in two additional states. A total of 285 bills and resolutions [had] passed legislatures; 23 of these bills [were] pending [the] Governor's approval and three bills were vetoed."[17] Only four states did not enact a single immigration law during this period: Alaska, Massachusetts, Michigan, and Ohio.[18]

At a time when sixty votes were needed and every vote counted, four senators who were on the record as supporting the DREAM Act did not vote in 2007. Senator John McCain (R-AZ), who had been instrumental in the failed effort at comprehensive immigration reform with Senator Edward Kennedy (D-MA), did not even vote, as he was in the throes of his unsuccessful presidential campaign and did not want to alienate his conservative base voters. Senator Kennedy was unavailable for the vote, as his health had taken a turn for the worse. Senator Barbara Boxer (D-CA) was unavailable, as extensive wildfires had broken out in her state and she was away from the nation's capital. Senator Christopher Dodd (D-CT), an early DREAM Act supporter, was also unavailable and did not vote.[19] Most unusual and disappointing was the action of Senator Arlen Specter (R-PA), who had been a supporter of the DREAM Act and who was considered to be among the most liberal Republicans in the Senate. He voted against the bill, on the credulity-straining grounds that if it were enacted it would impede the larger goal of comprehensive immigration reform.[20] On the Senate floor on October 24, 2007, he read the following remarks:

> Mr. President, I believe that the DREAM Act is a good act, and I believe that its purposes are beneficial. I think it ought to be enacted. But I have grave reservations about seeing a part of comprehensive immigration reform go forward because it weakens our position to get a comprehensive bill.
>
> Right now, we are witnessing a national disaster, a governmental disaster, as States and counties and cities and townships and boroughs and municipalities—every level of government—are legislating on immigration because the Congress of the United States is derelict in its duty to proceed.
>
> We passed an immigration bill out of both Houses last year. It was not conferenced. It was a disgrace that we couldn't get the people's business done. We were unsuccessful in June in trying to pass an immigration bill. I think we ought to be going back to it. I have discussed it with my colleagues.

I had proposed a modification to the bill defeated in June, which, much as I dislike it, would not have granted citizenship as part of the bill, but would have removed fugitive status only. That means someone could not be arrested if the only violation was being in the country illegally. That would eliminate the opportunity for unscrupulous employers to blackmail employees with squalid living conditions and low wages, and it would enable people to come out of the shadows, to register within a year.

We cannot support 12 to 20 million undocumented immigrants, but we could deport the criminal element if we could segregate those who would be granted amnesty only.

I believe we ought to proceed with hearings in the Judiciary Committee. We ought to set up legislation. If we cannot act this year because of the appropriations logjam, we will have time in late January. But as reluctant as I am to oppose this excellent idea of the Senator from Illinois, I do not think we ought to cherry-pick. It would take the pressure off of comprehensive immigration reform, which is the responsibility of the Federal Government. We ought to act on it, and we ought to act on it now.[21]

This turnabout by a previously supportive senior Republican senator, combined with the White House's efforts to defeat passage, essentially on the same grounds, became the kiss of death for the bill. The George W. Bush White House issued an insincere press release just prior to the Senate's DREAM Act vote, stressing the need for overall immigration reform and suggesting that the current legislation was too generous:

The Administration continues to believe that the Nation's broken immigration system requires comprehensive reform. This reform should include strong border and interior enforcement, a temporary worker program, a program to bring the millions of undocumented aliens out of the shadows without amnesty and without animosity, and assistance that helps newcomers assimilate into American society. Unless it provides additional authorities in all of these areas, Congress will do little more than perpetuate the unfortunate status quo. The Administration is sympathetic to the position of young people who were brought here illegally as children and have come to know the United States as home.

Any resolution of their status, however, must be careful not to provide incentives for recurrence of the illegal conduct that has brought the Nation to this point.[22]

Prior to his defection, Senator Specter was widely considered to be a safe "yes" vote on the DREAM Act, and his politics had evolved to the point where he would even switch parties in 2008 and become a Democrat.[23] Senator Kay Bailey Hutchison (R-TX), who anticipated running for governor of Texas against the incumbent, the Republican Rick Perry (who had signed into law the first state legislation to grant in-state tuition to the undocumented), voted for the DREAM Act and thereby reduced the risk of alienating Latino voters in her home state, who would now have to choose in the primary between two candidates who had supported the issue.[24] Observers, including Senate staff, noted that there had been several other possible votes that likely would have been available for the legislation if the required sixty votes were within shouting distance; these senators were willing to risk the wrath of critical constituents only if their votes would actually count.[25] The absences of Senators McCain and Kennedy, both champions of immigration reform generally, as well as the absences of Dodd and Boxer, the defection of Specter, and the administration's withholding of its support clearly doomed the star-crossed bill at the very last stages of maneuvering. There was evidence that Republicans, all of whom (except McCain) voted, also had not wanted to give what would likely be viewed as a legislative victory to the Democrats, or to appear to do so, with the national presidential election coming soon afterward.[26] Given that the DREAM Act had bipartisan sponsorship, there were signals that its enactment would be able to garner the sixty votes necessary to avoid a Senate filibuster. Its failure was a bitter pill to swallow.

The Republican presidential primary candidates began in earnest to accuse each other of weakness on immigration and of favoring an amnesty for the affected students.[27] By this time, FAIR, the Heritage Foundation, and restrictionist lawyers had also added to the brew, making it impossible for supporters to bring up the issue.[28] The fleeting, and perhaps best, opportunity for enacting the DREAM Act had passed, caught in the ironic pincers of being too much (for conservative legislators who feared being tarred as supporting amnesty) and too little (enacting it would torpedo the larger strategy of reforming overall immigration problems).

Had the DoD strategy been attempted either immediately after September 11, 2001, or soon thereafter, when support for the war efforts in Afghan and Iraq were greater, it is more likely that it would have passed. Terrorism overshadowed events, rendering international issues too hot to handle; several of the terrorists involved in the deadly 9/11 attacks were themselves out-of-status college students.[29] It is all the more remarkable that the various state DREAM acts were all undertaken after 2001, save for the original statute, which was signed into Texas state law before September 11 by Governor George Bush's successor. After President Barack Obama, an early cosponsor of the bill when he was in the US Senate, was elected president and assumed office in January 2009, his first major legislative initiatives were focused on dealing with the economic meltdown that began to surface politically in the late summer and fall of 2008; comprehensive health care and insurance reform would follow.[30] Senator Harry Reid (D-NV), the majority leader, indicated that he would not proceed with the next two major legislative subjects in piecemeal fashion, forcing climate change and immigration reform to evolve as comprehensive omnibus projects rather than addressing the various component parts such as DREAMers, their parents, and legal immigration changes.[31]

There was also a substantial wait until the Obama administration made its own immigration reform design clear. It was not until mid-November 2009 that DHS secretary Janet Napolitano made her first address on the subject of comprehensive immigration reform, and while she stressed the need to incorporate the undocumented "shadow" population through legalization provisions, the major emphasis appeared to be on border security and employment verification:

> Let me be clear: when I talk about "immigration reform," I'm referring to what I call the "three-legged stool" that includes a commitment to serious and effective enforcement, improved legal flows for families and workers, and a firm but fair way to deal with those who are already here. That's the way that this problem has to be solved, because we need all three aspects to build a successful system. This approach has at its heart

the conviction that we must demand responsibility and accountability from everyone involved in the system: immigrants, employers and government. And that begins with fair, reliable enforcement.[32]

Until the actual proposals were introduced—whether by Congress or by President Obama and the executive branch—everything had pointed to an omnibus approach, and the convolutions of the 2009–2010 health care reform strategy suggested that the most salient consideration would be which of the large scale systemic initiatives would be able to move forward and under what timing and calendar constraints they would emerge. Could climate control, economic and banking reform, immigration, and the continuing war efforts all move to the front burner? Or would they compete for political resources in serial fashion?[33]

Senator Charles Schumer (D-NY) had assumed responsibility for steering immigration reform through the Senate following the death of Senator Kennedy, and his remarks showed him to be much more conservative compared to Kennedy. For example, in public remarks he adopted actual restrictionist code words and rhetoric, making it clear that his first priority was to "secure the border," and he even touted language to signal and characterize the problems.[34] For example, in summer 2009 he gave a public lecture where he laid out his first principle, objecting even to widely employed terminology such as "undocumented workers":[35]

The first of these seven principles is that illegal immigration is wrong—plain and simple. When we use phrases like "undocumented workers," we convey a message to the American people that their Government is not serious about combating illegal immigration, which the American people overwhelmingly oppose.

Above all else, the American people want their Government to be serious about protecting the public, enforcing the rule of law, and creating a rational system of legal immigration that will proactively fit our needs rather than reactively responding to future waves of legal immigration. People who enter the United States without our permission are illegal aliens, and illegal aliens should not be treated the same as people who entered the United States legally.[36]

On the subject of the DREAM Act, his principles did not include specific reference to the topic, but he had voted for the bill in 2007, suggesting his inclination and support for this part of the larger issue, notwithstanding his rhetorical finger-wagging.[37] The draft versions of reform legislation included DREAM Act provisions buried inside larger omnibus overhaul approaches, hiding and drawing away from "legalization" or "amnesty" features.

Despite many opinions that the DREAM Act, once enacted, would clear the decks and show that bipartisan differences could be resolved, thereby leading to the larger, more comprehensive overhaul, this turned out to be wishful thinking. There had been a brief window in 2007 when this might have occurred, and the narrative recounted here shows that a little luck might have helped turn the corner: had Senator Kennedy been well, had Senator Specter not backed away, had the fires not broken out in California, had Senator Dodd voted, had there not been a presidential election looming. But it goes without saying that all legislation, not just that affecting immigration, has to face the cards on the table at the time of its consideration. President Obama had undertaken so many major initiatives, including an early and unexpected nomination of a Supreme Court justice,[38] that all the oxygen in the room was being inhaled. As one observer noted: "On February 24, [2009], Obama addressed Congress to explain his budget priorities and urge Congressional action on three key priorities: energy, health care, and education. . . . This three-part agenda, combined with other pending legislative initiatives (immigration reform, highway programs, banking system regulation) not mentioned in the address, was remarkably ambitious. President Obama's strategy was to begin by pushing for several major initiatives at once."[39]

The agenda items were not only "remarkably ambitious" but also inextricably interrelated. In another setting where President Obama was addressing the entire Congress, it was during his discussion of health care proposals that Representative Joe Wilson (R-SC) famously shouted out, "You lie!" regarding immigrant benefits.[40] If there ever had been a need to demonstrate the relationship among several volatile topics, surely this unprecedented breach of protocol was Exhibit A.[41] A final reason why comprehensive immigration reform appeared to require an omnibus and overarching legislative strategy was because the issue was simply one of such transcendent complexity, with so many interrelated moving parts, that it could not be incrementally reformed. While partisan politics will always be present, the bedfellows of immigration reform cannot be easily identified by the traditional scorecards.[42] In 2001, I would have taken any bet that immigration legislation introduced by Senators Orrin Hatch (R-UT) and the late Senator Kennedy would have been enacted into law; indeed, I did take that bet, and in print.[43] If cosponsorship was a determinative signaling device or leading indicator, the DREAM Act would be law today, and these young adults would be working their way toward a form of legalization.

However, even if legislation passed tomorrow, it would not affect the ability of states to grant resident tuition, to enable them to award state scholarships and grants, and to allow them to withhold enrollment. Thus, no matter the fate of omnibus immigration reform or the stand-alone DREAM Act, this issue would remain an agenda item at the state level. Gary Reich and Alvar Ayala Mendoza, in their thoughtful study of the unlikely passage of tuition legislation in conservative Kansas, noted that its successful enactment was due, in a traditional sense, to the careful framing of the issue not as amnesty to helpless children but as one of educating a vulnerable population and to the persistence and skill of its advocates:

> [The] local framing of in-state tuition is crucial. Advocates of in-state tuition in Kansas consistently couched their arguments in the local terms of Kansan children desiring an education. By contrast, the main opponent of HB 2008 employed an issue frame based on national immigration policy and terrorism to argue against the bill. The appeals to national immigration policy and terrorism did not appear to resonate with state legislators, nor were they supported by any major elected state official (for example, neither the governor nor the attorney general played a role in the debate over the bill). However, where concerns about immigration law and the threat of terrorism have more local salience for voters and elected officials (Arizona may be a relevant example), we would expect FAIR's arguments to be more effective. In this regard, national

immigration debates may work against proponents of in-state tuition in the future. In Kansas, debates about HB 2008 occurred in a climate in which illegal immigration was not as prominent a public policy issue as it would become just a year later, when the Bush administration's immigration reform bill prompted extensive media attention.[44]

Of course, all politics is local, and there are features evident in Kansas that were simultaneously unique and generic, as there have been in every state where the issue has been taken up, whether successfully, unsuccessfully, or somewhere between, as in the case of Oklahoma, where both the thrill of victory and the agony of defeat were evident in the partial rescission of the statute.[45] In this sense, the legislative strategy will have a different playbook in every state, even as the toolkit will have certain common instruments that may be deployed or not as local circumstances require. Indeed, this is the case of every statute ever enacted and is unremarkable in one very real sense.

However, at the federal level, where most immigration policy resides, the basics of the system are so complex, the policy issues are so politicized and intertwined, and the different coalitions are so evanescent that the polity cannot feed all the smaller parts through the legislative scheme and process one component at a time. At some point, and by all indications, legislation will likely pass in one form or another, and the subsequent, never-ending line of complex problems will be taken up. (See table 3.1.) These issues will have had their own narratives and legislative histories and their own arcs and trajectories. Immigration will continue to claim a permanent place on the congressional agenda, especially in a globalized world where the United States will require immigrants and immigrants will come. When a DREAM Act becomes law, the structural features of federal immigration legislation and state college tuition policies will necessitate coordinated and integrated state legislation for full implementation at the institutional level, thereby guaranteeing continued attention to the issue. The republic will survive, legislative work will get done, and our experiment in representative democracy will continue to evolve. And these *Plyler* children among us will have graduated from college and taken up their place in the larger community.

TABLE 3.1: DREAM Act and DACA congressional legislative history
(2001–2019)

(107TH CONGRESS) 2001–02:
    S. 1291, DREAM Act of 2001
    H.R. 1918, Student Adjustment Act of 2001

(108TH CONGRESS) 2003–04:
    S. 1545, DREAM Act of 2003
    S. Rept. 108-224—Amending the Illegal Immigration Reform Act of
      1996
    H.R. 1684, Student Adjustment Act of 2003

(109TH CONGRESS) 2005–06:
    S. 2075, DREAM Act of 2005
    H.R. 5131, American DREAM Act of 2006
    S. 2611, Comprehensive Immigration Reform Act of 2006

(110TH CONGRESS) 2007–08:
    S. 1348, Comprehensive Immigration Reform Act of 2007
    5/11/2007: Sponsor introductory remarks on measure. (CR
      S6007–6008)
    5/21/2007: Cloture on the motion to proceed invoked in Senate by Yea-
      Nay Vote. 69—23. Record Vote Number: 173. (consideration: CR
      S6387-6388)
    6/7/2007: Cloture on the bill not invoked in Senate by Yea-Nay
      Vote. 34—61. Record Vote Number: 204. (consideration: CR
      S7279-7280)
    Action By: Senate
    S. 774, Development, Relief, and Education for Alien Minors Act of
      2007
    H.R. 1221, EARN Act
    H.R. 1275, American DREAM Act
    S. 2205, DREAM Act 2007 [voted on, 44–52 (October 24, 2007)]
    S. Amdt. 2919 (DREAM Act of 2007) to H.R. 1585 (National Defense
      Authorization Act for Fiscal Year 2008)
    H.R. 1645—STRIVE Act of 2007
    S. 1348—Secure Borders, Economic Opportunity, and Immigration
      Reform Act of 2007
    06/07/2007 Cloture on amendment SA 1150, upon reconsideration, not
      invoked in Senate by Yea-Nay Vote. 45—50. Record Vote Number:
      206. (consideration: CR S7313; text: CR S7313)

(111TH CONGRESS) 2009–10

H.R. 4986, National Defense Authorization Act for FY 2008

01/28/2008: Became Public Law No: 110–181.

01/22/2018: Received in the Senate, read twice, considered, read the third time, and passed without amendment by Yea-Nay Vote. 91—3. Record Vote Number: 1. (consideration: CR S54–57)

01/16/2008: House. On motion to suspend the rules and pass the bill Agreed to by the Yeas and Nays: (2/3 required): 369—46 (Roll no. 11). (text: CR H76–257)

01/16/2008: DEBATE—The House proceeded with forty minutes of debate on H.R. 4986.

S. 729, DREAM Act of 2009

H.R. 1751, DREAM Act of 2009

03/26/2009: Sponsor introductory remarks on measure. (CR E797)

H.R.5281—Removal Clarification Act of 2010

7/27/2010 Passed House

12/03/2010 Passed Senate

12/08/2010 Resolving Differences

05/25/2010 House Subcommittee Hearings Held by House Judiciary Subcommittee on Courts and Competition Policy

5/12/2010 Sponsor introductory remarks on measure. (CR E827–828)

H.R. 6327, Citizenship and Service Act of 2010

H.R. 6497, DREAM Act of 2010

S. 3827, DREAM Act of 2010

S. 3932, Comprehensive Immigration Reform Act of 2010

S. 3962, DREAM Act of 2010

S. 3963, DREAM Act of 2010

S. 3992, DREAM Act of 2010

12/09/2010: Cloture motion on the motion to proceed to the bill rendered moot in Senate. (consideration: CR S8668)

12/09/2010: Motion to table the motion to proceed to the bill agreed to in Senate by Yea-Nay Vote. 59—40. Record Vote Number: 268. (consideration: CR S8668)

112TH CONGRESS (2011–12)

S. 6, Reform America's Broken Immigration System Act

S. 952, DREAM Act of 2011

S. 1258, Comprehensive Immigration Reform Act of 2011

H.R. 1842, DREAM Act of 2011

TABLE 3.1: (*cont.*)

113TH CONGRESS (2013–14)

S. 744, Border Security, Economic Opportunity, and Immigration Modernization Act

6/27/2013: Passed Senate with an amendment by Yea-Nay Vote. (68–32)

06/27/2013: Considered by Senate. (consideration: CR S5315–5317, S5317–5320, S5320–5329, S5357–5475)

06/07/2013: By Senator Leahy from Committee on the Judiciary filed written report. Report No. 113-40. Additional and Minority views filed.

05/22/2013: Hearings Held Prior to Referral by House Committee on the Judiciary.

05/22/2013: Committee on Small Business and Entrepreneurship. Hearings held.

05/07/2013: Committee on Homeland Security and Governmental Affairs. Hearings held. Hearings printed: S.Hrg. 113–254.

04/23/2013: Committee on the Judiciary. Hearings held. Hearings printed: S.Hrg. 113–875.

04/22/2013: Committee on the Judiciary. Hearings held. Hearings printed: S.Hrg. 113–875.

04/19/2013: Committee on the Judiciary. Hearings held. Hearings printed: S.Hrg. 113–44.

H.R. 15, Border Security, Economic Opportunity, and Immigration Modernization Act

11/21/2013: Sponsor introductory remarks on measure. (CR E1751–1753)

03/26/2014: Motion to Discharge Committee filed by Mr. Garcia. Petition No: 113-9. (Discharge petition text with signatures.)

114TH CONGRESS (2015–2016)

115TH CONGRESS (2017–2018)

S. 1615—DREAM Act of 2017

H.R. 1468—Recognizing America's Children Act

H.R. 3440—DREAM Act of 2017

H.R. 2071—American DREAM Promise Act

H.R. 1468—Recognizing America's Children Act

S. 1852—SUCCEED Act

H.R.4760—Securing America's Future Act of 2018 06/21/2018: failed by record vote 193 – 231

06/21/2018: On motion to recommit with instructions Failed by the Yeas and Nays: 191—234 (Roll no. 281).

06/21/2018: Considered under the provisions of rule H. Res. 954. (consideration: CR H5380–5438; text: CR H5380–5423)

06/21/2018: DEBATE—The House proceeded with one hour of debate on H.R. 4760.

06/21/2018: DEBATE—The House proceeded with ten minutes of debate on the motion to recommit with instructions. The instructions contained in the motion seek to require the bill to be reported back to the House with an amendment to replace the bill text with language found in H.R. 3440, the Dream Act of 2017.

H.R. 4796—USA Act of 2018

H.R. 4750—TPS Act

S. 2199—Border Security and Deferred Action Recipient Relief Act

S. 2367—USA Act of 2018

H.R. 4873—DACA Compromise Act of 2018 H.R. 6136—Border Security and Immigration Reform Act of 2018

06/27/2018: Failed by recorded vote: 121–301

06/21/2018: DEBATE—The House proceeded with one hour of debate on H.R. 6136.

S. 2464—Three-Year Border and DACA Extension Act

S. 128.—BRIDGE Act

116TH CONGRESS (2019-2020)

S. 197—A bill to provide for the confidentiality of information submitted in requests for deferred action under the deferred action for childhood arrivals program, and for other purposes.

H.R. 6—American Dream and Promise Act of 2019

S. 879—A bill to provide a process for granting lawful permanent resident status to aliens from certain countries who meet specified eligibility requirements, and for other purposes.

S. 1088—A bill to amend the Immigration and Nationality Act to require the President to set a minimum annual goal for the number of refugees to be admitted, and for other purposes.

In fall 2009, Representative Luis Gutiérrez (D-IL), the chief House proponent of the DREAM Act and immigration reform, introduced his immigration "Core Principles," as Senator Schumer had done, but immigration reform bills—either comprehensive or a standalone DREAM Act—were not gaining traction.[46] And the subject languished, with no indication of the more clandestine administrative efforts being undertaken with the forerunner of DACA.[47] In the 111th Congress, the House and Senate versions were dutifully filed and waiting in the queues.[48] In the US House, HR 1751 was introduced: "To amend the Illegal Immigration Reform and Immigrant Responsibility Act of 1996 to permit States to determine State residency for higher education purposes and to authorize the cancellation of removal and adjustment of status of certain alien students who are long-term United States residents and who entered the United States as children, and for other purposes." Its chief sponsor was Representative Howard L. Berman (D-CA), and it was introduced on March 26, 2009, with ten cosponsors. It was referred to the House Judiciary and House Education and Labor Committees; on May 14, 2009, it was referred to House subcommittee and, in turn, to the Subcommittee on Higher Education, Lifelong Learning, and Competitiveness. In the US Senate, S. 729 was introduced: "A bill to amend the Illegal Immigration Reform and Immigrant Responsibility Act of 1996 to permit States to determine State residency for higher education purposes and to authorize the cancellation of removal and adjustment of status of certain alien students who are long-term United States residents and who entered the United States as children, and for other purposes." Its chief sponsor was Senator Richard Durbin (D-IL), and it was introduced on March 26, 2009, with thirty-one cosponsors. On the same day, it was referred to the Senate Judiciary Committee. Although not everyone realized it at the time, this would become the closest precursor to the 2012 DACA policy of prosecutorial discretion as a standalone DREAM Act bill.[49]

Ted Kennedy's Senate seat was filled by a Republican who was seated in February 2010, giving Republicans forty-one seats in the Senate and the opportunity to mount filibusters with more regularity.[50] Notwithstanding this turn of events , the logjam broke slightly in March 2010 when President Obama made his own first formal announcement on immigration reform, linking it to the need for bipartisan support. More important, the Affordable Care Act was signed into law by use of the reconciliation process; Congress gave final approval to health care legislation without a single Republican vote.[51] The logjam appeared to back him in March 2010 when President Obama made his first formal announcement on immigration reform.

In fall 2010, at the urging of Latino groups and to jump-start the chimerical comprehensive immigration reform, Senator Harry Reid changed his mind and brought forward a standalone DREAM Act bill. The DREAM Act became an amendment to a Department of Defense bill (S. 3454, the "National Defense Authorization Act for Fiscal Year 2011"). He also added two other amendments: a repeal of the so-called Don't Ask, Don't Tell policy regarding the enlistment of gay and lesbian soldiers in the military, and an overhaul of the "secret hold" tradition in the Senate to require public disclosure when moving legislative actions forward. On September 21, 2010, the vote became hostage to the Don't Ask, Don't Tell controversy; the Republicans voted as a bloc rather than hand President Obama and the Democrats a victory on this issue; the cloture motion was rejected 43–56 (with a single absence).[52] Senator Reid himself voted against the motion after it was clear that he did not have the required sixty votes. (This vote against his own motion would allow Reid to call for reconsideration.) Even Republican supporters of the earlier legislation in the 2007 vote did not support the overall package in the 2010 effort, and two Democrats crossed over to vote against it as well.[53] Once again, the DREAM Act was tantalizingly close and followed many public stories in the media about undocumented college students; these news reports continued through the lame-duck session, where once again the votes were not there.

The third time may be the proverbial charm, but not in this subject matter. In the final days of the same Congress, the greatest disappointment occurred. On December 8, 2010, the House attached the DREAM Act (HR 6497) to another moving House bill, HR 5281, and passed it 216–198. This was the first time that the House had ever voted on a version of the DREAM Act since its introduction in 2001. Initially, the Senate was scheduled to take a procedural vote on its version of DREAM (S 3992), but instead Senate Democrats voted 59–40 to withdraw S 3992 and to focus on the bill passed on December 8 by the House. On December 18, 2010, the Senate took up the cloture motion (technically, the Motion to Invoke Cloture on the Motion to Concur in the House Amendment to the Senate Amendment No. 3 to H.R. 5281, the Removal Clarification Act of 2010).[54] Democratic backers of the legislation fell short of the sixty votes required to move the DREAM Act legislation forward, with a vote of 55–41 in favor.[55]

Five Democratic senators—Max Baucus (MT), Kay Hagan (NC), Ben Nelson (NE), Mark Pryor (AR), and Jon Tester (MT)—joined most Republicans in voting against the measure. Three Republican senators—Bob Bennett (UT), Richard Lugar (IN), and Lisa Murkowski (AK)—voted yes. Four other senators—Jim Bunning (R-KY), Judd Gregg (R-NH), Orrin Hatch (R-UT), and Joe Manchin (D-WV)—were not present for the vote. The ultimate ironies were that, in a separate vote, the Don't Ask, Don't Tell policy was repealed, and Senator Hatch, who had introduced the original legislation a decade earlier, was not in the chamber to vote for the DREAM Act.[56]

By Christmas 2010, the House, which was about to turn Republican after the November elections, was on the record for the DREAM Act, but the Senate (which was to remain controlled by Democrats but with fewer than the sixty who had been in office) could not deliver. Although standalone DREAM Act bills have since been introduced each term, no actual votes have been taken on this legislation in the intervening years. As will be discussed in chapter 6, when the Senate acted in June 2013 to pass comprehensive immigration reform, a section of that omnibus legislation (S. 744) incorporated DREAM Act features that would have allowed a pathway to citizenship for most DREAMers, but the Republican-led House did not take up any reform bill or any subsequent version of the DREAM Act. In a sense, the legislative program had a near-life experience but then lapsed into a comatose state, where it lay, like Sleeping Beauty, waiting for the kiss to awaken.

4

The Aftermath of the DREAM Act Defeats, State Developments

With regard to relief for DREAMers, while the federal legislation option was the best known and most politicized, actions at the state level increased substantially, and a number of developments occurred after the December 2010 failure in Congress.[1] Subsequent activities at the state level included Wisconsin (repealed resident tuition statute);[2] Maryland (passed resident tuition statute; "frozen" while certified for state ballot measure);[3] Rhode Island (state board responsible for residency tuition policy enacted rule allowing residency tuition in 2012);[4] Illinois (passed state statute allowing schools to award non–state-funded scholarships to the undocumented);[5] California (passed three state statutes: allowing schools to award non–state-funded scholarships, providing state financial assistance, and making special provisions for undocumented student leaders);[6] and Connecticut (passed resident tuition statute).[7] While Maryland placed the issue on the 2012 statewide ballot, there was an effort in California to do the same before the provisions of the new laws were to take effect in 2013; when the signatures were counted in early January 2012, there were not enough legitimate signatures to certify the measure to the November 2012 ballot.[8] In 2013, tuition statues were passed in Oregon, Colorado, and Minnesota, and Hawaii enacted an administrative procedure.[9] Rhode Island was the first state to enact residency tuition for undocumented college students by administrative action rather than by a statute, as tuition policy is set administratively in the state.[10]

From 2010 through 2013, litigation occurred in California,[11] Nebraska,[12] and Texas,[13] upholding state statutes against restrictionist efforts to eliminate the recent tuition provisions. In New Jersey[14] and Florida,[15] the states were sued due to policies that restricted even citizen residents from receiving residency or financial aid if their parents were out of status. Litigation also was filed in Maryland[16] and New York[17] on associated residency tuition issues. In addition to these expansive accommodationist initiatives, designed to incorporate undocumented college students into their communities, there have been states that have done the opposite—enacting statutes or policies to prevent the undocumented from receiving resident tuition (redundant, as sections 1621 and 1623 require affirmative passage of "state law[s]" to trigger the statutes)[18] (see appendix 1)—and a small number of states ban them outright, including Alabama,[19] Indiana,[20] and Ohio,[21] which did so in 2011 (for these, see appendix 2). The 2011 Alabama bill would have restricted even refugees from enrolling, and it was enjoined by a federal district court judge.[22] Additional Alabama provisions affecting K–12 students and requiring the state to "inventory" such children were not enjoined by the trial court but was by the Eleventh Circuit.[23] Existing New Jersey policy denied state financial aid to a student who was a US citizen but whose mother was undocumented.[24] Suit was filed on this issue in 2011.[25] On October 20, 2011, the Southern Poverty Law Center filed *Ruiz v. Robinson*,[26] which would require Florida to extend its in-state tuition rates to citizen residents who qualify, even if their parents are undocumented.[27] In a major development, in late 2010, the California Supreme Court overturned a state appellate court,[28] which had the effect of upholding the state's residency statute, thereby exempting undocumented immigrant students from paying nonresident tuition at California state schools, a policy in place since 2001.[29] There have been other stutter-steps and half-steps in states on the topic of such residency statutes, both accommodationist and restrictionist.[30]

During the pendency of these various state actions, the 2012 GOP presidential primary race heated up, providing an unexpected national debate on the issue of undocumented college students.[31] In the early stages of the 2011 campaign period, Texas governor Rick Perry, who had signed the original accommodationist state law in 2001, drew the attention of his opponents, all of whom aligned themselves against his record.[32] When he withdrew from the race in early 2012, virtually all observers noted that his poor performance in the debates[33] as well as his earlier actions concerning the tuition matter (and his spirited defense of those actions) hurt him with voters and the public.[34] Buoyed by his leaving the race, the remaining candidates piled on against his views and indicated their opposition to the DREAM Act.[35] During the course of the Republican campaign, among ethnic and immigration politics, the DREAM Act was excoriated.[36]

In April 2011, Senator Harry Reid and twenty-one other Democratic senators published a letter they sent to President Barack Obama urging him to use executive discretion and authority to stop deportations and removals of undocumented young people—those who grew up in the United States or have been residing here for many years—who would have benefitted from the DREAM Act. The cosigners said in the letter that they would bring the DREAM Act back to the Senate for a vote, but the Republican-led House was likely this time to block the bill,[37] a reversal of the previous December 2010 bill, when the House passed the bill but the Senate failed to gain the sixty senators it needed.[38] Senator Chuck Schumer, who was leading the Senate effort to enact the bill as chair of the Senate Judiciary Subcommittee on Immigration, Refugees, and Border Security, sent his own letter to Department of Homeland Security secretary Janet Napolitano, calling on her not to target DREAM Act–eligible young people for deportation.[39] Although Napolitano said that the students were "not the [Department's] priority,"[40] she insisted that no category of prosecutorial discretion would be employed for groups of individuals: "I am not going to stand here and say that there are whole categories that we will, by executive fiat, exempt from the current immigration system, as sympathetic as we feel towards them."[41]

In June 2011, with the release of what came to be known as the "Morton Memo," and in August and November 2011, there were developments in the issue of deferred action and the extent to which the Obama administration would extend a form of prosecutorial discretion to DREAM Act students and others in the country without legal status.[42] The Obama administration undertook a test-case review of immigration cases in Baltimore and Denver with an eye toward freezing deportations of unauthorized residents who had no criminal records and then expanding the program of prosecutorial discretion nationwide.[43] The plans were to favor the elderly, children who have been in the country more than five years, students who came to the United States under the age of sixteen and were enrolled in a college degree program, and victims of domestic violence:[44] their pending deportations could be put on hold under the test program as low-priority populations.[45] In the predictable thermodynamics of immigration politics, however, there was an equal and opposite reaction against employing such discretion, particularly for the population of potential DREAM Act enrollees. In addition, deferred action, however advantageous in stopping the clock or in throwing sand into the deportation and removal gears, is not a true or final resolution of undocumented immigration status and would likely leave many DREAMers unassisted and ineligible for any ultimate change in their legal status. The uncertainty and complexity had made the status quo very frustrating for many observers, particularly the affected students.

Moreover, there were many potentially eligible students who had grown frustrated at the slow pace and their lack of options during college and after graduation, and with a series of large public marches in 2006 they began a systematic practice of outing and revealing themselves to authorities in public fashion. This brought attention to the students—negative and positive—but even over time it has not created any valence for revisiting the failed 2010 federal legislation.[46] That avenue was closed due to the Republican Party's intransigence on enacting any legislation for which President Obama could claim credit and the symmetrical decision by the president to run for another term, with one campaign theme being the inability or unwillingness of Congress to do its legislative and governance work, especially the Republican House and, to a lesser degree, the Democratic Senate.[47] It was a surprise on June 15, 2012, therefore, when the administration, prior to the start of the presidential campaign season, announced the establishment of a generous deferred action policy: Deferred Action for Childhood Arrivals. On the thirtieth anniversary of *Plyler v. Doe*—the 1982 case in which the US Supreme Court ruled that states could not deny funds for the education of children of unauthorized immigrants[48]—the president announced a halt to the deportation of some undocumented immigrants who came to the United States as children and had graduated from high school or served in the military.[49] While its outlines were unclear and it was certainly not as robust as any of the previous decade's DREAM Act proposals, this program was an entirely new initiative, carved from prosecutorial discretion clay, and for the first time in many years the DREAMers could have hope.

5

The DREAM Act and Prosecutorial Discretion

The Birth of DACA

In furtherance of a lifelong indulgence with rock and roll, I have developed a playful series of research and policy analyses on the topic of the law and business of rock and roll, one I conduct for various audiences and with continuing legal education credit for entertainment lawyers.[1] Among the many fascinating topics are the adhesion contracts that many young artists sign in their early ambition and naïveté;[2] a number of riveting cases that have arisen over the years with deceased and living artists;[3] the growing number of technological advances that affect the ownership and distribution of musical resources to the large number of user destinations; public policy and regulation concerning music; musical references hidden in judicial opinions; and the very large intersection of rock and roll and immigration law—or the flow of international artists into and from the United States in the globalized world that is today's genre.[4] Among this treasure trove of materials, I discuss the relationship between rock and roll and deferred action, in the person of one of my most beloved musical influences, the late former Beatle John Lennon, whose legal troubles in the 1970s gave rise to the doctrine of deferred action (at the time, also called "prosecutorial discretion" and "nonpriority status"), as he and his wife Yoko Ono attempted to remain in the United States despite Lennon's earlier drug conviction in the United Kingdom.[5]

Their lawyer, Leon Wildes, has recounted the extensive and complicated history of the case, which became a struggle to determine the existence of applicable agency discretion and the extent to which it could be employed in Lennon's attempt to remain in the United States, where they were searching for Yoko Ono's daughter, who had been snatched by Ono's former husband and could not be found:

Lennon came to the United States as a visitor in August 1971, and was permitted to remain until late February 1972. At that time the INS instituted deportation proceedings against him as an alleged overstay. Lennon claimed that the proceedings were instituted for political reasons. Among other things, he requested a grant of nonpriority status.

Nonpriority status is a euphemism for an administrative stay of deportation which effectively places an otherwise deportable alien in a position where he is not removed simply because his case had the lowest possible priority for INS [now DHS] action. Traditionally, the status was accorded to aliens whose departure from the United States would result in extreme hardship. Lennon and artist Yoko Ono, his wife, had come to this country to fight contested custody proceedings concerning Kyoko, Ono's daughter by a prior marriage. Lennon and Ono were completely successful on the law, with courts in several jurisdictions awarding them custody of Kyoko. However the father absconded with the child and could not be found. In the midst of the frantic search for the child, Lennon and Ono were subjected to expulsion proceedings. They felt, accordingly, that the equities involved in their continued search for the child justified the application for nonpriority status. Hardship notwithstanding, nonpriority status was never even given consideration, and the deportation proceedings relentlessly advanced.

Commencing on May 1, 1972, through extensive correspondence with the INS, Lennon made every conceivable effort to obtain the records relevant to nonpriority procedures before instituting suit in federal court. However, after more than a year's correspondence, the records were not forthcoming. In fact, the Service stated that the data about nonpriority cases were "not compiled" although at no time did it deny the existence of either a nonpriority program or relevant records. Lennon's demands, made pursuant to the FOIA [Freedom of Information Act], continued until August 1973, with no response from the Service.[6]

When this legal action was undertaken, the salient rules on the various INS nonpriority classifications were in a hidden format, unknown and inaccessible to immigration attorneys: "The entire program was so shrouded in secrecy that a former District Director of the Immigration and Naturalization Service (INS) actually denied the existence of the program. . . . The situation was a classic example of secret law."[7] As Lennon's attorney noted, after the case, "this [Operations] Instruction was transferred from the unpublished Blue Sheets to the published White Sheets."[8] This made the Operations Instruction (OI) and its implementing details known to the practitioner community, and the resultant regularization of the practice resulted in more transparency in the process.[9] In its earlier existence, the INS's internal regulations were never made available and had carried little weight.[10] These more open provisions continued over two decades, with modifications and significant litigation, until 1997, when they were rolled into a revised and reformatted "Standard Operating Procedures" manual, one whose contents were public and available to the immigration bar.[11]

As another Beatles song had foretold, the Lennon matter was a "Long and Winding Road," one that, after the five-year struggle, permitted the musician to remain in the United States. It also shined light under the Freedom of Information Act on the internal practice of allowing INS officials to short-circuit a proceeding and assign low priority status to it, essentially letting it remain in a state of limbo without further action to remove the noncitizen.[12] In the 1970s, when this status came to light, remaining in the United States was an unalloyed positive feature, which diminished with the 1996 appearance of prohibitive and punitive three-year and ten-year bars on relief.[13] Therefore, the discovery of this discretionary status was a substantial practice tool for an immigration bar that has shrunk over the years, as Congress has, in a series of actions, squeezed much of the previously available discretion from the system and made relief unavailable except in substantially narrowed and limited circumstances.[14]

This shrinking (and intermittent expansion) of discretionary jurisdiction remain essentially the case to the present, forty-plus years after *United States v. Lennon*[15] and nearly a quarter-century after the Illegal Immigration Reform and Immigrant Responsibility Act,[16] the Antiterrorism and Effective Death Penalty Act (AEDPA),[17] and the Personal Responsibility and Work Opportunity Reconciliation Act,[18] all enacted by Congress in 1996. By every indication, even with exceptions, there is much less play in the statutory joints than had been the case before these statutes were passed.[19]

With these more detailed and punitive 1996 legislative provisions there was less discretion available to intending immigrants and noncitizens, and this reduction in the statutory authority to resolve cases led, perhaps inevitably, to heightened administrative agency authority to exercise residual prosecutorial flexibility.[20] Because no legislation as comprehensive as that affecting immigration and naturalization can pin down every detail or anticipate every development, a certain (and very large) amount of administrative discretion will always be available, but the balance of this determination has shifted dramatically and paradoxically to the agency,[21] as noted by professors Adam Cox and Cristina Rodriguez, who have written:

> [T]he Executive still has de facto delegated authority to grant relief from removal on a case-by-case basis. The Executive simply exercises this authority through its prosecutorial discretion, rather than by evaluating eligibility pursuant to a statutory framework at the end of removal proceedings. In fact, because these decisions are no longer guided by the INA's statutory framework for discretionary relief, the changes may actually have increased the Executive's authority.[22]

And the sea-changes occurred in immigration enforcement after the depredations of September 11, 2001, when national security and terrorism became of necessity an even larger part of the equation.[23] These acts of terrorism on the United States within its own borders immeasurably strengthened the executive's hand. Even with the rise of the multitude of post-9/11 immigration reform legislation and the rise of executive action, such as the growth and reorganization of the immigration function within what grew into the larger omnibus Department of Homeland Security, the die had been cast and additional centralization of the discretion function became evident.[24] Although the emergent Executive Office for Immigration Review (EOIR) immigration courts' function remained within the Department of Justice (DOJ), with accompanying substantive and administrative/jurisdictional responsibilities, observers have noted:

> [Choosing to] insulate decisions regarding relief from the prosecutorial arm of the immigration agencies has been undermined by the recent changes to the relief provisions. These changes have had the effect of shifting more aspects of the deportation decision back to Immigration and Customs Enforcement (ICE). Far from eliminating discretion, then,

the statutory restrictions on discretionary relief have simply consolidated this [remaining] discretion in the agency officials responsible for charging decisions. Prosecutorial discretion has thus overtaken the exercise of discretion by immigration judges when it comes to questions of relief.[25]

As the legislative record of 2010–2016 reveals, deep and growing enmity arose between the two major political parties, and it grew exponentially during the early years of the Donald Trump administration.[26] The Obama Administration apparently had determined that any forms of immigration reform would have to be modest and in the nature of nonlegislative, adjudicatory, administrative review and discretionary deferred action.[27] This was not minor tinkering or a forlorn concession but rather an important political insight that grasping the real levers of immigration reform were in fundamental fashion a powerful tool, especially if congressional commitment to immigration reform was not evident or, as during an election year, not possible. The truth is that every administration (and, for that matter, every administrative agency), regardless of the interaction with the legislative process and Congress, seeks to maximize the discretionary space available to it.[28] Seen in this light, this administrative law and legislative case study underscore the story of almost any complex administrative regime, with thick descriptive narrative to detail the case of DREAM Act–eligible undocumented college students.

A final appeal option for a failed immigration matter is, in effect, a piece of legislation that is so individualized or focused on a small party with humanitarian circumstances that it is labeled a "private relief bill";[29] it is legislation so daunting that Congress had passed only two such extraordinary measures in the years between 2005 and 2012.[30] The other remaining final avenue is discretion available to the immigration authorities, traditionally exercised as a form of relief from enforcement, allowing a favorable judgment within the zones of prosecutorial priorities.[31] One avenue of prosecutorial discretion and relief is deferred action, such as that sussed out by the earlier matter involving John Lennon.[32]

While the odds of getting a private relief bill enacted are always very small,[33] attempting to do so remains a legitimate part of an advanced cause of action for a client, especially one who has appealing characteristics and a compelling narrative arc to his or her story. Examples of successful private relief legislation include two stunning cases of hardship. One involved a would-be beneficiary whose mother had fled spousal abuse in Japan but died in a car crash before she was remarried to a US citizen (who was therefore not yet in a statutory position to confer any derivative status upon the boy).[34] The other was the widow of a US Marine who had married her telephonically—and not in person—and who was killed in action before they could technically consummate the long-distance virtual marriage.[35] (Ironically, at the time they married she was pregnant with his child, who was then born a US citizen after his father's death in combat.)[36] These extraordinary provisions are rare in part because they require unanimity and because the congressional committee rules for enacting them have become very strict and unavailing.[37] In addition, while they often can eventually lead to lawful permanent resident status, the mere introduction of a private relief bill no longer guaranteed that the case would even be permanently deferred or stayed.[38]

Deferred action is another form of immigration relief, but it is fundamentally a form of administrative function—in football terms, a "Hail Mary pass" to the immigration authorities rather than to Congress—and it (or a form of it) is widely available within DHS.[39] As one example of a successful deferred action, a young out-of-status child who had been brought by her parents to the United States from Brazil had been involved in a terrible multicar crash caused by foggy weather. Her parents, her older sister, an uncle, and her uncle's girlfriend died in the accident, and she was hospitalized with serious injuries.[40] Being orphaned in such a horrific way enabled her to obtain deferred action status and avoid removal in 2012,[41] although it is not clear what her eventual relief may have been: she would appear to qualify for special immigrant juvenile status, another form of extraordinary relief, available only for children in dire straits.[42]

Deferred action is available only at the discretion of the agency, and while the status could be requested by counsel, there is no formal application, and it was not a widely sought or widely available form of relief.[43] Immigration authorities treated deferred action as an act of "administrative choice by [Immigration and Customs Enforcement (ICE), Customs and Border Protection (CBP), and Citizenship and Immigration Services (CIS)]" to give some cases lower priority in appropriate circumstances "and [is] in no way an 'entitlement.'"[44] Even if it were extended, it serves merely to "freeze" the case and does not remove or reconstitute the underlying adjudication of the person's deportability.[45] It grants no other benefit, although it can include work authorization, and does not extend to family beneficiaries or even immediate relatives.[46] In essence, each deferred action case and its constituent parts must be made on their own facts and circumstances.[47]

In a technical sense, deferred action has no formal group eligibility, such as its close nonstatutory cousin, Deferred Enforced Departure (DED, formerly known as Extended Voluntary Departure)[48] or its statutory cousin Temporary Protected Status (TPS),[49] which may be extended to groups for long periods of time and in similarly compelling circumstances.[50] Deferred action is predominantly a case-by-individual-case determination. DED and TPS, however, do accord work authorization and other privileges and arise from the same humanitarian motivation.[51] Deferred action can occasionally morph or be stretched into a group concept, as in 2005 when Hurricane Katrina closed New Orleans colleges and made it impossible for international students to remain continuously enrolled in course work, disrupted their studies, and, in a number of cases, displaced them to other cities.[52] At that time and for those circumstances, US Citizenship and Immigration Services (USCIS) issued "Interim Relief" guidelines and was flexible in allowing the affected colleges and students to waive certain requirements and procedures.[53] Statutory provisions as well as USCIS guidelines outlining a form of deferred action also have been enacted for so-called U visas, which are available to certain individuals without status who have experienced violence or who have been victims of crime.[54] The use of "Humanitarian Parole," which does not count as a formal means of entry into the United States, also functionally resembles deferred action status and may be granted on a case-by-case basis, often for emergency medical treatment or other humanitarian purposes.[55] This was a condition ill-suited for these DREAMers, who in most cases were brought into the country a number of years earlier and either surreptitiously entered without inspection or arrived legally such as tourists and then over-stayed (often with parents) the limits of their visa stays.

Eligibility for deferred action had originally appeared at 242.1(a)(22)(A)–(D) of the OI, but the OI was administratively withdrawn in 1997 and removed from the *Inspector's Field Manual*. Several instructions were replaced by 8 C.F.R. § 274a.12(c)(14): deferred action is "an act of administrative convenience to the government which gives some cases lower priority."[56] A decade later, the agency ombudsman recommended to the USCIS that it publish the criteria and application guidelines for deferred action, that the data be gathered in a systematic fashion, and that they be made publicly available to establish a regular review of the decisions ("to ensure that like cases are decided in like manner"),[57] but none of these had occurred. The previous OI, OI 242.1(a)(22), had required data to be gathered and kept, in large part so that the cases could not languish and be kept open for long periods of time:

> The district director will sign the form personally and set forth the basis for making the recommendation. Interim or biennial reviews will be conducted to evaluate whether approved cases should be continued or removed from the deferred-action category. Each regional commissioner must maintain current statistics on deferred-action cases, with the data readily available upon request. Statistics must be kept on the numbers of: (i) cases in the deferred-action category at the beginning of the fiscal year; (ii) recommendations received in the fiscal year to date; (iii) recommendations approved; (iv) recommendations denied; (v) cases removed from the deferred-action category; and (vi) deferred-action cases pending at the end of the fiscal year.[58]

In subsequent law review articles, Lennon's attorney provided an invaluable scholarly service by publishing previously unavailable data on the use of deferred action in the files made available to him.[59] Writing in 2004, attorney Wildes found:

> Aside from the records of cases recently approved, removed, and denied deferred action status, sixty-three cases that were approved between 1959 and 1991 were included in the files. These old cases contained forms indicating that a biennial review had taken place and that the statuses of the cases remained the same; thus, it was determined that the cases should be maintained in deferred action classification.
>
> A major shortcoming of the current data is that it contains fewer cases, only 332 from the eastern region and 167 cases from the central region, as opposed to the 1843 cases nationwide analyzed in the original 1976

[Wildes] article. Of the 332 eastern cases, 8 were denied deferred action status and 28 were removed from the category entirely, meaning that approximately 89% of the cases were granted. None of the cases from the central region were removed. However, 19 were denied. Thus, approximately 89% of those cases were granted.[60]

In a 1997 study of deferred action and private relief bills, Robert Hopper and Juan P. Osuna noted how rare prosecutorial discretion was: "In the Western Region of the INS, there were 131 deferred-action cases pending at the beginning of fiscal year (FY) 1995. Favorable recommendations for deferred action were sent to the regional commissioner in only 22 of those cases. In the Central Region, only 49 deferred-action cases were pending at the beginning of FY 1995. Finally, in the Eastern Region, there were 106 deferred-action cases still pending as of December 1995. Only five cases had been approved."[61]

The record-keeping has gotten no better or more transparent, and the agency has found itself being able to please no one: restrictionists do not want deferred action expanded, while accommodationists want deferred action widened and deepened.[62] Because the data are so spotty and irregular, neither side can say with certainty which form of perdition has occurred.[63]

Professor Shoba Sivaprasad Wadhia, heir to the Wildes deferred action scholarship throne, has conscientiously attempted to gather more recent deferred action data and has persisted through several years of the immigration authorities doing a poor job of making data available and busily releasing radar chaff to hide the complete data and decisions.[64] For example, in one remarkable stretch of persistence—including FOIA requests, phone calls, and dogged follow-up—she emerged with partial and incomplete deferred action records from FY 2003 through FY 2010, having requested them individually from each USCIS regional service center and field office:

> The remaining qualitative data within the 270-page PDF document included 118 identifiable deferred action cases. It was difficult to label a case as tender or elder age because much of the data lacked identifiers. However, when a field included the word "minor," "infant," or a specific age (e.g., eighty-nine-year-old), the case was calculated as involving tender or

elder age for purposes of this analysis. It should also be mentioned that some of the cases approved, pending, or unknown contained little to no factual information and, as a consequence, were not identified as bearing any of the "positive" factors listed above. The outcomes for many of these cases were unknown because the field was blank or there simply was not a field in the log maintained by a particular office. Many of the cases also had outcomes that were marked as "pending." Of the 118 cases, fifty-nine (59/118 or fifty percent) were pending or unknown; forty-eight (48/118 or 40.7%) were granted; and eleven (11/118 or 9.3%) were denied.

Among the 107 cases approved, pending, or unknown, fifty (50/107 or 46.7%) involved a serious medical condition, nineteen (19/107 or 17.8%) involved cases in which the applicant had USC [U.S. Citizen] family members, twenty-two (22/107 or 21.5%) involved persons who had resided in the United States for more than five years, and thirty-two (32/107 or 29.9%) cases involved persons with a tender or elder age. Many of these cases (29/107 or 27.1%) involved more than one "positive" factor. For example, many of the cases (10/107 or 9.3%) involved both a serious medical condition and USC family members. Likewise, many of the cases (21/107 or 19.6%) involved both tender or elder age and a serious medical condition.

Among the forty-eight granted cases, twenty-four (24/48 or 50%) involved a serious medical condition; ten (10/48 or 20.8%) involved cases in which the applicant had USC family members; four (4/48 or 8.3%) involved persons who had resided in the United States for more than five years; and thirteen (13/48 or 27.1%) cases involved persons with a tender or elder age. Many of these cases (12/48 or 25%) involved more than one "positive" factor. For example, four (4/48 or 8.3%) of the cases involved both a serious medical condition and USC family members. Likewise, ten (10/48 or 20.8%) of the cases involved both tender or elder age and a serious medical condition.[65]

In a surprising turn of events, whereas the Bush administration employed deferred action an average of 771 times for the years 2005 through 2008, during the first two years of the Obama administration (2009 and 2010) the pace dropped to 661 per year on average.[66] In response to the GOP's insistence that the border be "tightened" before discussion of comprehensive immigration reform could take place, US Immigration and Customs Enforcement (ICE) under the new Democratic admin-istration seriously advanced enforcement measures and, by 2010, was deporting almost 400,000 people annually, more than any in history.[67] Yet, disagreement over what the enforcement metrics would include, divisive 2012 election-year politics, and the unwillingness of any South-west border state Republican senator to take the lead on such policies brought the DREAM Act to a stall and resulted in no bipartisan trac-tion on the larger issue.[68] Senator John McCain, historically a moderate and conciliator on the subject, took a sharp turn to the right when he unsuccessfully ran for the presidency in 2008, and after losing to Barack Obama he never again spent his political capital on this issue.[69] In 2018, he died from a similar form of brain cancer to that which had killed his friend Ted Kennedy.[70]

By 2011, and with the inability of the Obama administration to get the DREAM Act through Congress, it had become clear that the only pathway for any movement on resolving the inchoate and liminal status of the large number of noncriminal undocumented persons was that of internal administration, including the tools available for prosecuto-rial discretion, or the small number of nonstatutory and other nonreg-ulatory mechanisms.[71] At the time, reports began to indicate that the combination of a slowed economy, increased border security, and re-strictionist state statutes had reduced the number of undocumented im-migrants in the country,[72] and even citizen children were being removed with their parents who were in unauthorized status.[73] DHS began tele-graphing small signals regarding the administration's intent to reduce the many low-priority cases from the civil and immigration court case dockets and instead to focus on bigger game, including criminal aliens, terrorism and national security matters, and the larger border-securing devices that the Republicans had laid out as conditions precedent for agreeing to any legalization initiatives or other cooperative efforts.[74] By this time, a curious phenomenon had occurred. The administration had developed an impressive and successful enforcement regime, but it was one that had employed forms of prosecutorial discretion (such as de-ferred action) less often than had the predecessor Bush administration, resulting in historically high numbers of deportations and removals; still, the administration received no public credit for its successes from conservative critics.[75]

Secretary Napolitano noted accurately in March 2011 that the use of deferred action had fallen since the Bush years and that more unauthorized persons had been removed.[76] The numbers also revealed how immigration cases overall had clogged the system and ground it almost to a halt.[77] National data gathered by the Transactional Records Access Clearinghouse reported in August 2010 that the number of unresolved Executive Office for Immigration Review immigration cases before immigration judges were at their all-time high of approximately 250,000, averaging 459 days from notices to appear through resolution.[78]

Democratic members of the House and Senate began in the spring of 2011 to press for expanded use of deferred action, prosecutorial discretion, and other administrative means to allow DREAM Act students some form of relief from deportation, especially as hundreds had publicly outed themselves and made their undocumented status known to the larger community during the years of DREAM Act deliberations.[79] Additional news stories had begun to appear regularly about students without status being discovered in traffic court, random police encounters, and travel security.[80] Most of these stories cast the students in a favorable light, and a number of private and public resources were being made available, such as resident tuition for certain postsecondary-*Plyler* enrollees, financial aid for some, litigation that upheld the state resources, and public sympathy and solidarity with others, turning their status into a larger traditional civil rights identity and movement.[81]

Then, in June 2011, ICE director John Morton released directives announcing the expanded use of prosecutorial discretion in enforcement and began a pilot project process in two offices where additional legal review and discretion would be undertaken.[82] In August 2011, DHS established a joint DHS-DOJ working group to review and resolve the hundreds of thousands of cases then in the process of EOIR review.[83] In November 2011, DHS revealed additional details on how the review was to proceed and how the large number of cases would be whittled down to the most urgent and serious.[84] Six months after the several "Morton Memos" were issued, in January 2012, ICE had completed the prosecutorial discretion pilot project reviews in Denver and Baltimore and had determined that many low-priority cases could be identified and more attention paid as a result to the criminal and serious immigrant offenders in the system.[85]

Working with various immigration organizations and advocates, the administration began to lay out its plans and announced how prosecutorial discretion would be administered, how pending cases at various stages would be reviewed, and how lawyers and representatives could seek prosecutorial discretion for clients in the system.[86] The political thermodynamics of this complex initiative were quick to emerge and complicate the overall project.[87] Of course, there were many observers who were against any easing of the process or any review, labeling such a system a "back door amnesty," a view that ranged from political moderates who did not want to give federal agencies more authority to congressional actors who saw this increase in prosecutorial discretion as an end run around legitimate legislative options and the more limited regulatory procedures, one that they felt enabled the administration to act unilaterally.[88] And some political opportunists saw this as a chance to excoriate President Obama and to accuse him of pandering to Latino and other Democratic constituencies; nativists at the far right saw this as an act of perdition and political cowardice.[89] And those who wanted to extend the discretion further were unhappy and disappointed at what they considered to be a tepid, half-loaf response combined with unpopular security measures.[90]

In real life, the Morton Memo was not just one memorandum but collectively a series of memoranda promulgated before and after the June 17, 2011, memorandum on prosecutorial discretion with T and U visas.[91] Moreover, the Morton Memo is an administrative Rosetta Stone of policy and procedure, one that contains many interrelated sections and complex characteristics.[92] Even though this is obviously a mixed metaphor, it should be noted that the Morton Memo has many moving parts, including the basic concordance setting out priorities; the multiple and freighted meanings of the applicable terminology; the organizational ethos and structural capability of ICE to administer and adjudicate the many cases that are likely to be processed; and the many administrative and procedural transparency features that would be needed for all the parties involved—the immigrants and their families, their counsel and other advocates, the agency personnel, the political actors across all spectrums from the Obama administration through the broad middle of the polity to the restrictionist and nativist politicians.[93] A national discourse was getting under way, but in a presidential election year where anti-immigrant sentiment had already been openly on display this had been and was likely to continue as an ugly act in self-constituting the sovereign self.[94]

In chronological order, the collective Morton Memo subjects included: Guidance Regarding the Handling of Removal Proceedings of Aliens with Pending or Approved Applications or Petitions, August 20, 2010; Civil Immigration Enforcement Priorities for the Apprehension, Detention, and Removal of Aliens, March 2, 2011;[95] Exercising Prosecutorial Discretion Consistent with the Civil Immigration Enforcement Priorities of the Agency for the Apprehension, Detention, and Removal of Aliens, June 17, 2011;[96] Prosecutorial Discretion: Certain Victims, Witnesses, and Plaintiffs, June 17, 2011; Case-by-Case Review of Incoming and Certain Pending Cases, November 17, 2011; and other USCIS and EOIR memos.[97]

These policy documents set out the broad outlines of the comprehensive and overarching ICE prosecutorial discretion program, including the actual priority enforcement decision structure, the affected agency (and related agencies) personnel, the relevant factors to consider for exercising prosecutorial discretion, positive factors for exercising "particular care and concern," negative factors to be used in determining enforcement policies, and the timing or preferable points at which prosecutorial discretion might best be applied.[98] In addition, Morton indicated which of the many memoranda that had been issued by previous immigration officials would be incorporated into the new mix of priorities and which were to be rescinded or discarded.

The detailed criteria, even sketched in necessarily broad (and sometimes confusing and duplicative) strokes, showed the folk wisdom of both God and the Devil residing in the details of any complex scheme.[99] The broad outlines, carried across several administrations and incorporating many plusses and minuses from earlier organizational experiences and political priorities, were so generic as to be unnewsworthy and quotidian.[100] Of course, the mere announcement of such initiatives, which emphasized ongoing and previously established priorities as well as new emphases and policies, had the inevitable Heisenberg effect—the uncertainty principle where the very act of announcing an initiative draws attention to the topic and alters the position of the issue being observed.[101]

Leon Wildes and the law scholar Shoba Sivaprasad Wadhia, for example, have noted:

The Morton Memo also empowers Immigration and Customs Enforcement employees to consider cases for prosecutorial discretion early in the enforcement process and without relying on an affirmative request by an attorney. This clause is important because prosecutorial discretion has largely operated as a program reserved for seasoned private immigration attorneys with special relationships within the agency.

Nevertheless, critics believe the Morton Memo serves as a new backdoor "amnesty" or circumvention of Congress in the wake of failed congressional action on immigration. Select members of Congress have gone so far as to announce legislation to prevent the administration from exercising prosecutorial discretion. But that is politics. The importance of prosecutorial discretion was revealed long ago with the case of John Lennon. More than thirty-five years later, prosecutorial discretion continues to serve as a smart enforcement policy that allows the immigration agency to prioritize its limited resources and place sympathetic cases on the backburner. Ultimately, the impact of the Morton Memo is important and can be measured only with diligent oversight by the private bar, Congress and the agency's own watchdogs.[102]

The nativist columnist Michelle Malkin railed indelibly against the initiatives as examples of the "deadly '13 strikes you're out' policies of border-state prosecutors."[103] She saw the series of memos as a political ploy and a power play designed to accomplish administratively what the Obama administration could not do legislatively: enact any form of immigration reform that would provide some pathway for some unauthorized aliens to earn or become eligible for a more regularized status.[104]

And ICE is a large player in the scheme of immigration enforcement, but it is by no means the only participant. In January 2012, the US Border Patrol had announced a new plan to repatriate unauthorized Mexicans back to Mexico and "to begin imposing more serious consequences on almost everyone it catches from Texas to San Diego."[105] Labeled the "Consequence Delivery System," the proposed Border Patrol initiative prioritized apprehended immigrants into categories, from first-timers to criminal aliens with violent records.[106] Associated Press reports indicated that additional penalties were to be meted out and that these would "be severe for detained migrants and expensive to American taxpayers, including felony prosecution or being taken to an unfamiliar border city hundreds of miles away to be sent back to Mexico."[107] This new strategy was piloted in 2009 in Arizona, which had statewide restrictionist policies designed to discourage undocumented workers from establishing residence or working.[108] The program, if expanded, would be expensive, overpopulate local and state prison facilities, and tax the enforcement efforts that had already been overwhelmed by the new metrics of increased border security.[109] Even with moderate enforcement, immigration cases had saturated court dockets in the Southwest.[110]

Among individual immigration courts, and considering only those with at least 1,000 pending cases, the immigration court with the fastest buildup during FY 2011 was in Oakdale, Louisiana, where pending cases jumped 45 percent. The San Antonio, Texas, court ranked second, with a growth spurt of 40 percent during this year. New Orleans (up 33 percent), Houston (up 31 percent), and Phoenix (up 28 percent) rounded out the remaining top five locations experiencing the highest growth rates in case backlogs. Las Vegas was next, with a growth rate of 27 percent.[111] And when examining the actual wait times (from start to final resolution of cases already docketed),[112] the data from the Transactional Records Access Clearinghouse showed: "Wait times continue to be longest in California with 666 days, up from 660 days three months ago. Massachusetts average wait times declined to 603 days from 617 days over the same time period. Utah stayed in third place, with an average time of 563 days pending cases have been waiting in the Salt Lake City Immigration Court-up from 537 days three months ago."[113]

Meanwhile, other comprehensive enforcement initiatives such as the ICE Secure Communities Program,[114] designed to coordinate multiagency cooperation and resource-sharing, were operational since March 2008, but a number of state officials withdrew or attempted to limit their participation in the multilateral consortia as they had from section 287(g) cooperative arrangements. In other words, these relationships were complex, fluid, and highly politicized.[115]

Moreover, no war can be waged without support of its infantry, and ICE employees on the ground did not support initiatives that would have led to more targeted enforcement and more prosecutorial discretion resources.[116] Supporting an overwhelming vote of no-confidence in ICE director John Morton and other top officials, the AFL-CIO National Immigration and Customs Enforcement Council, representing approximately 7,000 ICE officers and other employees, showed displeasure with the direction of ICE's efforts in June 2010, well before the increased accommodationist initiatives that became evident in the administration's support of the DREAM Act and the summer 2011 Morton Memos.[117] They thought the proposed resource allocation would undermine enforcement authority and reward illegal behavior.[118] While labor disagreement with management has a long and complicated history in the United States, such enmity and animosity—not over working conditions or conservative efforts to undermine labor unions but rather basic organizational goals and legal strategy for executing the fundamental mission direction—was unusual, and certainly it was not likely to be efficacious for smooth implementation of the changed discretionary policies and programs.[119]

While the staff reaction to a different mix of enforcement and adjudications or processing persons for permanent residence in the country more clearly embraced the enforcement function of the house, this emphasis was a relatively recent development within the agency,[120] one that was likely increased due to the DHS reorganization and the increased general emphasis on immigration control as national security and border security in the war on terrorism.[121] As one internal measure of this mixed-function issue, ICE began to deploy Fugitive Operations Teams, which were responsible for locating and apprehending persons whose presence in the United States was considered to be unauthorized, either through legal entry and subsequent violations (such as overstaying a visa's terms) or through crossing a border without inspection.[122]

In addition, worksite enforcement had become a higher priority for ICE, and thousands of arrests were being made each year as a measure of this mission—over and above the policing efforts by the agency charged with actually securing the border, US Customs and Border Protection (CBP), which grew from approximately 4,000 agents each year in the early 1990s to more than 21,000 in FY 2011 and more than 19,000 in 2018.[123] These figures do not include the extensive support staff and administrative CBP staff.[124] One scholar who has carefully examined this shifting mission remarked on the rise in residential and workplace enforcement in ICE: "Together, the surge in residential and workplace enforcement actions has been breathtaking and inconsistent with the agency's historical focus on serious offenders and genuine threats to national security."[125]

This mission creep is a problematic evaluation issue across many governmental agencies and complex administrative structures, and the extensive scholarship in these areas points to issues of professional competence and institutional capacity.[126] Taking on new jurisdictions or having complex adjudicatory powers can reveal serious fault lines in large governmental organizations.[127] For example, if comprehensive immigration reform is ever enacted, it would require a substantial increase on the naturalization and evaluation side, even while the enforcement functions would need to be enhanced in the post-9/11 world.[128] If the sign of a mature intellect is the ability to hold incongruous and nuanced positions or ideologies, so it is with administrative agencies. ICE functions under the relatively new DHS umbrella, and it has taken on enhanced apprehension and policing and enforcement functions, which pose internal dissension and persistent tensions with the more ameliorative incorporation and constitutive obligations.[129] Prosecutorial discretion and deferred action perform a fluid, lubricating role in mediating among these conflicting strains within the organization and across agencies, such as coordination with the Department of Labor's employment expertise.[130]

Perhaps as an indication of this mediating dimension, there is evidence that ICE was using deferred action as a means of negotiating and settling litigation that involved excessive force or embarrassing public mistakes by immigration authorities. For example, in Connecticut in 2007, soon after the city of New Haven had announced a voluntary municipal registration card to be available to all residents irrespective of immigration status, ICE agents and police arrested without warrants almost a dozen Latino men who were not authorized to be in the country.[131] After the men obtained pro bono legal counsel, and following several years of processing the matter, in 2012 ICE offered all the plaintiffs either immigration relief or termination of their pending deportation proceedings; the settlement also paid compensation of $350,000.[132] ICE conceded no admission of liability or fault but settled the matter for discretionary purposes and because the men were not criminal aliens and fit the deferred action–priority criteria.[133] More widespread use of dormant discretionary latitude undoubtedly leads to less litigation and fewer monetary settlements.[134]

ICE began an overall practice trial run that ended on January 13, 2012, designed to keep the "new low priority cases from clogging the immigration court dockets."[135] In this capacity, ICE attorneys were ordered to review all "incoming cases in immigration court" as well as other cases making their way through the ICE master calendar docket to employ the "more focused [Morton] criteria" to identify cases that were "most clearly eligible and ineligible for a favorable exercise of discretion."[136]

As test cases for the new policy approached, the Denver and Baltimore trial runs were informative and promising but also illustrative of the many problems that the revised policies present to all involved.[137] In what one observer called a "lightning review,"[138] Denver prosecutors set aside much of their ongoing workloads, among the busiest in the nation, and worked around the clock during December 2011 and January 2012 to sift through the nearly 8,000 cases in one stage or another of deportation proceedings then pending before the local immigration courts and to apply the principles outlined in the Morton Memos.[139] This review resulted in the identification of more than 1,300 pending cases (16.4 percent, or one-sixth) the lawyers considered low priority, ranging from DREAM Act–type students outed in routine traffic infractions to an unauthorized worker who had been married for nearly a dozen years to a US citizen and who had been employed while using someone else's Social Security information.[140] The actual review, while overwhelming the sixteen lawyers and staff who conducted it over the holidays, was undertaken on a short timetable due to the trial nature of the experiment, cleared out many cases, and relieved the crush on the six immigration judges who averaged more than 1,300 cases each with an average of eighteen months in the queue per case.[141] The review in Baltimore was on a smaller scale but had somewhat similar results, with 366 cases of the total 3,759 (9.7 percent) sorted for deferred action recommendations to close or terminate cases.[142]

Picking this low-hanging fruit had consequences, however. To be sure, other court and agency business had been put on hold during the review, but the concentration of professional effort was quite impressive and efficacious, especially in the initial test of the complex new policy.[143] While the larger union problems that surfaced earlier are of obvious concern for carrying out any wholesale revision of policy and procedure, especially when the objections are about the usual workload/employee matters as well as the overall direction and focus of agency enforcement initiatives, any changes in administrative organizational procedures would require commitment of the entire staff from top to bottom and from lawyers and nonlawyer professionals.[144] There were promising early reports that the immigration staff lawyers were pleased with their increased discretion and authority to settle cases that would have continued to pour in, discretion that their companion criminal prosecutors routinely employed to manage criminal pleadings and to reduce criminal dockets.[145] The routine administration of justice in all areas requires focusing resources on the most important and dangerous cases and offenders, and lawyers make dozens of decisions each week to pursue or not to pursue matters and to assign priority to enforcement efforts.[146] Removing and accelerating such a large part of the docket become attractive incentives for government lawyers to participate in such efforts.

As essential as it is to get administrative buy-in and cooperation of agency staff for any major program initiative, perhaps equally important is the need to harness the energies of the large and varied immigration bar: the lawyers and other professionals who represent the immigrants in the processes, as well as the array of nongovernmental organizations (NGOs) and other actors in the large universe of immigration adjudication in the United States.[147] While they surely share in the hope that these revised processes and policies will result in better and expedited results for their undocumented and possibly deportable clients, the metrics of success and efficacy are harder to agree on, much less to measure.[148]

Even successful instances of awards of prosecutorial discretion or other forms of relief, while welcome, still leave many noncitizens in an odd limbo—a situation surely better than the status quo ante, with its own unique and extraordinary hardships, but in some ways an equally frustrating and unresolved place.[149] Administrative closure, the primary form of prosecutorial discretion available under these reviews, does not automatically award any status except a promise of delaying the case and not moving forward immediately with removal efforts.[150] To be sure, this is better than not receiving the status; it is not nothing. However, the fortunate recipients still are likely ineligible for driver's licenses, other governmental identification, any governmental benefits, any waivers from other harsh penalties such as the bars to reentry that likely affect most of them, any employment authorization, any adjustment of status opportunities, or, in truth, any movement forward to a more permanent status or permission to remain in the country.[151] A number of noncitizens have received only temporary reprieves of one or two years with no discernible end in sight for a change in their status.[152] For example,

DHS played hardball with the important Employment Authorization Document (EAD) process, indicating that even successful cases being administratively closed would be ineligible for EAD unless they have a fresh and "independent basis" for such work authorization, such as that which would be embedded within a pending adjustment of status or application for asylum.[153] Truth be told, if these noncitizens had plausible cases for asylum or other forms of relief, they would have invoked them already, quite apart from the revised DHS initiative and the Morton Memos.[154] Because the discretion regime is designed over the long haul to integrate noncitizens into the society of eventual citizens, not providing work authorization always seemed ill-advised and shortsighted, particularly for DREAM Act–eligible students who were ready to begin their careers. Almost certainly, they were poor. Moreover, as long as restrictionists were loudly challenging any such use of discretion, the more expansive version should have been issued. Doing less than is possible within existing practice seems completely feckless and underachieving, especially with the relentless criticism that is occurring in any event.[155] In the increasing number of states that have enacted restrictionist statutes, these "sleeping beaut[ies]"[156] might not be able to attend public colleges, participate in adult education or GED classes, or take English-language instruction offered or subsidized by public funds.[157] Their ineligibility for these incorporating and mediating programs would isolate them even further into their liminal status[158] and make it more difficult for them to become members of the society that they were on the verge of joining permanently.[159]

In addition, the immigration bar had reason to believe that the proposed deferred action initiative was not likely to be an improvement and for a truly ironic reason: If these clients and others like them are deemed to be eligible for any form of prosecutorial discretion, why would they accept the deferred action half-loaf when they might push for the real prize—permanent relief through one of the other means, such as special juvenile immigrant status, or one of the other inchoate waiver forms available to immigration judges and immigration officials?[160] An article described one Denver lawyer's opinion:

> In many cases, lawyers for illegal immigrants are not accepting prosecutors' offers because the immigrants have good chances of winning legal

residency in court. Laura Lichter, the president-elect of the American Immigration Lawyers Association, who practices in Denver, said ICE could have done far more to reduce backlogs by rapidly completing those strong cases. "It is a major undertaking," she said of the docket review. "But it is also a major lost opportunity."[161]

It was not clear that they will be able to secure better results for their clients unless deferred action and prosecutorial discretion were to be broadened and more fully implemented; worse, government decision-makers may then decide to play hardball with the cases that were not resolved and accorded such status.[162] This blowback would have likely harmed other clients and made it more difficult to advise clients to roll the dice with limited results and no eventual resolution.[163] And if more lawyers calculate that they could have done better for their clients and actually achieved a form of relief with traction, one that offered more hope and opportunities than would the vague status of deferred action and prosecutorial discretion, they may be tempted to play a dangerous game of chicken with immigration judges and government lawyers. In other words, taking the easy cases off the table would, to ICE, signal that they have already given all the deals they are going to give, while to lawyers on the other side of the bar, taking these cases off the table but offering no final disposition could signal business as usual on an expedited but insincere basis. In a contest where slowing the process down could gain some tactical advantages or simply enable a client to remain in the country longer, such a result might prove less efficacious than the current situation and would further clog the court dockets.[164]

In other words, the inevitable distrust and stalemates may return with a vengeance, with both sides more convinced than ever that cooperation and flexibility are in neither side's interest. Simply parking these cases off the docket will not resolve them absent additional discretion or finality. Most clients are not John Lennon, who had widespread positive media coverage and enormous financial and social resources.[165] In the stark arithmetic of immigration enforcement, unless both sides trust each other and actually plea-bargain with some authority, the entire enterprise would collapse. The inability to resolve the 16 percent of deferred action cases satisfactorily might make the remaining 84 percent virtually impossible to adjudicate.[166] Expanded to all of the approximately

400,000 national cases pending would mean that between 40,000 and 64,000 cases could be affected by the enhanced review (assuming the 10 percent to 16 percent figures played out in the remaining districts).[167] Without some form of final resolution, which is in the hands of a variety of review authorities, this population would still be in limbo at the least until additional security and criminal checks could be completed and then again until an actual form of relief became available and was applied to the noncitizen. The limbo would be extended until a form of comprehensive immigration reform eventually evolved.[168] As was seen, while President Obama was reelected, the GOP held majorities in the House and Senate, thwarting any immigration overhaul; indeed, it was in this precarious balance that President Obama enacted DACA.

Of course, life also continued for ICE and the other players in this drama. Even if the cohort were removed through streamlined additional review, there would have been the remaining individuals who would have their fates determined in the continuing process and under the traditional review procedures. And although Congress never acted, and may not ever enact such legislation, additional special reviews may be required for either a military legalization procedure (such as those that appeared to surface in late 2011 and early 2012 to provide immigration status for military service) or another round for the DREAM Act with military beneficiaries or standalone. These will be even more complex cases, as the beneficiaries will be entitled to enhanced status with a likely detailed condition-precedent determination process that will have to be layered on.[169] In many respects, these would be a salutary development even if targeted toward a subset of all the undocumented in the United States. But the trial runs in Denver and Baltimore have shown the many difficulties in planning, implementation, and operationalization of immigration legislation and the symmetrical effects upon the immigration bar and private organizations and NGOs to gear up for the legal representation, advocacy, and litigation sure to result.[170] DACA was enacted and grew spectacularly for over four years, after which it was tragically scapegoated by the surprising turn of events that led to the Republicans winning the House, Senate, and White House in 2016 (this is autopsied in the final two chapters). DACA was cut down in its prime, and instead of morphing into a significant playbook for a form of comprehensive immigration reform it became a pawn in national politics.[171]

TABLE 5.1: Number of Form I-821D, consideration of Deferred Action for Childhood Arrivals, by fiscal year, quarter, intake, and case status for fiscal years 2012–2018 (July 31, 2018)

Period	Requests by intake and case status						
	Intake[1]				Case review[6]		
	Requests accepted[2]	Requests rejected[3]	Total requests received[4]	Average accepted/ day[5]	Approved[7]	Denied[8]	Pending[9]
Fiscal Year—Total							
2012	152,431	5,395	157,826	3,629	1,680	-	150,751
2013	427,617	16,350	443,967	1,697	470,351	10,968	97,025
2014	238,900	24,887	263,787	952	158,330	20,990	156,538
2014 Initial	122,460	19,064	141,524	488	136,100	20,987	62,333
2014 Renewal	116,440	5,823	122,263	464	22,230	3	94,205
2015	448,857	35,474	484,331	1,781	509,969	21,350	73,902
2015 Initial	85,304	7,150	92,454	338	90,633	19,069	37,861
2015 Renewal	363,553	28,324	391,877	1,443	419,336	2,281	36,041
2016	260,701	12,317	273,018	1,035	198,530	14,435	120,715
2016 Initial	73,351	1,151	74,502	291	52,706	11,399	46,237
2016 Renewal	187,350	11,166	198,516	744	145,824	3,036	74,478
2017	472,850	43,455	516,305	1,884	462,280	13,297	117,592
2017 Initial	45,596	44	45,640	182	47,274	9,232	35,219
2017 Renewal	427,254	43,411	470,665	1,702	415,006	4,065	82,373
2018	187,882	25,916	213,798	899	255,262	10,598	39,413
2018 Initial	1,697	2	1,699	8	23,264	6,835	6,798
2018 Renewal	186,185	25,914	212,099	891	231,998	3,763	32,615
Total Cumulative	2,189,238	163,794	2,353,032	1,451	2,056,402	91,638	39,413
Total Cumulative Initial	908,456	49,156	957,612	602	822,008	78,490	6,798
Total Cumulative Renewal	1,280,782	114,638	1,395,420	849	1,234,394	13,148	32,615

- Represents zero.

[1] Refers to a request for USCIS to consider deferred removal action for an individual based on guidelines

described in the Secretary of Homeland Security's memorandum issued June 15, 2012.
Each request is considered on a case-by-case basis.
See www.uscis.gov/childhoodarrivals.

[2] The number of new requests accepted at a Lockbox during the reporting period.

[3] The number of requests rejected at a Lockbox during the reporting period.

[4] The number of requests that were received at a Lockbox during the reporting period.

[5] The number of requests accepted per day at a Lockbox as of the end of the reporting period. Also note the average accepted per day for initial plus renewal will not equal the total average.

[6] The number of new requests received and entered into a case-tracking system during the reporting period.

[7] The number of requests approved during the reporting period.

[8] The number of requests that were denied, terminated, or withdrawn during the reporting period.

[9] The number of requests awaiting a decision as of the end of the reporting period.

[10] The overall number of receipts for Q2 remains consistent with the March 31, 2018, report. USCIS has adjusted the number of "initial" and "renewal" requests for certain necessary reclassifications of those requests.

TABLE 5.2: Number of Form I-821D, consideration of Deferred Action for Childhood Arrivals, by country of origin for fiscal years 2012–2018 (July 31, 2018)

Top countries of origin	Accepted to date[1]			Approved to date[2]		
	Initials	Renewals	Total	Initials	Renewals	Total
Grand total	908,456	1,280,782	2,189,238	822,008	1,234,394	2,056,402
Mexico	707,536	1,005,353	1,712,889	647,450	969,338	1,616,788
El Salvador	34,497	48,817	83,314	29,642	47,006	76,648
Guatemala	24,914	32,192	57,106	20,885	30,894	51,779
Honduras	22,696	30,315	53,011	19,086	29,172	48,258
Peru	9,832	15,255	25,087	9,276	14,725	24,001
South Korea	7,904	15,548	23,452	7,417	14,863	22,280
Brazil	8,629	11,578	20,207	7,601	11,200	18,801
Ecuador	7,796	10,899	18,695	6,862	10,449	17,311
Colombia	7,298	10,590	17,888	6,725	10,210	16,935
Philippines	5,127	7,998	13,125	4,782	7,749	12,531
Argentina	5,263	7,343	12,606	4,938	7,142	12,080
India	3,788	5,727	9,515	3,246	5,488	8,734
Jamaica	4,451	5,071	9,522	3,521	4,930	8,451
Venezuela	3,489	4,964	8,453	3,182	4,784	7,966
Dominican Republic	3,844	4,322	8,166	3,263	4,183	7,446
Uruguay	2,643	3,482	6,125	2,474	3,378	5,852
Bolivia	2,240	3,420	5,660	2,114	3,307	5,421
Costa Rica	2,290	3,282	5,572	2,097	3,148	5,245
Poland	2,007	2,740	4,747	1,862	2,656	4,518
Chile	1,908	2,809	4,717	1,792	2,721	4,513
Pakistan	1,949	2,771	4,720	1,725	2,660	4,385
Nicaragua	1,909	2,496	4,405	1,656	2,402	4,058
Tobago	2,442	1,719	4,161	2,095	1,706	3,801
Guyana	1,487	2,021	3,508	1,299	1,957	3,256
Unknown	1,604	1,852	3,456	1,255	1,652	2,907
All others	30,913	38,218	69,131	25,763	36,674	62,437

- Represents zero.

TABLE 5.2: (*cont.*)

Residence	Accepted to date[1]			Approved to date[2]		
	Initials	Renewals	Total	Initials	Renewals	Total
Total	908,456	1,280,782	2,189,238	822,008	1,234,394	2,056,402
California	246,430	279,317	525,747	229,004	275,468	504,472
Texas	142,771	149,298	292,069	127,396	147,376	274,772
New York	51,570	91,473	143,043	45,178	90,074	135,252
Florida	41,688	75,537	117,225	35,564	74,465	110,029
Illinois	46,330	49,676	96,006	43,396	48,880	92,276
New Jersey	26,542	41,523	68,065	23,422	40,931	64,353
Arizona	31,064	31,981	63,045	28,452	31,392	59,844
North Carolina	29,907	29,202	59,109	27,842	28,783	56,625
Georgia	29,086	30,819	59,905	24,869	30,329	55,198
Washington	20,009	23,466	43,475	18,449	23,139	41,588
Colorado	19,377	19,249	38,626	17,652	18,931	36,583
Virginia	14,377	21,516	35,893	12,798	21,168	33,966
Nevada	14,351	16,148	30,499	13,363	15,937	29,300
Maryland	11,868	17,921	29,789	10,349	17,641	27,990
Massachusetts	9,974	19,608	29,582	8,651	19,308	27,959
Oregon	12,225	12,713	24,938	11,526	12,523	24,049
Pennsylvania	7,493	14,848	22,341	6,475	14,626	21,101
Indiana	10,849	10,863	21,712	10,042	10,726	20,768
Utah	10,633	9,822	20,455	9,866	9,667	19,533
Michigan	7,587	12,189	19,776	6,819	11,974	18,793
Tennessee	9,445	9,649	19,094	8,524	9,507	18,031
Minnesota	7,127	9,861	16,988	6,524	9,683	16,207
Wisconsin	8,261	8,436	16,697	7,742	8,330	16,072
Connecticut	5,866	9,543	15,409	5,249	9,397	14,646
Oklahoma	7,573	7,763	15,336	7,012	7,674	14,686
Kansas	7,403	7,487	14,890	6,948	7,387	14,335
New Mexico	7,505	6,953	14,458	6,962	6,867	13,829
South Carolina	7,266	7,198	14,464	6,560	7,090	13,650
Ohio	5,484	8,882	14,366	4,762	8,724	13,486
Arkansas	5,680	5,520	11,200	5,203	5,432	10,635
Alabama	4,870	4,931	9,801	4,381	4,866	9,247
Missouri	3,995	5,281	9,276	3,688	5,218	8,906
Nebraska	3,852	4,284	8,136	3,494	4,213	7,707
Kentucky	3,523	4,162	7,685	3,160	4,107	7,267
Iowa	3,217	4,224	7,441	2,904	4,146	7,050
Idaho	3,430	3,592	7,022	3,207	3,537	6,744
Louisiana	2,496	3,730	6,226	2,165	3,678	5,843
Rhode Island	1,510	2,941	4,451	1,325	2,893	4,218

Residence	Accepted to date[1]			Approved to date[2]		
	Initials	Renewals	Total	Initials	Renewals	Total
Hawaii	861	3,458	4,319	709	3,398	4,107
Delaware	1,645	2,098	3,743	1,500	2,079	3,579
Mississippi	1,725	1,896	3,621	1,504	1,880	3,384
District of Columbia	988	2,019	3,007	840	1,994	2,834
Puerto Rico	575	2,261	2,836	423	2,224	2,647
New Hampshire	480	1,197	1,677	418	1,173	1,591
Wyoming	699	703	1,402	628	691	1,319
Alaska	216	872	1,088	179	863	1,042
South Dakota	316	546	862	275	535	810
Maine	148	634	782	125	620	745
Guam	115	649	764	95	640	735
North Dakota	151	571	722	122	563	685
Virgin Islands	168	420	588	112	406	518
West Virginia	160	380	540	134	372	506
Montana	93	287	380	80	277	357
Vermont	66	307	373	51	304	355
Armed Forces-Pacific	33	146	179	29	142	171
Armed Forces-Europe, Middle East, Africa, Canada	28	129	157	21	124	145
Armed Forces-Americas (except Canada)	19	84	103	14	84	98
Northern Mariana Islands	32	39	71	13	36	49
Palau	-	20	20	-	19	19
Not reported	17,304	190,460	207,764	13,813	159,883	173,696

[1] The number of requests that were accepted to date of the reporting period.

[2] The number of requests that were approved to date of the reporting period.

[3] All fields with less than 10 or a blank in the state field are included in the field "not reported."

NOTE: 1) Some requests approved or denied may have been received in previous reporting periods.

2) The report reflects the most up-to-date estimate data available at the time the report is generated.

3) Ranked by total approvals.

Source: Department of Homeland Security, U.S. Citizenship and Immigration Services, Enterprise Citizenship and Immigration Services Centralized Operation Repository (eCISCOR), July 2018.

6

Undocumented Lawyers, DACA, and Occupational Licensing

This chapter is an early reflection on several intersecting narratives, ones that exist in several dimensions, rather like the iconic Star Trek chess game that added depth and competing chessboards layered on top of each other.[1] Or, in a more earthly sense, I situate several legal narrative flows that exist in a tectonic fashion, cruising by each other to contain the earth's magma core but occasionally and spectacularly colliding and bumping up against each other, leaving fresh landscapes and jagged oceanic scars. How else can observers understand and reconcile the different stories of complex immigration categories, the architecture of occupational licensing, and the intersecting state and federal dimensions that form this Joycean novel? Who would have ever thought that an undocumented immigrant, without legal status in the United States, could be practicing law with the support of and accommodation by several institutions in California: the state bar licensing authority, the legislature, the governor's office, and the state supreme court?[2] Or that President Barack Obama's Department of Justice would argue against such a move?[3] And who could have predicted the Obama's fertile use in 2012 of Deferred Action for Childhood Arrivals, broadening the traditional narrow scope of discretionary administrative enforcement authority with the effect of transforming more than 750,000 undocumented youth into DACAmented youth[4]—after many years of record immigration enforcement, deportations, and removals of unauthorized adults and children?[5]

In this chapter, I gather for the first time basic immigration eligibility information that serves as statutory, administrative, common law, and local prerequisites for entering licensed professions, high and low. The framework sets out national data across all US jurisdictions (focusing on the admissions standards and citizenship/immigration status required for entry into medicine, nursing, attorney, and K–12 teaching professions) and then drills down on several large state jurisdictions in detailed case studies across dozens of licensed occupations in California, Texas, Illinois, and New York.[6] My research has not revealed any national studies—and I have looked everywhere and shagged any number of false leads—and the sheer size of such an enterprise has likely precluded others from this snipe hunt.

As befits a multijurisdictional dataset, I discovered that there are major inconsistencies, gaps, and mistakes regarding state occupational licensing laws, and virtually every state has multiple examples.[7] While no one could have anticipated the explosive growth occasioned by DACA and its unique vectors implicating occupational licensing, it is growing clear that most licensure or certification authorities have not thought through or reconsidered immigration and citizenship requirements for their professions in any systematic fashion.[8] Virtually all have some form of formal or informal citizenship admissions criteria, but as DACA and case law have revealed, this tectonic plate is shifting and disturbing other plates.[9] In geology, the earth's lithosphere—sublayers of the crust—moves in regular and punctuated fashion, creating continental drift, faults, and trenches across the globe.[10] Its counterpart in immigration and licensing law is the changing and moving universe of immigration law and the growing state regulation of labor and employment, thereby necessitating special tools of legal analysis.[11]

In this vein, I offer preliminary thoughts about the various immigration classifications implicated by business and occupational licensing.[12] Then, I set out to briefly describe the overall architectural features of licensing in US society, revealing multidimensional forces at play at the state and federal levels.[13] Finally, I situate the data, pointing out intuitive issues and a number of counterintuitive considerations that make a unified occupational licensing field-theory virtually impossible.[14] As a result, many jurisdictions will continue to muddle along, deciding challenges and mounting reforms on a case-by-case basis. Each of these areas has its own narrative flow, and the overall effect is confusing and ineffective. Even so, these data will assist all serious scholars, elected officials, and professional licensing authorities.

Setting aside refugee and asylum matters recently in the news,[15] US immigration policies and procedures break the world down into two large admissibility categories: family-related relationships spanning all dimensions of this comprehensive subject; and employment-based regimes, which govern the importation of labor and work eligibility.[16] Although these are obviously intertwined in many respects, the family and employment bases are parallel universes, almost Manichean in their ways.[17] Being a US citizen, whether by birthright or by naturalization, entitles that person to work at any job that is offered to her and for which she is eligible. (And that relationship to employment is in turn regulated by a myriad of labor, civil rights, and employment features.)[18] At the opposite end of the spectrum, a transient passing through the United States on a common carrier passenger laying over at an airport during a flight across the world would not earn employment authorization any more than if one were booking passage on a train that on its course traversed US and Canadian or Mexican borders.

But it is the many places across this possible spectrum of employment authorization, manifested in an Employment Authorization Document,[19] that predominate in this narrative. Most naturalized citizens move from lawful permanent resident status to citizenship, which can be derived from either a family-based or employment-based relationship. Lawful permanent residents are eligible for virtually all employment opportunities and licenses save a few outdated anomalies, such as being an optometrist in Puerto Rico,[20] or possible security-related employment on classified job sites where US citizenship may be a prerequisite.[21] In an increasingly complex and accommodating world, many persons also can, depending upon their eligibility and resources, maintain multiple citizenships or nationalities or can choose not to become citizens even if eligible to do so.[22] In *Nyquist v. Mauclet*, for example, the United States Supreme Court held that important college financial aid benefits could not be withheld from LPRs who had not chosen to invoke US citizenship,[23] as they are allowed to remain permanently in the country and participate in almost all civic activities save for voting in federal elections, holding certain offices, and the like.[24]

In addition, anyone admitted to the United States as an immigrant earns LPR status, whether they are admitted by the employment or family-based routes.[25] In turn, as LPRs, they are eligible for employment and most licensing.[26] Notwithstanding this constitutional equivalence between eligibility for citizens and permanent residents, a large number of occupational licensing requirements cite US citizenship as a prerequisite.[27] States that appear to limit occupational licensing to US citizens are ripe targets for an admissions case challenging the citizenship prerequisite.[28] Yet the data I present in the body of this study are riddled with such occupational admissions criteria waiting to be discovered by an otherwise eligible noncitizen applicant who would bring a legal challenge. These occupational admissions criteria revealed the parallel issue that a number of states are inconsistent in their formal application of state law, either by requiring immigration information not necessitated by operating statutes or by using inconsistent immigration categories across multiple licensing criteria.[29]

The next category would be the millions of persons who enter the country annually as nonimmigrants, temporarily admitted for temporary purposes, with alphabetical categories of visas from A to V.[30] These categories include a number of employment-related occupational authorizations, but many of the largest categories do not allow employment.[31] Some small categories of nonimmigrant visas allow no employment or US-derived salary save for traditional benefits and small intermittent stipends, such as a European or Latin American academic on a tourist visa who could give a series of lectures in United States colleges and lecture halls, occasioning travel support, honoraria, and meals.[32] A number of entertainers are allowed to enter the country for festivals or concerts where they are not paid but receive travel-related support, an example being music groups attending the annual South by Southwest music festival in Austin, Texas.[33] This arrangement was intersected by the Trump administration's 2017 travel ban, which disrupted these longstanding arrangements and left the affected music acts with last-minute cancellations even though their time in the country was donated and not paid for by stipends or salaries; they were denied permission to perform and even to enter the country on standard nonimmigrant visas.[34]

Given the many millions who enter the country each year on non-employment nonimmigrant visas, most cannot work or be employed by US employers while in the country, affecting categories of tourists or certain family members who are not extended employment authorization.[35] In most instances, the Department of Homeland Security is required to determine whether a nonimmigrant admitted into the country may be employed, self-employed, or ineligible to work.[36] Certain nonimmigrants will have employment authorization in their DHS-assigned class of admission (such as performers, who are free in most instances to strike deals with entertainment venues), while other nonimmigrants may have employment authorization but only with specific employers (such as religious organization workers), with no freelancing allowed; if they were to lose their position, they would be removable.[37] Although all are technically temporary, their eligibility to work can last for many years and decades as long as the terms are properly maintained and the requirements are adhered to.[38] Almost all of these employment relationships exist in a zone maintained and administered by the DHS and the Department of Labor.[39] As noted, some nonimmigrants, such as tourists or crew members, may not be employed and cannot apply for employment authorization while in the United States.[40]

While there is much more to fill in about how this vast array operates, I am sketching these to show the overall mechanics—and why occupational licensing matters.[41] There are additional categories that involve and can enable such noncitizen-status persons to hold employment.[42] A variety of loosely connected status and inchoate categories could be set out as ones with PRUCOL (permanently residing under color of law) characteristics.[43] Although the formal category was abolished by the Personal Responsibility and Work Opportunity Reconciliation Act of 1996, it still remains in play through its functional equivalent of qualified aliens, such as those in the country as refugees before their LPR status is accorded after the requisite waiting period or asylum-seekers whose cases are being determined.[44] These PRUCOL noncitizens are allowed to remain in the United States until their cases are resolved, usually with EAD during the pendency of the determination, and after resolution of the matter.[45] Inherent in these determinations is that the person is "known to the government," and some are otherwise eligible for public benefits, sometimes including "lawful presence," an important category that suspends deportation until after a formal process that can take many years and, in effect, freezes their illegality and removability.[46]

It is exactly at this point that DACA figures into the picture, and "on the thirtieth anniversary of *Plyler v. Doe*—the 1982 case in which the U.S. Supreme Court ruled that states could not [charge tuition] for the education of schoolchildren of unauthorized immigrants—[President Obama in 2012] announced a halt to the deportation of some undocumented immigrants who came to the United States as children and ha[d] graduated from high school."[47] Unfortunately, it was not the stalled DREAM Act, which would have created a path to citizenship for some immigrants who came to the United States as children and have been admitted to college or registered under the Selective Service Act.[48] The president's decision to fashion DACA, which used existing powers of prosecutorial discretion reaching back to the earlier John Lennon case, was old wine in a new wineskin, one that became surprisingly resilient and transformative.[49] The policy did not create a pathway to LPR or citizenship, as the DREAM Act would have done, but instead deferred deportation for renewable two-year periods. More to the points under discussion, it gave the recipients several important benefits: EAD, a Social Security number (SSN), and "lawful presence" such as that which existed for a number of the PRUCOL noncitizens.[50]

The FAQ section of DACA's policies and procedures clearly states:

> Although action on your case has been deferred and you do not accrue unlawful presence (for admissibility purposes) during the period of deferred action, deferred action does not confer any lawful status.[51]
>
> The fact that you are not accruing unlawful *presence* does not change whether you are in lawful *status* while you remain in the United States.[52] However, although deferred action does not confer a lawful immigration status, your period of stay is authorized by the Department of Homeland Security while your deferred action is in effect and, for admissibility purposes, you are considered to be lawfully present in the United States during that time.[53] *Individuals granted deferred action are not precluded by federal law from establishing domicile in the U.S.*[54]
>
> Apart from the immigration laws, "lawful presence," "lawful status" and similar terms are used in various other federal and state laws.[55]

Within the first week of the DACA program application, which began on August 15, 2012, tens of thousands of these students surfaced, and by the end of the Obama administration in January 2017 more than 750,000 DACA recipients had been screened and admitted into being "DACAmented," with virtually all renewing after the two-year period.[56] A number of court challenges followed, beginning within six months, when disgruntled ICE employees filed suit in federal court and lost.[57] Also, in a complex series of cases concerning second-round extensions, there were no successful substantive challenges to DACA or the president's discretionary immigration authority.[58]

Undocumented immigrants eligible for DACA flocked to its programs, triggering a number of issues having to do with the EAD authority.[59] These issues include challenges from immigrant rights groups such as the Mexican American Legal Defense and Educational Fund, (MALDEF) which challenged Nationwide Insurance, a major national insurance services company, when it would not admit DACA recipients into its management program, even those with EAD, on the grounds that such work authorization was of limited duration and contingent.[60] In an important settlement, Nationwide agreed to admit otherwise qualified DACA recipients to apply and be considered for the management trainee program.[61] This signaled to other would-be or hesitant employers that they were not violating federal law by hiring such employees; in fact, they would be violating the law by *not* considering for employment fully qualified individuals with permission to work in the United States.[62]

Building on the 2012 success, President Obama in November 2014 set out the Immigration Accountability Executive Action (which would have widened DACA and expanded the program from two years to three), as well as the Deferred Action for Parents of Americans and Lawful Permanent Residents (DAPA) initiative for the parents of US citizens and lawful permanent residents who met certain criteria.[63] As unpopular as the successful DACA program had proven to its opponents, it had been tested several times and was found to be legal, including collateral DACA-related benefits such as resident college tuition[64] and driver's licenses issued to DACA recipients, by almost every court that reviewed the issue.[65] But behind *Plyler* and DACA was a narrative that innocent children should not be punished for actions undertaken by their parents, and in such a narrative parents morphed into lawbreakers and villains, resulting in an all-out war on DAPA when officials attempted to give them any DACA-like relief.[66]

Almost immediately, the restrictionist sheriff of Maricopa County, Arizona, Joseph Arpaio, sued in a Washington, DC, federal court to enjoin the DACA extension and the DAPA program,[67] and twenty-six state attorneys general filed a similar case in federal court in Brownsville, Texas.[68] Sheriff Arpaio's lawsuit was dismissed, and on appeal the dismissal was upheld by a three-judge panel of the DC Circuit Court of Appeals. The Supreme Court denied certiorari on the sheriff's appeal, ending the matter.[69]

However, the Texas federal court preliminarily enjoined both initiatives: the DACA expansion (including its extension to three years upon renewal) and DAPA.[70] The Department of Justice appealed,[71] and the Fifth Circuit Court of Appeals panel upheld Judge Andrew Hanen's ruling in a 2–1 decision.[72] The Supreme Court—absent the recently deceased Justice Antonin Scalia—tied 4–4, upholding the district court's original temporary restraining order and returning the case to Brownsville.[73] When the Trump administration took office in January 2017, there was no actual ruling on the constitutionality of DACA, its extension to three years, or DAPA.[74] The Trump administration, as has been detailed in other chapters, attempted to rescind DACA, but a series of court decisions thwarted the attempt. However, there will come a time when the current DACA recipients will no longer be able to avail themselves of the program's benefits because a form of relief not yet in sight has preempted the field or because the DACA program is rescinded within a legal framework. The status quo ante therefore held, with no further formal action to rescind taken by the Trump administration on DACA despite confusing developments that led to the removal of a small number of DACA recipients and accusations that others were ineligible.[75] No one has been able to join DACA since the attempted rescission, shrinking the field further.

After a flurry of cases concerning DACA, the question also became: How are the hundreds of thousands of DACAmented students to be treated given that their new benefits rendered them eligible to remain in college and to move into licensed occupations and other employment?[76] In addition, there were still many college students who were undocumented and ineligible for DACA due to a variety of reasons such as age, inability to meet the criminal tests, or inability to be admitted into or afford college—the pathway to DACA.[77] These undocumented students or undocumented persons were unable to navigate DACA and thus were unauthorized to receive employment authorization, SSNs, or the other collateral benefits of DACA such as "lawful presence."[78] They were, in effect, removable once they were known to the government or came into governmental sights.[79] Of all the immigration categories, individuals with similar circumstances as these students might find work yet have no legal status, no lawful presence, and no prospects of ever being able to adjust their liminal illegality into a pathway to citizenship or even to the safer confines of DACA.[80]

Federal and State Jurisdictions and Occupational Licensing Governance—California Lawyers as a Case Study

This brief review masks many important features that matter but are required to situate the data at the heart of this project.[81] The complex worlds of occupational licensing have many features in common, but each specific area has its own top-to-bottom features grounded in state statutes, regulations, common law, and trade practices.[82] For example, lawyer licensing is usually the domain of state statute, but in a number of states the details are determined by a state bar authority, a separate licensing authority (such as a state board of law examiners or bar examiners), the state's supreme court, or an amalgam of the various decision makers.[83] A long-standing tradition of self-governance within law licensure has given much discretion to the final arbiter in each state to determine who may join the profession and have permission to practice law in that jurisdiction, making it a very complicated pathway and journey that is made all the more difficult by the effect of reciprocal bar admissions across state borders, where sophisticated legal practices often require multistate licensing and federal and state eligibility to try complex cases and negotiate transactions.[84] In addition, some fields of specialized law are predominantly federal, such as immigration law and patent law, and therefore these federal practice areas will implicate certain federal bar admissions requirements.[85]

This is evident in the most populous state, California, where there is a state statute that sets out provisions for the state bar, which is governed by a board of trustees.[86] Its provisions include: Title 1. Global Provisions; Title 2. Rights and Responsibilities of Members; Title 3. Programs and Services; Title 4. Admissions and Educational Standards; Title 5. Discipline, Title 6. Governance; Title 7. Miscellaneous Provisions; and the California Rules of Professional Conduct.[87] The State Bar Act is set out by the California *Business & Professions Code Div. 3–Professions and Vocations Generally, Ch. 4–Attorneys* and codifies the practice of law in California.[88] The state bar exam and admissions procedures are administered by the Committee of Bar Examiners.[89] (I include this outline in some detail to give a sense of how complex the overall licensure and maintenance of licenses can be. The actual topics run over a dozen pages, simply outlining the subject matter.)[90]

This is just one occupational licensing architecture, albeit a highly regulated arrangement and, in some respects, a protectionist scheme designed to limit the important medallion to a limited number of seekers.[91] In this welter of complex governance in California law admissions, there had been no reference to or requirement of immigration status or citizenship until 2008, in effect allowing undocumented students to take and pass the bar and truthfully answer all the questions posed for admission and membership.[92] If and when they met all the eligibility criteria they were admitted, in small numbers, and formed a Dream Bar Association.[93] Discussions with California scholars and bar admissions personnel have estimated that between one and two dozen such undocumented lawyers had been licensed in the state prior to the case of Sergio Garcia, who was born in 1977 in Mexico of Mexican parents.[94]

Garcia was residing in California without legal status, although he had lived in the United States almost all his life and continuously since 1994.[95] Due to the complexities of US immigration law, his undocumented father had earned LPR status and eventually became a US citizen, but due to long queues in lines for Mexican dependents his son Sergio had been waiting for nearly twenty years for an adjustment of status.[96] This PRUCOL-like limbo is indicative of the oftentimes cruel and senseless nature of immigration to the United States, especially in its slow crawl for would-be beneficiaries from oversubscribed countries such as Mexico.[97]

When DACA was enacted in 2012, Garcia was too old to apply, but he received his law degree from Cal Northern School of Law in May 2009. He sat for and passed the July 2009 California bar examination, a year after the Committee of Bar Examiners began asking for immigration information on its application. As the California Supreme Court summarized:

> [The Committee] has submitted the name of Sergio C. Garcia (hereafter Garcia or applicant) for admission to the State Bar. In conjunction with

its certification, the Committee has brought to the court's attention the fact that Garcia's current immigration status is that of an undocumented immigrant, and has noted that the question whether an undocumented immigrant may be admitted to the State Bar is an issue that has not previously been addressed or decided by this court. We issued an order to show cause in this matter to address the question.[98]

Our order to show cause requested briefing on a number of issues raised by the Committee's motion to admit Garcia to the State Bar, including the proper interpretation of a federal statute—section 1621 of title 8 of the United States Code (hereafter section 1621)—that generally restricts an undocumented immigrant's eligibility to obtain a professional license but that also contains a subsection expressly authorizing a state to render an undocumented immigrant eligible to obtain such a professional license through the enactment of a state law meeting specified requirements.[99] Very shortly after we held oral argument in this matter, the California Legislature enacted a statute that was intended to satisfy this aspect of section 1621 and the Governor signed that legislation into law. (Bus. & Prof. Code, § 6064, subd. (b); Stats. 2013, ch. 573, § 1, enacting Assem. Bill No. 1024 (2013–2014 Reg. Sess.) as amended Sept. 6, 2013.) The new legislation became effective on January 1, 2014.[100]

In light of the recently enacted state legislation, we conclude that the Committee's motion to admit Garcia to the State Bar should be granted.[101]

The new statute provided in section 6064:

(a) Upon certification by the examining committee that the applicant has fulfilled the requirements for admission to practice law, the Supreme Court may admit the applicant as an attorney at law in all the courts of this state and may direct an order to be entered upon its records to that effect. A certificate of admission thereupon shall be given to the applicant by the clerk of the court.[102]

(b) Upon certification by the examining committee that an applicant who is not lawfully present in the United States has fulfilled the requirements for admission to practice law, the Supreme Court may admit that applicant as an attorney at law in all the courts of this state and may direct an order to be entered upon its records to that effect. A certificate of admission thereupon shall be given to the applicant by the clerk of the court. *(Amended by Stats. 2013, Ch. 573, Sec. 1. Effective January 1, 2014.)*[103]

It is a fascinating narrative and makes California the first state to affirmatively grant authorization for an undocumented person (one "who is *not* lawfully present in the United States") to be licensed to practice law.[104] Florida has passed a similar law, but it is limited to applicants—like those with DACA—who are "lawfully present,"[105] not undocumented, and New York has had similar administrative law actions to allow DACA recipients to practice law in that state.[106] And, as becomes evident in the study data, some states are like pre-2008 California and ask no immigration questions.[107] Thus, there can be no immigration lies or equivocations. Given the rising costs of legal education and other forms of professional education, the uncertainties of DACA, the tantalizing reach of comprehensive immigration reform, and the continuing refinement of collateral legal issues, it is not clear how these issues will play out. But it is clear that some number of law students, medical students, and others with postbaccalaureate qualifications will come forth in jurisdictions that have immigration policies and practices that will have to be clarified or modified in the case of these nascent professionals.[108]

And it is not too early to anticipate some second-order issues that likely might arise even once admissions may be granted.[109] For example, the comity arrangement of reciprocity that has arisen for multistate law practice (wherein attorneys from one state can gain admittance to practice in another state) will bog down if no other state accepts such members whose immigration status is not the same as the reciprocal state's requirements—even with reciprocity language on the books.[110] If they are undocumented attorneys, they will not have work authorization; being hired may place them and their employers at risk, leaving them with a restricted number of employment opportunities outside the solo practice of law.[111] There are sometimes additional filters required for a comprehensive practice such as permission to practice before a federal tribunal or entity.[112] In Garcia's case, the Department of Justice entered into the amicus fray[113] and argued that he should not be admitted to the state practice based upon the department's reading of section 1621 on which the California Supreme Court ruled—notwithstanding the exceptions spelled out in some detail:

§ 1621. Aliens who are not qualified aliens or nonimmigrants ineligible for State and local public benefits

(a) In general
(b) Notwithstanding any other provision of law and except as provided in subsections (b) and (d) of this section, an alien who is not—
  (1) a qualified alien (as defined in section 1641 of this title),
  (2) a nonimmigrant under the Immigration and Nationality Act, or
  (3) an alien who is paroled into the United States under section 212(d)(5) of such Act for less than one year, is not eligible for any State or local public benefit (as defined in subsection (c) of this section) . . .
(c) "State or local public benefit" defined
  (1) Except as provided in paragraphs (2) and (3), for purposes of this subchapter the term "State or local public benefit" means—
    (A) any grant, contract, loan, professional license, or commercial license provided by an agency of a State or local government or by appropriated funds of a State or local government; . . .
(d) State authority to provide for eligibility of illegal aliens for State and local public benefits

A State may provide that an alien who is not lawfully present in the United States is eligible for any State or local public benefit for which such alien would otherwise be ineligible under subsection (a) of this section only through the enactment of a State law after August 22, 1996, which affirmatively provides for such eligibility.[114]

In light of the fact that California did exactly this for lawyers, a "professional license . . . provided by an agency of a State or local government or by appropriated funds of a State or local government" triggers the exception to the federal prohibition.[115] And because DACA provides "lawful presence" to its recipients, this provision is not even applicable for the undocumented; the provision to allow licenses could be triggered by any state that enacts state law, whether by statute or other operation of law, for the undocumented (without lawful presence) or the DACA-mented (with lawful presence).[116] This reveals the extent to which federal and state laws interact in licensing and immigration governance and in very a complicated fashion regarding DACA.[117]

Parsing these high-caste occupational law licensing immigration criteria would require book-length observations, but highlighting several examples here from the national dataset will suffice to make the point that this is a rich diet, one with many tasty morsels evident and larders full of ripe fruit.[118] To continue the theme of attorney licensing, consider just four states, starting in alphabetical order:

Alabama

"Only a person who is a citizen of the United States or, if not a citizen of the United States, a person who is legally present in the United States with appropriate documentation from the federal government, may be licensed to practice law in this state." This broad categorization could include many non-immigrants who were "legally present," and DACA provides the requisite "lawful presence," technically making it possible in theory for the DACAmented and others with a variety of immigration categorizations to become licensed.[119]

Alaska

"The application shall be made under oath and contain such information relating to the applicant's age, residence, addresses, citizenship, occupations, general education, legal education, moral character and other matters as may be required by the Board"; however, the application must contain the applicant's social security number. This state is silent on required immigration status, provided the applicant has a SSN—available to DACA recipients; it is not clear if an Individual Taxpayer Identification Number (ITIN) could suffice.[120]

Arizona

"If a US citizen, a copy [is required] of your birth certificate, passport information page, valid driver's license, completed I-9, or certificate of naturalization (copies allowed). If not a citizen of the USA, copies of official documentation of immigration status." This is a particularly inconsistent requirement in a state that has been an active litigant on both sides of benefits-eligibility in the immigration and especially the DACA context. But the technical eligibility language ("If not a citizen of the USA, copies of official documentation of immigration status") covers a number of immigration categories, and is unclear on its reach. As just one pertinent example, any non-immigrant student or tourist could provide such documentation.[121]

Arkansas
"Candidates may be a United States citizen, an alien lawfully admitted for permanent residence, or an alien otherwise authorized to work or study lawfully in the United States." This requirement appears to cover the waterfront, but the last phrase ("or an alien otherwise authorized to work or study lawfully in the United States") would appear to enable licensing for both DACA recipients, who are "authorized to work," or some F-1 students. Even the seemingly-straightforward language of being "authorized to . . . study lawfully in the United States" is not definitive, as many categories of non-immigrants may enroll to study, not only the two most common F-1 or M-1 visa categories.[122]

There are more landmines dotting this field, given that states deploy proxy measures as substitutes or elaborations for immigration status requirements, not always anticipating how the measures can change over time (such as DACA or collateral legislation) or how imperfect or imprecise terminology can be ("students," "SSN holders," or "lawful presence").[123] Again, DACA became the perfect vehicle for broad eligibility, as states likely had no intent or plans to admit DACA recipients given that the program began in 2012, and no one could have predicted the growth or even understood that a person like Sergio Garcia could arise and challenge the complex and intricate pathways, much less that the country's largest state would act in private relief fashion to accommodate his application through legislation in the midst of a state court trial on that very matter of eligibility.[124] In light of the large political divide over immigration-related employment, it is unlikely that Alabama intended for the DACAmented or even other noncitizens (except LPRs) to become licensed attorneys in the state.[125] After all, Alabama was embroiled in substantial litigation about college tuition for undocumented residents, and the state's ethos has unlikely changed since that litigation.[126]

In this vein, the Alaska requirement that would-be lawyers present SSNs predated DACA and its provisions for SSNs, but a variety of tax and employment transactions require either one's SSN or an Individual Taxpayer Identification Number (ITIN), which is a tax-processing number issued by the Internal Revenue Service.[127] The IRS uses ITINs for persons who are required to have a US taxpayer identification number but who are ineligible to obtain an SSN.[128] ITINs are issued to all non-LPR/US citizen comers, no matter their immigration status, because even the undocumented or certain noncitizens have filing or reporting obligations under the Internal Revenue Code.[129] Technically, SSNs and ITINs serve a limited purpose for tax reporting and do not provide EAD, Social Security or other benefits, or eligibility for Earned Income Tax Credits.[130] At the same time, both are an unlikely and imprecise measure of immigration licensing eligibility.[131]

Of course, the practice of law is not alone in its high status and its detailed educational and other licensing criteria.[132] Becoming a licensed physician is, in many respects, even more fraught with immigration implications due to the large number of foreign-trained physicians (including US citizens, LPRs, and international scholars).[133] Thus, there is a very exacting immigration-related series of federal licensing requirements built into the medical practice field, but a review of the statutory medical doctor eligibility and admissions criteria reveals similar confusion and imprecision[134] resulting in a comprehensive architecture that is both too much and too little with regard to citizenship criteria.

Here, I highlight four state jurisdictions (representing the last four in alphabetical order) and their immigration categorizations for admission into the medical field:

West Virginia

"In order to comply with federal law, the West Virginia Board of Medicine is obligated to inform each applicant or licensee from whom it requests a Social Security Number that disclosing such number is MANDATORY in order for this Board to comply with the requirements of the federal National Practitioner Data Bank and the Healthcare Integrity and Protection Data Bank. If this Board should be required to make a report about one of its applicants or licensees to either of these data banks, it must report that individual's Social Security Number."[135]

Wisconsin

There is no specific immigration status indicated, but a SSN or Employer Identification Number is required in the Application Form. If the SSN is not provided, form 1051, an Affidavit, is required to explain why the SSN was not provided on the application. Applicants must answer a question about immigration status in the application form: "CERTIFICATION OF LEGAL STATUS: I declare under penalty of law that I am (check one): A citizen or national of the United States, or, A qualified alien or nonimmigrant lawfully present in the United States who is eligible to receive this professional license or credential as defined in the Personal Responsibility and Work Opportunities Reconciliation Act of 1996, as codified in 8 U.S.C. § 1601 et. Seq. (PRWORA) . . . Should my legal status change during the application process or after a credential is granted, I understand that I must report this change to the Wisconsin Department of Safety and Professional Services immediately."[136]

Wyoming

"Except as otherwise specifically provided by statute, a board or commission authorized to establish examination, permit or license application requirements for any profession or occupation regulated under this title shall require applicants for new licenses, certificates of registration or renewals of licenses or certificates to include the applicant's social security number on the application form."[137]

Washington, DC

The SSN is required on the application form, but the statute has no specific required immigration status reference.[138]

As was evident in the lawyer-licensing world, similar nomenclature and proxy issues arise in the context of medical practice.[139] Wisconsin has unusually detailed immigration language, but its fulcrum is the SSN, and it adds the Employer Identification Number (EIN), which is usually issued by the IRS for limited tax administration purposes associated with principal businesses in the United States.[140] Because the EIN is available to a wide range of individuals with a variety of immigration categories,[141] Wisconsin's detailed immigration requirement is rendered less restrictive than it seems on its face.

To license an applicant to the practice of nursing, the neighboring states of Alabama, Mississippi, and Arkansas vary from high to low.[142] Alabama has among the strictest immigration criteria: "An alien who is not lawfully present in the United States and who is not defined as an alien eligible for public benefits under 8 U.S.C. § 1621(a) or 8 U.S.C. § 1641 shall not receive any state or local public benefits."[143] The phrase "public benefits" is defined as including professional licenses: "An applicant for a license . . . a citizen of the United States or, if not a citizen of the United States, a person who is legally present in the United States with appropriate documentation from the federal government."[144] DACA enrollment would meet this requirement, as would a number of other immigrant and nonimmigrant classifications. Mississippi statutorily requires the applicant to have an SSN, while Arkansas has no immigration criteria.[145] Nonetheless, the entrance to nursing practice in Arkansas at the Licensed Practical Nurse (LPN) and Registered Nurse (RN) levels is administered by a uniform application bank process—a commercial service deceptively named "easyNCLEX.com"—that requires a "valid Social Security Number," even if the Arkansas nursing eligibility statute specifies no such requirement.[146] Again, these examples show the as-applied differences between the actual authorization language and the practical gatekeeping-form passageways.[147]

New York, like many other states, has a widespread and detailed administrative scheme for its many hundreds of occupational licenses. It also maintains an unusually decentralized form of governance, including several domains within so-called Current Licenses available through the comprehensive NYS License Center Portal.[148] This online portal aggregates many licenses for Agriculture, Forestry, and Fisheries; Construction; Education; Finance and Insurance; Food Service and Processing; Health Care; Manufacturing; One-Time Permits; Real Estate; Recreation; Retail; Services, Transportation and Public Utilities; and Wholesale, as well as additional permits and licenses for more than a hundred agencies, from the Adirondack Park Agency to the Workman's Compensation Board.[149]

Furthermore, the New York Department of State governs another roster of occupations:[150]

TABLE 6.1: New York Department of State Division of Licensing Services: index of licensees and registrants

Alarm Installer	Apartment Information Vendor
Apartment Sharing Agent	Armored Car Carrier
Armored Car Guard	Athlete Agents
Bail Enforcement Agent	Bedding
Central Dispatch Facility	Document Destruction Contractor
Document Destruction Contractor Branch Office	Hearing Aid Dispenser
Hearing Aid Dispenser Business	Home Inspection
Notary Public	Private Investigator
Proprietary Employer Of Security Guards	Real Estate Appraiser
Security Guard	Telemarketer Business
Ticket Reseller	Ticket Reseller Branch Office
Watch Guard And Patrol Agency	

In addition, the New York State Department of Education governs hundreds of other permits, some of which are episodic or recreational (Seven-Day Fishing License or One-Day Fishing License; Aircraft One Time) but it also includes licenses by which residents can make their living, such as Lifetime Licenses for hunting & fishing, trapping, bow hunting, and even muzzle-loading privileges.[151] The issuing agencies involve the Departments of Agriculture and Markets, the Department of Environmental Conservation, the State of New York, Taxation and Finance, and Motor Vehicles, among others.[152]

Some of the sample occupational licenses include: Appearance Enhancement Natural Hair Stylist; Brewer Tasting; Bulk and Package Hauler; Milk Dealer; and Special Entertainer's Permit (for Minors).[153] In a 2015 study, Janet M. Calvo found almost thirty occupations governed by the New York Education Law and the Department of Education that had no statutory immigration limitations among the many hundreds of such licensed occupations.[154] As she noted:

> Title VIII of the New York Education Law does not require citizenship or immigration category for twenty-nine professions. Therefore, New York State law does not require that an individual be in any particular immigration category to obtain a license for the following listed professions. Even with these omissions, she found widespread "as-applied" *de*

facto requirements, either by the actual application forms that asked for immigration status or through the website portal's stated citizenship restrictions: Yet, the application forms published on the New York State Department of Education's website restrict licensing applications to limited categories of non-citizens.[155]

Calvo's findings corroborated the data I examined above, and had she detailed all of the state's occupations and licenses she would have elaborated upon more than the twenty-nine she listed from the single agency.[156] While not every state or jurisdiction is as large and decentralized as New York's statutory and administrative regimes, the outlines and patterns are evident at every layer across all fields high and low.[157] Put starkly, the actual technical details of implementation do not often track the legal underpinnings; indeed, there is a substantial slip between the authorizing cup and the as-applied lip.[158]

Over the years, New York has prompted several important immigration cases involving licensure and benefit eligibility, including the DACA bar admissions matter allowing Cesar Vargas to obtain a license to practice law,[159] *Mauclet*,[160] and *Dandamudi*.[161] Tracking these cases and their implementation, Calvo also documented that New York Education Law Title VIII does not require any citizenship or immigration category for an additional nine professions.[162] The statutes regarding these nine professions specifically state that an individual does not require US citizenship and do not include an immigration category requirement.[163] However, the application forms published on the New York State Department of Education's website restrict licensing applications for these nine occupations from limited categories of noncitizens.[164]

Finally, Calvo's analysis of thirteen New York Education Law Title VIII occupations noted that licenses were restricted to citizens and lawful permanent residents—even after the immigration requirements were struck down as unenforceable under the terms of the *Dandamudi* litigation.[165] Even though there are no enforceable immigration-based legislative restrictions on these professions, "the application forms published on the New York State Department of Education's website restrict licensing applications to limited categories of non-citizens."[166] Having immersed myself in these data and these literatures, I moved from a sense of satisfaction in gathering the information to a sense of growing dread as I began to delve into the various inconsistencies, mistakes, gaps, and confusion—both in the actual governance language and the "as-applied administration" of immigration eligibility across occupational licensing in many fields, whether elite or accessible.[167]

The dread enveloped me as I began to recognize how difficult it would be to theorize on these admissions requirements and how complex a project this was going to be.[168] Of course, I knew it would not be easy, but I assumed that more thoughtful attention and precision in eligibility requirements would have developed over time (in part because of my own deep dives into legal education and eligibility for my own profession of law).[169] I have been involved in law school accreditation, law licensure, and assessments of moral character and fitness for bar eligibility and, in some detail (in New York, California, and Florida), dealt with undocumented and DACAmented applicants.[170] Even so, I was unprepared for the actual requirements I unearthed, much like my students and various educators and licensing professionals with whom I have discussed these matters on my way to gathering the data. There are almost as many needed footnotes as there are categories. I have been shocked at the unanticipated absence of immigration criteria in a substantial number of professions and in a number of jurisdictions, as well as the multiple ways in which the formal requirements do not mesh with actual implementation.[171] It will require more detailed, almost anthropological case studies in hundreds of data cells to reconcile the formal criteria with the data routinely required. What passes for quotidian applications forms—such as immigration status questions or SSNs—can pose formidable barriers to noncitizens.[172]

The uncertainty over immigration reform and the fate of DREAMers, as well as the tightened immigration scrutiny practiced since the Trump administration took office in January 2017, have made the entire process more complex and uncertain—certainly more so compared to other presidential transitions.[173] With regard to immigration, there is more instability in the system, more litigation in the courts, and more polarization in the polity, all further contributing to the confusion and apprehension.[174] I suspect that additional attention will be paid to these crucial intersections and that changes will occur to the higher- and lower-caste professions at the state and federal levels.[175] By the time the dust settles, there will be more than 750,000 DACA recipients making their intrepid way through the occupational pathways available to them; their progress will be punctuated and uncertain.[176] As has been shown with the examples of bar membership in three of the largest states, the progress could be a regression to the mean of restrictionism but could just as easily turn toward accommodation and incorporation, recouping the investment occasioned by *Plyler*'s promise.[177]

The national dataset reveals national examples of occupational licensing laws across dozens of fields and states, nearly all of which appear to require US citizenship notwithstanding federal and state litigation that has struck down such a high entry bar.[178] In other words, there has been a widespread failure to enact statutes and practices that conform to the broader eligibility requirements at play in the employment field.[179] At the very least, various accreditation and licensing authorities and legislatures have not done the necessary work to smooth out the inconsistencies or to regularize the various anomalies.[180]

Observers are left with the clear impression of the need for recodification or restatements, profession by profession, especially as employment and immigration laws continue to slide along tectonic plates, causing gaps and ridges.[181] One of the glories of the US immigration system is not that it breaks down or is unfair—both of which are demonstrably accurate—but that it works well much of the time. Given the early returns on occupational licensing and the intersection with immigration, there is reason to hope.[182] There is surely reason to improve.[183]

The 2016 Election of Donald Trump, the Rescission of DACA, and Its Aftermath

Following a letter from a small number of immigration law professors, led by UCLA professor Hiroshi Motomura in 2012, President Barack Obama used his prosecutorial discretion to establish DACA (Deferred Action for Childhood Arrivals) on June 15, 2012, the fortieth anniversary of *Plyler v. Doe*.[1]

This policy enabled applicants who had arrived in the country before the age of sixteen and who met certain criteria to receive DACA, which included a Social Security number, work authorization, permission to leave and reenter the country, and "lawful presence" on a renewable two-year basis provided they complied with all the requirements.[2] Despite widespread misgivings about the requirement that DACA applicants share such information and biometrics data with the government, more than 750,000 students became "DACAmented" recipients.[3] In November 2014, President Obama doubled down, extending a similar form of discretionary relief to certain undocumented parents with US citizen children (Deferred Action for Parents of Americans, or DAPA) and extending the two-year DACA periods to renewable three-year periods.[4]

As noted earlier, Texas and a number of other states with Republican governors and/or attorneys general brought suit to enjoin the expansion features of the program. *United States v Texas* resulted in a 4–4 Supreme Court decision, the tie in effect upholding the trial judge and Fifth Circuit rulings that the DAPA codicil violated presidential authority.[5] The Supreme Court was down to eight members following the death of Associate Justice Antonin Scalia and the abject refusal of the United States Senate's Republican majority leader, Mitch McConnell, to schedule a hearing for President Obama's replacement nominee, Merrick Garland, for the final ten months of Obama's term, eventually leading to President Trump's appointment of Neil Gorsuch to the vacancy.[6] The case reverted back to the trial judge, who kept jurisdiction over the technically unresolved original DACA program. With the new administration in 2017, events overtook the program, which was still in existence even as uncertainty hovered over the program's reach and provenance.

Despite the many court challenges examined in previous chapters and allied cases spawned by the program, DACA was a self-financed and wildly successful program, one that gave temporary shelter to the many students, including the ability to obtain professional licenses, such as those described in chapter 6. It spawned dozens of books and hundreds of articles.[7] In its first half-dozen years, it also spawned dozens of lawsuits, directly concerning and defining the program, and with collateral litigation affecting its relationship with various public benefits or other features (recall appendix 3).

The national election of Donald J. Trump to the presidency, however, promised to threaten the existence of DACA and immigration generally, as candidate Trump had mounted a divisive and nativist campaign against all things Obama, including this signature initiative.[8] On September 5, 2017, Attorney General Jefferson B. Sessions announced he would terminate DACA, saying that the program was illegal and exceeded the presidential authority.[9] The administration eventually issued guidelines for phasing out DACA and announced that it would not review new applications.[10] Within a short period of time, a number of states and immigration advocates filed suits challenging the proposed DACA rescission.[11] In effect, the Trump administration indicated that it did not feel that such a large program could be created without Congress enacting legislation and that it did not believe that the executive action of inherent prosecutorial discretion and authority existed.

There ensued a complex series of court challenges that were litigated against the backdrop of radical, restrictionist administrative actions undertaken by the Trump administration to drastically reduce legal immigration, to enact harsher enforcement policies against illegal immigration, and to undertake nativist challenges to certain groups. Such actions included restricting entry to travelers from several predominantly-Muslim countries (the "Muslim Ban"), ramping up workplace raids to apprehend undocumented workers, reducing the number of refugees allowed to enter the country annually, rescinding Temporary Protected Status that had been in place for several other Caribbean and Latin American countries, and, most visibly, enacting a "zero tolerance" policy that separated parents from children, leading to public outcry and a turnabout that slowed the separations as pictures of crying children and the resulting public disapproval forced President Trump's hand.[12] Of course, additional advocates threw more sand into the gears even as the president took to the airwaves and social media to incite the public narrative, which took a nasty, racist, and xenophobic turn (including his excoriating asylum-seekers as "thugs," "murderous gang members," and "rapists" traveling from south of the US-Mexico border in what he labeled as an ominous and menacing "caravan" that would attempt to cross the border in "hordes").[13] Daily stories featured President Trump's tweets such as the one he circulated on June 22, 2018: "Republicans should stop wasting their time on immigration until after we elect more senators and congressmen/women in November."[14] Partly to deflect attention away from the incarcerated and removed children already in this country, the Republican-led House voted on several iterations of relief for the separated children, including proposed legislation that included DACA relief.[15] Twice in June 2018 Congress failed to enact legislation that would have both addressed and resolved the vague status of DACA and allowed these DREAMers a pathway to permanent residence.[16]

During this period, the United States Supreme Court ruled in a 5–4 vote that the travel ban was not unconstitutional.[17] Later that same week, Justice Anthony Kennedy announced he would retire in the summer of 2018, giving President Trump a second vacancy to fill, which he did in the hotly debated nomination of Judge Brett Kavanaugh of the DC Circuit, who was approved on a 50–48 vote in the Senate.[18] The confluence of these various immigration events, highlighted by the president's many tweets excoriating Democrats for not approving billions of dollars to build a wall separating the US border with Mexico, as well as his regaining his footing after the ignominious attention drawn to the children and caged facilities, roiled the waters so much that consensus could not be maintained to get either chamber of Congress to enact a DREAM Act bill.[19]

The primary challenges to the Trump administration's DACA rescission took three different paths originating in litigation filed in California, New York, and the District of Columbia. The original challenge to DAPA was also remanded to the original trial court in Brownsville, Texas, where it had been languishing after the Supreme Court's 4–4 nondecision.[20]

In January 2018, a federal district court in the Northern District of California issued a preliminary injunction and ordered DHS to continue the DACA program extension, although no new DACA applications were authorized.[21] The court first described the history of deferred action and discretionary prosecutions in the immigration context, including a reference to the rescission of DACA and the newly proposed DAPA. The court parsed administrative law precedents and determined that Attorney General Sessions's DACA rescission was reviewable by an Article III court and also found a mistake of law.[22] He wrote:

> In short, what exactly is the part of DACA that oversteps the authority of the agency? Is it the granting of deferred action itself? No, deferred action has been blessed by both the Supreme Court and Congress as a means to exercise enforcement discretion. Is it the granting of deferred action via a program (as opposed to ad hoc individual grants)? No, programmatic deferred action has been in use since at least 1997, and other forms of programmatic discretionary relief date back to at least 1956. Is it granting work authorizations coextensive with the two-year period of deferred action? No, aliens receiving deferred action have been able to apply for work authorization for decades. Is it granting relief from accruing 'unlawful presence' for purposes of the INA's bars on reentry? No, such relief dates back to the George W. Bush Administration for those receiving deferred action. Is it allowing recipients to apply for and obtain advance parole? No, once again, granting advance parole has all been in accord with pre-existing law. Is it combining all these elements into a program? No, if each step is within the authority of the agency, then how can combining them in one program be outside its authority, so long as the agency vets each applicant and exercises its discretion on a case-by-case basis? Significantly, the government makes no effort in its briefs to challenge any of the foregoing reasons why DACA was and remains within the authority of the agency. Nor does the government challenge any of the statutes and regulations under which deferred action recipients obtain the foregoing benefits.[23]

Judge Hanen's ruling in Brownsville had affected DACA and DAPA nationally beyond his court's jurisdiction; similarly, the California court's restoration of the status quo ante enabled DACAmented students to renew their applications for two years until the program was changed or terminated.[24] The California court did not allow the proposed three-year renewals, but it did continue the two-year renewals and extended the program features implicating work authorization and lawful presence. The advance parole provision, which had allowed DACA recipients to leave the country and return with permission, was also knocked out, eliminating a small loophole that enabled some DACA recipients in this transitional zone to adjust status and become lawful permanent residents.[25] The judge also restored the removal proceedings that had been used against a small number of DACA recipients who had not met the terms of continuing in the program (e.g., by not notifying USCIS of address changes, not making satisfactory progress in school, committing offenses that precluded renewal, and the like). A steady stream of media stories began to surface with such rescissions, which remained in place nevertheless and rendered the formerly DACAmented ineligible to sustain their lawful presence; some were deported.[26]

On January 16, 2018, the Trump administration appealed the lower court's decision to the United States Court of Appeals for the Ninth Circuit.[27] Two days later, the administration attempted to expedite the case by simultaneously petitioning the Supreme Court to skip the standard appellate process and consider the case directly on general "public interest grounds," which the Court refused to do on February 26, 2018.[28] (Such expedited requests are rarely granted absent emergency situations.)

During this period of Ninth Circuit uncertainty, on February 13, 2018, the Eastern District of New York also enjoined the proposed DACA rescission. Using language similar to the California refusal, it issued a similar nationwide injunction prohibiting DHS from moving forward with the DACA rescission and employed essentially similar reasoning, adding that not doing so would "cause irreparable harm."[29]

Two months later on April 24, 2018, in a case brought by Princeton and several elite universities, as well as the NAACP, the American Federation of Teachers, and the AFL-CIO (*Trustees of Princeton University et al. v. United States et al.*), the federal district court for the District of Columbia produced yet a third order enjoining the DACA rescission. It not only incorporated the California and New York district court rationales but also further determined that the proposed rescission lacked even "scant legal reasoning" to end the program.[30] It froze its own injunction through a *vacatur* action, which was to dissolve in ninety days. After that DACA was to go forward with the renewals (as had been effectuated with the other federal course decisions), and unless DHS could produce a legally sufficient reason the backlog of DACA recipients who had not been allowed to apply would be allowed to do so, effectively continuing the program.[31] It was not clear what fate other features—such as advance parole and others—would find. The congressional failures to enact a DREAM Act provision in the face of open hostility and inconsistent support and withdrawals of support from the president did not portend a successful passage of either DACA or a DREAM Act that had a pathway for eventual permanent residency or long-term US citizenship. It was also hard to believe that the administration, which had not even been able to properly end a discretionary program, would not learn to shoot straight and eventually end DACA once and for all. The renewals had added at least two rounds of extensions for those already enrolled, but no new DACA determinations would have eventually killed off the program or shrunk it through attrition and frustration. DHS disarray had also blurred its administrative vision and acumen.[32]

DHS secretary Kirstjen Nielsen complied with the April order by submitting a three-page memo that reiterated earlier arguments that DACA was "illegal" and that the administration could end the program because it did not wish to administer such a legally deficient program. She also reiterated the administration line that the structure of DACA was not nuanced or individualized and that it amounted to a large-scale amnesty. Her memo noted: "It is critically important for DHS to project a message that leaves no doubt regarding the clear, consistent, and transparent enforcement of the immigration laws against all classes and categories of aliens."[33]

The DHS position under the Trump administration had been inconsistent, and it was essentially circular: in essence, Secretary Nielsen argued that the Obama administration undertook to establish this program as a stopgap measure because it recognized that the Congress was not going to act on behalf of DREAMers and because immigration was a mess by anyone's measure—and so DACA was illegal. This version not only misconstrued the nature of discretionary decision-making, clearly evident in any number of other Trump initiatives—in immigration, foreign policy, and pardon policy—but also assumed illegality as the only basis for such a program:

> In addition, DHS should only exercise its prosecutorial discretion not to enforce the immigration laws on a truly individualized, case-by-case basis. While the DACA policy on its face did allow for individual considerations, a categorical deferred-action policy, at the very least, tilts the scales significantly and has the practical effect of inhibiting assessments of whether deferred action is appropriate in a particular case. Without the DACA policy, DHS may consider deferred action on a case-by-case basis, consistent with the INA. Moreover, considering the fact that tens of thousands of minor aliens have illegally crossed or been smuggled across our border in recent years and then have been released into the country owing to loopholes in our laws—and that pattern continues to occur at unacceptably high levels to the detriment of the immigration system—it is critically important for DHS to project a message that leaves no doubt regarding the clear, consistent, and transparent enforcement of the immigration laws against all classes and categories of aliens. All of those considerations lead me to conclude that Acting Secretary Duke's decision to rescind the DACA policy was, and remains, sound as a matter of both legal judgment and enforcement policy discretion.[34]

In September 2018 in the Second Circuit, attorneys general from seventeen states took issue with the June 2018 memo by Secretary Nielsen—which she had released to comply with an April order from a US district judge that required DHS to answer why DACA should not be resumed—in which she averred that DHS had persuasively argued the case (essentially by repeating that it was "illegal"). The state attorneys general took issue, arguing that the memo had not been made part of the appellate record and that the federal government was simply wrong: "The June 2018 memorandum is outside the administrative record, and even if it were properly before this court, its substance is insufficient to cure the defects in defendants' [original] September 2017 decision to end DACA."[35] They also alleged that the district court judge had been persuaded enough by their challenges under equal protection and the Administrative Procedure Act (APA) to enjoin any DACA rescission by DHS. In addition, they called out President Trump for his many anti-immigrant and anti-Mexican tweets and public comments, noting that his "demonstrated animus, together with his participation in the decision to end DACA, raises a plausible inference of invidious discrimination."[36]

This reasoning essentially undergirded the "zero tolerance" policy that the Trump administration began in summer 2018 under which unauthorized parents with children who crossed the border or sought asylum at the borders were separated from their infants and children, creating an entire legion of "unaccompanied alien minors" who were housed separately in makeshift facilities, some of them tent cities, in the summer heat and humidity.[37] While the ensuing public outcry caused the administration to blink and rescind the policy (which it had falsely insisted was necessitated by "Democrats' laws"), the circularity was revealed and a crisis of uncertainty was created. The policy was stayed by federal courts, and the children were ordered to be returned to their parents.[38] After nightly barrages of photos and audiotapes of crying children, mass public demonstrations and political advocacy grew through July 4, 2018. President Trump, for one of the few times in his presidency, made a midcourse correction and withdrew his policy as federal judges ordered the administration to reunite the children and minors separated from their parents; such timetables were not met by DHS.[39]

It was against this backdrop of many moving parts that the DREAM Act provisions went down to defeat in Congress. By the close of the 115th Congress, thirteen DACA and DREAM Act bills were introduced in those two years (2017–18), and only two came to a vote, both times unsuccessfully, in the House of Representatives.[40] The Senate never considered such legislation or voted on it. The issue died ignominiously, lost in the swirl of opposition from Trump and Sessions and the international issues concerning Russia, North Korea, and even allies such as Canada and the G-7, which together burned up all the oxygen in the foreign affairs atmosphere.[41] To accommodationists, there was an ironic sense that the political pushback and judicial restraining orders against the president's rescission kicked the can down the road, making legislation less urgent after the initial news cycle played out; restrictionists simply waited out the momentum and sympathy, and any chance for legislation effectively died.

Although it may be correct that the morning is most dark just before the dawn, there was little hope with regard to DACA, predominantly because the Trump administration continued its war against DACA on all fronts: legal, regulatory, legislative, and narrative. This included threatening to end birthright citizenship; weaponizing the Census Bureau's data on citizenship; limiting the number of refugees to be admitted into the country; singling out the "caravan" of potential asylum-seekers from Central America; and fashioning an Armageddon defense of sealing off the border by deploying more military personnel than have been deployed overseas since the post-9/11 wars and police actions (including Iraq, Iran, Yemen, Afghanistan, and elsewhere).[42] This comprehensive nativist agenda was designed to reverse immigration trends and to make it harder for many immigrants, particularly those from Latin American and South America, to raise legitimate claims for asylum or to seek relief—even types of relief that were promised by international law and US treaty obligations.[43] And at the end of the day, DACAmented students still found themselves in limbo, anxious over their uncertain status and legal future. DACA as it was then being enforced would not allow new people to apply, and the entire episode cast a pall over the continued employment eligibility and professional occupational licensing authority for current DACA recipients.

Following the national midterm elections in November 2018 the Senate remained in Republican hands but the House came under Democrat control, and there were important developments in DACA litigation.[44] The Ninth Circuit acted to continue the nationwide injunction that had resuscitated DACA in its original form and its renewal provisions, but it also kept in place the prohibitions against new members, resulting in a modern form of the Civil War widows' fund, a cohort that added no recipients and winnowed out those who failed to reapply or who became ineligible for renewals due to disqualifying reasons such as a criminal conviction or failure to abide by program rules. The Ninth Circuit court did make an important new finding, holding that DACA had been a lawful exercise of presidential discretion, and the three-judge panel denied the administration's claims that the original provisions were unlawful or that they were "arbitrary and capricious."[45] The administration had also argued that, under the APA and underlying immigration statutes, its rescission was unreviewable by courts. The panel also found that DACA recipients would likely succeed on their claims that the termination had been improperly undertaken and that they would also likely prevail on their equal protection claims: "The government's decision to rescind DACA is subject to judicial review" and "[t]he government may not simultaneously both assert that its actions are legally compelled, based on its interpretation of the law, and avoid review of that assertion by the judicial branch, whose 'province and duty' it is 'to say what the law is'" (citing *Marbury v. Madison* and *Heckler v. Chaney*).[46]

Following Judge Hanen's 2015 action to strike down DAPA and certain DACA features—such as the proposal to authorize renewals for three years rather than two—his ruling was upheld by the US Fifth Circuit Court of Appeals; on appeal to the Supreme Court, the justices tied 4–4, effectively upholding it. The Administration claimed it had the authority to shut down DACA, which it announced it would do in September 2017.[47] Collateral cases on DACA from other circuit courts had enjoined any additional changes in DACA and had enjoined any dismantling of DACA . And the request of the administration to receive expedited review by the Supreme Court would not be resolved for several years, even when certiorari was granted and whether or not President Obama's discretionary powers would be upheld. On this point, a panel sitting on the Ninth Circuit had found that the DACA plaintiffs were more likely than not to succeed on their national origin and equal protection claims, which they determined to be more convincing than the travel ban–related facts in *Trump v. Hawaii*, where majority-Muslim countries were targeted (minus US ally Saudi Arabia):

> We therefore conclude that DACA was a permissible exercise of executive discretion, notwithstanding the Fifth Circuit's conclusion that the related DAPA program exceeded DHS's statutory authority. DACA is being implemented in a manner that reflects discretionary, case by case review, and at least one of the Fifth Circuit's key rationales in striking down DAPA is inapplicable with respect to DACA. With respect for our sister circuit, we find the analysis that seemingly compelled the result in Texas entirely inapposite. And because the Acting Secretary was therefore incorrect in her belief that DACA was illegal and *REGENTS OF THE UNIV. OF CAL. v. USDHS* had to be rescinded, plaintiffs are likely to succeed in demonstrating that the rescission must be set aside.[48]

The Ninth Circuit's ruling did not affect the February 2018 national injunction preserving DACA issued by the US district court judge Nicholas Garaufis in Brooklyn, which was also on appeal. Even more important, on April 24, 2018, the US district court judge John D. Bates in Washington, DC, ordered the Trump administration to resume taking new DACA applications from those who were eligible under the original criteria; this decision to continue the status quo ante was stayed while on appeal.[49]

Supreme Court observers were likely to notice that any expedited case would require extraordinary efforts to complete the record, which had been incomplete. In January 2018, Judge William Alsup in California agreed with five different DACA-related plaintiff groups and enjoined the Trump administration from rescinding DACA and required that those applicants who had already received DACA benefits could continue to reapply for two-year renewals until the matter was concluded, either legislatively or upon resolution of the cases wending their way through the various circuits.[50] Immediately following this district court ruling, the administration sought expedited Supreme Court review to bypass the circuit court of appeals; in February 2018 certiorari was denied.[51] In May 2018, the Ninth Circuit panel heard the appeals and, as noted, refused to strike down DACA. But the administration must have taken some solace that the circuit panel did not rule that there was no way to end the program but that the administration needed to do so without resting its decision on the program's reputed illegality:

> To be clear: we do not hold that DACA could not be rescinded as an exercise of Executive Branch discretion. We hold only that here, where the Executive did not make a discretionary choice to end DACA—but rather acted based on an erroneous view of what the law required—the rescission was arbitrary and capricious under settled law. The government is, as always, free to reexamine its policy choices, so long as doing so does not violate an injunction or any freestanding statutory or constitutional protection.[52]

In other words, this Gang That Couldn't Shoot Straight had undermined its undeniable ability to shut down DACA by poor lawyering and by coming into court with the wrong argument. DACA proponents and DACA recipients were adamant that the discretionary program was legal because DHS and USCIS had the inherent authority to determine their own prosecutorial priorities.[53] The Trump administration simply asserted the program's illegality, adding well over two years' worth of renewable DACA permission. The panel determined: "The government may not simultaneously both assert that its actions are legally compelled, based on its interpretation of the law, and avoid review of that assertion by the judicial branch, whose 'province and duty' it is 'to say what the law is.'"[54]

Judge Hanen in Brownsville, who had blocked the implementation of the Obama administration's DAPA program and adjustments to DACA in 2015—which resulted in the 4–4 tie—in August 2018 moved to Houston, where the Southern District of Texas was headquartered. Surprisingly, however, he did not issue the injunction against DACA that many observers had expected. Rather, while remaining certain that DACA was illegal, and that it was within the Trump administration's power to withdraw it upon its individual expired renewals, Judge Hanen wrote an opinion employing a Humpty Dumpty metaphor: "Here, the egg has been scrambled. To try to put it back in the shell with only a preliminary injunction record, and perhaps at great risk to many, does not make sense nor serve the best interests of the country."[55] As to the endgame, he determined: "This court does not like the outcome of this case, but is constrained by its constitutionally limited role to the result that it has reached. Hopefully, the Congress and the president will finally get their job done."[56] On this unexpected note, DACA rolled on to its uncertain future, with all the cases in all the circuits allowing DACAmented recipients to continue in their previous frozen state with permission to work and lawful presence but no clear pathway to lawful permanent resident status.

Ironically, the Trump administration's knee-jerk and visceral opposition to DACA, as well as its surprising and ineffective litigation theories, had mousetrapped the administration and breathed life into DACA and the 750,000 DACA recipients. By now, they were taking their place as licensed members of the professional class, including lawyers, doctors, teachers, and other occupations. By Thanksgiving 2018, Democrats were readying to govern the House of Representatives, but no reasonable observer could predict with confidence what would happen.[57]

In the weeks before Thanksgiving 2018, two headlines appeared in the national press and immigration trade press, linking two surprising developments: "GOP leaders aim to avert shutdown over wall funding, but Trump makes no promises" in the *Washington Post*,[58] and "Koch Groups Push For 'Dreamer' Protections In Spending Bill," in *Law360*,[59] a specialized immigration publication. At this time there was a looming budget battle during which the federal government was about to run out of money, necessitating an embarrassing shutdown of all but the most essential federal offices.[60] The fulcrum was whether or not the president would get the money he was demanding to build his southern border wall. He had run on building the wall during his campaign, but he had also promised it would be paid for by Mexico—an invitation that the country did not accept. Even so, modernization and expansion of the existing areas that had been fenced for years was undertaken, and by FY2019 there was a confrontation between President Trump and Congress. The House was reverting to the Democrats, who wanted no part of such a budget; the Trump administration and some members of the Republican Party saw that the appropriations role would within months be undertaken by the resurgent Democrats, who had won nearly forty more congressional seats against GOP incumbents or vacancies.[61] Because all budget and spending legislation must originate in the House of Representatives, there were urgent negotiations and posturing in evidence.

The *Post* story noted:

> Sen. Richard J. Durbin (Ill.), the No. 2 Senate Democrat, said Thursday that he doesn't anticipate Democrats agreeing to more than the $1.6 billion they've already signed off on for the 2019 fiscal year . . . 'I don't see it. I think we've taken a position which is reasonable. We've given this administration more money than they can spend, and I don't see it,' Durbin said. 'If there are variables and things that are offered to us, of course we'll consider them, but I think our position is pretty sound and understandable.
>
> Durbin, a longtime champion of permanent protections for immigrants brought illegally to the country as children, said he was not aware of talks to make a deal on those 'dreamers' in exchange for money for Trump's wall. Such deals have been attempted repeatedly under Trump's presidency only to collapse in the end.

[Texas Senator John] Cornyn and other Republicans say they are open to such a deal now, but it appears unlikely to come together in the short time lawmakers have ahead of the Dec. 7 deadline.[62]

In the middle of this fray, *Law360* on November 15, 2018, reported:

Advocacy groups backed by the conservative Koch brothers have urged bipartisan lawmakers to prioritize Deferred Action for Childhood Arrivals recipients in a spending bill for the 2019 fiscal year that also proposes funding for border security.

In a letter from Tuesday, the Koch-affiliated Americans for Prosperity, Freedom Partners and the Libre Initiative said that Congress should find a permanent fix for DACA beneficiaries, known as Dreamers, as part of the spending bill due by Dec. 7, when the current continuing resolution passed by Congress expires.

The letter, addressed to Speaker Paul Ryan, R-Wis., Senate Majority Leader Mitch McConnell, R-Ky., Senate Minority Leader Chuck Schumer, D-NY, and House Minority Leader Nancy Pelosi, D-Calif., urges them to "seize this opportunity" in the coming weeks to push for permanent relief to the some 800,000 undocumented immigrants who came to the U.S. as children.

"These young people, brought here as children, continue to live in uncertainty as their status is in jeopardy," the groups wrote. "Their ability to plan for the future and contribute to the nation remains limited until Congress passes legislation resolving their legal status. Lawmakers can provide that certainty to them, their families, and their communities by reaching across the aisle on this important bipartisan effort—now."

Established in 2012, DACA has offered deportation relief and work authorization to these young immigrants, but in September 2017, the Trump administration attempted to terminate the program, asserting that former President Barack Obama's creation of the program constituted an unlawful overreach of his executive authority. But earlier this month, the Ninth Circuit left in place its nationwide injunction keeping the program alive, finding that Obama's creation of the program was a legitimate exercise of executive discretion.

Ahead of the bill's December deadline, the House and Senate will debate over immigration issues, including the issue of additional funding for the border wall with Mexico, according to the letter. With Democrats claiming control of the House in the midterm elections, the groups say that a compromise deal that provides a solution for the Dreamers may now be in sight.

"A legislative compromise that pairs a permanent solution for the Dreamers with additional funding for border security has again been proposed," the groups wrote. "We believe such a compromise can be passed and enacted into law with broad bipartisan support. We stand ready to work with you or any lawmaker toward this goal."[63]

This surprising development from outspoken conservative business leaders, urging a program to provide a standalone legislative DREAM Act and to fund increased border security and some wall construction, tilled the soil for compromise, but chess pieces do not have the independence or agency to move themselves or to capture the king. DREAMers, by definition, lack the legal status that would accord them the right to vote. Nonetheless, they were very active, well organized, and intent on seizing control of their own narrative and in serving as the resistance to the Trump administration and Congress, which had failed them in reaching their ultimate goal—a comprehensive immigration reform bill or, failing that, a legislative answer for improving their own liminal status—even if they could not reach for sufficient levers that might regularize the status of parents who lacked the semifirm but slippery footing accorded them by DACA.[64] As it turned out, these rhetorical flourishes did not materialize into legislative support, and the fecklessness of President Trump and the Republicans resulted in no traction for the appropriations struggle over wall funding. Even the Democrats seemed more intent on scoring points over the president on wall construction money but with no explicit linkage to the DREAMers.

And DACA was itself still under attack from the Trump administration, which was trying to rescind the Obama-era program. But in an almost comical twist, DHS and DOJ had become reminiscent of *The Gang That Couldn't Shoot Straight*, the 1969 novel[65] and 1971 film[66] about incompetent gangsters who were ludicrously incapable of murdering the Mafia don at the heart of the story despite repeated and more extreme measures.

The first two years of the Trump administration saw several immigration-related departments announce plans to abolish DACA only to fail spectacularly in their attempts to pull the plug. The proper way would have been to announce such intentions in the *Federal Register* and then reverse-engineer the discretionary steps that had been employed to create the original program. First, it would have to spell out its objections to DACA (and to DAPA, if it wanted to drive a stake into that heart) and follow the logic that, if it had been discretionary to begin the program, then so would be its ending; that it had been a successful pilot project but had run its course and would be used as a model for immigration reform if the time came.[67] After all, the Republicans had held all three of the bodies—the House, Senate, and the presidency. Moreover, with two new appointments seated on the Supreme Court, the Trump administration had turned a balanced Court into one with a solid conservative majority (depending upon the issue). Democrats would be hard-pressed to hold the line because they were in the minority and the rescission logic would have been irresistible.

If a president could prioritize his enforcement efforts and create DACA, another president could invoke the same overall process by deemphasizing that enforcement strategy and endorsing another. For example, he could have given higher priority to protecting US jobs and proposed to reduce the numbers of refugees or students or whatever. This cruel logic could hardly be denied had the Trump Administration followed the proper steps and dismantled the program, stressing its own discretionary enforcement priorities. As an example, it could have highlighted legal immigration or business-related, nonimmigrant options that would have allowed fewer permanent resident pathways, shrunk refugee numbers (an annual statutory presidential prerogative), and done away with DACA and other interim provisions (including Temporary Protected Status).[68] Discretionary priorities can and will change with new administrations, but at the very least the proper steps must be taken to do so; federal courts were providing some resistance and pushback on the administration's immigration priorities.

Instead, the immigration authorities simply announced that they would simply no longer grant DACA to eligible DREAMers and would let the 750,000–plus "DACAmented" recipients shrink as their two-year renewals would no longer be made available (and likewise with regard to their advance parole permission to leave the country and return with permission). With this meat-cleaver approach and a flurry of Twitter-generated Trump instructions and remarks,[69] no orderly end was proposed to ease this popular group of high-achieving and accomplished young students armed with lawful presence (if not lawful *status*) into some inchoate form of relief. The callous admonition of 2012 Republican presidential candidate Mitt Romney that DREAMers should simply "self-deport," a ludicrous proposition at the time, had become the default resolution.[70] There were conflicting signals sent that the DREAMers would be accommodated, but no legislation was actually introduced or sponsored by the GOP-held House or Senate or the administration, which could have waved a wand and resolved the impasse by a meaningful and sincere option.

After the legal machinery was begun by private organizations and law firms to throw sand into the gears of disassembling DACA or starve it of oxygen and administrative clarity, several lawsuits bought sufficient time to restore renewal of existing DACA applicants as their two-year terms expired, but there were no opportunities for newly eligible DREAMers to apply for or receive DACA and its benefits. The administration had been too clever by half, and as a result it did little more than snatch defeat from the jaws of victory by blithely assuming that, if it said so, DREAMers would simply roll over and die and that their supporters would capitulate. Indeed, the Texas litigation was only one of the various ribbons of cases, and DACA rescission was squarely in the sights of other federal judges who disallowed any material changes to the process and who ordered that the two-year renewals be continued if and until there was an authoritative end brought to the program.[71]

So the abrupt about-face in DACA tied the program's fate to a variety of other political goals, the most notable being President Trump's decision, announced by dozens of his tweets and other public announcements, to tie DACA to a deadline[72] and then to funding for his wall.[73] He had the determination that he would actually build a brick-and-mortar wall structure on the southern border with Mexico and that Mexico would pay for it. What he could not wring out of the congressional budgeting process, he began speaking and tweeting about, invoking emergency powers due to the House's constitutional requirement that it "originate" funds[74] and in turn "appropriate" money "drawn from the Treasury."[75] In other words, because he could not get Congress to fund the wall (even during the first two years of his term, when Democrats had no effective control over the chambers of Congress), he first attempted a partial government shutdown,[76] which predictably blew up in his and the GOP's faces when it lasted over a month and when it ended at Congress's hand, with him being forced to accept less appropriations money than had been on the table before the shutdown.[77]

Over time, and even as the Republican-led House refused to appropriate money for such a wall, his fiercest public right-wing partisans urged him to insist that such a structure was so important that US taxpayers should finance it[78] rather than the predictably reluctant Mexicans.[79]

This Mexican standoff froze much of the year-end government spending process and led to the longest shutdown in history (thirty-five days),[80] which one news report characterized as evidence of the gang not being able to shoot straight: "[T]he government shutdown morphed into a downpour, a winter storm of disruption, dysfunction and desperation that shocked stubborn politicians into action."[81] This painted the president into a corner because he had said he would shoulder the shutdown and not blame Democrats for it, a promise he immediately repudiated.[82] In addition, when the public saw the increasingly desperate nightly specter of flight controllers, IRS employees, Coast Guard employees, TSA security at jam-packed airports, FBI agents resorting to food banks for subsistence provisions, and others becoming one paycheck away from losing their homes or cars,[83] it overwhelmingly cast the blame on President Trump.[84]

It didn't help when his clueless and wealthy cabinet members proved to be tone-deaf, such as suggesting for nightly news broadcasts that furloughed workers should cash-in idle investments or take out personal loans to feed families and pay utility bills in the middle of dangerous weather and snowstorms plaguing much of the nation at the time.[85] The Democrats hung together and, having retaken the House, unanimously refused to support the president and the GOP leadership, giving Democrats considerable leverage to enact or block legislation to fund the government even for a short period.[86]

The president made an offer to Congress that wrapped into the mix a Band-Aid fix for DACA, but the fix would have only kicked the can down the road for a period of time, and it was not taken seriously.[87] In effect, the various slowdowns of the unsuccessful administration DACA rescission had resulted in a temporary extension anyway, adding years to the enjoined program's life. The various federal courts had frozen it for what would prove to be several years; each extension allowed DACA-mented students (and workers, once they finished their schooling and used the employment authorization benefits) two more years, renewable until eligibility was no longer able to be renewed.[88] This gave additional leverage to the Democrats: the extra breathing space meant that they did not have to give the president his hollow victory of tying DACA to the passage of the stalled budget.

While this linkage would likely have helped break the impasse, it was in the interests of Democrats to make the other antagonists squirm (such as widely characterizing the breakdown as "Trump's furlough" and "Trump's Wall")[89] and to remind voters and the public that the president had prompted the furloughs by refusing to sign the budget bill and by tying the fate of all forward progress to the wall money that he had not been able to earmark earlier.[90] With shared governance, he was going to have to deal with the Democrats rather than simply tweet in frustration and demonize them. And it was clear that the wall itself did not inspire support from either Congress or the general public.[91] And after all the annoyance and economic loss tied to the partial governmental shutdown, he was back to an even smaller deal than he had walked away from at the beginning; he absorbed virtually all the blame and had less to show for the painful delays.[92]

Over the 2018 Christmas holidays, when Trump could not wring billions for wall construction out of the congressional budgeting process, he began speaking and tweeting about invoking emergency powers; he was casting about to save face, appear strong and resolute, and placate his supporters. When all else fails, there is always The Wall, the President's symbolic promise and the "national security" gift that keeps on giving.[93] There have been few presidents who so relentlessly shifted positions while adeptly sensing the messaging that can be used to communicate with base voters.[94] For her part, Speaker-elect Nancy Pelosi drew on her considerable political and legislative expertise, even refusing to allow the anxious president to present the annual State of the Union address in the House chambers. She played hardball, withholding the one significant venue capable of holding the annual message, with all its pomp and ceremony.[95] He wanted the House chambers and begrudgingly acknowledged he had been outflanked, but he also peevishly cancelled a congressional oversight trip overseas to remind Democrats who controlled their travel funds on federal transport planes.[96] Holding the televised event in a local university gym or a local football stadium was not the same, and the president backed down, finally signing the short-term legislation to start the federal funds flowing again.[97] But he was smarting from the humiliating negotiations she forced him into, and he accelerated his insistence that he would invoke his emergency powers to redeploy other unexpended funds for the wall.[98] For several months over the 2018–2019 holidays, the national discourse was about the promised wall and how to fund it even though Congress (including Republicans) had refused to provide the money.[99] The public discussions were almost existential: What is a wall? Is it a metaphor or a barricade? Alternative memes arose, such a "steel slats," "my big, beautiful wall," and, perhaps most bizarre, "they can call it oranges."[100] This extended game of financial chicken continued with no resolution. President Trump was increasingly beleaguered by Special Counsel Robert Mueller's successful indictments and convictions or guilty pleas from former Trump associates.[101] He felt encircled and angry, especially when reporters and other observers saw parallels with Watergate, which had brought down President Richard Nixon by threatening impeachment and likely conviction in the Senate for his criminal misdeeds.[102]

All these various feints came to a head on March 14, 2019, the deadline for the Senate to vote on the emergency declaration Joint Resolution. On that day, with a dozen Republicans joining the unified Democratic senators, providing a 59–41 margin, Congress sent the passed bill to the president for his signature; he vetoed the bill, the first in his two-plus years of being president.[103] Not only did this cause a serious constitutional showdown over the scope of the emergency powers, which have seriously eroded congressional governance and authority; the defection of so many Republicans showed the personal and philosophical commitments they had to consider regardless of the politics of the actual event.[104] Undoubtedly, Republicans were considering what lengths a Democratic president could use this precedent. Perhaps an emergency declaration to effectuate climate-control powers or some other shibboleth, foreseeing a what's-good-for-the-goose-is-good-for-the-gander logic after an election that would restore the presidency to the Democrats?[105] His veto cast into stark relief how divided the various bodies were, with a bevy of Democrats (including at least half a dozen incumbent or would-be senators) already declared as presidential candidates for the elections less than two years away in 2020.[106] The Republicans who supported the president's declaration also knew they were weakening their own hand because the wall (and whatever manifestation of a barrier it represented) was supported only by Trump and his most avid members of the Republican base.[107] A large majority of the public considered it to be an expensive waste of time and resources. Democrats seized the more realistic mantra that the country needed more and better border security but not an actual wall, for which they would appropriate not a single dollar.[108] This intransigence required the president to ramp up his emergency decree and to propose taking unspent money from their appropriated purposes to build the wall. He also authorized federal military troops to undertake construction and border improvements, as well as repairs of fencing and the like, but not a mile of expensive wall construction. Every House member elected from districts along the southern border was on the record opposing any form of wall.[109]

The vote not only constituted a sharp rebuke of the president's promise to circumvent the constitutional appropriation powers reserved to Congress; the redirection of billions of dollars was sure to trigger lawsuits challenging his emergency declaration to violate long-established separation of powers over a rhetorical wall that he determined to be such a national emergency that it would prompt this crisis. Even supporters had urged him not to pursue this course, and even those who voted to support him were voting against their own interests and, in many instances, those of constituents who had been chimerically promised that any wall would be paid for by Mexico.[110]

Of the many remarks prompted by these events, perhaps none was more pointed as that spoken by Senator Lamar Alexander of Tennessee, an influential force in the Republican Party who voted against the president: "Never before has a president asked for funding, Congress has not provided it, and the president then has used the National Emergencies Act of 1976 to spend the money anyway." He continued: "The problem with this is that after a Revolutionary War against a king, our nation's founders gave to Congress the power to approve all spending so that the president would not have too much power. This check on the executive is a crucial source of our freedom."[111] The president lashed out at defectors and the Democrats who had thwarted his plans and who were widely viewed as having handed him a substantial setback: "It's pure and simple: it's a vote for border security, it's a vote for no crime," Mr. Trump told reporters ahead of the vote, which he declared on Twitter to be "a vote for Nancy Pelosi, Crime and the Open Border Democrats!"[112]

Meanwhile, the earlier DACA suits were wending their way through the various courts, and the maneuvers continued behind the scenes. However, ironically, even hard-line Judge Andrew Hanen was essentially forced to allow the various strands of the case to play themselves out, conceding the case would have to return to the Supreme Court.[113] This complicated case may resolve the temporary DACA program if legislation were not to be enacted.[114] This provided more time for DACA renewals to roll out, although it was clear that this temporary program, born in the Obama administration's discretion, would live on for several years even as its long-term survival prognosis was virtually nil. Even if the Democrats took over the presidency, it had become clear even to its supporters that DACA—however successful and ameliorative it had been—was on a form of life support and was chronically poised to be one court decision or proper sideswipe away from dying. Comprehensive immigration reform—elusive since the Immigration Reform and Control Act of 1986—was not in the immediate cards.[115] Dozens of DREAM Act bills had come and gone in every session since the first version was introduced in 2001.[116] DACA lived a charmed life until it didn't, and it was left by the courts and the Trump administration to suffer a death by a thousand cuts.

After the Senate vote, President Trump used his veto power to veto the Joint Resolution,[117] and the votes to override were not there.[118] Through his veto the president won the battle, but legal actions challenging the bona fides of the emergency declaration and failures of governance may have resulted in his losing the war. On the subject of war and national security threats, two former senior intelligence chiefs wrote with apparent concern and sorrow:

[A]n informed and honest assessment of the facts demonstrates that there is no national security crisis. We offer this assessment as former government officials with decades of experience in security, intelligence and law enforcement, serving Democratic and Republican presidents alike. And we are not alone in this assessment. As dozens of our former colleagues with national security experience serving administrations of both parties recently made clear in a declaration: "under no plausible assessment of the evidence is there a national emergency today that entitles the president to tap into funds appropriated for other purposes to build a wall at the southern border." Even the president, in his remarks announcing his plan to declare a national emergency, admitted he "didn't need to do this," and that he would simply rather build his wall "much faster." The president and administration officials, however, have at various times pointed to "thousands" of terrorists seeking to cross the southern border and to an "invasion" of criminals and drugs to conjure up a crisis and to justify invoking emergency authorities. These claims are false.[119]

The claims may have been false, and Trump might very well have gotten the funds he wanted by other, less-fraught means, but the contest served to divert attention from his personal legal problems and embarrassments at the time, as well as the loss of the House of Representatives, which was beginning to exert substantial oversight. But none of this mattered for DREAMers, whose fate had woven in and out of this year-long set of skirmishes, with no pathway forward for improving the hand dealt them. Indeed, looked at in hindsight, the president scapegoated Mexicans generally and then held DACA and the DREAMers hostage to his idea of fencing off Mexico from the United States. After all, DACA was being ended because his administration sought to end it with no endgame in sight. The DREAMers' one positive development, DACA, was on death's door, and heroic measures were being administered on its (and their) behalf, with no long term recovery or prospects in sight. The DREAM Act, first introduced in 2001, was no closer to passage than it had been almost two decades earlier. DREAMers had incontestably kept their part of the bargain that had been forged with their government: they studied, worked hard against all odds, participated in civic affairs like the citizens they longed to become, began to acquire licenses and professions, paid their taxes, and trusted that their doing so would earn them the chance to adjust their status. If anything, success almost within their grasp gave them the cruelest form of thwarted hope: dashed dreams and an exquisite sense of betrayal. Eventually, the US Supreme Court granted certiorari and on November 12, 2019, heard the case, for which more than a thousand advocates, including 125 immigration law professors, signed amicus briefs for and against the DACA rescission.[120]

Conclusion

Awakening from the DREAM

Once I undertook to write this book, I stumbled across just how many times the image of a "DREAM" had entered the various slipstreams of discourse. Indeed, using "slipstream" leads me to Van Morrison's incomparable "Astral Weeks" ("If I ventured in the slipstream/ Between the viaducts of your dream"),[1] but forms of the word have fueled popular and rock music for many years, from the Everly Brothers ("All I Have to Do Is Dream"),[2] to Bruce Springsteen ("Dream Baby Dream"),[3] to Beyoncé ("Sweet Dreams"),[4] to John Lennon "# 9 Dream."[5] Although the word does not appear in the title, Lennon's 1971 "Imagine" has the evocative "dreamer" reference ("Imagine there's no heaven/It's easy if you try. . . . /You, you may say/I'm a dreamer, but I'm not the only one/I hope some day you'll join us/And the world will be as one . . .").[6]

Onstage, one could look to Shakespeare's *Hamlet*, Act 3, scene 1, where Hamlet famously ponders:

> To be, or not to be: that is the question:
> Whether 'tis nobler in the mind to suffer
> The slings and arrows of outrageous fortune,
> Or to take arms against a sea of troubles,
> And by opposing end them? To die: to sleep;
> No more; and by a sleep to say we end
> The heart-ache and the thousand natural shocks
> That flesh is heir to, 'tis a consummation
> Devoutly to be wish'd.
> To die, to sleep;
> To sleep: perchance to dream: ay, there's the rub . . .[7]

The stage has provided numerous DREAM references, including Pedro Calderon de la Barca's 1635 *La vida es sueño*[8]:

> Yo *sueño* que estoy aquíde estas prisiones cargado, y *soñé* que en otro estadomás lisonjero me vi.¿Qué es la vida? Un frenesí.¿Qué es la vida? Una ilusión,una sombra, una ficción,y el mayor bien es *pequeño*: que toda la vida es *sueño*, y los *sueños, sueños* son.

"LIFE IS A DREAM," TRANSLATED FROM THE SPANISH BY
MICHAEL A. OLIVAS:

> I dream that I am here
> of these imprisonments charged,
> and I dreamed that in another state
> I saw myself more flattering.
> What is life? A frenzy.
> What is life? An illusion,
> a shadow, a fiction,
> and the greatest good is small:
> that all of life is a dream,
> and dreams, are only dreams.

And I borrowed Langston Hughes's 1951 poem "Harlem, What happens to a dream deferred?"[9] for a law review article:[10]

> Does it dry up
> like a raisin in the sun?
> Or fester like a sore
> And then run?
> Does it stink like rotten meat?
> Or crust and sugar over
> like a syrupy sweet?
>
> Maybe it just sags
> like a heavy load.
>
> *Or does it explode?* . . .

There are so many more, but readers get the idea and may have their own favorites. But gilding the lily is not productive, as the DREAM Act's failure to thrive has tantalized undocumented students for many years. I recently heard from a retiring colleague with whom I worked on the 1980s *Leticia "A"* litigation, who recalled the twists and turns and sadly said: "Did you ever think that we'd still be fighting for these things?" Well, no, not really, as I figured the issue would resolve itself at the federal level, especially after 2001, when such a federal bill was introduced, only to reappear annually but never to take root in the soil. As I was completing my edits for this book, I was scolded online by a DREAMer about my admonition that I could not represent her or answer specific legal questions by email. Sternly, she admonished me: "I think my question could have been more specific—as an immigration law and policy expert in the law school field, have you seen this issue before in other law schools that have DACAmented students wanting to get a clinical experience during their senior year? How was it resolved? Do we, [my law school] and the dean, need to worry about this? In my humble opinion, I do not think this matter necessitates a lawyer; I think what it needs are immigration law professors and experts in the field, who can provide that advice to deans facing similar questions with their DACA students." God, you just have to love them, even if they are being rude and presumptuous and humble and asynchronous in their emailing me late at night, insistent that I answer her query right then and there.

With my own presence in addressing this issue, which reaches back to my graduate school days forty years ago and Ohio state residency tuition statutes,[11] this has not been a leisurely stroll through memory lane but instead a reminder to myself and my readers that progress is very slow and takes constant effort. Dr. Martin Luther King popularized an earlier such thought, noting: "The arc of the moral universe is long, but it bends towards justice."[12] I do not offer the suggestion that a more fair immigration system is impossible, and I will be the first to acknowledge that the United States has made strides, of which DACA and its successes are clearly one such example (or, even better, 800,000 such examples).

But after such a long career focusing on this topic and devoting much of my professional attention to the subject, I fear that time is slipping away—and not just for me. After all, I am a US birthright citizen, born overseas of US citizen parents. But it just shouldn't be so hard. Because the country has become so polarized, and even though all genuine polls indicate sympathy and widespread support for DREAMers to regularize their unauthorized status, they languish and have been cruelly whip-sawed. This book began as a hopeful birth announcement, but it ends as a dirge. As I wrote this, my mind flew back to seminary high school days and a poet whom I had adored but whom I had forgotten, Edna St. Vincent Millay. She also wrote about dirges in "Dirge Without Music":

> I am not resigned to the shutting away of loving hearts in the hard
>   ground.
> So it is, and so it will be, for so it has been, time out of mind:
> Into the darkness they go, the wise and the lovely. Crowned
> With lilies and with laurel they go; but I am not resigned.
>
> Lovers and thinkers, into the earth with you.
> Be one with the dull, the indiscriminate dust.
> A fragment of what you felt, of what you knew,
> A formula, a phrase remains,—but the best is lost.
>
> The answers quick and keen, the honest look, the laughter, the love,—
> They are gone. They are gone to feed the roses. Elegant and curled
> Is the blossom. Fragrant is the blossom. I know. But I do not approve.
> More precious was the light in your eyes than all the roses in the
>   world.
>
> Down, down, down into the darkness of the grave
> Gently they go, the beautiful, the tender, the kind;
> Quietly they go, the intelligent, the witty, the brave.
> I know. But I do not approve. And I am not resigned.[13]

While she is writing about death's universality, her line "Gently they go, the beautiful, the tender, the kind; Quietly they go, the intelligent, the witty, the brave" just as easily could have been referring to DREAMers, who deserve better than they have been accorded. I know. But I do not approve. And I am not resigned.

ACKNOWLEDGMENTS

Gestation, and a Beautiful Boy

Of the sixteen books I have written, this DREAM Act project has been in gestation the longest in all senses of the word "gestate." First, I moved to Houston in 1982, just as *Plyler v. Doe* was decided by the Supreme Court.[1] I have poured out much of my research, and my heart, in a series of articles reconceived in what became the first full-length book on the case, which appeared thirty years after the decision. In that 2012 book, I dug deeply into MALDEF archives at Stanford University, detailed the convoluted case, and dubbed it the "apex of immigrants' rights."[2] That turn of phrase led one historian following the case and its place in the firmament to cite me in *The New Yorker*,[3] a citation initiation into the scholars' ranks and into my favorite magazine in the world, something that had never come my way since my first book in 1975. But even early on, as I met and watched these *Plyler* kids make their way through the public schools to which they were entitled, I wondered about post-secondary *Plyler* eligibility and sponsored the first national academic conference on the subject in 1986, where it became clear that a number of structural impediments were in the way of their enrollment—unlike that of their citizen classmates whose passages were easy-peazy. I even wrote the first law review article anyone wrote on the undocumented transition from K–12 to college,[4] setting my eventual sights on nearly a dozen successors, some of which I harvested for *Perchance to DREAM*.

Soon after, in what now seems like a lifetime ago, an unexpected comprehensive immigration relief law (the Immigration Control and Reform Act of 1986, or IRCA) was enacted by Congress and signed by a conservative lion, President Ronald Reagan.[5] So the problem was, for the most part, resolved by the legalization provisions, and the students began to enroll in college—not because their undocumented status gave them free rein but because they were eligible for the runup to lawful permanent residence, the step before naturalization or ripening into US citizens. (Now *those* were the high-water marks for immigrant rights, as litigation and additional legislation fleshed out the new language and the application of the omnibus legislation.) I taught dozens of workshops, consulted with a number of colleges and community groups, and trained many of my education and law students to enter this burgeoning field. I planned this book, which I knew would take a long time; on this, I was correct.

What the polity giveth, the polity can taketh as well, and the 1990s saw a swing back to nativist and restrictionist politics, where ground zero was California and its anti-immigrant Proposition 187,[6] which features in several chapters (as do several rollbacks of immigration policy that tightened loopholes and turned the clock back, specifically PWORA[7] and IIRIRA).[8] And all these were led by a person running for president on a platform that insistently drew its attention to supposed immigrant perfidy and scapegoating, Pete Wilson, the former mayor of San Diego, US senator, and California governor from 1991 until 1999.[9] As chapter 1 presents in grim detail, there were wide swings in California immigrant college student policies, which ultimately led to complete bans on resident tuition, the means by which these undocumented students were able to enroll in the state's inexpensive but academically superior postsecondary institutions.

Even with a number of court cases that arose during that period, it remained largely a California issue. This was because the student numbers had not yet swelled to the 800,000 in evidence today, with the rise of DACA, the transformative prosecutorial discretion employed by the Obama administration in 2012, and California had so many inexpensive public colleges. In addition, the schools had seized on *Plyler*'s mandate and produced so many Mexican American students. But it had also become a national issue, with dozens of states staking out directions in residency requirements and even financial aid for these students.[10] I wanted readers to be able to follow my tracks and resources, so I doubled down on footnotes, producing an unusually high number and unapologetically drawing on so many resources and other scholars across domains and subject matters.

At that point, the book I had planned on the DREAM Act got set aside as DACA's swift ascent became evident, but it also drew raw energy that I just feared would not end up well, notwithstanding my own late conversion to DACA and its transformative generosity. After all, even without any clear path after DACA status, these youths received Social Security numbers, employment authorization, a chance to leave the country and return under advance parole, and, perhaps most important, "lawful presence," which froze their immigration transgressions so that they could remain in the United States and not be deported while in good DACA standing.[11] This development swamped all previous efforts to serve DREAMers, as the undocumented students had come to be known, so the book's gestation period entered its second life. Undocumented immigrants were becoming transformed and reconstituted into DACAmented adults in a growing and thriving enterprise, one that gave hope to observers that its successes were the trial run for a DREAM Act that might legalize their inchoate status and ripen into a form of permanency, perhaps a preliminary legal step not unlike the 1986 IRCA prelude to lawful permanent residency and then full US citizenship.

The narrative tide had also turned as states began to allow these graduates presented full academic and professional credentials to enter the professions, including the most prized ones such as attorneys, teachers, and medical doctors. Once again this was led by California, where an undocumented law school graduate sought admission to the state bar and prevailed when the state actually crafted what became an almost a private relief bill to admit him, with the California Supreme Court ratifying his wish with a state law that would allow him to practice. In an interesting twist, he had aged out of DACA and thus had been unable to avail himself of its occupational provisions.[12] Other states acted either by legislation (as in Florida)[13] or by administrative procedure and a case (as in New York), to allow eligible DACAmented law school graduates to become lawyers after taking the state bar examination and passing it.[14] A parallel track of conservative thought and advocacy for simplifying occupational certification also arose, and the strange bedfellows arrangement actually led to calls for a DREAM Act–type of legislation by this previously restrictionist sector. The line of thinking arose was exemplified by the advocacy of the Koch brothers;[15] their support of Donald Trump and the support of a majority of the Electoral College led to his unforeseen win as president in the 2016 election, a campaign that included what can only be described as a coarsened attack on immigrants, particularly Mexicans, who made up the vast majority of DACA recipients.[16] This wing of the increasingly conservative and nativist Republican Party seemed an unusual birthplace for progressive reforms in the immigration architecture of occupational licensing. I looked at this in detail in chapter 6, revealing data from a national survey of immigration entry requirements to licensing in all states, as well as granular state studies in major receiver states. And I found that not all states even exercise immigration criteria for admission into various professions, certainly never figuring that hundreds of thousands of DACA recipients would present their credentials with the expectation that they could work and remain in the country.

President Trump's appointment of the long-time restrictionist senator Jeff Sessions (R-AL) as attorney general[17] added fuel to the nativist fires; within the first year of his term the Department of Homeland Security, which housed DACA, and the Department of Justice were attempting to dismantle the signature discretionary program of President Obama, DACA.[18] A year later, in 2018, a virtual impasse had occurred, as detailed in chapter 7. And although the DACA rescission had been tied up in courts and extended to allow renewals, no new DACA applicants were being allowed or processed, thereby cutting off any possible options for those who either had not yet aged into the program or who for one reason or another had not yet applied when the program closure was enacted. As applications to this program foundered, dozens of court cases were wending their way forward, and a funereal pall was cast over DACA.[19] Extending the gestation period, the complex rendering that had been my birth announcement book had now morphed yet again into a triage or autopsy.

In January 2016, I found myself unexpectedly called into service as a college president, taking me out of my usual routine. I was to preside over and learn from serving as CEO of the University of Houston–Downtown (UHD), the comprehensive and second-largest baccalaureate institution in Houston, which itself was about to become the third-largest city in the nation. Ironically, UHD is an exemplar of an Hispanic Serving Institution, with a majority of the students being Latino, predominantly of Mexican origin; more than 600 of them were DACA-mented, attending college on undocumented resident tuition and grants that I had been involved in drafting and advocating in 2001.[20] Indeed, within a week after the November 2016 presidential election, against the fear of the Trump win and the enactment of the Texas state law that legislated against "sanctuary campuses,"[21] I brought my immigration law colleagues and my former law students—now immigration lawyers—to the UHD campus for extensive workshops, where we outlined and discussed the foreseeable future and promised we would make whatever legal assistance we could available to them. When I left one of the activities to return to my office for another event, I was disconsolate and was cheered only somewhat when a DACA student got on my elevator and reassured me, "Presidente Olivas, Llegamos tan cerca" (We came so close), consoling me, where it was my job to console and serve him. By a large measure, this injection of real-life hardship directly into my book narrative was the worst day of my accidental life as a college president.

When I returned to teaching law after the UHD sojourn, I rededicated myself to this book, and not a week has passed since where I was not reading, interviewing, filing, and writing. Oh, yes, and rewriting. So here it is, after several gestation periods, starts, false starts, and a delayed birth. My patient publisher, Clara Platter, who had been so generous as each phase came and then went, gently inquired about my plans. I had completed the large-scale national study of occupational licensing and immigration requirement (the data that form the spine of chapter 6), and I assured her I could have it in her hands by Thanksgiving 2018, which I did even as events continued to spool out with the unpredictable Trump administration, the recalcitrant Republican Congress, and the resurgent 2018 midterm elections in which the Democrats improbably took control of the House of Representatives.[22] President Trump has several times said he wanted to sign a DREAM Act but then behaved in a manner more consistent with his nativist public remarks, stopping the negotiations in their tracks.[23] At any point since he took office, he could have become serious, interceding with Republican legislators to make this possible and to counter his clear anti-immigrant narrative and actions. And when Mexico embarrassed him by unsurprisingly rejecting his insistence that they would pay for the objectionable wall, the DREAM Act and any formalization of DACA were consigned to the attic where positive but star-crossed legislation goes to moulder.

Although his lyrics were reportedly cribbed from another, earlier source, the late Beatle John Lennon, who actually makes several immigration-related appearances in this book's treatment of deferred action, wrote the lovely song "Beautiful Boy (Darling Boy)," including the famous line: "Life is what happens to you while you're busy making other plans."[24] In truth, for over a decade and a half, not a day of making other plans has gone by when I didn't think about or write down a few lines or snatches of ideas, interview and meet with DREAMers, e-file and synthesize news stories and the emerging research literature, polish my footnotes and sources, or teach immigration and higher education. I dedicate this book to the thousands of DREAMers I have met, taught, and admired. Even when they disregarded my advice and outed themselves or did something else transgressive, it was clear to me that we were very lucky to live in a country that accorded them wingspan and flight. Of course, some of them flew too close to the sun and lost their status, but most have thrived and kept their part of the bargain. As liminal as their status is, I can only contrast their fate with the fate of children and their families in the so-called "caravan," which arrived in the middle of militarized and armed US border and tear gas was used to repel them.[25]

I acknowledge a long line of research assistants and students who have worked with me on different parts of this project, including a number who are now educators or immigration civil rights lawyers: Judge Lisa Luis, President Sister Helene Monahan, Jacob Monty, Lorie Hutensky, Celina Moreno, Kristen Werner, Deterrean Gamble, Eric Munoz, Amaury Nora, Richard Padilla, Caren DeLuccio, Eglantine Pauverel Moss, Angeline Gallivan, Nancy M. Molina, Rocio Rodriguez Ruiz, Bryce Romero, and the late Nancy Snyder-Nepo and the late Celia Figueroa. A number of faculty and practice colleagues have shared their scholarship with me and commented on my research: Shoba Sivaprasad Wadhia, Kevin R. Johnson, N'Dri Assie-Lumumba, Janet Calvo, Nancy Morawetz, Margaret Stock, Daniel M. Kowalski, Stephen Legomsky, Benjamin Marquez, Leticia Saucedo, Francine Lipman, Jose Luis Perez, Peter Schuck, Michael Klein, Alina Das, Jennifer Chacon, Yocel Alonso, and David Martin. My listing several of them inevitably means I will have to apologize to those I have inadvertently missed. At New York University Press, I acknowledge Clara Platter, Ediberto Roman, Veronica Knutson, Marybeth Jarrad, Laura Ewen, and my estimable copy editor Martin Coleman. At UH and UHLC, I learned from my interaction with Lauren E. Schroeder, Harold P. Bradford, Deborah Y. Jones, Professor Augustina H. Reyes, Professor Geoffrey Hoffman, President Renu Khator, Dean Leonard Baynes, Professor Amanda Watson, Robert Clark, Chris Dykes, Dan Donahue, and especially the erstwhile Katy Stein Badeaux, for whom no missing footnote or reference is too daunting. I owe thanks to Governor Bill Richardson and Brooke Lange, fellow New Mexicans.

And if it is not absolutely clear, I acknowledge the various DREAMers with whom I have interacted over the years whose work and perseverance have inspired. Telling their stories has been very satisfying and life-affirming. I dedicate this book to them and pray for their lives and those of their intrepid families to improve. Their gain will be ours.

State Laws Allowing Undocumented College Students to Establish Residency, 2019

* allowing financial aid and residency
+ repealed

* * Texas, H.B. 1403, 77th Leg., Reg. Sess. (Tex. 2001) [amended by S.B. 1528, 79th Leg., Reg. Sess. (Tex. 2005), relating to student financial aid]; TEX. EDUC. CODE ANN. § 54.052 and 54.053
* * California, A.B. 540, 2001–02 Cal. Sess. (Cal. 2001); CAL. EDUC. CODE §68130.5; A.B. 30 (2011), (amending CAL. EDUC. CODE §68130.7 and adding §66021.7, relating to nonstate funded scholarships); A.B. 131, October 8, 2011 (amending Section 68130.7 of and adding Sections 66021.6, 69508.5, and 76300.5 to the Education Code, relating to state financial aid); A.B. 844, October 8, 2011 (amending Section 72023.5 and adding Sections 66016.3 and 66016.4 to the Education Code, relating to state financial aid to certain student leadership positions); S.B. 1210, Ch. 742 (2014) (amending CAL. EDUC. CODE §§ 70030 et seq., providing DREAM loans); S.B. 68, Ch. 496 (2017) (amending CAL. EDUC. CODE § 68130.5. (expanding in-state tuition eligibility); A.B. 343, Ch. 491 (2018) (amending CAL. EDUC. CODE § 68075.6 (exempts students with special immigrant visas and refugees exempted from paying nonresident tuition fees)).
* Utah, H.B. 144, 54th Leg., Gen. Sess. (Utah 2002); UTAH CODE ANN. § 53B-8–106; Utah S.B. 253 (Utah 2015), UTAH CODE ANN. § 63G-12–402 (2015).
* New York, S. B. 7784, 225th Leg., 2001 NY Sess. (NY 2002); N.Y. EDUC. LAW §355(2)(h)(8)
* * Washington, H.B. 1079, 58th Leg., Reg. Sess. (Wash. 2003); WASH. REV. CODE. ANN. § 28B.15.012; and S.B. 6523, 63d Leg., Reg. Sess. (Wash. 2014); 2014 Wash. Sess. Laws ch. 1; amending WASH. REV. CODE § 28B.92.010 (2014) (relating to state financial aid), H.B. 1488, 65th Leg., Reg. Sess. (Wash. 2018), Wash. Sess. Laws ch. 204, amending WASH. REV. CODE § 28B.118.010, 28B.145.030, and 28B.15.012.

Oklahoma, S.B. 596, 49th Leg., 1st Reg. Sess. (OK 2003) [+financial assistance provisions rescinded, Oklahoma Taxpayer and Citizen Protection Act of 2007 (H.B. 1804)]; OKLA. STAT. ANN. TIT. 70, § 3242

Illinois, H.B. 60, 93rd Gen. Assemb., Reg. Sess. (Ill. 2003); 110 ILL. COMP. STAT. ANN. [amended by S.B. 2085, 97th Gen. Assemb., Reg. Sess. (Ill. 2011), relating to nonstate funded scholarships; 110 ILL. COMP. STAT. ANN.]

Kansas, H.B. 2145, 2003–2004 Leg., Reg. Sess. (KS 2004); K.S.A. §76–731a

*New Mexico, S.B. 582, 47th Leg. Reg. Sess. (2005); N.M. STAT ANN. §21-1-1 [allowing resident tuition and financial assistance]

Nebraska, L.B. 239, 99th Leg. 1st Sess. (Neb. 2006); NEB. REV. STAT ANN. § 85–502

+Wisconsin, 2009 Assembly Bill 75 (2009 WISCONSIN ACT 28); WIS. STAT. § 36.27 [repealed by AB 40, June 26, 2011]. State of Wisconsin Executive Budget for 2019–21 (proposed; allowing resident tuition for University of Wisconsin System (Feb. 28, 2019, https://doa.wi.gov/budget/SBO/2019-21%20Executive%20Budget%20Complete%20Document.pdf)).

Maryland, S.B. 167, 2011 Leg., Reg. Sess. (Md. 2011); MD. CODE ANN. § 15–106.8 ["suspended," pending state referendum: MD Const. XVI, Sec. 2] [Ballot measure approved in general election, November, 2012]; S.B. 532, 2018 Leg., Reg. Sess. (Md. 2018); amending MD. CODE ANN. EDUC. § 18–303.2 and 18–1401 (Md. 2018) [exempts Dreamers from out of state tuition].

Connecticut, H.B. 6390, 2011 Leg., Reg. Sess. (Conn. 2011); CONN. GEN. STAT. § 10a-29; H.B. 6844 (2015) Conn. Public Act No. 82, CONN. GEN. STAT. § 10a-29 [reducing 4 year requirement to 2 years]; S.B. 4, Conn. Public Act No. 18–2 (2018) [opening access to financial aid for some undocumented students].

*Oregon, H.B. 2787, 77th Leg., Reg. Sess. (Or. 2013); 2013 Or. Laws Ch. 17, § 2; OR. REV. STAT. § 351.641 (2013); S.B. 932 (2015) Or. Laws ch. 846, OR. REV. STAT.. §§ 348.180, 348.283, 348.303, 348.320, 351.641 [financial aid and scholarships: Sec. 8 (effective 2016–2017 academic year); Sec. 9 (special appropriation for 2015–2016 academic year)]; S.B. 1563, 79th leg., Reg. Sess. (Or. 2018), Or. Laws Ch. 122; amending Or. Rev. Stat. § 352.287 [Removes requirement that students who are not citizens or lawful permanent residents apply for official federal identification document to be eligible for exemption from paying nonresident tuition at public universities].

*Colorado, S.B. 13–033, 69th Gen. Assemb., 1st Reg. Sess. (Co. 2013); amend-
ing COLO. REV. STAT. § 23-7-110 and COLO. REV. STAT. § 24–76.5–103
[allowing resident tuition and financial assistance]

Minnesota, S.F. 1236, 88th Leg., 2013 Minn. Laws 75; MINN. STAT. § 135A.043
(2014)

Florida, 2014 Fla. Sess. Law Serv. Ch. 2014–62, FLA. STAT. § 1009.26 (2014)
(waiving out of state fees for undocumented students).

New Jersey, S. 2479, 215th Leg., 1st Ann. Sess., N.J. STAT. ANN. § 18A:62–4.4
(West Supp. 2014); S. 699, 219th Leg. (2018), N.J. STAT. ANN. § 18A:71B-2.1
(West) [prohibits discrimination against eligible students based on their
immigration status].

UNIVERSITY POLICIES

Hawaii, Univ. Hawaii Board of Regents Policies, 6.209 [allowing resident
tuition and financial assistance].

Maine, Univ. Maine System Board of Trustees, [in-state tuition for those with
DACA status].

Michigan, Univ. Michigan System Board of Regents, 2013, https://ro.umich.
edu/tuition-residency/residency [expanding eligibility for in-state tuition
to students who attended middle and high school in state, regardless of
immigration status].

Rhode Island, S. 5.0, R.I. Board of Governors for Higher Education, September 26, 2011.

NOTES: DEVELOPMENTS AND DACA ISSUES (AS OF APRIL 2019)

In several states, there are ongoing legislative efforts or cases involved
in implementing these residency and financial aid issues. In New Jers-
ery, an administrative action has been filed to implement financial aid
for citizen children of undocumented parents, following A.Z. v. Higher
Education Assistance Authority, 427 N.J. Super. 389, 398 (App. Div.
2012): www.aclu-nj.org/legaldocket/petition-rule-making-regarding-
student-eligibility-financial-aid [N.J.A.C. 9A:9-2-2(a)(1)]. Ironically, in
one of the more unnecessary legislative efforts in this entire area, Tennessee does not allow undocumented or DACA students to establish
residency, but it became the only state to assure that citizen children
are eligible for both status benefits irrespective of the immigration status of their parents: http://wapp.capitol.tn.gov/apps/BillInfo/Default.

aspx?BillNumber=SB2115&ga=108 (legislation and legislative history). This superfluous statute makes it the obverse of New Jersey's, which does not accord these children financial aid. In New York, a settlement was reached in the residency case, Strum, et al. v. SUNY, et al. (Index No. 2011/00064) (regarding out-of-state students who attended high school in the state): www.suny.edu/tuitionsettlement.

In addition, some states have allowed DACA recipients who meet durational requirements to establish residency status, on the premise that they are lawfully present and not undocumented; examples include Massachusetts. In the Arizona v. MCCCD case, a state judge ruled that Maricopa County Community College must accord resident tuition to eligible DACA recipients, and the Arizona Board of Regents extended the resident tuition policy to the other state colleges: Statement, Arizona Board of Regents, *ABOR Statement on In-State Tuition for DACA Students* (May 7, 2015). Superior court opinion reversed and remanded; court of appeals opinion affirmed in part and vacated in part. In 2018, the Arizona Supreme Court held that students under DACA were not "lawfully present" in the United States for purposes of receiving public benefits and thus were not eligible for in-state college tuition. Arizona ex rel. Brnovich v. Maricopa Cty. Cmty. Coll. Dist. Bd., 243 Ariz. 539 (2018).

Other states such as Ohio have ruled that individual public colleges in those states are eligible to make the determination about DACA recognition for resident tuition. In a small number of states, public institutions are charged by law or administrative regulation with devising their own admissions standards and resident tuition policies, as in Michigan. The University of Michigan, as one example, has adopted a policy that allows certain undocumented students who attended the state's middle schools and high schools to establish resident tuition. Not all Michigan public colleges in the state have adopted accommodationist resident tuition policies. In Washington State, the attorney general has ruled that DACA students may establish residence and eligibility for state financial aid: www.law.uh.edu/ihelg/documents/DACA-FinancialAid.asp.

APPENDIX 2

States Restricting Access to Postsecondary Education for Undocumented/DACA Students through April 2019

BY STATUTE

Alabama, H.B. 56, 2011 Leg., Reg. Sess. (Ala. 2011); ALA. CODE § 31-13-8
[added section barring undocumented students from enrolling in or attending any institutions of postsecondary education; enjoined by federal
district court October 2011]. The issue was rendered moot after legislature
removed the second sentence of the code section, limiting enrollment to
aliens who "possess lawful permanent residence or an appropriate nonimmigrant visa under 8 U.S.C. § 1101, et seq." *Id.* The district court enjoined
section 8 in its entirety on the grounds that it constituted an unconstitutional classification of aliens. After that ruling, the legislature amended section 8 to remove the second sentence entirely, defining "lawful presence" as
requiring lawful permanent residence or a nonimmigrant visa.

Hispanic Interest Coal. of Alabama v. Governor of Alabama, 691 F.3d 1236,
1242 (11th Cir. 2012). Code section amended in 2012 by Ala. Act 2012–491,
p. 1410, § 1.

Arizona, S.C.R. 1031, § 3, Proposition 300, approved election Nov. 7, 2006, eff.
Dec. 7, 2006 (Ariz. 2006); ARIZ. REV. STAT. ANN. § 15–1803 [amended to
ban in-state tuition for undocumented students].

Georgia, S.B. 492, 149th Gen. Assemb., Reg. Sess. (Ga. 2008); GA. CODE
ANN. § 20-3-66(d) [amended to ban in-state tuition for undocumented
students]. In Olvera v. Univ. Sys. of Ga.'s Bd. of Regents [http://efast.gaap-
peals.us/download?filingId=e2388b2a-b4c8-488b-b18a-7625bfd5dc03], the
Board of Regents was sued to implement DACA as meeting the eligibility
criteria for resident tuition. "In this case, a group of college students, including Miguel Angel Martinez Olvera, who are not United States citizens
and who are grant beneficiaries of the Deferred Action for Childhood
Arrivals program (DACA), filed a declaratory judgment action against

the University System of Georgia's Board of Regents and its members in their official capacities (collectively, the Board) seeking a declaration that they are entitled to in-state tuition at schools in the University System of Georgia. The trial court granted the Board's motion to dismiss on the ground that sovereign immunity bars the action, and the Court of Appeals affirmed the trial court. Olvera v. Univ. Sys. of Georgia's Bd. of Regents, 331 Ga. App. 392, 771 S.E. 2d 91 (2015). We affirm." Olvera v. Univ. Sys. of Georgia's Bd. of Regents, 298 Ga. 425, 425 (2016).

Indiana, H.B. 1402, 2011 Gen. Assemb., Reg. Sess. (Ind. 2011); IND. CODE ANN. § 21-14-11 [added Chapter 11 to Title 21, banning in-state tuition for undocumented students].

Ohio, 129th General Assembly File No. 28, HB 153, § 101.01; O.R.C. 3333.31 (D), (E) (2011) [banning in-state tuition for undocumented students].

Missouri, H.B. 2003, 97th Gen. Assemb., 2d Reg. Sess. (Mo. 2014): "[N]o funds shall be expended at public institutions of higher education that knowingly offer a tuition rate to an unlawfully present covered student pursuant to 173.1110, RSMo, that is less than the tuition rate charged to citizens or nationals of the United States whose residence is not in Missouri" (www.house.mo.gov/billtracking/bills141/biltxt/truly/HB2003T.htm); and S. B. 224 ("To repeal section 160.545, RSMo, and to enact in lieu thereof one new section relating to eligibility criteria for reimbursements from the A+ schools program") [Legislature overrode governor's veto by a two-thirds vote in both the House and Senate: H.J. of Mo., 98th Gen. Assemb., Veto Sess. 27 (2015); S.J. of Mo., 98th Gen Assemb., Veto Sess. 12 (2015)].

Montana, 2011 Mont. Laws 1238 [ratified by state ballot measure, November 2012; amending MONT. CODE ANN. § 20-25-502 (2009), eff. 1/2013] [enjoined by federal court, 6/2014]. Legislative Referendum 121, codified at MONT. CODE ANN. § 1-1-411 (West), was found to be preempted by federal law by the Montana Supreme Court. Montana Immigrant Justice All. v. Bullock, 383 Mont. 318 (2016): "[W]e affirm the District Court's June 20, 2014 Order granting MIJA's motion for summary judgment to the extent it found LR 121 was preempted by federal law, and we reverse the District Court's Order to the extent it found § 1-1-411(3), MCA, was severable and not preempted."

South Carolina, H.B. 4400, 117th Gen. Assem. Reg. Sess. (S.C. 2008); S.C. CODE ANN. § 59-101–430 [added section 430 to bar undocumented students from attending public institutions of higher learning and also to bar them from being able to receive in-state tuition].

BY POLICY OR REGULATION

Georgia Board of Regents, October 2010
Section 4: Student Affairs

4.1.6 Admission of Persons Not Lawfully Present in the United States

A person who is not lawfully present in the United States shall not be eligible for admission to any University System institution which, for the two most recent academic years, did not admit all academically qualified applicants (except for cases in which applicants were rejected for non-academic reasons).

Source: www.usg.edu/policymanual/section4/C327/#p4.1.6_admission_of_pe%20rsons_not_lawfully_present_in_the_united_states (affecting Georgia College & State University, Medical College of Georgia, Georgia State University, Georgia Institute of Technology, and University of Georgia)

4.3.4 Verification of Lawful Presence

Each University System institution shall verify the lawful presence in the United States of every successfully admitted person applying for resident tuition status, as defined in Section 7.3 of this Policy Manual, and of every person admitted to an institution referenced in Section 4.1.6 of this Policy Manual.

Source: www.usg.edu/policymanual/section4/C329/#p4.3.4_veri%20 fication_of_lawful_presence

University of North Carolina Board of Governors:

CHAPTER 700

700.1.4[G]

Guidelines on the Admission of Undocumented Aliens

Undocumented aliens are eligible to be considered for admission as undergraduates at UNC constituent institutions** based on their individual qualifications with limitations as set out below:

1. An undocumented alien may be considered for admission only if he or she graduated from high school in the United States.

**The North Carolina School of Science and Mathematics admits and enrolls only legal residents of the state of North Carolina. See G.S. 116–235: www.northcarolina.edu/apps/policy/index.php?section=700.1.4%5BG%5D.

2. Undocumented aliens may not receive state or federal financial aid in the form of a grant or a loan.

3. An undocumented alien may not be considered a North Carolina resident for tuition purposes; all undocumented aliens must be charged out-of-state tuition.

4. All undocumented aliens, whether or not they abide in North Carolina or graduated from a North Carolina high school, will be considered out of State for purposes of calculating the 18 percent cap on out of State freshmen pursuant to Policy 700.1.3.

5. When considering whether or not to admit an undocumented alien into a specific program of study, constituent institutions should take into account that federal law prohibits the states from granting professional licenses to undocumented aliens.

APPENDIX 3

Cases Involving Citizens, Residency, Tuition Benefits/Status, and the DREAM Act & DACA (through April 2019)

DIRECT CHALLENGES TO THE DACA PROGRAM

Arpaio v. Obama, 27 F. Supp. 3d 185 (D.D.C. 2014) (striking down AZ sheriff challenge to DACA), *aff'd* 797 F.3d 11 (D.C. Cir. 2015), *cert. denied*, 136 S. Ct. 900 (Jan 16, 2016, No. 15–643).

United States v. Juarez-Escobar, 25 F. Supp. 3d 774 (W.D. Pa. 2014) [Memorandum Opinion and Order of Court Re: Applicability of President Obama's November 20, 2014 Executive Action on Immigration to this Defendant].

Texas v. United States, 86 F. Supp. 3d 591 (S.D. Tex. Feb. 16, 2015) (enjoining DHS from implementing DAPA), *emergency stay denied*, 2015 WL 1540022 (S.D. Tex. Apr. 7, 2015), *aff'd*, 787 F.3d 733 (5th Cir. May 26, 2015), *preliminary injunction aff'd*, 809 F.3d 134 (5th Cir. Nov. 9, 2015), *aff'd* 136 S. Ct. 2271 (June 23, 2016), *pet. for rehearing denied*, 137 S.Ct. 285 (Oct. 3, 2016). *dismissal order*, ECF no. 471(Sept. 8, 2017).

Judicial Watch, Inc. v. U.S. Dep't of Justice, 20 F. Supp. 3d 260 (D.D.C. 2014) (Court upholds FOIA Exemption 5 withholding of privileged DACA deliberative memos).

Crane v. Napolitano, 920 F. Supp. 2d 724 (N. D. Tex. 2013) (challenge to DACA dismissed under Civil Service Reform Act ("CSRA")), *aff'd*, 783 F.3d 244 (5th Cir. 2015).

Common Cause v. Biden, 909 F. Supp. 2d 9 (D.D.C. 2012) (dismissing Senate debate/filibuster rules, re immigration reform), *affirming* 748. F.3d 1280 (D.C. Cir. 2014), *cert. denied*, 135 S. Ct. 451 (2014).

Texas v. United States, No. 18-cv-00068 (S.D. Tex. filed May 1, 2018), *motion for summary judgment pending*, ECF no. 356 (Feb. 4, 2019).

CHALLENGES TO BENEFIT/STATUS DENIAL RE: USC CHILDREN OF
UNDOCUMENTED PARENTS

Herrera v. Finan, 176 F. Supp. 3d 549 (D.S.C. 2016), *aff'd*, 709 Fed. Appx. 741
(4th Cir. 2017) (denying challenge to in-state residency requirement).

Ruiz v. Robinson, 892 F. Supp. 2d 1321 (S.D. Fla. 2012) (FL resident tuition case
concerning USC children and undocumented parents).

A.Z. ex rel. B.Z. v. Higher Educ. Student Assistance Auth., 48 A.3d 1151 (N.J.
Super. Ct. App. Div. 2012) (NJ financial aid case concerning USC children
and undocumented parents); consolidated with Cortes v. Higher Educ.
Student Assistance Auth., No. A-2142–11-T1 (N.J. Super. Ct. App. Div. 2012).

Consent Decree, Student Advocates for Higher Educ. v. Bd. of Trs. of Cal.
State Univ., No. CPF-06–506755 (Cal. Super. Ct. Apr. 19, 2007).

IMMIGRATION-RELATED CHALLENGES TO FINANCIAL AID/
RESIDENCY, INCLUDING DACA

Doe v. Curators of Univ. of Missouri, No. 15BA-CV03499 (Mo. Cir. Ct. filed
Oct. 13, 2015), dismissed without prejudice, Oct. 24, 2017.

Doe v. St. Louis Cmty. Coll., No. 15SL-CC03511 (Mo. Cir. Ct. filed July 11, 2017),
appeal filed, July 1, 2016.

Mashiri v. Dep't of Educ., 709 F.3d 1299 (9th Cir. 2013), *amended and superseded on denial of rehearing,* 724 F. 3d 1028 (9th Cir. 2013)

Hispanic Interest Coal. of Alabama v. Governor of Alabama, 691 F. 3d 1236
(11th Cir. 2012), *cert. den.* Alabama v. U.S., 133 S. Ct. 2022 (2013).

Marderosian v. Topinka, No. 1:12-cv-2262 (N.D. Ill. June 19, 2012) (challenge
to Illinois in-state tuition law for undocumented students) [withdrawn,
re-filed as Ardash Marderosian Trust v. Quinn, No. 1:12-cv-06869, 2013 WL
5405705 (N.D. Ill. Sept. 25, 2013) (challenge to Illinois scholarship law for
undocumented student scholarship fund, including scholarship funded by
original gift)].

Complaint for Declaratory Relief, Orellana v. State Council of Higher Educ.
for Virginia, No. CL13003086–00 (Va. Cir. Ct. Dec. 17, 2013) (seeking to
have DACA recipients considered eligible for resident tuition, unopposed
motion for nonsuit granted Feb. 12, 2014).

Olvera v. Univ. Sys. of Georgia's Bd. of Regents, 771 S.E.2d 91 (Ga. Ct. App.
2015) (affirming trial court dismissal of action seeking to have DACA
recipients considered eligible for resident tuition), *affirmed,* 782 S.E.2d 436.
(Ga. 2016).

Martinez v. Regents of the Univ. of California, 241 P.3d 855 (Cal. 2010), *cert. den.* 131 S.Ct. 2961 (June 6, 2011) (upholding CA resident tuition policy for undocumented students).

Arizona v. Maricopa Cnty. Cmty. Coll. Dist. Bd. ("MCCCD") No. CV-2013–009093 (Ariz. Super. Ct. May 5, 2015) (DACA recipients are "lawfully present" for the purposes of Prop 300 and in-state tuition rates), *rev'd*, 395 P.3d 714 (Ariz. Ct. App., June 21. 2017), *appeal filed*, CV-17–0215-PR (Ariz. Aug. 21, 2017).

Doe v. Maryland State Bd. of Elections, No. O2-C11–163050 (Md. Cir. Ct. Feb. 17, 2012) (unsuccessful challenge to the state ballot measure "freezing" the 2011 Maryland Dream Act implementation), *aff'd on appeal*, Doe v. Maryland State Bd. of Elections, 53 A.3d 1111 (Md. 2012).

Immigration Reform Coal. of Texas (IRCOT) v. Texas, 706 F. Supp. 2d 760 (S.D. Tex. 2010) (removed to state court); IRCOT's Notice of Nonsuit, Immigration Reform Coal. of Texas v. Hegar, No. 2009–79110 (281st Dist. Ct., Harris County, Tex. Dec. 10, 2015) (dismissing original suit); re-filed as Lone Star Coll. Sys. v. Immigration Reform Coal. of Texas (IRCOT), 418 S.W.3d 263 (Tex. App.—Houston [14th Dist.] 2013) (standing and procedural issues). Lone Star College System v. Immigration Reform Coalition of Texas (IRCOT), No. 14–0031, 2013 WL 5655882, [Tex.App.—Hous. [14th Dist., Oct. 17, 2013 (opinion withdrawn and superseded on denial of rehearing), Lone State Coll. Sys. v. IRCOT, 418 S.W.3d 263 (Tex. App.—Houston 14th Dist. Nov. 26, 2013, pet. filed).

Philips v. Bd. of Trustees of Montgomery Coll., No. C-342882 (Md. Cir. Ct. Aug. 16, 2011) (dismissing challenge to Montgomery College tuition policy for undocumented in-district residents).

Mannschreck v. Clare, No. CI 10–8 (Neb. Dist. Ct. Dec. 17, 2010) (striking down challenge to Nebraska residency statute).

Dominguez v. Texas, No. 5:07-cv-00549 (W.D. Tex. Nov. 6, 2008) (settlement agreement with notice of withdrawal regarding TX veterans college benefit).

Day v. Sebelius, 376 F. Supp. 2d 1022 (D. Kansas, 2005); Day v. Bond, 500 F. 3d 1127 (10th Cir. 2007) (dismissing challenge to Kansas state residency requirement).

Colotl Coyotl v. Kelly, No. 17-cv-01670 (N.D. Ga., dismissed and settled by plaintiff, May 28, 2018).

No. 17–12668, 2019 WL 1050886 (11th Cir. Mar. 6, 2019) (federal law allowed
states such as GA to ban DACA students from enrolling, on grounds they
are not "lawfully present").

DACA CHALLENGES TO DRIVER'S LICENSE POLICIES

Arizona Dream Act Coal. v. Brewer, 757 F.3d 1053 (9th Cir. 2014), *aff'd on
remand*, 81 F.Supp.3d 795 (D. Ariz. 2015), *opinion amended and superseded
on denial of rehearing en banc*, 855 F.3d 957 (9th Cir. 2017), *cert. denied*,
138 S. Ct. 1279 (2018). (Arizona driver's license ban in Arizona; defendants
permanently enjoined from enforcing any policy or practice by which the
Arizona Department of Transportation refuses to accept Employment Authorization Documents, issued under DACA, as proof that the document
holders are authorized under federal law to be present in the United States
for purposes of obtaining a driver's license or state identification card).

One Michigan v. Johnson, No. 2:12-cv-15551 (E.D. Mich. Dec. 19, 2012) (challenge to Michigan policy of denying driver's licenses to DACA recipients
(dismissed after Michigan reversed policy).

Hernandez v. Heineman, No. CI-13–2124 (Neb. Dist. Ct. June 10, 2013) (challenge to Nebraska policy of denying driver's licenses to DACA recipients),
remanded to district court, No. 4:14-CV-3178, 2014 WL 7331928 (D. Neb.
Dec. 19, 2014).

Valenzuela v. Ducey, 329 F. Supp. 3d 982 (D. Ariz. 2018) (Arizona's policy of denying driver's licenses, or requiring additional documentation before issuing
licenses, to noncitizens with federally issued EADs containing the code (c)
(14) violated the Supremacy Clause, permanent injunction granted).

OCCUPATIONAL LICENSING/BAR ADMISSIONS, DACA OR
UNDOCUMENTED

In re Sergio Garcia on Admission, 315 P.3d 117 (Cal. 2014) (recognizing CA
statute to admit undocumented applicant to CA bar).

In re Florida Bd. of Bar Examiners, 134 So. 3d 432 (Fla. 2014) (not admitting
DACA applicant to FL bar).

In re Vargas, 10 N.Y.S. 3d. 579 (N.Y. App. Div. 2015) (application granted).

Juarez v. Nw. Mut. Life Ins. Co., 69 F. Supp.3d 364 (S.D.N.Y. Nov. 14, 2014), *appeal withdrawn*, No. 15–790 (2d Cir. June 4, 2015), *order amended* 2014 WL
127772237 (S.D.N.Y. Dec. 30, 2014 (allegations of refusal to recognize EAD
for hiring sufficient to state § 1981 claim).

Rodriguez v. Procter & Gamble Co., No. 17-cv-22652 (S.D. Fla., filed July 17, 2017) (proposed class action alleging P&G categorically denies non-citizen job applicants employment with the company in the United States if they are not U.S. permanent residents, refugees, or individuals granted asylum) (case ongoing, including April 17, 2019 request for class certification).

CHALLENGES TO END OF DEFERRED ACTION FOR CHILDHOOD ARRIVALS PROGRAM

Batalla Vidal v. Baran, 279 F. Supp. 3d 401 (E.D.N.Y. 2018) (granting preliminary injunction).

Batalla Vidal v. Nielsen, 291 F. Supp. 3d 260 (E.D.N.Y. 2018) (motions to dismiss granted in part, denied in part).

New York v. Trump, No. 17-cv-05228 (E.D. N.Y., filed Sept. 6, 2017) (On November 9, 2017 the following claims were dismissed: Second claim for relief (Due Process Clause—Information-Use Policy); Third claim for relief (Equitable Estoppel—Information-Use Policy); Seventh claim for relief (Due Process Clause—Notice)=).

Regents of Univ. of California v. United States Dep't of Homeland Sec., No. C-17–05211 2017 WL 4642324 (N.D. Cal. Oct. 17, 2017), *mandamus denied*, 875 F.3d 1177 (9th Cir. Nov.16, 2017), *stay denied*, 875 F.3d 1177 (9th Cir. Nov. 21 2017), *cert. granted, vacated and remanded*, 138 S. Ct. 443 (Dec. 20, 2017), *remanded to district court*, 877 F.3d 1080 (9th Cir. 2017), *on remand* No. C-17–05211, 2018 WL 339144 (N.D. Cal. Jan. 9, 2018), *granting preliminary injunction*, 2018 WL 5833232 (9th Cir. Nov. 8, 2018), *affirming grant of preliminary injunction*, 908 F.3d 476 (9th Cir. 2018).

In re United States, 875 F.3d 1177 (9th Cir. 2017), 138 S. Ct. 443 (U.S. 2017) (Granting certiorari, the Supreme Court held that the District Court, before ordering the Government to complete the administrative record, was required to consider the Government's threshold arguments regarding reviewability under the APA and jurisdiction under the Immigration and Nationality Act (INA).

City & County of San Francisco v. Trump, 17–16886, 2018 WL 1401847, at *1, (9th Cir. Jan. 4, 2018), *dismissing appeal as moot*.

Garcia v. United States, No. 17-cv-05380 (N.D. Cal. 2017), resolved by *In re* United States, 875 F.3d 1177 (9th Cir. 2017), 138 S. Ct. 443 (U.S. 2017).

NAACP v. Trump, 315 F. Supp. 3d 457 (D.D.C. 2018), *dismissing appeal as moot*, 2018 WL 1401847 (9th Cir. Jan. 4, 2018).

Massachusetts v. U.S. Dep't of Homeland Sec., No. 17-cv-12022 (D. Mass, filed Oct. 17, 2017) (matter ongoing).

Casa De Maryland v. U.S. Dep't of Homeland Scc., 284 F. Supp. 3d 758 (D. Md. 2018) (government's motion for summary judgment granted in part, denied in part), *appeal filed*, May 8. 2018).

In re Elaine Duke, 2018 WL 33351 (E.D.N.Y. Jan. 8, 2018) (granting motion to certify appeal).

Princeton Univ. v. U.S. Dept. of Homeland Sec., 315 F. Supp. 3d 457 (D.D.C. 2018), *dismissing appeal as moot,* 2018 WL 1401847 (9th Cir. Jan. 4, 2018).

Georgia Latino Alliance for Human Rights et al v. Alford, No. 1:16-CV-00757 (N.D. Ga. Mar. 9, 2016), (matter stayed pending the resolution of the appeal in Estrada v. Becker. Appeal No. 17–12668).

Estrada v. Becker, No. 1:16-CV-3310, 2017 WL 2062078 (N.D. Ga. May 15, 2017), *appeal pending,* No. 17–12668.

Rigoberto Rivera Hernandez, et al. v. C. Dean Alford, et al., No. 2016-cv-274418 (Ga. Super. Ct. Dec. 30, 2016), *ruling in favor of plaintiff DACA recipients, appeal pending,* No. A17A1124.

APPENDIX 4

Immigration-Related Issues: New York State Education Department Licenses

No statutory limitations based on immigration category	Specific language that citizenship is not a requirement and no immigration related criteria	Limiting licenses for professions declared unconstitutional
Acupuncturist: N.Y. Educ. Law § 8214 (McKinney) http://www.op.nysed.gov/prof/ acu/acu1.pdf	Interior Design: N.Y. Educ. Law § 7304 (McKinney) http://www.op.nysed.gov/prof/ id/intdesform1.pdf	Chiropractor: N.Y. Educ. Law § 7504 (McKinney) http://www.op.nysed.gov/prof/ chiro/chiro1.pdf
Athletic Trainer: N.Y. Educ. Law § 8355 (McKinney) http://www.op.nysed.gov/prof/ at/at1.pdf	Architect: N.Y. Educ. Law § 7904 (McKinney) http://www.op.nysed.gov/prof/ arch/arch1.pdf	Certified Shorthand Reporter: N.Y. Educ. Law § 6604 (McKinney) http://www.op.nysed.gov/prof/ csr/csr1.pdf
Audiologist: N.Y. Educ. Law § 8206 (McKinney) http://www.op.nysed.gov/prof/ slpa/sla1.pdf	Occupational Therapist: N.Y. Educ. Law § 7904 (McKinney) http://www.op.nysed.gov/prof/ ot/ot1.pdf	Dentist: N.Y. Educ. Law § 6609 (McKinney) http://www.op.nysed.gov/prof/ dent/dent1.pdf
Clinical Laboratory Technologist: N.Y. Educ. Law § 8605 (McKinney) http://www. op.nysed.gov/prof/clt/clt1.pdf	Occupational Therapist Assistant: N.Y. Educ. Law § 7124 (McKinney) http://www.op.nysed.gov/prof/ ot/ot1.pdf	Dental Hygienist: N.Y. Educ. Law § 7206 (McKinney) http://www.op.nysed.gov/prof/ dent/dh1.pdf
Cytotechnologist: N.Y. Educ. Law § 8605 (McKinney) http://www.op.nysed.gov/prof/ clt/clt1.pdf	Ophthalmic Dispensing: N.Y. Educ. Law § 7104 (McKinney) http://www.op.nysed.gov/prof/ od/od1.pdf	Engineer: N.Y. Educ. Law § 7206-a (McKinney) http://www.op.nysed.gov/prof/ pels/pe1.pdf
Clinical Laboratory/ Histological Technician: N.Y. Educ. Law §§ 8606, 8606-a (McKinney) http://www.op.nysed.gov/prof/ clt/cyt1.pdf	Optometrist: N.Y. Educ. Law § 7004 (McKinney) http://www.op.nysed.gov/prof/ optom/opt1.pdf	Land Surveyor: N.Y. Educ. Law § 7324 (McKinney) http://www.op.nysed.gov/prof/ pels/lsurv1.pdf
Dental Assistant: N.Y. Educ. Law § 8004 (McKinney) http://www.op.nysed.gov/prof/ dent/dent-rdfl1.pdf	Podiatrist: N.Y. Educ. Law § 7603 (McKinney) http://www.op.nysed.gov/prof/ pod/pod1.pdf	Landscape Architect: N.Y. Educ. Law § 7804 (McKinney) http://www.op.nysed.gov/prof/ larch/landarch1.pdf
Dietitian/Nutritionist: N.Y. Educ. Law § 8705 (McKinney) http://www.op.nysed.gov/prof/ diet/diet1.pdf	Psychologist: N.Y. Educ. Law § 7404 (McKinney) http://www.op.nysed.gov/prof/ psych/psych1.pdf	Massage Therapist: N.Y. Educ. Law § 6524 (McKinney) http://www.op.nysed.gov/prof/ mt/mt1.pdf

No statutory limitations based on immigration category	Specific language that citizenship is not a requirement and no immigration related criteria	Limiting licenses for professions declared unconstitutional
Medical Physicist: N.Y. Educ. Law § 6541 (McKinney) http://www.op.nysed.gov/prof/medphys/mp1.pdf	Certified Public Accountant: N.Y. Educ. Law § 6554 (McKinney) http://www.op.nysed.gov/prof/cpa/cpa1.pdf	Physician: N.Y. Educ. Law § 6955 (McKinney) http://www.op.nysed.gov/prof/med/med1.pdf
Physician Assistant: N.Y. Educ. Law § 6541 (McKinney) http://www.op.nysed.gov/prof/med/pa1.pdf		Midwife: N.Y. Educ. Law § 6704, 6711 (McKinney) http://www.op.nysed.gov/prof/midwife/mid1.pdf
Specialist Assistant: N.Y. Educ. Law § 8403 (McKinney) http://www.op.nysed.gov/prof/med/sa1.pdf		Pharmacist: N.Y. Educ. Law § 6711 (McKinney) http://www.op.nysed.gov/prof/pharm/pharm1.pdf
Mental Health Practitioner: N.Y. Educ. Law § 8403 (McKinney) http://www.op.nysed.gov/prof/mhp/mft1.pdf		
Family Therapist: N.Y. Educ. Law § 8404 (McKinney) http://www.op.nysed.gov/prof/mhp/mft1.pdf		
Creative Arts Therapist: N.Y. Educ. Law § 8405 (McKinney) http://www.op.nysed.gov/prof/mhp/cat1.pdf		
Psychoanalyst: N.Y. Educ. Law § 6905 (McKinney) http://www.op.nysed.gov/prof/mhp/psyanl1.pdf		
Registered Nurse: N.Y. Educ. Law § 6905 (McKinney) http://www.op.nysed.gov/prof/nurse/nurse1.pdf		
Licensed Practical Nurse: N.Y. Educ. Law § 6910, 6911 (McKinney) http://www.op.nysed.gov/prof/nurse/nurse1.pdf		
Certification for Nurse Practitioners and Clinical Nurse Specialists: N.Y. Educ. Law § 8609 (9) (McKinney) http://www.op.nysed.gov/prof/nurse/np1.pdf; http://www.op.nysed.gov/prof/nurse/cns1.pdf		

No statutory limitations based on immigration category	Specific language that citizenship is not a requirement and no immigration related criteria	Limiting licenses for professions declared unconstitutional
Perfusionist permit: N.Y. Educ. Law § 6734 (McKinney) http://www.op.nysed.gov/prof/perfusion/perf5.pdf		
Physical Therapist: N.Y. Educ. Law § 6734 (McKinney) http://www.op.nysed.gov/prof/pt/pt1.pdf		
Physical Therapist Assistant: N.Y. Educ. Law § 8505 (McKinney) http://www.op.nysed.gov/prof/pt/pt1.pdf		
Polysomnographic Technologist (authorization): N.Y. Educ. Law § 8504 (McKinney) http://www.op.nysed.gov/prof/polysom/polysom1.pdf		
Respiratory Therapist: N.Y. Educ. Law § 8504 (McKinney) http://www.op.nysed.gov/prof/rt/rt1.pdf		
Respiratory Technician: N.Y. Educ. Law § 7704 (McKinney) http://www.op.n.gov/prof/rt/rt1.pdf		
Social Worker Master: N.Y. Educ. Law § 7704 (McKinney) http://www.op.nysed.gov/prof/sw/lmsw1.pdf		
Clinical Social Worker: N.Y. Educ. Law § 8206 (McKinney) http://www.op.nysed.gov/prof/sw/lcsw1.pdf		
Speech Pathologist/Audiologist: N.Y. Educ. Law § 8804 (2) (McKinney) http://www.op.nysed.gov/prof/slpa/sla1.pdf		
Licensed Behavior Analyst: N.Y. Educ. Law § 8804 (1) (McKinney) http://www.op.nysed.gov/prof/aba/aba1.pdf		
Certified Behavior Analyst Assistant: N.Y. Educ. Law § 8305 (McKinney) http://www.op.nysed.gov/prof/aba/aba1.pdf		

NOTES

CHAPTER 1. COLLEGE RESIDENCY, RACE, AND REACTION

1 *Wisconsin ex rel. Priest v. Regents of the Univ.*, 11 N.W. 472 (Wis. 1882) (upholding institution's right to charge out-of-state surcharge).

2 *See generally* Michael A. Olivas, *Administering Intentions: Law, Theory, and Practice in Postsecondary Residency Requirements*, 59 J. Higher Educ. 263 (1988).

3 Jonathan D. Varat, *State "Citizenship" and Interstate Equality*, 48 U. Chi. L. Rev. 487 (1981); James N. Morgan, *Tuition Policy and the Interstate Migration of College Students*, 19 Res. Higher Educ. 183 (1983).

4 *See, e.g.*, Olivas, *Administering Intentions*; David Palley, *Resolving the Nonresident Student Problem: Two Federal Proposals*, 47 J. Higher Educ. 1 (1976); Robert Carbone, *Alternative Tuition Systems* (1974); Robert Carbone, *Students and State Borders* (1973).

5 Robert Carbone, *Resident or Nonresident? Tuition Classification in Higher Education*, 2 (Education Commission of the States [ECS], Denver 1970).

6 D.C. Code Ann. § 31-601 (1993); *see, e.g.*, Olivas, *Administering Intentions*, at 287–90 (App. I).

7 *See generally* Christopher T. Corson, *Reform of Domicile Law for Application to Transients, Temporary Residents and Multi-Based Persons*, 16 Colum. J. L. & Soc. Probs. 327 (1981); Harald Bauder, *Domicile Citizenship, Human Mobility and Territoriality*, 38 Progr. in Hum. Geog. 9 (2014).

8 Corson, *Reform of Domicile Law*.

9 *Restatement (Second) of Conflict of Laws* § 11(2) ("Every person has a domicile at all times and, at least for the same purpose, no person has more than one domicile at a time.").

10 *Id.; see also* Gary S. Josephs, *A Checklist for Determining Domicile*, Prac. Law., July 15, 1981, at 55; Adam B. Schiff, Comment, *State Discriminatory Action Against Nonresidents: Using the Original Position Theory as a Framework for Analysis*, 22 Harv. J. Legis. 583 (1985).

11 *Id.; see also* Joseph A. Bollhofer, Comment, *Disenfranchisement of the College Student Vote: When a Resident Is Not a Resident*, 11 Fordham Urb. L.J. 489 (1983) (reviewing voting practices affecting students who live in campus housing); Matt Dempsey, *Confusion for Prairie View A&M Students on the Last Day for Voter Registration*, Hous. Chron., Oct. 9, 2018, www.houstonchronicle.com (reviewing student voter suppression at HBCUs). *See generally* Benjamin Highton, *Voter*

Identification Laws and Turnout in the United States, 20 Ann. Rev. Pol. Sci. 149 (2017) (reviewing effects of voter identification as a tool of voter suppression, especially directed at African American and Latino voters).

12 *See generally* Patricia M. Lines, *Tuition Discrimination: Valid and Invalid Uses of Tuition Differentials*, 9 J.C. & U.L. 241 (1982–83); Varat, *State "Citizenship."*

13 For example, because the intent requirement cannot be measured or enforced until after the educational resource is consumed (i.e., after graduation or the completion of studies), the true metric is likely to manifest too late. In an earlier work, I proposed a time-shifting alternative that would tie tuition benefits to a rebate after the completion of studies. Olivas, *Administering Intentions*, at 284–85. Those loud sounds are people running away from this good idea.

14 For example, a student could simultaneously establish residence in one or more of the following: the "home state," the school state, the parents' state(s), or a holiday or summer job location.

15 *See, e.g., Frame v. Residency Appeals Comm.*, 675 P.2d 1157 (Utah 1983).

16 *See, e.g.,* Carbone, *Borders*; Michael A. Olivas, *The Rise of Nonlegal Legal Influences*, in *Governing Academia* 258–75, 267–70 (Ronald G. Ehrenberg ed., Cornell Univ. Press 2004) (reviewing consortial arrangements).

17 Michael A. Olivas, *Postsecondary Residency Requirements: Empowering Statutes, Governing Types, and Exemptions*, 16 Coll. L. Dig. 268 (1986).

18 Youngblood Henderson, *The Question of Nonresident Tuition for Tribal Citizens*, 4 Am. Ind. L. Rev. 47 (1976) (analyzing residency classifications that conflict with domicile determinations for reservation Indians).

19 Tex. Educ. Code Ann. §§ 54.052, 54.059, 54.063 (West 1995). For an extreme example, Texas provides nonresident tuition waivers for federal prisoners incarcerated in Texas correctional facilities provided the inmate designates a Texas domicile. Op. Tex. Att'y Gen. No. H-559 (Mar. 20, 1975).

20 *See* Texas Higher Education Coordinating Board, *An Evaluation of Exemption and Waiver Programs in Texas*, Oct. 2006, www.thecb.state.tx.us.

21 There are regular threats and posturing about these provisions, especially with regard to immigration. For example, in April 1993 a bill was introduced in the Texas legislature to address the problems of intending permanent residents or persons permanently residing under color of law (PRUCOL), but it died in committee. *See* H.B. No. 2510 Introduced Version, 73rd Reg. Sess., Apr. 28, 1993. For excellent studies of PRUCOL aliens, *see* Peter L. Reich, *Public Benefits for Undocumented Aliens: State Law into the Breach Once More*, 21 N.M. L. Rev. 219 (1991); John W. Guendelsberger, *Equal Protection and Resident Alien Access to Public Benefits in France and the United States*, 67 Tul. L. Rev. 669 (1993); Robert Rubin, *Walking a Gray Line: The "Color of Law" Test Governing Noncitizen Eligibility for Public Benefits*, 24 San Diego L. Rev. 411 (1987). For more recent vintage, *see* Julian Aguilar, *Dan Patrick Again Targeting In-State Tuition for Undocumented Students*, Tex. Trib., Sept. 9, 2016, www.texastribune.org.

22 For details of the waivers, *see* Tex. Educ. Code Ann. § 54.052(h), *Economic Development & Diversification In-State Tuition for Employees*, https://gov.texas.gov.

23 *See, e.g.,* Olivas, *Administering Intentions*, at 276–78 (likening practices to "one-hoss shay").

24 The discussion of discretionary practices was taken from my previous work, *Administering Intentions*; Michael A. Olivas, Plyler v. Doe, Toll v. Moreno, *and Postsecondary Admissions: Undocumented Adults and "Enduring Disability,"* 15 J.L. & Educ. 19 (1986); as well as more recent research, Michael A. Olivas, *Within You Without You: Undocumented Lawyers, DACA, and Occupational Licensing*, 52 Valparaiso Univ. L. Rev. 65–164 (2017).

25 Olivas, *Enduring Disability*, at 42–44.

26 Olivas, *Administering Intentions*, at 287–90.

27 *Dunn v. Blumstein*, 405 U.S. 330 (1972) (striking down one-year voter registration residency requirement); *see also* Bollhofer, *Disenfranchisement*.

28 *Dunn*, 405 U.S. at 333–36 & nn. 3–6 (reviewing difficulties in residency determinations and cases requiring reasonable accommodations). *See also* Highton, *Voter*.

29 Olivas, *Administering Intentions*, at 274–77 (analyzing problems of evidence and burden of proof in residency/domicile determinations).

30 The leading "irrebuttable presumption" case arose in the area of postsecondary residency requirements. *Vlandis v. Kline*, 412 U.S. 441 (1973) (striking down irrebuttable presumptions in out-of-state college applications). *Vlandis* remains the leading SCOTUS case in residency determinations and rebuttable presumptions. But hope springs eternal. *See, e.g.,* Hannah McCann, *Privileged for Being Stationary: Why the Practice of Differentiating Between In-State and Out-of-State Tuition Rates Is Unconstitutional*, 4 Belm. L. Rev. 279 (2017) (arguing that *Vlandis* is unconstitutional and outmoded).

31 *Toll v. Moreno*, 458 U.S. 1, 9–10 (1982) (striking down state college residency requirement for G-4 aliens on preemption grounds).

32 The requirement was that a Texas resident be "gainfully employed." Tex. Educ. Code Ann. § 54.052(e) (West 1995). This requirement has been finessed to mean "substantially," "more than part-time," "non-work study," or "not a public charge" (i.e., not on welfare). I chaired the University of Houston Residency Appeals Committee for more than twenty-five years, and we adjudicated hundreds of cases every year from students who felt they had met the Texas criteria.

33 Anne Ryman, *Community Colleges Don't Plan to Appeal Ruling Denying In-State Tuition to DACA Students*, Ariz. Rep., May 22, 2018, www.azcentral.com; Rachel Leingang, *Big Drop in "Dreamers" Enrolled at Maricopa Community Colleges After Tuition Ruling*, Ariz. Rep., Sept. 24, 2018, www.azcentral.com.

34 457 U.S. 202 (1982), aff'g *Doe v. Plyler*, 628 F.2d 448 (5th Cir. 1980), aff'g *Doe v. Plyler*, 458 F. Supp. 569 (E.D. Tex. 1978). For careful studies following soon after the decision, *see* Jose A. Cardenas & Albert Cortez, *The Impact of* Plyler v. Doe *Upon Texas Public Schools*, 15 J.L. & Educ. 1 (1986) (finding Plyler had a "minimal" impact upon Texas schools, with a greater impact upon urban areas and certain

border districts); Manuel Garcia y Griego, *The Rights of Undocumented Mexicans in the United States After* Plyler v. Doe: *A Sketch of Moral and Legal Issues*, 15 J.L. & Educ. 57 (1986) (reviewing normative obligations to undocumented aliens in the United States).

35 According to the Texas state Education Code:

(a) All children who are citizens of the United States or legally admitted aliens and who are over the age of five years and under the age of 21 years on the first day of September of any scholastic year shall be entitled to the benefits of the Available School Fund for that year.

(b) Every child in this state who is a citizen of the United States or a legally admitted alien and who is over the age of five years and not over the age of 21 years on the first day of September of the year in which admission is sought shall be permitted to attend the public free schools of the district in which he resides or in which his parent, guardian, or the person having lawful control of him resides at the time he applies for admission.

(c) The board of trustees of any public free school district of this state shall admit into the public free schools of the district free of tuition all persons who are either citizens of the United States or legally admitted aliens and who are over five and not over 21 years of age at the beginning of the scholastic year if such persons or his parent, guardian or person having lawful control resides within the school district.

Tex. Educ. Code Ann. § 21.03 (Vernon Supp. 1981), cited in *Plyler*, 457 U.S. at 201 n.1.

36 *Id.* It is not surprising that such anti-Mexican legislation would have originated in Texas, a jurisdiction widely regarded to have "a legacy of hate engendered by the Texas Revolution and the Mexican American War." Guadalupe San Miguel, *"Let Them All Take Heed": Mexican Americans and the Campaign for Educational Equality in Texas, 1910–1981* (Univ. Texas Press 1987); *see generally* Arnoldo De Leon, *They Called Them Greasers* (Univ. Texas Press 1983). According to historians, this history of conflict has "generated distrust and dislike between Anglos and Texas Mexicans. Most important, it shaped Anglo attitudes towards Mexicans by (a) justifying the inferior status to which they were relegated, (b) legitimizing the stereotype of Mexicans as 'eternal enemies' of the state, and (c) encouraging their denigration. Additionally this legacy undergirded the historical attitude of Anglo disparagement of Mexican culture and the Spanish language." San Miguel, *"Let Them All Take Heed,"* at 32. *See also* Cynthia F. Orozco, *No Mexicans, Women, or Dogs Allowed: The Rise of the Mexican American Civil Rights Movement* (Univ. Texas Press 2009).

37 *Plyler*, 457 U.S. at 227.

38 *Id.*

39 *Id.* at 226 ("We perceive no national policy that supports the State in denying these children an elementary education.").

40 *Toll v. Moreno*, 458 U.S. 1 (1982).

41 Olivas, *Enduring Disability. Nyquist v. Mauclet*, 432 U.S. 1 (1977), had been the first Supreme Court postsecondary education case construing a state statute affecting permanent resident college students. *Nyquist* struck down a New York State statute that prohibited permanent resident aliens from receiving college tuition assistance benefits. *Id.* at 12.

42 This case went through several different incarnations. The following is a complete history of the Toll case: *Moreno v. Univ. of Md.*, 420 F. Supp. 541 (D. Md. 1976), *aff'd without op. sub nom.Moreno v. Elkins*, 556 F.2d 573 (4th Cir. 1977), question certified, 435 U.S. 647 (1978), certified question answered, *sub nom., Toll v. Moreno*, 397 A.2d 1009 (Md.), answer conformed to, 441 U.S. 458 (per curiam), on remand, 480 F. Supp. 1116 (D. Md. 1979), later proceeding, 489 F. Supp. 658 (D. Md. 1980), *aff'd sub nom., Moreno v. Univ. of Md.*, 645 F.2d 217 (4th Cir. 1981) (per curiam), *aff'd sub nom., Toll v. Moreno*, 458 U.S. 1 (1982).

43 In pertinent part: "This Constitution, and the laws of the United States . . . shall be the supreme Law of the Land." U.S. Const. art. VI, cl. 2.

44 *Toll*, 458 U.S. at 17, 20.

45 *Moreno v. Toll*, 489 F. Supp. 658 (D. Md. 1980).

46 *Moreno v. Univ. of Md.*, 645 F.2d 217 (4th Cir. 1981) (per curiam).

47 *Toll*, 458 U.S. at 13–17, 20.

48 *Moreno v. Univ. of Md.*, 420 F. Supp. 541, 544, 548, 554 (D. Md. 1976).

49 *Elkins v. Moreno*, 435 U.S. 647 (1978).

50 *Id.* at 668–69.

51 *Toll v. Moreno*, 397 A.2d 1009, 1019 (Md. 1979).

52 *Toll v. Moreno*, 441 U.S. 458 (1979) (per curiam).

53 *Id.*

54 *Id.* at 461–62.

55 *Moreno v. Toll*, 489 F. Supp. 658 (D. Md. 1980).

56 *Id.* at 668.

57 *Id.* at 667–68.

58 *Moreno v. Univ. of Md.*, 645 F.2d 217, 220 (4th Cir. 1981) (per curiam).

59 *Takahashi v. Fish & Game Comm'n*, 334 U.S. 410 (1948) (states cannot impose discriminatory burdens on aliens), cited in *Toll*, 458 U.S. at 10–11.

60 *Graham v. Richardson*, 403 U.S. 365 (1971) (states may not impose regulations upon aliens if the burdens are not contemplated by Congress), cited in *Toll*, 458 U.S. at 12.

61 *De Canas v. Bica*, 424 U.S. 351 (1976) (Court upheld state law regulating employment of undocumented immigrants), cited in *Toll*, 458 U.S. at 13.

62 *Toll*, 458 U.S. at 12–13 (quoting *De Canas*, 424 U.S. at 358 n.6). Justice Brennan agreed that the Court had previously upheld legislation limiting the "participation of noncitizens in the States' political and governmental functions." *Id.* at 12 n.17 (citations omitted).

63 *Id.* at 14.

64 *Id.* at 16 (citations omitted). Moreover, Maryland law had tracked the federal exemption. *See id.* at 15 n.22.

65 *Id.* at 16. Justice O'Connor dissented from this characterization but concurred in the opinion "insofar as it holds that the state may not charge out-of-state tuition to nonimmigrant aliens who, under federal law, are exempt from both state and federal taxes, and who are domiciled in the State." *Id.* at 24. (O'Connor, J., concurring in part and dissenting in part).

66 *Id.* at 24–28 (O'Connor, J., concurring in the result).

67 *Id.* at 19–24 (Blackmun, J., concurring).

68 *Id.* at 29–30 (Rehnquist, J., dissenting) (construing *Graham v. Richardson*, 403 U.S. 365 (1971)).

69 *Id.* at 33 (Rehnquist, J., dissenting).

70 *Id.* at 33 (Rehnquist, J., dissenting) (emphasis deleted).

71 *See* T. Alexander Aleinikoff, *Citizens, Aliens, Membership and the Constitution,* 7 Const. Commentary 9 (1990) (examining discrepancies in treatment of aliens in equal protection theory); T. Alexander Aleinikoff, *Federal Regulation of Aliens and the Constitution,* 83 Am. J. Int'l L. 862 (1989) (criticizing judicial deference toward immigration legislation); Gerald M. Rosberg, *The Protection of Aliens from Discriminatory Treatment by the National Government,* 1977 Sup. Ct. Rev. 275 (1977) (same). Flash-forward to the Trump administration, and any fair reading will say that many people have been thinking long and hard about deferred action and the larger subject: prosecutorial discretion. *See, e.g.,* David S. Rubenstein, *Taking Care of the Rule of Law,* Geo. Wash. L. Rev. 168 (2018); Shoba S. Wadhia, *Immigration Enforcement and the Future of Discretion,* 23 R. Wms. Univ. L. Rev. 2 (2018).

72 *Toll,* 458 U.S. at 17–18.

73 Md. Rev. Code Ann., Tax-Gen. Sec. 280a (1977).

74 *Toll,* 458 U.S. at 7 (quoting App. to Pet. for Cert. 173a-174a).

75 *Toll,* 458 U.S. at 16 (quoting Brief for Petitioners 23).

76 Michael A. Olivas, *What the "War on Terror" Has Meant for U.S. Colleges and Universities, in Doctoral Education and the Faculty of the Future* 249–58 (Ronald G. Ehrenberg & Charlotte V. Kuh eds., Cornell Univ. Press 2009); a revised edition was published in the trade press: *Colleges Should Think Twice About Exporting Their Programs,* Chron. Higher Educ., Nov. 7, 2008, www.chronicle.com/article/ Colleges-Should-Think-Twice/30571 (evidence of major disruptions, stemming from U.S. PATRIOT Act, for domestic students and especially international students).

77 "[W]e cannot conclude that Congress ever contemplated that a State, in the operation of a university, might impose discriminatory tuition charges and fees solely on account of the federal immigration classification." *Toll,* 458 U.S. at 17.

78 IRCA (1986) provided additional independent nonimmigrant status for relatives of employees of international organizations or long-term (sixteen years or more) G holders. 8 U.S.C.A. § 1101(a)(15)(N) (West 1995); 8 U.S.C.A. § 1101(a)(27)(I) (West 1995). *See, e.g., Nyquist v. Mauclet,* 432 U.S. 1 (1977) (state financial aid pro-

gram requirement cannot compel resident alien to become citizen). *See generally* Janette Fenn Maxwell, Comment, *An Alien's Constitutional Right to Loan, Scholarships and Tuition Benefits at State Supported Colleges and Universities*, 14 Cal. W. L. Rev. 514 (1979).

79 *Wong v. Board of Trustees*, 125 Cal. Rptr. 841 (1st Dist. 1975) (omitted in official reporter by order of California Supreme Court, January 15, 1976) (denying equal protection challenge to requirement that aliens hold permanent resident status for one year prior to determination of residence).

80 In Texas, as in many states, nonimmigrants such as K-visa holders (fiancées or fiancés) and L holders (intracompany transferees) are more easily accorded residence for tuition purposes since federal immigration law does not require them to maintain a domicile in their home country. 8 U.S.C.A. § 1101 (a)(15)(K)(L)(West 1995). Nonimmigrants on student visas set out in section (F), by contrast, are required to maintain their original domicile in their home country. 8 U.S.C.A. § 1101(a)(15)(F)(West 1995). Thus, by the terms of the F-visa application, they are not accorded permission to relinquish this domicile. Unless they make an adjustment to another visa, they must return home or leave the United States at the end of their nonimmigrant stay, no matter how long they remain in that visa status.

81 Tentative Decision, No. 588982-5 (Cal. Super. Ct., Alameda Cty., Apr. 3, 1985); Judgment (May 7, 1985); Statement of Decision (May 30, 1985) (*Leticia "A" I*); Clarification, May 19, 1992 (*Leticia "A" II*). All subsequent references are to the May 30, 1985, Statement of Decision, unless otherwise noted.

82 *Id.* at 1–4. The California State University and College System, which had also employed the University of California System practice, was similarly enjoined from continuing in that practice. *Id.* at 9. The reinstated judgment, however, allocated the trial costs to the UC system. *Id.* at 7.

83 *Id.* at 6.

84 Immigration and Naturalization Act of 1952, Pub. L. No. 82–44, 66 Stat. 163 (codified and amended at 8 U.S.C. §§ 1101–1525 (1995)).

85 Cal. Educ. Code § 68062(h) (West 1995) (citations deleted). Some of this section draws on Michael A. Olivas, *Storytelling Out of School: Undocumented College Residency, Race, and Reaction*, 22 Hast. Const. L.Q. 1019 (1995), and, as noted, personal experience in the matters.

86 Cal. Educ. Code § 68018 (West 1995).

87 Cal. Educ. Code § 68062 (a) (West 1995).

88 Cal. Educ. Code § 68062 (d) (West 1995).

89 Cal. Educ. Code § 68061 (West 1995).

90 "The legislative history of Education Code section 68062, subdivision (h), demonstrates that the Legislature did not intend to, and the subdivision does not, permit undocumented aliens to establish residence for tuition purposes in California's public institutions of higher education." 67 Op. Cal. Att'y Gen. 241, 241 (1984).

91 *Leticia "A,"* No. 588982-4, slip op. at 2 (May 7, 1985).

92 "It is neither applicable to the facts nor appropriate to the legal issues in this case." *Leticia "A" I*, No. 588982-4, slip op. at 6 (Apr. 3, 1985).

93 *Id.*

94 *Plyler*, 457 U.S. at 227 n.22.

95 "In sum, education has a fundamental role in maintaining the fabric of our society." *Plyler*, 457 U.S. at 221.

96 *Leticia "A" I*, No. 588982-4, slip op. at 4.

97 *Id.* at 8.

98 *Id.* (emphasis deleted from original).

99 *Id.* at 5.

100 67 Op. Cal. Att'y Gen. 241 n. 11. In footnote 11, the attorney general's opinion notes, "It is possible that this interpretation of the statute raises constitutional issues of equal protection. (*See Plyler*, 457 U.S. 202.) We have not been asked and have not considered such questions." *Id.*

101 *Leticia "A,"* No. 588982-4, slip op. at 9.

102 *Id.* Several of the original plaintiffs, including Leticia "A," had changed their status during the course of the litigation. The original eight plaintiffs thereby shrank to four. By 1993, all had adjusted their status by one or another means. Telephone interviews with Multicultural Education, Training, and Advocacy (META) and Mexican American Legal Defense and Educational Fund (MALDEF) staff in San Francisco, Calif. (Oct. 12, 1993).

103 *Leticia "A" I*, No. 588982-4, slip op. at 9–10 (Apr. 3, 1985).

104 No. C607748 (Cal. Super. Ct., L.A. Cty. May 30, 1990), *aff'd sub nom., Board of Regents of Univ. of Cal. v. Superior Ct.* (*Bradford II*), 276 Cal. Rptr. 197 (Cal. Ct. App. 1990), *rev. den.*, 1991 Cal. LEXIS 1367 (Cal. 1991). Bradford argued he had been forced to resign for his action, but the court held that he had "voluntarily quit his position" over the policy. Carol McGraw, *UC Worker Who Quit over Fees Policy Loses Bid to Get Job Back*, L.A. Times, Aug. 29, 1990, at B3.

105 *Id.* (citing Cal. Educ. Code § 68062(h)).

106 Brief for Appellant, at 12–13, *Leticia "A,"* No. 588982-2; interviews with CSU legal staff, July 11, 1992 (discussing CSU's long-standing policy of allowing undocumented to establish domicile, dating back to 1985; identities withheld upon request).

107 Larry Gordon, *Immigrants Face Cal State Fee Hike*, L.A. Times, Sept. 9, 1992, at A3, A20 (decision "could affect 800 of the 361,000 Cal State students"); Gary Libman, *Losing Out on a Dream?*, L.A. Times, Jan. 23, 1992, at E3, E11 ("The [Bradford] decision will affect only about 100 UC students but about 14,000 at state community colleges, officials estimate."). California public college students total over 2 million, including over 1.5 million in the community colleges. Alice C. Andrews & James W. Fonseca, "Community Colleges in the United States: A Geographical Perspective" (Washington, D.C.: Association of American Geographers 1998).

108 Auditor General of California, *A Fiscal Impact Analysis of Undocumented Immigrants Residing in San Diego County* 119–20 (1992). The report did not estimate the

undocumented students in the UC or community colleges in San Diego County because those students were being required to pay out-of-state tuition. *Id.* at 120.

109 Gordon, *Immigrants*, at A3 (estimating that only 14,000 of 1.5 million CCC students were undocumented). MALDEF officials have insisted that even these numbers overestimated the true enrollment, as most undocumented students could not afford to pay either in-state or out-of-state tuition and were hesitant to enroll in college and risk subjecting themselves to detection and possible deportation by the INS.

110 No. C607748 (Cal. Super. Ct., L.A. Cty. May 30, 1990) (David P. Yaffe, J.), cited in *Bradford II*, 276 Cal. Rptr. 197, 199 (Cal. Ct. App. 1990). All references to the *Bradford I* opinion are as they are cited in *Bradford II*.

111 *Id.*

112 *Bradford II*, 276 Cal. Rptr. at 199.

113 *Id.*

114 *Id. See also* interviews with California State University legal staff, Long Beach, Calif., June 1992.

115 *Id.* at 200.

116 *Id.* at 201–02.

117 *Leticia "A" II*, No. 588982-4, May 19, 1992 (as clarified).

118 *Id.* Judge Kawaichi ordered that the CSU be enjoined from denying in state residency benefits "to persons solely on the basis of their undocumented immigration status." *Id.* He also reiterated his earlier ruling that the undocumented students "shall be afforded a full and fair opportunity to demonstrate the bona fides of their residency." *Id.*

119 I and others encouraged the CSU chancellor at the time, Dr. W. Ann Reynolds, not to appeal the 1985 ruling but to begin enrolling the students who were otherwise eligible to attend. During the pendency of the *Leticia "A"* litigation, UC officials did not charge nonresident tuition to the plaintiffs or others in their same status. Interview with Dr. W. Ann Reynolds, CSU Chancellor, in Long Beach, Calif., 1985.

120 *See, e.g., infra* note 235.

121 *American Ass'n. of Women (AAW) v. Board of Trustees of the Cal. St. Univ.*, No. BC061221, slip op. at 7 (Cal. Super. Ct., L.A. Cty. Sept. 28, 1992), *aff'd* 38 Cal. Rptr. 2d 15 (Cal. Ct. App. 1995). By this time, Dr. Barry Munitz was chancellor of the CSU system. I and others urged him not to appeal Judge Kawaichi's clarification. CSU also chose not to appeal *Leticia "A" II*. (I refreshed legal memories with him in person in October 2018.)

122 *Id.* at 1.

123 *Id.* at 6–7. Essentially, Judge O'Brien held that because CSU had not appealed the original *Leticia "A"* ruling to an appellate court, the appellate *Bradford* decision should trump the trial court. *Id.* at 7. At the time the *Leticia "A" II* and *AAW* cases were occurring, UC was in the papers on a regular basis for the exorbitant retirement package paid the retiring UC president, as well as for pending cuts in the

UC proposed state budget. For a small sampling of the negative press stories, see a series of articles by Louis Freedberg in the *San Francisco Chronicle*: *UC Retirement Deal for Gardner Assailed*, S.F. Chron., Apr. 3, 1992, at A1; *How UC Regents Tried to Downplay the Gardner Deal*, S.F. Chron., Apr. 16, 1992, at A1; *Gardner Successor Gets Similar Pay Package, UC Compensation over $400,000 a Year*, S.F. Chron., July 30, 1992; *Gardner Leaves UC with Plan to Close Huge Budget Gap*, S.F. Chron., Sept. 19, 1992, at A1. *See also* Debra Saunders, *Fat Left to Trim on Wilson's Plate*, S.F. Chron., Nov. 2, 1992, at A14.

124 AAW, No. BC061221, slip op. at 9.

125 *Id.* at 7, 8 ("Bradford has cast a different light on CSU's process and Section 68062(h) which should be decided at the appellate level . . . [and] Leticia 'A' is essentially a finished case with different parties and a different threshold issue relating to Section 62062(h)").

126 *Id.* at 9.

127 *Id.*

128 Telephone interview with UC legal office, Jan. 10, 1993 (identities withheld upon request).

129 *Id.* at 9.

130 *Bradford II*, 276 Cal. Rptr. at 200–01; AAW, No. BC061221, slip op. at 4–6.

131 *Leticia "A" II*, No. 588982-4, slip op. at 18 (May 19, 1992).

132 *Bradford II*, 276 Cal. Rptr. at 201 ("We do not interpret the federal immigration statutes, therefore, as authorizing, or not precluding, the establishment of domicile here by those whose very presence is unlawful.").

133 Cal. Educ. Code § 68062(h) (West 1995) ("An alien, including an unmarried minor alien, may establish his or [her] residence, unless precluded by the Immigration and Nationality Act from establishing domicile in the United States") (emphasis added; citations omitted).

134 *Bradford II*, 276 Cal. Rptr. at 200–01.

135 *Toll*, 435 U.S. 647 (1978).

136 *See Elkins v. Moreno*, 435 U.S. 647, 668–69 (1978) (G-4 holders can be US domiciliaries).

137 *Cabral v. State Bd. of Control*, 169 Cal. Rptr. 604 (Cal. Ct. App. 1980) (undocumented can establish California residency for purposes of state Victims of Violent Crimes Act standing).

138 *Bradford II*, 276 Cal. Rptr. at 201.

139 *See generally Toll*, 458 U.S. 1 (1982).

140 *Bradford II*, 276 Cal. Rptr. at 201.

141 In the Toll case's earlier incarnation, *Elkins v. Moreno*, 397 A.2d 1009 (Md. 1979), the Maryland court certified that under state law G-4 aliens were able to acquire and demonstrate domicile. *Id.* at 1019.

142 In *Plyler*, the Court held that the undocumented "might be granted federal permission to continue to reside in this country, or even to become a citizen . . . [and enjoy] an inchoate federal permission to remain." 457 U.S. at 226. In addition, the

Court struck down the Texas statute that functionally resembled the California provision, noting: "A State may not, however, accomplish what would otherwise be prohibited by the Equal Protection Clause, merely by defining a disfavored group as nonresident. And illegal entry into the country would not, under traditional criteria, bar a person from obtaining domicile within a State." *Id.* at 227 n.22. I have often thought that this counterintuitive insight was the genuine key to *Plyler* and the rights of the undocumented, whether adults or children. *See* Michael A. Olivas, *No Undocumented Child Left Behind:* Plyler v. Doe *and the Education of Undocumented Children* (New York University Press 2012).

143 *Woodby v. INS*, 385 U.S. 276, 286 n.19 (1966).

144 462 U.S. 919 (1983) (finding that legislative veto provisions violated separation of powers).

145 8 U.S.C.A. § 1254(a)(1) (West 1995). In *INS v. Phinpathya*, 464 U.S. 183 (1984), the Court upheld the strict residence requirements even though the holding meant that a three-month absence constituted ineligibility for suspension of deportation. This harsh result led to the Fifth Circuit denying suspension to an alien who had resided in the United States for twelve consecutive years minus one night. *Sanchez-Dominguez v. INS*, 780 F.2d 1203 (5th Cir. 1986). Congress in turn decided that the "continuous" standard was being construed too literally and amended section 1254 to enable aliens to have "brief, casual and innocent" absences as long as they "did not meaningfully interrupt the continuous physical presence." 8 U.S.C.A. § 1254(b)(2) (West 1995). In short, it is clear that Congress not only assumes that domicile can be acquired by deportable aliens but also requires that domicile be established in the United States for these adjustments or reliefs from deportation.

146 8 U.S.C.A. § 1259 (West 1995). The 1972 cutoff date was established by IRCA. Unlike the other "legalization" provisions, registry enables the alien to become a permanent resident immediately without the intermediate "Temporary Resident Status." 8 U.S.C.A. § 1255a (West 1995).

147 *Id.* Suspension of deportation and registry provisions are two excellent devices to regularize the status of otherwise deportable immigrants, but they are by no means the only such provisions. *See* Paul B. Hunker III, *Cancellation of Removal or Cancellation of Relief—the 1996 IIRIRA Amendments: A Review and Critique of Section 240A(A) of the Immigration and Nationality Act*, 15 Geo. Immigr. L.J. 1 (2000).

148 *See generally Castillo-Felix v. INS*, 601 F.2d 459, 464 (9th Cir. 1979) ("To establish domicile, aliens must not only be physically present here, but must intend to remain"); *Lok v. INS*, 681 F.2d 107, 109 (2d Cir. 1982) (finding undocumented alien established domicile "when he established an intent to remain") (citations omitted).

149 Olivas, *No Undocumented Child*.

150 461 U.S. 321 (1983).

151 Tex. Educ. Code Ann. § 21.031 (Vernon 1995).

152 *Martinez v. Bynum*, 461 U.S. 321 (holding that Texas could charge tuition to alien children if families were not domiciled in the state). *See also Matter of Sanchez*, 17 I&N Dec. 218 (BIA 1980) (eligibility for suspension of deportation requires establishment of domicile in the United States).

153 The various forms of relief do not distinguish among the various forms of becoming undocumented. For example, under INA § 212 (c), 8 U.S.C. § 1182(c), relief would be available to undocumented aliens whether they entered illegally under their own power, were brought here illegally by their parents, or entered as nonimmigrants and then did something to violate the terms of their visas (e.g., switching schools without permission or not maintaining full-time student status). This argument exceeds the scope of this article, but it seems clear that the greatest moral and legal claims to equitable relief can be made by aliens whose parents surreptitiously brought them into the country. The children in this example have the domicile of their parents (or custodial parent, if only one), and once they reach majority age they can establish their own independent domicile through operation of law. Thus if there is a "clean hands" argument to be made in either a court or a legislature, these children are innocent of any illegal entry. *Plyler* mooted this point, in any event. 457 U.S. at 228–30 (striking down state's rationales for regulating immigration).

154 *Leticia "A" II*, No. 588982-4, slip op. at 4–5.

155 Testimony of Dr. Leo Chavez, anthropology professor at UC Irvine, in *Leticia "A" I*, No. 588982-4, Transcript, at 26–34; and *Leticia "A" II*, No. 588982-4, slip op. at 2–4 (children are brought to the United States without any plans for them to enroll in college).

156 *See generally* the text at notes 145–47.

157 *Toll*, 458 U.S. at 17.

158 *Bradford II*, 276 Cal. Rptr. at 201 (citations omitted).

159 8 U.S.C.A. § 1255a (h) (West 1995).

160 *INS Issues Guidelines on School Approval Petitions*, Inter. Rel. 347-48, 361–67 (Mar. 14, 1994) (Revised INS School Approval Guidelines). *See* Janet M. Calvo, *Alien Status Restrictions on Eligibility for Federally Funded Assistance Programs*, 16 N.Y.U. Rev. L. & Soc. Change 395 (1987–88).

161 *See generally* Kevin R. Johnson, *An Essay on Immigration Politics, Popular Democracy, and California's Proposition 187: The Political Relevance and Legal Irrelevance of Race*, 70 Wash. L. Rev. 629, 634 (1995).

162 *See League of United Latin Am. Citizens (LULAC II) v. Wilson*, 997 F. Supp. 1244, 1261 (C.D. Cal. 1997) (striking down virtually all of Proposition 187).

163 The full text of Proposition 187 appears in *League of United Latin Am. Citizens (LULAC II) v. Wilson*, 908 F. Supp. 755, 787–91 (C.D. Cal. 1995). There is extensive literature on the events leading to, and following from, this ballot initiative. *See generally* Evangeline G. Abriel, *Rethinking Preemption for Purposes of Aliens and Public Benefits*, 42 UCLA L. Rev. 1597 (1995); Linda S. Bosniak, *Opposing Prop. 187: Undocumented Immigrants and the National Imagination*, 28 Conn. L. Rev. 555

(1996); Richard A. Boswell, *Restrictions on Non-Citizens' Access to Public Benefits: Flawed Premise, Unnecessary Response*, 42 UCLA L. Rev. 1475 (1995); Lolita K. Buckner Inniss, *California's Proposition 187—Does It Mean What It Says? Does It Say What It Means? A Textual and Constitutional Analysis*, 10 Geo. Immigr. L.J. 577 (1996); Kevin R. Johnson, *Public Benefits and Immigration: The Intersection of Immigration Status, Ethnicity, Gender, and Class*, 42 UCLA L. Rev. 1509 (1995); Stephen H. Legomsky, *Immigration, Federalism, and the Welfare State*, 42 UCLA L. Rev. 1453 (1995); Hiroshi Motomura, *Immigration and Alienage, Federalism and Proposition 187*, 35 Va. J. Int'l L. 201 (1994); Gerald L. Neuman, *Aliens as Outlaws: Government Services, Proposition 187, and the Structure of Equal Protection Doctrine*, 42 UCLA L. Rev. 1425 (1995); Michael A. Olivas, *Preempting Preemption: Foreign Affairs, State Rights, and Alienage Classifications*, 35 Va. J. Int'l L. 217 (1994); Peter H. Schuck, *The Message of Proposition 187*, 26 PAC. L.J. 989 (1995); Frederick J. Boehmke, *The Initiative Process and the Dynamics of State Interest Group Populations*, 8 State Pol. & Pol'y Q. 362 (2008). Some of the fuller studies include, *e.g.*, Vanessa A. Baird, *Answering the Call of the Court: How Justices and Litigants Set the Supreme Court Agenda* 73–82 (Univ. Virginia Press 2007); Robin Dale Jacobson, *The New Nativism: Proposition 187 and the Debate Over Immigration* (Univ. Minnesota Press 2008).

164 *LULAC I*, 908 F. Supp. 755; *LULAC II*, 997 F. Supp. 1244. For a review of the residency issues leading up to this time, and the result of *LULAC, see* Libman, *Losing Out on a Dream?*, at E3 ("The [*Bradford*] decision will affect only about 100 UC students but about 14,000 at state community colleges, officials estimate"); Gordon, *Immigrants*, at A3 ("[The *Bradford*] decision could affect 800 of the 361,000 Cal State students."). At the time, California public college students totaled nearly 2 million, including more than 1.36 million in the community colleges. Sacramento: California Postsecondary Education Commission, *Student Profiles, 1994*, at table 1-5, www.cpec.ca.gov.

165 *Chiles v. United States*, 69 F.3d 1094 (11th Cir. 1995); *Padavan v. United States*, 82 F.3d 23 (2d Cir. 1966); *New Jersey v. United States*, 91 F.3d 463 (3d Cir. 1996); *Arizona v. United States*, 104 F.3d 1095 (9th Cir. 1997); *Texas v. United States*, 106 F.3d 661 (5th Cir. 1997).

166 *Id. Chiles*, 69 F.3d 1094; *Padavan*, 82 F.3d 23; *New Jersey*, 91 F.3d 463; *Arizona*, 104 F.3d 1095; *California v. United States*, 104 F.3d 1086 (9th Cir. 1997); *Texas*, 106 F.3d 661. Notwithstanding these cases, which all the states lost, it was a complex issue. For example, in 1993 Texas did not even spend all of its federal dollars allocated for immigrant program support and actually returned $90 million unspent to the government. *See* James Cullen, Editorial, *Blame the Newcomers*, Tex. Observer, Aug. 19, 1994, at 2–3.

167 For an authoritative review of the 1996 legislative histories and restrictionist efforts leading to the Personal Responsibility and Work Opportunity Reconciliation Act of 1996 and Illegal Immigration Reform and Immigrant Responsibility Act of 1996, written by an observer-participant, *see* Philip G. Schrag, *A Well-Founded*

Fear: The Congressional Battle to Save Political Asylum in America, 141–44, 178–82, 244–45 (Routledge 2000). While *Plyler* provided constitutional protection to the undocumented children from state laws, the case did not apply in similar fashion to congressional legislation. For other thoughtful studies of *Plyler* and the issues of federal preemption, *see generally* Peter H. Schuck, *The Transformation of Immigration Law*, 84 Colum. L. Rev. 1 (1984); Stephen H. Legomsky, *Fear and Loathing in Congress and the Courts: Immigration and Judicial Review*, 78 Tex. L. Rev. 1615 (2000); Gerald L. Neuman, *Jurisdiction and the Rule of Law After the 1996 Immigration Act*, 113 Harv. L. Rev. 1963 (2000).

168 Personal Responsibility and Work Opportunity Reconciliation Act of 1996 (PRWORA), Pub. L. No. 104-193, 110 Stat. 2105 (1996) (codified as amended in scattered sections of 2, 5, 7, 8, 10, 11, 13, 15, 20, 21, 25, 26, 28, 29, 31, 42 U.S.C.); Illegal Immigration Reform and Immigrant Responsibility Act of 1996 (IIRIRA), Pub. L. No. 104-208, 110 Stat. 3009 (1996) (codified as amended in scattered sections of 8, 18 U.S.C.).

169 8 U.S.C.A. § 1621 (West 2010); *see* 8 U.S.C.A. § 1623 (West 2010).

170 *League of United Latin Am. Citizens v. Wilson* (*LULAC II*), 997 F. Supp. 1244 (C.D. Cal. 1997) (finding the majority of Proposition 187 preempted by previously enacted federal legislation).

171 *LULAC II*, 997 F. Supp. at 1253.

172 Patrick J. McDonnell, *Davis Won't Appeal Prop. 187 Ruling, Ending Court Battles*, L.A. Times, July 29, 1999, at A1; Patrick J. McDonnell, *Prop. 187 Talks Offered Davis Few Choices*, L.A. Times, July 30, 1999, at A3.

173 Tex. Educ. Code Ann. § 54.052 (Vernon 2005). *See* Sara Hebel, *States Take Diverging Approaches on Tuition Rates for Illegal Immigrants*, Chron. Higher Educ., Nov. 30, 2001, at A22.

174 *See* Kevin R. Johnson, *September 11 and Mexican Immigrants: Collateral Damage Comes Home*, 52 DePaul L. Rev. 849, 852–65 (2003); Michael A. Olivas, *IIRIRA, the DREAM Act, and Undocumented College Student Residency*, 30 J.C. & U.L. 435, 457–63 (2004); Olivas, *What the "War on Terror" Has Meant*. For a study of the larger issue of terrorism, *see* Louis Fisher, *The Constitution and 9/11: Recurring Threats to America's Freedoms* (Univ. Press of Kansas 2008).

175 Table 3.1.

CHAPTER 2. 2001–2010 STATE DREAM ACTS AND LITIGATION

1 The Development, Relief, and Education for Alien Minors Act (DREAM Act) is known as such in the Senate. The DREAM Act of 2005, S. 2075, 109th Cong. (2005). In the House, the proposed legislation was known as the American Dream Act. The American Dream Act of 2006, H.R. 5131, 109th Cong. (2006). (See Table 3.1.)

2 A 2006 Migration Policy Institute (MPI) study estimated that approximately 50,000 undocumented college students were enrolled, either full time or part time, and would be eligible for permanent status under the DREAM Act. Jeanne

Batalova & Michael Fix, *New Estimates of Unauthorized Youth Eligible for Legal Status Under the DREAM Act*, Oct. 2006, www.migrationpolicy.org (accessed from homepage by searching keywords "backgrounder DREAM Act"). These data do not include persons who might be eligible for the act's military options for legalization. For additional data, *see also* Elizabeth Redden, *Data on the Undocumented*, Inside Higher Ed, Mar. 17, 2009, www.insidehighered.com; Jeffrey S. Passel & D'Vera Cohn, Pew Hispanic Center, *A Portrait of Unauthorized Immigrants in the United States* iv (2009), http://pewhispanic.org. ("[A]mong unauthorized immigrants ages 18 to 24 who have graduated from high school, half (49%) are in college or have attended college. The comparable figure for U.S.-born residents is 71%."); Dawn Konet, Migration Policy Institute, *Unauthorized Youths and Higher Education: The Ongoing Debate*, Sept. 2007, www.migrationinformation.org; Raphael Lewis, *In-State Tuition Not a Draw for Many Immigrants*, Bos. Globe, Nov. 9, 2005, at A1.

3 *See* Michael A. Olivas, *Immigration-Related State and Local Ordinances: Preemption, Prejudice, and the Proper Role for Enforcement*, U. Chi. Legal F. 27 (2007); Steven G. Calabresi & Lena M. Barsky, *An Originalist Defense of* Plyler v. Doe, BYU L. Rev. 225–329 (2017); Emily R. Crawford, *The Ethic of Community and Incorporating Undocumented Immigrant Concerns into Ethical School Leadership*, 53 Educ. Admin. Q. 147 (2017).

4 *Plyler v. Doe*, 457 U.S. 202, 230 (1982). *See* Michael A. Olivas, Plyler v. Doe: *The Education of Undocumented Children, and the Polity*, in *Immigration Stories* 197 (David Martin & Peter Schuck eds., 2005); *see also* María Pabón López, *Reflections on Educating Latino and Latina Undocumented Children: Beyond* Plyler v. Doe, 35 Seton Hall L. Rev. 1373 (2005); Jaclyn Brickman, Note, *Educating Undocumented Children in the United States: Codification of* Plyler v. Doe *Through Federal Legislation*, 20 Geo. Immigr. L.J. 385 (2006). Historically, Texas is widely considered to have been the most restrictive and nativist toward its Mexican-origin population. *See, e.g.*, Cynthia E. Orozco, *No Mexicans, Women, or Dogs Allowed: The Rise of the Mexican American Civil Rights Movement* (Univ. Texas Press 2009).

5 *See generally* Batalova & Fix, *New Estimates*.

6 In a series of articles, I have tracked these developments through various legislative fits and starts. *See generally* Michael A. Olivas, *Storytelling Out of School: Undocumented College Residency, Race, and Reaction*, 22 Hast. Const. L.Q. 1019 (1995); Michael A. Olivas, *IIRIRA, the DREAM Act, and Undocumented College Student Residency*, 30 J.C. & U.L. 435 (2004); Michael A. Olivas, *Lawmakers Gone Wild? College Residency and the Response to Professor Kobach*, 61 SMU L. Rev. 99 (2008); Michael A. Olivas, *Undocumented College Students, Taxation, and Financial Aid: A Technical Note*, 32 Rev. Higher Educ. 407 (2009); Michael A. Olivas, *The Political Economy of the DREAM Act and the Legislative Process: A Case Study of Comprehensive Immigration Reform*, 55 Wayne L. Rev. 1757 (2009); Michael A. Olivas, Plyler's *Political Efficacy*, 45 UC-D. L. Rev. 1 (2011); Michael A. Olivas & Kristi L. Bowman, Plyler's *Legacy: Immigration and Higher Education in the 21st*

Century, 2011 Mich. St. L. Rev. 261 (2011); Michael A. Olivas, *Dreams Deferred: Deferred Action, Prosecutorial Discretion, and the Vexing Case(s) of DREAM Act Students*, 21 Wm. & Mary Bill Rts J. 463 (2012). See also Stella M. Flores, *State Dream Acts: The Effect of In-State Resident Tuition Policies and Undocumented Latino Students*, 33 Rev. High. Educ. 239, 239 (2009) (*"Plyer v. Doe* . . . addressed only the educational and secondary schools . . . and did not address state or federal actions regarding the postsecondary opportunities of undocumented students.").

7   Michael A. Olivas, *The Political Economy of Immigration, Intellectual Property, and Racial Harassment: Case Studies of the Implementation of Legal Change on Campus*, 63 J. Higher Educ. 570, 573–77 (1992); Victor C. Romero, *Postsecondary School Education Benefits for Undocumented Immigrants: Promises and Pitfalls*, 27 N.C. J. Int'l L. & Com. Reg. 393 (2002); Victor C. Romero, *Noncitizen Students and Immigration Policy Post-9/11*, 17 Geo. Immigr. L.J. 357 (2003); Neeraj Kaushal, *In-State Tuition for the Undocumented: Education Effects on Mexican Young Adults*, 27 J. Pol'y Analysis & Mgmt. 771 (2008). *See generally* Karen Engle, *The Political Economy of State and Local Immigration Regulation: Comments on Olivas and Hollifield, Hunt & Tichenor*, 61 SMU L. Rev. 159 (2008); Edward D. Vargas, *In-State Tuition Policies for Undocumented Youth*, 23 Harv. J. Hisp. Pol. 43 (2010–11); Theresa Lyon Little & Donald Mitchell Jr., *A Qualitative Analysis of Undocumented Latino College Students' Movement Towards Developing Purpose*, 42 Rev. High. Educ., 137 (2018).

8   Batalova & Fix, *New Estimates*.

9   *See League of United Latin Am. Citizens v. Wilson (LULAC II)*, 997 F. Supp. 1244, 1261 (C.D. Cal. 1997) (striking down virtually all of Proposition 187). *See generally* Kevin R. Johnson, *An Essay on Immigration Politics, Popular Democracy, and California's Proposition 187: The Political Relevance and Legal Irrelevance of Race*, 70 Wash. L. Rev. 629, 634 (1995); Ruben J. Garcia, Comment, *Critical Race Theory and Proposition 187: The Racial Politics of Immigration Law*, 17 Chicano-Latino L. Rev. 118, 120–22 (1995).

10 The full text of Proposition 187 appears in *League of United Latin Am. Citizens v. Wilson (LULAC II)*, 908 F. Supp. 755, 787–91 (C.D. Cal. 1995). There is extensive literature on the events leading to, and following from, this ballot initiative. *See generally* Evangeline G. Abriel, *Rethinking Preemption for Purposes of Aliens and Public Benefits*, 42 UCLA L. Rev. 1597 (1995); Linda S. Bosniak, *Opposing Prop. 187: Undocumented Immigrants and the National Imagination*, 28 Conn. L. Rev. 555 (1996); Richard A. Boswell, *Restrictions on Non-Citizens' Access to Public Benefits: Flawed Premise, Unnecessary Response*, 42 UCLA L. Rev. 1475 (1995); Lolita K. Buckner Inniss, *California's Proposition 187—Does It Mean What It Says? Does It Say What It Means? A Textual and Constitutional Analysis*, 10 Geo. Immigr. L.J. 577 (1996); Kevin R. Johnson, *Public Benefits and Immigration: The Intersection of Immigration Status, Ethnicity, Gender, and Class*, 42 UCLA L. Rev. 1509 (1995); Stephen H. Legomsky, *Immigration, Federalism, and the Welfare State*, 42 UCLA L. Rev. 1453 (1995); Hiroshi Motomura, *Immigration and Alienage,*

Federalism and Proposition 187, 35 Va. J. Int'l L. 201 (1994); Gerald L. Neuman, *Aliens as Outlaws: Government Services, Proposition 187, and the Structure of Equal Protection Doctrine*, 42 UCLA L. Rev. 1425 (1995); Michael A. Olivas, *Preempting Preemption: Foreign Affairs, State Rights, and Alienage Classifications*, 35 Va. J. Int'l L. 217 (1994); Peter L. Reich, *Environmental Metaphor in the Alien Benefits Debate*, 42 UCLA L. Rev. 1577 (1995); Peter H. Schuck, *The Message of Proposition 187*, 26 PAC. L.J. 989 (1995). Some of the fuller studies include, *e.g.*, Vanessa A. Baird, *Answering the Call of the Court: How Justices and Litigants Set the Supreme Court Agenda* 73–82 (Univ. Virginia Press 2007); Robin Dale Jacobson, *The New Nativism: Proposition 187 and the Debate over Immigration* (Univ. Minnesota Press 2008); Frederick J. Boehmke, *The Initiative Process and the Dynamics of State Interest Group Populations*, 8 State Pol. & Pol'y Q. 362 (2008).

11 *LULAC I*, 908 F. Supp. 755; *LULAC II*, 997 F. Supp. 1244. For a review of the residency issues leading up to this time and the result of *LULAC*, *see* Olivas, *Storytelling Out of School*; Gary Libman, *Losing Out on a Dream? Education: Tuition Changes Cloud Future for Illegal Immigrants Who Had Hopes of Attending UC Schools, Other State Colleges*, L.A. Times, Jan. 23, 1992, at E3 ("The [*Bradford*] decision will affect only about 100 UC students but about 14,000 at state community colleges, officials estimate."); Larry Gordon, *Immigrants Face Cal State Fee Hike*, L.A. Times, Sept. 9, 1992, at A3 ("[The Bradford] decision could affect 800 of the 361,000 Cal State students."). At the time, California public college students totaled nearly 2 million, including over 1.36 million in the community colleges. Sacramento: California Postsecondary Education Commission, *Student Profiles, 1994*, at table 1-5.

12 *Chiles v. United States*, 69 F.3d 1094 (11th Cir. 1995); *Padavan v. United States*, 82 F.3d 23 (2d Cir. 1966); *New Jersey v. United States*, 91 F.3d 463 (3d Cir. 1996); *Arizona v. United States*, 104 F.3d 1095 (9th Cir. 1997); *Texas v. United States*, 106 F.3d 661 (5th Cir. 1997).

13 *Chiles*, 69 F.3d 1094; *Padavan*, 82 F.3d 23; *New Jersey*, 91 F.3d 463; *Arizona*, 104 F.3d 1095; *California v. United States*, 104 F.3d 1086 (9th Cir. 1997); *Texas*, 106 F.3d 661. Notwithstanding these cases, which all the states lost, it was a complex issue. For example, in 1993, Texas did not even spend all of its federal dollars allocated for immigrant program support and returned $90 million unspent to the government. *See* James Cullen, Editorial, *Blame the Newcomers*, Tex. Observer, Aug. 19, 1994, at 2–3.

14 Olivas, *Plyler v. Doe:The Education of Undocumented Children, and the Polity*, at 212–13. For an authoritative review of the 1996 legislative histories and restrictionist efforts leading to the Personal Responsibility and Work Opportunity Reconciliation Act of 1996 and Illegal Immigration Reform and Immigrant Responsibility Act of 1996, written by an observer-participant, *see* Philip G. Schrag, *A Well-Founded Fear: The Congressional Battle to Save Political Asylum in America* 141–44, 178–82, 244–45 (Routledge 2000). While *Plyler* provided constitutional protection to the undocumented children from state laws, the case did not apply

in similar fashion to congressional legislation. For other thoughtful studies of *Plyler* and the issues of federal preemption, *see generally* Peter H. Schuck, *The Transformation of Immigration Law*, 84 Colum. L. Rev. 1 (1984); Stephen H. Legomsky, *Fear and Loathing in Congress and the Courts: Immigration and Judicial Review*, 78 Tex. L. Rev. 1615 (2000); Gerald L. Neuman, *Jurisdiction and the Rule of Law After the 1996 Immigration Act*, 113 Harv. L. Rev. 1963 (2000).

15 Personal Responsibility and Work Opportunity Reconciliation Act of 1996 (PRWORA), Pub. L. No. 104-193, 110 Stat. 2105 (1996) (codified as amended in scattered sections of 2, 5, 7, 8, 10, 11, 13, 15, 20, 21, 25, 26, 28, 29, 31, 42 U.S.C.); Illegal Immigration Reform and Immigrant Responsibility Act of 1996 (IIRIRA), Pub. L. No. 104-208, 110 Stat. 3009 (1996) (codified as amended in scattered sections of 8, 18 U.S.C.).

16 8 U.S.C.A. § 1621 (West 2010); *see* 8 U.S.C.A. § 1623 (West 2010).

17 *League of United Latin Am. Citizens v. Wilson (LULAC II)*, 997 F. Supp. 1244 (C.D. Cal. 1997) (finding the majority of Proposition 187 preempted by previously enacted federal legislation).

18 *LULAC II*, 997 F. Supp. at 1253.

19 Patrick J. McDonnell, *Davis Won't Appeal Prop. 187 Ruling, Ending Court Battles*, L.A. Times, July 29, 1999, at A1; Patrick J. McDonnell, *Prop. 187 Talks Offered Davis Few Choices*, L.A. Times, July 30, 1999, at A3.

20 Tex. Educ. Code Ann. § 54.052 (Vernon 2005). *See* Sara Hebel, *States Take Diverging Approaches on Tuition Rates for Illegal Immigrants*, Chron. Higher Educ., Nov. 30, 2001, at A22. *See also* Andrew Guy, *Big Man on Campus: Law Professor Fights for Issues Dear to His Heart*, Hous. Chron., June 4, 2001, at A1.

21 *See* Kevin R. Johnson, *September 11 and Mexican Immigrants: Collateral Damage Comes Home*, 52 DePaul L. Rev. 849, 852–65 (2003); Olivas, *IIRIRA*, at 457–63; Michael A. Olivas, *What the "War on Terror" Has Meant for U.S. Colleges and Universities, in Doctoral Education and the Faculty of the Future* 249–58 (Ronald G. Ehrenberg & Charlotte V. Kuh eds., Cornell Univ. Press 2009). For a study of the larger issue of terrorism, *see* Louis Fisher, *The Constitution and 9/11: Recurring Threats to America's Freedoms* (Univ. Press of Kansas 2008).

22 *See, e.g.*, Table 3.1.

23 *See* Olivas, *IIRIRA*, at 456.

24 *Id. See Strong Illegal Immigration Bill Biggest Legislative Achievement*, Post & Courier (Charleston, S.C.), June 7, 2008, at A10.

25 S.C. Code Ann. § 59-103-5 (West 2009); South Carolina General Assembly, 117th Session (2007–8), www.law.uh.edu (detailing the state's regulatory interpretation of the law).

26 *See, e.g.*, J. Austin Smithson, Comment, *Educate then Exile: Creating a Double Standard for Plyler Student Who Wants to Sit for the Bar Exam*, 11 Scholar 87 (2008). *See generally* Chapter 6 in this volume.

27 *Id.*; Susan Carroll, *Immigrant Spends Life Looking Over Her Shoulder*, Hous. Chron., Nov. 28, 2009, at B1 (describing an undocumented schoolteacher who

fears deportation after spending most of her life in the United States). This is also an issue with immigrants throughout the regime of legal immigration. *See, e.g.,* Jeanne Batalova & B. Lindsay Lowell, *Immigrant Professionals in the United States,* 44 Soc'y 26 (2007).

28 Batalova & Fix, *New Estimates.* The total college enrollment in the United States in 2007 was over 18 million students. U.S. Dep't of Educ., Nat'l Ctr. for Educ. Statistics, Digest of Educ. Statistics (2008), http://nces.ed.gov. *See The Ohio State University,* www.osu.edu.

29 *See* Table 3.1.

30 *Letter from Daniel J. Popeo, Chairman and General Counsel, Washington Legal Foundation & Richard A. Samp, Chief Counsel, Washington Legal Foundation, to Daniel Sutherland, Officer for Civil Rights and Civil Liberties, Dep't of Homeland Sec.,* Aug. 9, 2005, www.wlf.org.

31 Jody Feder, Congressional Research Service, *Unauthorized Alien Students, Higher Education, and In-State Tuition Rates: A Legal Analysis* 6 (2008), www.digitalcommons.ilr.cornell.edu.

32 *Letter from Jim Pendergraph, Executive Director, Office of State and Local Coordination, U.S. Immigration & Customs Enforcement, to Thomas J. Ziko, Special Deputy Attorney General,* N.C. Dep't of Justice, July 9, 2008, cited in K. M. Manuel, *Unlawfully Present Aliens, Higher Education, In-State Tuition, and Financial Aid: Legal Analysis* (Washington, D.C.: Congressional Research Service 2014), at 17.

33 *Id.* at footnote 115.

34 *Martinez v. Regents of the University of California,* 50 Cal. 4th 1277 (2010).

35 *Day v. Sebelius,* 376 F. Supp. 2d 1022, 1039–40 (D. Kan. 2005) (denying standing to challengers and upholding residency requirement allowing undocumented aliens to establish residency). *See also* Gary Reich & Alvar Ayala Mendoza, *"Educating Kids" Versus "Coddling Criminals": Framing the Debate over In-State Tuition for Undocumented Students in Kansas,* 8 St. Pol. & Policy Q. 177 (2008).

36 *Day,* 376 F. Supp. 2d 1022. There was also an unsuccessful attempt in 2006 to repeal the statute. Chris Moon, *Immigrant Tuition Vote Typifies Fragile Statehouse Ties,* Topeka Capital-Journal, Feb. 17, 2006, at A1.

37 *Day v. Bond,* 500 F.3d 1127, 1136–40 (10th Cir. 2007). Because the trial judge removed the governor as a defendant, the case at the Tenth Circuit was styled as *Day v. Bond.*

38 *Day v. Bond,* 500 F.3d 1127 (10th Cir. 2007), *cert. denied,* 128 S. Ct. 2987 (2008).

39 Cal. Educ. Code § 68130.5 (West 2002). The California Assembly bill became California Education Code Section 68130.5. *See* Ralph W. Kasarda, *Affirmative Action Gone Haywire: Why States Granting College Tuition Preferences to Illegal Aliens are Preempted by Federalism,* 2009 BYU Educ. & L.J. 197, 210 (2009).

40 *Martinez v. Regents of Univ. of Cal.,* No. CV 05-2064, 2006 WL 2974303 (Cal. App. Dep't Super Ct. 2006) (orders on demurrers, motion to strike, and motions by proposed interveners).

41 Cal. App. Dep't. Super. Ct. 2006 (dismissing challenge to state residency statute), *rev'd*, 83 Cal. Rptr. 3d 518 (Cal. App. 3d 2008), *superseded by* 198 P.3d 1 (Cal. 2008) (granting respondents' petition for review); *see* Kristen Miller & Celina Moreno, Martinez v. Regents: *Mis-Step or Wave of the Future*, www.law.uh.edu.

42 *Martinez*, 198 P.3d 1.

43 *Id.* ("[p]etition for review filed by respondents . . . is granted").

44 *Id.*

45 Cal. Educ. Code § 68040 (West 2010).

46 *Student Advocates for Higher Educ. v. Trustees, Cal. State Univ.*, No. CPF-06-506755 (Cal. App. Dep't Super Ct. Feb. 26, 2007). The state agreed to discontinue the practice and entered into a consent decree, so the matter was resolved in favor of the plaintiffs. *See* Cal. Educ. Code § 68040 (West 2010); Cal. Code Regs. tit. V, § 41904 (2010). The above-mentioned case challenged Cal. Educ. Code § 68040, Cal. Code Regs. tit. V, § 41904, and the state constitution. Full disclosure: then and now, I was a member of the Board of the Mexican American Legal Defense and Educational Fund (which was a party to this challenge) and participated in the litigation and settlement discussions at the board level.

47 There is a growing technical and policy literature on the issue of the taxation and financial services for undocumented persons, including college students. *See, e.g.*, Paula N. Singer & Linda Dodd-Major, *Identification Numbers and U.S. Government Compliance Initiatives*, 104 Tax Notes 1429 (2004); Staff of Joint Comm'n on Taxation, Present Law and Background Relating to Individual Taxpayer Identification Numbers (ITINs) 3 (2004) ("[T]he [Internal Revenue Code] does not contain special rules regarding the treatment of illegal aliens, or the tax identification number requirements with respect to illegal aliens."); Francine J. Lipman, *The Taxation of Undocumented Immigrants: Separate, Unequal, and Without Representation*, 9 Harv. Lat. L. Rev. 1 (2006); Cynthia Blum, *Rethinking Tax Compliance of Unauthorized Workers After Immigration Reform*, 21 Geo. Immigr. L.J. 595 (2007); John Coyle, *The Legality of Banking the Undocumented*, 22 Geo. Immigr. L.J. 21 (2007); Michael A. Olivas, *Undocumented College Students, Taxation, and Financial Aid: A Technical Note*, 32 Rev. Higher Educ. 407 (2009). A detailed 2009 US Government Accountability Office study noted the complexity of the federal process but did not address the related immigration issues. Gov't Accountability Office, *Fed. Student Aid: Highlights of a Study Group on Simplifying the Free Application for Fed. Student Aid* (2009), www.gao.gov.

48 Student Advocates for Higher Educ., No. CPF-06–506755.

49 *Id.*

50 Op. Colo. Att'y Gen. No. 07-03 (2007); Allison Sherry, *Tuition Tussle Takes Shape*, Denv. Post, Aug. 15, 2007, at A1, www.denverpost.com. *Also see Memorandum from Ronald C. Forehand, Senior Assistant Att'y General, Chief, Education Section to Lee Andes, State Council of Higher Educ. for Va.*, Mar. 6, 2008. In Virginia, citizen applicants of undocumented parents were the subject of an attorney general memo; the memo advised its client colleges to deal with these students on a case-

by-case basis for residency tuition purposes. *See also* Susan Kinzie, *The University of Uncertainty: Va. Children of Illegal Immigrants Lack In-State Status*, Wash. Post, Mar. 14, 2008, at B1; Susan Kinzie, *U-VA Accepts Residency Claim*, Wash. Post, Mar. 24, 2008, at B5. *See generally* Sherry, *Tuition Tussle Takes Shape*, at A1.

51 *A.Z. ex rel. B.Z. v. Higher Educ. Student Assistance Auth.*, 48 A.3d 1151 (N.J. Super. Ct. App. Div. 2012) (N.J. financial aid case concerning USC children and undocumented parents); consolidated with *Cortes v. Higher Educ. Student Assistance Auth.*, No. A-2142-11-T1 (N.J. Super. Ct. App. Div. 2012).

52 *Ruiz v. Robinson*, 892 F. Supp. 2d 1321 (S.D. Fla. 2012) (Fla. resident tuition case concerning USC children and undocumented parents).

53 Tex. Educ. Code Ann. § 54.053 (Vernon 2009) (enacted by S.B. 1528). The full text of S.B. 1528 is www.statutes.legis.state.tx.us. *See also* Juan Castillo, *After Delay, Bill Challenging In-State Tuition Law All but Dead*, Austin Am.-Statesman, May 10, 2007, at B1. In 2001, Gov. Rick Perry had signed the original legislation that established H.B. 1403: www.uh.edu. *See* Tex. Educ. Code §54.053 (Vernon 2005) (enacted by S.B. 1528).

54 *Id.* Susan Carroll, *Texas Lawmaker Challenges In-State Tuition Law*, Hous. Chron., Oct. 30, 2008, at B1; *Texas Attorney General Considers Payment of In-State Tuition by Undocumented Immigrants*, 86 Inter. Releases 2029 (2009); Melissa B. Taboada, *Should Illegal Immigrants Receive In-State Tuition?*, Austin Am.-Statesman, July 25, 2009, at B1. *See* Op. Tex. Att'y Gen. No. GA-0732 (2009), www2.texasattorney-general.gov.

55 H.B. 1403 was signed into law by Gov. Rick Perry, the Republican who succeeded Gov. George W. Bush's term and was then elected to his own terms. Clay Robison, *Budget Hits Include Judges' Pay Hike*, Hous. Chron., June 18, 2001, at 1A (describing the 2001 legislative session review of tuition revenue and the expected economic impact of the statute). In January 2007, Gov. Perry (then reelected to his second full term) indicated that he would not support any bills that overturned this legislation, including the revised version, S.B. 1528. Matthew Tresaugue & R. G. Radcliffe, *The Legislature: Illegal Immigrants May See Tuition Hike*, Hous. Chron., Jan. 11, 2007, at B1; Clay Robison & R. G. Ratcliffe, *Perry to Stick by Law Giving Tuition Breaks to Illegal Immigrants*, Hous. Chron., Jan. 12, 2007, at B4.

56 Op. Tex. Att'y Gen. No. GA-0347 (2005); Op. Tex. Att'y Gen. No. GA-0445 (2006). *See* Rosanna Ruiz, *Veterans Fight for Tuition Money from State*, Hous. Chron., June 30, 2007, at B7; Associated Press, *Immigrant Veterans Sue for Waivers on Tuition*, Hous. Chron., June 29, 2007, at B4. Ironically, Texas took a right turn after Gov. Perry left office, while California has clearly renounced its earlier bellwether nativist policies. *See* Tory Johnson, *The State Immigration Laws You Should Know About*, Immigration Impact, Jan. 24, 2018, http://immigrationimpact.com/2018/01/24/state-lawmakers-more-immigration-laws (reviewing legislation introduced or enacted, across categories); Todd Hutchinson, *Texas AG Hits San Antonio with Anti-Sanctuary Cities Lawsuit*, Law360.com, Nov. 30, 2018, www.law360.com (reviews lawsuits involving state "sanctuary city" and "sanctuary campus" laws).

57 In 2008, following the suit filed by MALDEF, *Dominguez v. State of Texas*, Attorney General Greg Abbott reversed his position. Dominguez case materials, 2008, http://maldef.org. *See* Hernan Rozemberg, *Texas Vets Get Tuition Back*, San Antonio Express-News, Jan. 16, 2008, at 1B; Lisa Falkenberg, *This Just In: AG Finds the Constitution*, Hous. Chron., Jan. 16, 2008, at B1. *See also* Matthew B. Allen, Comment, *The Unconstitutional Denial of a Texas Veterans Benefit*, 46 Hous. L. Rev. 1607 (2010).

58 N.M. Stat. § 21-1-1.2 (West 2009). I consulted with the state senator introducing this bill and the legislative counsel involved in drafting the statute. I also testified before the senate committee holding hearings on the legislation and was involved in discussions with the governor who signed it into law and his staff. *See* Press Release, Governor Bill Richardson, *Gov. Richardson Signs Bill Prohibiting Discrimination in Admission and Tuition Policy of New Mexico Post Secondary Educational Institutions Based on Student's Immigration Status* (Apr. 8, 2005), www.governor. state.nm.us.

59 Validity of Tuition Statute, Utah Code Ann. § 53B-8-106 (2006). *See* Deborah Bulkeley, *A Law Granting In-State Tuition to Undocumented Students Is Legally Sound*, Deseret News, Feb. 2, 2006, at A1; Deborah Bulkeley, *Measure to Repeal Tuition Break for Illegals Is Back*, Deseret Morning News, Feb. 9, 2007, at B4.

60 Utah Code Ann. § 53B-8-106 (West 2009) (remained unaffected by 2008 restrictionist law, S.B. 81); S.B. 110th Utah Cong. (2008), http://le.utah.gov. *See* Deborah Bulkeley, *Efforts to Repeal Immigrant Tuition Law Hit Speed Bump*, Deseret Morning News, Feb. 7, 2008, at A1; Bulkeley, *Measure to Repeal Tuition Break*; Deborah Bulkeley & Lisa Riley Roche, *Immigrant Tuition Repeal Removed from Bill*, Deseret Morning News, Feb. 13, 2008, at B7.

61 In 2007, Sen. Orrin Hatch was then the cosponsor of the DREAM Act. It is likely that his not being a cosponsor of the 2005 version was due in part to having a primary opponent for reelection. He was reelected to the Senate by a wide margin in 2006, but the FAIR website continued to label the DREAM Act as his bill and characterized it (in 2007) as "a giveaway to illegal aliens." For votes and statements of Sen. Orrin Hatch (R-Utah), *see* www.hatch.senate.gov; *see also* Press Release, Federation for American Immigration Reform, *The "DREAM Act": Hatch-ing Expensive New Amnesty for Illegal Aliens*, Oct. 23, 2003, www.fairus.org; Olivas, *Storytelling Out of School*, at 456–57 (in this 2004 article, I had wrongly assumed that Sen. Hatch's cosponsorship would likely hasten passage; like Rick in the movie *Casablanca*, "I was misinformed").

62 Yvonne Abraham, *Immigrant Tuition Bill Defeated*, Bos. Globe, Jan. 12, 2006, at A1; Emelie Rutherford, *House Scraps Tuition Deal for Illegal Immigrants' Kids*, Bos. Herald, Jan. 12, 2006, at A15.

63 Matt Viser & Maria Sacchetti, *Patrick Mulls New Tack on Immigrant Tuition: May Try to Bypass Wary Legislature*, Bos. Globe, Jan. 11, 2008, at B1; Elyse Ashburn, *Massachusetts Plan for Free Community Colleges Meets with Skepticism*, Chron. Higher Educ., June 15, 2007, at A22.

64 Maria Sacchetti, *Tuition Aid to Illegal Immigrants Falters: Patrick Declines to Act on Behalf of Graduates*, Bos. Globe, May 22, 2008, at B1.

65 H.F. 1083, 85th Leg. Sess. (Minn. 2007), www.revisor.mn.gov (accessed from homepage by entering legislation title in search).

66 Jean Hopfensperger, *Immigration Proposals Clash: The Governor and DFL Law-makers Offered Differing Views on Issues Involving the State's Immigrants*, Star Tribune (Minneapolis), Feb. 15, 2007, at 5B (reviewing DREAM Act legislative proposals in Minnesota). For the text, *see* H.F. 1083, 85th Leg. Sess. (2007). The bill analysis can be found at www.leg.state.mn.us. In 2014, S.F. 1236, 88th Leg., 2013 Minn. Laws 75; Minn. Stat. § 135A.043 (2014) was enacted.

67 H.F. 1083, 85th Leg. Sess. (Minn. 2007), www.revisor.mn.gov. For a good story on the overall legislation (but, to my point, one that does not specifically mention this issue), *see* Megan Boldt, *2008-09 Minnesota Budget—Reluctant Governor OKs School Spending: Bill Adds $794 M over 2 Years, Restores Aid for Special Education*, St. Paul Pioneer Press, May 31, 2007, at B1.

68 S.F. 1989, 85th Leg. Sess. (Minn. 2007) (providing details on the bill actually passed).

69 Alejandra Rincon, *Undocumented Immigrants and Higher Education: Si Se Puede!* 65–74 (LFB Scholarly Pub. 2008).

70 *Id.* (reviewing city community college policies before the 2001 Texas statute, H.B. 1403). *See generally* Vicky J. Salinas, Comment, *You Can Be Whatever You Want to Be When You Grow Up, Unless Your Parents Brought You to This Country Illegally: The Struggle to Grant In-State Tuition to Undocumented Immigrant Students*, 43 Hous. L. Rev. 847 (2006).

71 Rincon, *Undocumented Immigrants*, at 65–74.

72 Many, if not most, states reported at this time to have flat or declining appropria-tions to their two-year colleges and substantially increased enrollments. *See, e.g.,* Jennifer Gonzalez, *State Directors of Community Colleges See Bleak Financial Times Ahead*, Chron. Higher Educ., Sept. 24, 2009, at A20. A community college in Boston became so overcrowded it started midnight classes for students who are workers on the swing shift. *Id.*; Abby Goodnough, *New Meaning for Night Class at 2-Year Colleges*, N.Y. Times, Oct. 27, 2009, at A1; Lisa W. Foderaro, *Two-Year Col-leges, Swamped, No Longer Welcome All*, N.Y. Times, Nov. 11, 2009, at A17. For an analysis of state higher education funding and its decline, *see* Michael K. McLen-don, James C. Hearn & Christine G. Mokher, *Partisans, Professionals, and Power: The Role of Political Factors in State Higher Education Funding*, 80 J. Higher Educ. 686 (2009) (documenting pattern declines in funding). More recently, enroll-ments in two-year colleges have declined. *See* Ashley A. Smith, *No Bottom Yet in 2-Year College Enrollments*, Inside Higher Ed, June 21, 2018, www.insidehighered. com.

73 Colo. Att'y Gen. Op. No. 06-01/HE-HE-AGBBT (2006).

74 Colo. Att'y Gen. Op. No. 07-03/HE-HE-AGBCF (2007), www.coag.gov (accessed from homepage by entering document title in search).

75 *Id.* at 2; *see* Sherry, *Tuition Tussle Takes Shape*, at A1. Several years later, the state enacted resident tuition and financial aid for the undocumented who met certain criteria: Colorado, S.B. 13-033, 69th Gen. Assemb., 1st Reg. Sess. (Co. 2013); amending Colo. Rev. Stat. § 23-7-110 and Colo. Rev. Stat. § 24-76.5-103.

76 Taylour Nelson, *PSD Says Program That Helps Undocumented Students Is Legal*, Fort Collins Coloradan, Aug. 16, 2007, at 1A. *See, e.g.*, Perry Swanson, *Suthers: Kids of Illegal Immigrants Can Be Eligible for In-State Tuition*, Colo. Springs Gaz., Aug. 15, 2007, at A1.

77 L.B. 239, 99th Leg., 2d Sess. (Neb. 2005), www.nebraskalegislature.gov (accessed from homepage by selecting "search past legislation," then selecting "99th legislature" and entering keyword "LB239") *See also* Martha Stoddard, *Legislators Split on Immigrant Tuition*, Omaha World-Herald, Dec. 29, 2005, at A1; Ruth Marcus, *Immigration's Scrambled Politics*, Wash. Post, Apr. 4, 2006, at A23. In 2010, Kris Kobach filed suit in Nebraska state court to overturn the legislation (*Mannschreck v. Univ. of Nebraska*), and a bill (L.B. 1001, 2010) was introduced to repeal the statute. *See* Margery A. Beck, *Kris Kobach, Kansas Secretary of State Candidate, Sues Nebraska over Immigrant Tuition Law*, Kans. City Star, Jan. 26, 2010; Barb Shelly, *Kris Kobach's War on Undocumented College Students*, Kans. City Star, Jan. 26, 2010. I served as an expert witness to the state of Nebraska in this case.

78 *Fight for Rights: Tens of Thousands March for Immigration Reform*, Chi. Tribune, Mar. 13, 2006, at 8.

79 *See* James Sterngold, *500,000 Throng L.A. to Protest Immigrant Legislation*, S.F. Chron., Mar. 26, 2006, at A1. *See also* Walter J. Nicholls, *The DREAMers: How the Undocumented Youth Movement Transformed the Immigrant Rights Debate* (Stanford Univ. Press 2013); Sasha Costanza-Chock, *Out of the Shadows, Into the Streets! Transmedia Organizing and the Immigrant Rights Movement* (MIT Press 2014); Maria Chavez, Jessica L. Lavariega Monforti & Melissa R. Michelson, *Living the Dream: New Immigration Policies and the Lives of Undocumented Latino Youth* (Paradigm Pub. 2015); Liana Gamber-Thompson & Arely M. Zimmerman, *DREAMing Citizenship: Undocumented Youth, Coming Out, and Pathways to Participation*, in *By Any Media Necessary: The New Youth Activism* 186–218 (Henry Jenkins, Sangita Shresthova, Liana Gamber-Thompson, Neta Kligler-Vilenchik & Arely M. Zimmerman eds., New York University Press 2016).

80 *See Fight for Rights*, Chi. Tribune, Mar. 13, 2006, at 8. *See generally* Bill Ong Hing & Kevin R. Johnson, *The Immigrant Rights Marches of 2006 and the Prospects for a New Civil Rights Movement*, 42 Harv. C.R.–C.L. L. Rev. 99 (2007); Sylvia R. Lazos Vargas, *The Immigrant Rights Marches (Las Marchas): Did the "Gigante" (Giant) Wake Up or Does It Still Sleep Tonight?* 7 Nev. L.J. 780 (2007); Raquel E. Aldana, *Silent Victims No More? Moral Indignation and the Potential for Latino Political Mobilization in Defense of Immigrants*, 45 Hous. L. Rev. 73, 92–97 (2008).

81 S.B. 160, Leg. Sess. (Cal. 2005–06).

82 *See* http://gov.ca.gov; *see also* Scott Jaschik, *Post-DREAM Strategies*, InsideHigh-
    erEd.com, Oct. 29, 2007. *See* Carla Rivera, *Budget Cuts Hit Broad Swath of Cal
    State*, L.A. Times, Nov. 29, 2009, at A1.

83 During the same time as the discussions about undocumented Virginians and
    citizen children with undocumented parents were occurring, the Virginia legisla-
    ture established in-state tuition eligibility for those holding an immigration visa
    or those classified as political refugees in the same manner as any other resident
    student. Under these new provisions, students with temporary or student visa
    status were ineligible for Virginia resident status and thus were also ineligible for
    in-state tuition. Va. Code Ann. § 23-7.4 (West 2009).

84 *See* Ben Neary, *Governor Signs Key Bills*, Casper Star-Tribune, Mar. 11, 2006.

85 *See, e.g.*, Stephen Majors, *Immigrant Tuition Bill Fails Again*, Bradenton Herald,
    Apr. 21, 2006, at A1. Florida and Arizona were the only states among the major
    receiver states that have never accorded residency tuition status to the undocu-
    mented. The states' Section 529 plans are also open only to US citizens or "resi-
    dent aliens" as purchasers or as beneficiaries; *see* www.myfloridaprepaid.com. *See
    also* Dana Boone, *Her College Dream Is Slipping Away*, Des Moines Reg., Apr. 11,
    2006, at 1A; Jennifer Jacobs, *Iowans Learn to Deal with Immigration*, Des Moines
    Reg., Dec. 7, 2006, at 1A. *See also* Stoddard, *Legislators Split*, at A1. Florida eventu-
    ally came around and even gave DACAmented residents the right to practice law.
    See Chapter 6 in this volume.

86 Oklahoma Taxpayer and Citizen Protection Act of 2007 (H.B. 1804). (See Appen-
    dix 2.) In January 2008, the state's board of regents issued a memo and regulations
    outlining the new policies. *See* Valerie Jobe, *Immigration Reform Would Affect
    OCCC*, Okla. City Comm. Coll. Pioneer, Apr. 2, 2007, at 1.

87 *See* Susan Simpson & Michael McNutt, *New Immigration Law Is Raising Questions
    for Many*, The Daily Oklahoman, May 10, 2007, at A1. For an excellent summary
    of the various backstories on the enactment and partial repeal of the Oklahoma
    statute, *see* Elizabeth McCormick, *The Oklahoma Taxpayer and Citizenship
    Protection Act: Blowing Off Steam or Setting Wild-Fires?*, 23 Geo. Immigr. L.J. 293
    (2009). Mississippi also provides an interesting but not unique example of how
    the complexities of immigration and college residency law intersect imperfectly.
    In 1974, a 1972 Mississippi state statute, § 37-103-23, which held that "[a]ll aliens
    are classified as nonresidents," was declared unconstitutional but was never repro-
    mulgated in accordance with the court ruling. *Jagnadan v. Giles*, 379 F. Supp. 1178,
    1182 (D.C. Miss. 1974), *affirmed in part on other grounds*, 538 F.2d 1166 (5th Cir.
    1976), *cert. denied*, 432 U.S. 910 (1977). Therefore, as of 2010 there was no Missis-
    sippi statute that specifically addressed how various immigrants were to be treated
    for tuition. The state did promulgate a residency statute in 2006, but it did not ad-
    dress the immigration anomaly. Miss. Code Ann. § 37-103-7 (West 2009). In 2007,
    two attorney general opinions were issued, filling in some of the longtime gaps,
    especially following the federal provisions of 8 U.S.C. § 1621 (2000) and 8 U.S.C.
    § 1623 (2000), but the undocumented were determined not to be eligible for the

resident tuition, barring any change in the state statute. Op. Att'y Gen. Miss. No. 2007-00416 (Sept. 7, 2007); Op. Att'y Gen. Miss. No. 2007-00416 (Aug. 13, 2007).

88 Press Release, State of Connecticut, *Governor Rell Vetoes Bill to Provide In-State Tuition to Illegal Aliens*, June 26, 2007, www.ct.gov. Advocacy by Yale legal clinic students led to the unsuccessful push for resident tuition for the undocumented, although DACA students were accorded such status. Eileen FitzGerald, *Group Works to Improve Undocumented Student Aid*, Newstimes.com, May 2, 2014, www. newstimes.com.

89 Dirk Perrefort, *Filibuster Blocks Tuition Bill*, News-Times (Danbury, Conn.), Mar. 16, 2007, at A1; Stacey Stowe, *Bill Giving Illegal Residents Connecticut Tuition Rates Is Vetoed by the Governor*, N.Y. Times, June 27, 2007, at C14.

90 Brian Feagons, *Valedictorian in a Paradox*, Atl. J.-Const., May 30, 2007, at B1.

91 S.B. 529, Leg. Sess. (Ga. 2007). For additional discussion of the legislation in Georgia, *see* Brian Feagans, *Illegals to Lose In-State Tuition*, Atl. J.-Const., Dec. 16, 2006, at A1; Feagans, *Valedictorian in a Paradox*, at B1; Brian Feagans, Mary Lou Pickel & Anna Varela, *A Fierce Divide: Georgia's New Law on Illegal Immigrants Looks Strict, but Is It a Real Crackdown?*, Atl. J.-Const., June 30, 2007, at A1; Andrea Jones & James Salzer, *Student Residency Mistakes Cost State*, Atl. J.-Const., Dec. 14, 2007, at E1; Brian Feagans, *"I Can't Do What I Really Want to Do,"* Atl. J.-Const., Dec. 16, 2007, at D7. *See generally* Kristina M. Campbell, *Local Illegal Immigration Reform Act Ordinances: A Legal, Policy, and Litigation Analysis*, 84 Denv. U. L. Rev. 1041, 1059–60 (2007) (discussing the litigation arising from Georgia's anti-immigrant statute).

92 Yvonne Wingett, *Arizona's Colleges Struggle to Enforce New Tuition Statute*, Ariz. Rep., Jan. 3, 2007, at A1; Yvonne Wingett & Matthew Benson, *Migrant Law Blocks Benefits to Thousands*, Ariz. Rep., Aug. 2, 2007, at A1; Yvonne Wingett & Richard Ruelas, *ASU Helps Migrants Find Tuition*, Ariz. Rep., Sept. 8, 2007, at A1; Mariana Alvarado Avalos, *Law Shuts Out Some Students*, Ariz. Daily Star, Aug. 10, 2008, at B1; Renee Schafer Horton, *119 UA Students Reclassified as Out-of-State*, Tucson Citizen, Jan. 1, 2008, at A1. *See generally* Anne Ryman & Lesley Wright, *ASU Plans to Lay Off Faculty to Save Cash*, Ariz. Rep., Oct. 28, 2008, at A1; Eric Kelderman, *At the U. of Arizona, Goals Collide with Reality*, Chron. Higher Educ., Mar. 27, 2009, at A1.

93 Wingett & Ruelas, *ASU Helps Migrants*.

94 John Faherty & Maxine Park, *ASU Ends Scholarships for Illegal Immigrants*, Ariz. Rep., Feb. 16, 2008, at A1; Sara Hebel, *Arizona's Colleges Are in the Crosshairs of Efforts to Curb Illegal Immigration*, Chron. Higher Educ., Nov. 2, 2007, at A15; Katherine Mangan, *Arizona State U. Reclassifies 207 Students as Out of State*, Chron. Higher Educ., Jan. 8, 2008; Katherine Mangan, *Thousands of Arizona College Students Denied In-State Tuition*, Chron. Higher Educ., Jan. 9, 2008; Jesse McKinley, *Arizona Law Takes a Toll on Nonresident Students*, N.Y. Times, Jan. 27, 2008, at A13. In 2008–09, there was a midyear cutback of 18 percent in the Arizona State University budget. For a discussion of this, *see* Jonathan J. Cooper,

Undocumented Immigrants Spend Millions Extra on Tuition, DiverseEducation. com, Aug. 10, 2009, http://diverseeducation.com. While Arizona has resisted all accommodationist legislation or policies, it has begun to lose the cases involving 2012's DACA (for example, driver's licenses). Howard Fischer, *Arizona Ends Court Appeal, Will Issue Driver's Licenses to All Deferred-Action Recipients*, Capitol Media Services, Jan. 23, 2019, https://tucson.com.

95 H.B. 269, 94th Gen. Assemb., 1st Sess. (Mo. 2007) ("[H.B. 269 would] prohibit the admission of unlawfully present aliens to public institutions of higher education."). Tim Craig, *Va. House Approves Bill on Illegal Immigration: Aim Is to Block Access to State, Local Funds*, Wash. Post, Jan. 31, 2007, at A1; Tim Craig, *Va. Republican Bill Would Bar Illegal Immigrants from College*, Wash. Post, Aug. 30, 2007, at A1. For a review of the general history of this issue in Virginia, *see* Kerry Brian Melear, *Undocumented Immigrant Access to Public Higher Education: The Virginia Response*, 194 West Educ. L. Reporter 27 (2005). Virginia is interesting for a number of reasons, including its history as the one post-IIRIRA state challenged by the undocumented for the right claimed by a state to *withhold* this benefit (the converse of the Kansas federal case and the California state case). Virginia's law denying the benefit was upheld. *Doe v. Merten*, 219 F.R.D. 387, 396 (E.D. Va. 2004) (holding that Virginia undocumented students cannot be styled anonymously); *Equal Access Educ. v. Merten*, 305 F. Supp. 2d 585, 603, 614 (E.D. Va. 2004) (holding that state could enact laws denying resident tuition), *dismissed by* 325 F. Supp. 2d 655, 660, 673 (E.D. Va. 2004) (granting defendants' motion for summary judgment, finding that students do not have standing absent evidence that they were denied admission due to immigration status); *see also* Nathan G. Cortez, *The Local Dilemma: Preemption and the Role of Federal Standards in State and Local Immigration Laws*, 61 SMU L. Rev. 47 (2008).

96 S.B. 1230 Gen. Assemb. (Mo. 2008).

97 H.B. 1463, 94th Gen. Assemb. (Mo. 2007). H.B. 1463 would "prohibit the admission of unlawfully present aliens to public institutions of higher education." *See also* Eugene McCormack, *Missouri*, Chron. Higher Educ., Aug. 31, 2007, at 68 (Almanac issue).

98 *Id.*; S.B. 1230 Gen. Assemb. (Mo. 2008), permitted www.senate.mo.gov (accessed from homepage by selecting "Session Information," then "Past Sessions," then "2008," then "S.B. 1230"); *see also* David A. Lieb, *Missouri Lawmakers Have Big Issues Left on Last Day*, Jefferson City News-Tribune, May 16, 2008; Chris Blank, *Missouri Lawmakers Approve Crackdown on Illegal Immigrants*, Jefferson City News-Tribune, May 16, 2008; Didi Tang, *Colleges to Start Checking Legal Residency*, Springfield News-Leader, Nov. 3, 2008, at 1A (discussing developments in Missouri).

99 *Id.* Tang, *Colleges* at 1A.

100 *Martinez v. Regents of Univ. of Cal.*, No. CV 05-2064, 2006 WL 2974303.

101 *Merten*, 217 F.R.D. 387 (E.D. Va. 2004).

102 *Day v. Sebelius*, 376 F. Supp. 2d 1022 (D. Kan. 2005).

103 In Virginia, an attorney general memo does not have the binding force that an
attorney general opinion carries but is considered advisory to the requestor and to
other state officials who encounter similar situations. Several Virginia colleges in
the past appeared to have allowed undocumented students to enroll and establish in-state residency tuition, prompting different legislative proposals in both
2008 and in 2009. The legislature considered strengthening the current statute to
ban the practice but also considered legislation to permit a subgroup of undocumented students who met a heightened standard to receive in-state tuition. The
legislation died in 2009, with no changes enacted. For additional discussion on
the issue in Virginia, *see* Olympia Meola, *Colleges' Admittance of Illegals Opposed*,
Richmond Times-Dispatch, Jan. 18, 2008, at A1; Jim Nolan, *Va. Senate Backs Bill
to Restrict Tuition Benefits for Illegal Immigrants*, Richmond Times-Dispatch, Jan.
27, 2009, at A4; *What's Happening at the Legislature?*, Richmond Times-Dispatch,
Jan. 28, 2009, at A6; State Council for Higher Educ. for Va.; Martha Stoddard, *A
Tougher Proposal on Immigration; Gov. Dave Heineman and a State Senator Want
State and Local Law Enforcement Agencies to Aid Homeland Security*, Omaha
World-Herald, Jan. 22, 2008, at A1.

104 Deborah Bulkeley, "Efforts to Repeal Immigrant Tuition Law Hit Speed Bump,"
Deseret Morning News, Feb. 7, 2008; Bulkeley & Roche, *Immigrant Tuition Repeal*.

105 Mark Binker, *Illegal Immigrants' Tuition Pays Way*, News & Record (Greensboro,
N.C.), Mar. 20, 2009, at B1.

106 *See* Kristin Collins, *Feds: College: OK for Illegal Immigrants*, News & Observer
(Raleigh, N.C.), May 10, 2008, at A1; Kristin Collins, *Illegals May Enjoy a Brief
College Life*, News & Observer (Raleigh, N.C.), Aug. 15, 2008, at B3; Scott Jaschik,
New Twist on Immigrant Students in NC, InsideHigherEd.com, July 28, 2008,
http://insidehighered.com (discussing the May 2008 action by the North Carolina
Community College System to ban students who could not document legal im-
migration status from enrolling).

107 *Letter from Jim Pendergraph*.

108 Jennifer Gonzalez, *North Carolina Community Colleges to Resume Enrolling Illegal
Immigrants*, Chron. Higher Educ., Sept. 18, 2009; Katherine Mangan, *Community
Colleges in North Carolina Close Doors to Illegal Immigrants*, Chron. Higher Educ.,
Aug. 18, 2008; Kristin Collins, *Colleges Profit from Illegal Immigrants*, News &
Observer (Raleigh, N.C.), Mar. 25, 2009, at B3.

109 *See* Ark. Att'y Gen. Op. No. 2008-109 (2008) (explaining that higher education
admission in Ark. is open to undocumented aliens); *Arkansas Att. Gen. Opines
That Undocumented Individuals May Enroll in States, Public Colleges and Universities*, 85 Interpreter Releases 2519 (Sept. 22, 2008); Doug Thompson, *Bill for
In-State Tuition for Undocumented Students Falters in Committee*, Morning News
(Little Rock, Ark.), Mar. 23, 2009 (explaining that the immigrant tuition bill died
in the Senate committee); John Brummett, *Beebe Rallies, Falls Short on Tuition*,
Ark. News, Mar. 28, 2009. Soon after AG Beebe became Gov. Beebe, he upped the
ante by outing the colleges. Laura Kellams, *State's Colleges Warned About In-State*

Tuition, Ark. Democrat Gaz., May 23, 2008, at A1; John Brummett, *Shame, Shame,* Ark. News, Mar. 26, 2009, at A13.

110 Desiree Hunter, *Board Bars Illegal Immigrants from Junior Colleges*, Press-Register, Sept. 26, 2008, at B2; Katherine Mangan, *Alabama Board Bars Illegal Immigrants from State's 2-Year Colleges*, Chron. Higher Educ., Sept. 25, 2008.

111 Ovetta Wiggins, *Immigrant Tuition Bill Falters in Md. Senate*, Wash. Post, Apr. 7, 2007, at B1; John Wagner, *Session Winds Up, Bringing Benefits for Working Class*, Wash. Post, Apr. 12, 2007, at GZ-1. As an example, Maryland S.B. 41 was introduced but was not enacted into law:

> To qualify for an exemption from paying nonresident tuition, an individual must have attended a secondary school in the State for at least two years; have graduated from a high school in the State or received the equivalent of a high school diploma in the State; register as an entering student at a public institution of higher education in Maryland no earlier than the fall 2008 semester; provide documentation that the individual or the individual's parent or guardian has had Maryland income tax withheld during the year prior to high school graduation; and make application to attend the institution within three years of high school graduation. An individual who qualifies for the exemption and is not a permanent resident must also provide an affidavit stating that the individual will file an application to become a permanent resident within 30 days after becoming eligible to do so.

Fiscal and Policy Note, Sen. Harrington, www.mlis.state.-md.us; Maryland, S.B. 167, 2011 Leg., Reg. Sess. (Md. 2011); Md. Code Ann. § 15-106.8 ("suspended," pending state referendum: MD Const. XVI, Sec. 2.) The ballot measure was approved in the next general election, in November 2012, making it the first residency policy elected into being.

For discussion regarding the issue in Colorado, *see* Hank Lacey, *Legal Experts Dispute King's, GOP Certainty That Immigrant Bill Violates Federal Law*, Denver Statehouse Examiner, Mar. 12, 2009 (news report concerning Colorado tuition bill); Jeffery Wolf, *Colo. Senate Rejects Illegal Immigrant Tuition*, Denv. Post, Mar. 4, 2009, at B10 (editorial endorsing Colorado DREAM Act); Elise A. Keaton, Center for Policy & Entre., *Tuition Equity Legislation: Investing in Colorado High School Graduates Through Equal Opportunity to Postsecondary Education* (2008). Several Virginia colleges in the past appeared to allow undocumented students to enroll and establish in-state residency tuition, prompting different legislative proposals in both 2008 and in 2009. The legislature considered strengthening the current statute to ban the practice but also considered legislation to permit a subgroup of undocumented students who met a heightened standard to receive in-state tuition. The legislation died in 2009 without implementing any changes. Nate Jenkins, *Activists Blast Governor's Immigration Bill as Bigoted*, Lincoln Journal-Star, Jan. 23, 2008, at B1; *see also* H.B. No. 308, 127th Gen. Assemb. (Ohio 2007–08); Kirk Semple, *In New Jersey, Bills Offering In-State Tuition to Illegal Immigrants Face a Fight*, N.Y. Times, Apr.

20, 2009, at A20; State of New Jersey, Dep't of the Public Advocate, N.J. State DREAM Act. In 2014, New Jersey enacted resident tuition for undocumented students. *New Jersey*, S. 2479, 215th Leg., 1st Ann. Sess., N.J. Stat. Ann. § 18A:62-4.4 (West Supp. 2014).

112 *See* Appendix 1; S.C. Code Ann. § 59-103-430, 2009. *See* Yvonne Wenger, *Sanford Signs Broad Illegal Immigration Law*, Post & Courier (Charleston, S.C.), June 5, 2008, at A1. The state's Commission on Higher Education, in a memorandum dated January 16, 2009, determined that 2008 Act 280 (S.C. Illegal Immigration Reform Act, 2008 S.C. Acts 2325) did not prohibit the "issuance of transcripts to non-verified students," as they are not a "benefit." *Memorandum from S.C. Comm'n on Higher Educ., Issuance of Transcripts to Non-Verified Students* (Jan. 16, 2009), at 2.

113 *See generally* Eddy Ramírez, *Should Colleges Enroll Illegal Immigrants?*, U.S. News & World Rep., Aug. 17, 2008, at 46; Mary Beth Marklein, *Illegal Immigrants Face Threat of No College*, USA Today, July 6, 2008, at A1; Elizabeth Redden, *For the Undocumented: To Admit or Not to Admit*, Inside Higher Ed, Aug. 18, 2008, www.insidehighered.com; Katherine Mangan, *Most Colleges Knowingly Admit Illegal Immigrants as Students, Survey Finds*, Chron. Higher Educ., Mar. 17, 2009; Megan Eckstein, *In-State Tuition for Undocumented Students: Not Quite Yet*, Chron. Higher Educ., May 8, 2009, at A19; William Perez, *We Are Americans: Undocumented Students Pursuing the American Dream* (Stylus Pub. 2009).

114 Patrick McGee, *Colleges See Rise in Illegal Aliens*, Fort Worth Star-Telegram, July 21, 2005, at B1 ("More than 5,400 students benefited from the tuition law last spring [2006], up from 393 in 2001, according to the Texas Higher Education Coordinating Board."). *See also* Ashley Eldridge, *Array of Students Pay In-State Costs Under 2001 Bill*, Daily Texan, July 31, 2005, at 1. The Texas Coordinating Board, responsible for maintaining the data, reported in 2007:

> How many students has this affected? The number of students qualifying under these provisions is relatively small. The full population of students reported as residents under the residency provisions of TEC 54.052(a)(3) totaled 9,062 students in fall 2007. The state's public institution total enrollment that term was 1,102,572. Therefore, the TEC 54.052(a)(3) students represented slightly more than eight tenths of one percent of the public institution enrollment.

Tex. Higher Educ. Coordinating Bd., *Residency and In-State Tuition, Statistical Report* (2007), www.thecb.state.tx.us. My own regular discussions with the Coordinating Board staff have suggested that nearly 10,000 different students employed this provision in the approximately ten years since it was enacted (and before DACA), including citizens and permanent residents who graduated from the state's high schools and met the durational residency criterion. *See also* Chris Vogel, *The DREAM Act Might Be Dead, but These Kids' Hopes Are Not*, Hous. Press, June 17, 2008; Elizabeth Redden, *Success Obscured by Controversy*, InsideHigherEd.com, Apr. 24, 2009, www.insidehighered.com.

115 *See generally Washington Extends Resident Student Tuition Rate to Certain Non-immigrants,* 86 Interpreter Releases 1786 (2009); *Undocumented Students Face Barriers to Higher Education,* Physorg.com, Apr. 21, 2009; Kate Riley, *Harvesting a DREAM,* Seattle Times, June 5, 2009, at A12. In addition, as has happened a number of times, a very sympathetic undocumented college student surfaced, bringing attention to himself at some risk. Lornet Turnbull, *Scramble to Help UW Graduate Who's an Illegal Immigrant,* Seattle Times, Sept. 30, 2009, at B1. For a few of the many examples, *see, e.g.,* Press Release, Sen. Chris Dodd, *Dodd to Sponsor Rare Private Bill Preventing Haitian Girl's Deportation* (July 16, 2004) (discussing Sen. Dodd's sponsorship of a 2004 private relief bill for undocumented Haitian college student and urging passage of DREAM Act); *see also* Julia Preston, *In Increments, Senate Revisits Immigrant Bill,* N.Y. Times, Aug. 3, 2007, at A1; Paul Basken, Kelly Field & Sara Hebel, *Bush's Legacy in Higher Education: A Matter of Debate,* Chron. Higher Educ., Dec. 19, 2008, at A14.

116 Editorial, *In-State Tuition; Don't Kick Around Children of Immigrants,* Sacr. Bee, Dec. 26, 2005, at B4 (reporting that, in 2005, of the total 208,000 UC students, 1,339 received the A.B. 540 exemption, including 407 undocumented immigrants); Josh Keller, *State Legislatures Debate Tuition for Illegal Immigrants,* Chron. Higher Educ., Apr. 13, 2007, at A28; Josh Keller, *U.S. Citizens Reap Unintended Benefit from California's Immigrant-Tuition Law,* Chron. Higher Educ., Dec. 6, 2009, at A1.

117 Wis. Stat. Ann. § 36.27 (West 2009). *See* Georgia Pabst, *Some Illegal Immigrants Will Be Able to Get In-State Tuition,* Journal Sentinel (Milwaukee, Wis.), June 30, 2009, at B3. After two years of resident tuition, Wisconsin abruptly turned right and repealed the short-lived program, which had enrolled only several hundred undocumented college students. *See* 2009 Assemb. B. 75 (2009 Wisconsin Act 28); Wis. Stat. § 36.27, repealed by A.B. 40, June 26, 2011.

118 *See* www.njleg.state.nj.us (N.J. bill, 2010); RI H.B. 7172 (Rhode Island 2010 In-State Tuition Bill); *see also* Adrienne Lu, *N.J. Bill on In-State Tuition for Illegal Immigrants Advances,* Phil. Inquirer, Jan. 5, 2010, at A1; Lisa Fleisher & Trish G. Graber, *Right to In-State Tuition for Illegals Advances,* Star Ledger, Jan. 5, 2010, at News-22; Jeff Diamant, *In-State Tuition for Illegal Immigrants Fizzles,* Star Ledger, Jan. 12, 2010, at N.J.-16; Jonathan Tamari, *N.J. Legislature Denies In-State Tuition for Illegal Immigrants,* Phil. Inquirer, Jan. 12, 2010, at B1; Anastasia R. Mann, *Garden State Dreams: In-State Tuition for Undocumented Kids* (New Jersey Policy Perspective report, 2010), www.njpp.org; Susan Carroll, *In-State Rates for Illegal Immigrants Attacked; Group Says Texas Violating Federal Law by Allowing Such Tuition Breaks; LAWSUIT: Texas Led the Way,* Hous. Chron., Dec. 16, 2009, at B1; Margery A. Beck, *Lawsuit Targets Nebraska's Immigrant-Tuition Law,* Lincoln Journal-Star, Jan. 25, 2010, www.journalstar.com; Shelly, *Kris Kobach's War;* Martha Stoddard, *In-State Tuition Repeal Unlikely,* Omaha World-Herald, Feb. 2, 2010, www.omaha.com; JoAnne Young, *Senators Hear Arguments on Repealing Nebraska Dream Act,* Lincoln Journal-Star, Feb. 2, 2010.

119 J. Louis Brandeis (dissenting) in *New State Ice Co. v. Liebmann*, 285 U.S. 262, 311 (1932): "There must be power in the States and the nation to remould, through experimentation, our economic practices and institutions to meet changing social and economic needs. I cannot believe that the framers of the Fourteenth Amendment, or the States which ratified it, intended to deprive us of the power to correct the evils of technological unemployment and excess productive capacity which have attended progress in the useful arts.

"To stay experimentation in things social and economic is a grave responsibility. Denial of the right to experiment may be fraught with serious consequences to the nation. It is one of the happy incidents of the federal system that a single courageous State may, if its citizens choose, serve as a laboratory; and try novel social and economic experiments without risk to the rest of the country."

CHAPTER 3. THE DREAM ACT IN CONGRESS AND
FEDERAL DEVELOPMENTS

1 147 Cong. Rec. 8581 (2001) (statement of Sen. Orrin Hatch). S. 1291, 107th Cong. (2001) (as introduced in the Senate); S. 1291, 107th Cong. (2001) (as reported in the Senate); Student Adjustment Act of 2001, H.R. 1918, 107th Cong. (2001) (as introduced in the House).

2 DREAM Act of 2003, S. 1545, 108th Cong. (2003) (as introduced in the Senate); DREAM Act of 2003, S. 1545, 108th Cong. (2003) (as reported in the Senate); Student Adjustment Act of 2003, H.R. 1684, 108th Cong. (2003) (as introduced in the House); S. Rep. No. 108-224 (2004) (as reported by S. Comm. on the Judiciary) (regarding the proposed amendment of the Illegal Immigration Reform Act of 1996); DREAM Act of 2005, S. 2075, 109th Cong. (2005) (as introduced in the Senate); American Dream Act of 2006, H.R. 5131, 109th Cong. (2006) (as introduced in the House); Comprehensive Immigration Reform Act of 2006, S. 2611, 109th Cong. (2006) (as placed on calendar in the Senate).

3 Comprehensive Immigration Reform Act of 2007, S. 1348, 110th Cong. (2007).

4 *Id.*; DREAM Act of 2007, S. 774, 110th Cong. (2007) ("[t]o amend the Illegal Immigration Reform and Immigrant Responsibility Act of 1996 to permit States to determine State residency for higher education purposes and to authorize the cancellation of removal and adjustment of status of certain alien students who are long-term United States residents and who entered the United States as children, and for other purposes"); Educ. Access for Rightful Noncitizens (EARN) Act, H.R. 1221, 110th Cong. (2007) (as introduced in the House) ("[t]o provide for cancellation of removal and adjustment of status for certain long-term residents who entered the United States as children."); Am. Dream Act, H.R. 1275, 110th Cong. (2007) (as introduced in the House) ("[t]o amend the Illegal Immigration Reform and Immigrant Responsibility Act of 1996 to permit States to determine State residency for higher education purposes and to authorize the cancellation of removal and adjustment of status of certain alien students

who are long-term United States residents and who entered the United States
as children, and for other purposes"); DREAM Act, S. 2205, 110th Cong. (2007)
(as placed on calendar in the Senate) (a bill "[t]o authorize the cancellation of
removal and adjustment of status of certain alien students who are long-term
United States residents and who entered the United States as children, and for
other purposes"). A motion not to proceed was voted on October 24, 2007. The
bill terminated with a vote of 52 to 44. *Id.*

5 *See* The Future of Undocumented Immigrant Students: Hearing on Comprehensive Immigration Reform Before the H. Subcomm. on Immigration, Citizenship,
Refugees, Border Security & Int'l Law, 110th Cong. (2007), transcript, votes, and
committee transcript excerpts, http://judiciary.house.gov.

6 Security Through Regularized Immigration and a Vibrant Economy (STRIVE)
Act of 2007, H.R. 1645, 110th Cong. (2007); 2007 STRIVE hearing, http://judiciary.
house.gov.

7 DREAM Act, S. 2205, 110th Cong. (2007) (including details of the vote).

8 Eligibility for Title IV Program Assistance for Victims of Human Trafficking,
Information for Financial Aid Professionals, May 11, 2006, http://ifap.ed.gov.

9 *Letter from Jim Pendergraph, Executive Director, Office of State and Local Coordination, U.S. Immigration & Customs Enforcement, to Thomas J. Ziko, Special
Deputy Attorney General,* N.C. Dep't of Justice, July 28, 2008, www.nacua.org.

10 *See, e.g.,* Kris W. Kobach, *Immigration Nullification: In-State Tuition and
Lawmakers Who Disregard the Law,* 10 N.Y.U. J. Legis. & Pub. Pol'y 473, 477,
517, 521 (2006–07). *See also* Kris W. Kobach, The Heritage Found., *The Senate
Immigration Bill Rewards Lawbreaking: Why the DREAM Act Is a Nightmare,*
Backgrounder No. 1960 (2006). Then-professor Kobach apparently suffers
from recurring dreams—he also characterized the 2007 comprehensive im-
migration reform proposals as a "nightmare." Kris W. Kobach, The Heritage
Found., *The Senate Immigration Bill: A National Security Nightmare,* Web-
memo No. 1513 (2007), www.heritage.org. In 2010, he filed suit in Nebraska
state court to overturn the legislation (*Mannschreck v. Univ. of Nebraska*).
See Margery A. Beck, *Kris Kobach, Kansas Secretary of State Candidate, Sues
Nebraska Over Immigrant Tuition Law,* Kans. City Star, Jan. 26, 2010; Barb
Shelly, *Kris Kobach's War on Undocumented College Students,* Kans. City Star,
Jan. 26, 2010; Julia Preston, *A Professor Fights Illegal Immigration One Court
at a Time,* N.Y. Times, July 21, 2009, at A10. Margery A. Beck, *Lawsuit Targets
Nebraska's Immigrant-Tuition Law,* Lincoln Journal-Star, Jan. 25, 2010, www.
journalstar.com; Martha Stoddard, *In-State Tuition Repeal Unlikely,* Omaha
World-Herald, Feb. 2, 2010, www.omaha.com; JoAnne Young, *Senators Hear
Arguments on Repealing Nebraska Dream Act,* Lincoln Journal-Star, Feb. 2,
2010.

11 Andorra Bruno, Cong. Research Serv., *Unauthorized Alien Students: Issues and
"Dream Act" Legislation,* Report RL33863 (2008), http://trac.syr.edu. *See also* Jody
Feder, *Congressional Research Service, Unauthorized Alien Students, Higher Educa-*

tion, and In-State Tuition Rates: A Legal Analysis (2008), www.digitalcommons.ilr. cornell.edu.

12 *See* Elizabeth Redden, *A Message to Prospective Undocumented Students*, Inside Higher Ed, Oct. 16, 2008, www.insidehighered.com(reporting that Vassar is open to undocumented students); Am. Assn. of Collegiate Registrars and Admissions Officers (AACRAO), *Undocumented Students in the U.S.: Admission and Verification* (2009), www.aacrao.org; Nat'l Immigration Law Ctr., *Basic Facts About In-State Tuition for Undocumented Immigrant Students* (2009).

13 Roberto Gonzalez, Coll. Bd., *Young Lives on Hold: The College Dreams of Undocumented Students* (2009); Megan Eckstein, *College Board Announces Support for Immigration Bill*, Chron. Higher Educ., Apr. 22, 2009; Megan Eckstein, *In-State Tuition for Undocumented Students: Not Quite Yet*, Chron. Higher Educ., May 8, 2009, at A19; Anastasia R. Mann, *Garden State Dreams: In-State Tuition for Undocumented Kids* (New Jersey Policy Perspective report, 2010), www.njpp.org.

14 For several careful studies of the various legislative developments, *see generally* Maria Arhancet, *Developments in the Legislative Branch: Platforms of Presidential Candidates Regarding Immigration Reform*, 21 Geo. Immigr. L.J. 507 (2007) (outlining Republican and Democratic presidential candidates' positions on immigration); Keun Dong Kim, *Current Development in the Legislative Branch: Comprehensive Immigration Reform Nixed*, 21 Geo. Immigr. L.J. 685 (2007) (reporting on a failed immigration bill); Jeffrey N. Poulin, *Development in the Legislative Branch: The Piecemeal Approach Falls Short of Achieving the DREAM of Immigration Reform*, 22 Geo. Immigr. L.J. 353 (2008) (reporting on the failure of the DREAM Act in 2007). The national press kept up a steady drumbeat, much of it remarkably positive. *See, e.g.*, Miriam Jordan, *Illegal at Princeton*, Wall St. J., Apr. 15, 2006, at A1; Joseph Berger, *Debates Persist over Subsidies for Immigrant College Students*, N.Y. Times, Dec. 12, 2007, at B8; Michael Luo, *Romney's Words Testify to Threat from Huckabee*, N.Y. Times, Dec. 2, 2007, at YT 29; Martin Ricard, *Students Stage Mock Graduation to Advocate for Undocumented*, Wash. Post, June 24, 2009, at B2.

15 The National Conference of State Legislatures (NCSL) compiles legislative data on a variety of subjects, including state-level enactments of immigration laws, which showed in the first six months of 2009 that all but four states passed such laws, most of them restrictionist. *See* Immigrant Pol'y Project, *State Laws Related to Immigrants and Immigration* (2009), www.ncsl.org.

16 *Id. See* Jorge M. Chavez & Doris Marie Provine, *Race and the Response of State Legislatures to Unauthorized Immigrants*, 63 Annals Am. Acad. Pol. & Soc. Sci. 78 (2009), http://ann.sagepub.com (analyzing NCSL data). Perhaps by definition, state legislators and their organizations are very conservative, as is made evident by the extraordinary data in the regular NCSL tabulations. But in an interesting eclipse with liberal and progressive observers, the NCSL has taken the official position that federal law preempts state and local law immigration enforcement efforts: "NCSL holds firmly that states do not have 'inherent authority' to enforce

federal civil immigration law. We also oppose efforts to perpetuate this myth of 'inherent authority' indirectly by shifting federal responsibility of immigration enforcement to state and local law officers through the criminalization of any violation of federal immigration law." Nat'l Conference of State Legislatures, Immigration Reform—Official Policy (2009), www.ncsl.org (NCSL policy on preemption). For example, *compare* Peter J. Spiro, *The States and Immigration in an Era of Demi-Sovereignties*, 35 Va. J. Int'l L. 121 (1994), *with* Michael A. Olivas, *Preempting Preemption: Foreign Affairs, State Rights, and Alienage Classifications*, 35 Va. J. Int'l L. 217 (1994).

17 Immigrant Policy Project, *State Laws Related to Immigrants and Immigration*, www.ncsl.org/research/immigration/state-laws-related-to-immigration-and-immigrants.aspx.

18 *Id.*

19 McCain's absence was widely regarded as strategic, as he was in the thick of a Republican primary fight. *See, e.g.*, Stephen Dinan, *McCain Caters to GOP Voters*, Wash. Times, Oct. 31, 2007, at A1 (stating that "Sen. John McCain has quietly been piling up flip-flops," citing previous DREAM Act support). Sen. Kennedy, recovering from surgery at the time of the cloture vote, died from a brain tumor on August 25, 2009, at the age of seventy-seven. John N. Broder, *Social Causes Defined Kennedy, Even at the End of a 46-Year Career in the Senate*, N.Y. Times, Aug. 26, 2009, at A1. *See also* Press Release, Sen. Chris Dodd, *Dodd to Sponsor Rare Private Bill Preventing Haitian Girl's Deportation* (July 16, 2004) (discussing Sen. Dodd's sponsorship of a 2004 private relief bill for undocumented Haitian college student and urging passage of DREAM Act); Julia Preston, *Measure Would Offer Legal Status to Illegal Immigrant Students*, N.Y. Times, Sept. 20, 2007, at A1 (Sen. Dodd securing private relief legislation for undocumented college student).

20 DREAM Act of 2007: Hearing on S. 2205, 110th Cong. S13305 (2007) (excerpt from Sen. Arlen Specter's statement on the Senate floor regarding the DREAM Act).

21 *Id.*

22 Office of Mgmt. & Budget, *Statement of Administrative Policy: S. 2205—Development, Relief, and Education for Alien Minors Act of 2007* (2007), www.whitehouse.gov.

23 Carl Hulse & Adam Nagourney, *Specter Switches Parties*, N.Y. Times, Apr. 28, 2009, at A1. Of course, these political alliances are fleeting and malleable. *See, e.g.*, Carl Hulse, *Democrats Gain as Stevens Loses His Senate Race*, N.Y. Times, Nov. 19, 2008, at A1 (politics of Sen. Joe Lieberman's switch from Democrat to Independent); Katharine Q. Seelye, *Specter Feels Squeeze from New Friends and Old*, N.Y. Times, Jan. 27, 2010, at A12.

24 James C. McKinley Jr., *Governor's Race Exposes Republican Rift in Texas*, N.Y. Times, Aug. 14, 2009, at A11 (discussing differences between Perry and Hutchison); Robert Draper, *It's Just a Texas-Governor Thing*, N.Y. Times Mag., Dec. 6, 2009, at 30–5; James C. McKinley Jr., *Texas Senator Now a Challenger Lagging in*

Polls, N.Y. Times, Feb. 21, 2010, at A14. In March, she lost the Republican primary race to Perry. James C. McKinley Jr. & Clifford Krauss, *"Yes" for Texas Governor Is "No" to Washington*, N.Y. Times, Mar. 3, 2010, at A1 (Perry defeated Hutchison in primary without a runoff).

25 Discussions with Staff Attorneys, National Immigration Law Center, Mexican American Legal Defense and Educational Fund (Sept. 27, 2007). *See also* Julia Preston, *Measure on Legal Status for Immigrant Students Blocked*, N.Y. Times, Sept. 28, 2007, at A1; Elizabeth Redden, *DREAM Act Vote on Tap*, Inside Higher Ed, Oct. 24, 2007, www.insidehighered.com.

26 *See* Julia Preston, *Bill for Immigrant Students Fails Test Vote in Senate*, N.Y. Times, Oct. 25, 2007, at A16.

27 Sara Hebel, *Candidates Grapple with How to Expand Access to College*, Chron. Higher Educ., Sept. 14, 2007, at A17.

28 *See* Matthew Spalding, Heritage Found., *Getting Reform Right: The White House's Immigration Initiative, Web Memo* (2007); Preston, *Bill for Immigrant Students Fails*; Kobach, *Lawbreaking*. I do not suggest that all conservative views are of one accord on this topic or any other. Some of the more libertarian views, for example, advocate for more open borders, legalization, and increased immigration for both higher-end and lower-skill jobs. *See, e.g.*, Daniel Griswold, Cato Inst., Ctr. for Trade Pol'y Stud., *Comprehensive Immigration Reform: Finally Getting It Right*, Free Trade Bull. No. 29, at 1 (2007).

29 Michael A. Olivas, *IIRIRA, the DREAM Act, and Undocumented College Student Residency*, 30 J.C. & U.L. 435, 436 (2004). *See also* Leonard M. Baynes, *Racial Profiling, September 11, and the Media: A Critical Race Theory Analysis*, 2 Va. Sports & Ent. L.J. 1, 17–21 (2002) (detailing accounts of several hijackers). The student visas of two of the hijackers were actually approved exactly six months after they took over the planes. *See generally* Laura Khatcheressian, *FERPA and the Immigration and Naturalization Service: A Guide for University Counsel on Federal Rules for Collecting, Maintaining and Releasing Information About Foreign Students*, 29 J.C. & U.L. 457, 466–7 (2003).

30 *See, e.g.*, Fareed Zakaria, *The Post-American World* (2008); Richard Florida, *How the Crash Will Reshape America*, Atlantic Monthly, Mar. 2009, at 44; Andrew Ross Sorkin, *Too Big to Fail: The Inside Story of How Wall Street and Washington Fought to Save the Financial System from Crisis—and Themselves* (2009); John Cassidy, *How Markets Fail: The Logic of Economic Calamities* (2009). *See* Gregory Koger, *Making Change: A Six-Month Review*, The Forum, July 2009, www.bepress.com(reviewing first six months of Obama legislative agenda); *see also* John M. Broder, *Obama Hobbled in Fight Against Global Warming*, N.Y. Times, Nov. 16, 2009, at A1. *See also* Daniel J. Tichenor, *Navigating an American Minefield: The Politics of Illegal Immigration*, The Forum, July 2009, www.bepress.com. By early 2010, these efforts had stalled in Congress. David M. Herszenhorn & Robert Pear, *Democrats Put Lower Priority on Health Bill*, N.Y. Times, Jan. 27, 2010, at A27; Paul Kane & Shailagh Murray, *Democrats*

Confused About Road Forward, Wash. Post, Jan. 29, 2010, at A1; Carl Hulse & Sheryl Gay Stolberg, *His Health Bill Stalled, Obama Juggles an Altered Agenda*, N.Y. Times, Jan. 29, 2010, at A1.

31 Kelly Field, *Deal Is Reached on Immigration Bill Affecting Students, Says Senate Leader*, Chron. Higher Educ., Nov. 24, 2008. Sen. Reid's views were set out at his website and in remarks he made at a national Latino organization in 2008: http://reid.senate.gov (website and remarks). In addition, on June 24, 2009, at Georgetown University Law Center, Sen. Reid's chief immigration staff counsel, Serena Houl, addressed a group of immigration professionals and outlined the senator's plans and legislative strategies. A webcast recording of her remarks can be found at www.law.georgetown.edu.

32 Janet Napolitano, Sec'y of Homeland Sec., Remarks at Center for American Progress (Nov. 13, 2009), video www.americanprogress.org; *see also* Lee Hockstader, *Immigration Awaits Its Turn*, Wash. Post, Sept. 13, 2009, at A23; Julia Preston, *White House Plan on Immigration Includes Legal Status*, N.Y. Times, Nov. 14, 2009, at A10; Spencer S. Hsu, *Obama Presses Congress to Rework Immigration Laws*, Wash. Post, Nov. 14, 2009, at A16.

33 In 2010, health care and insurance reform efforts both stalled. *See* Herszenhorn & Pear, *Democrats Put Lower Priority on Health Bill*, at A27; Kane & Murray, *Democrats Confused*, at A1; Hulse & Stolberg, *His Health Bill Stalled*, at A1. *See also* Sewell Chan, *Dodd Calls Obama Plan Too Grand*, N.Y. Times, Feb. 3, 2010, at B1 (banking and financial institutions reform bogged down).

34 Sen. Schumer, *Keynote Speaker at the Immigration Law and Policy Conference*, Migration Policy Institute (June 24, 2009), http://schumer.senate.gov (accessed from homepage by searching keywords "reform principles") (website), and www.law.georgetown.edu (accessed from homepage by searching keywords "Schumer webcast") (GULC webcast).

35 *Id.*

36 *Id.*

37 For details of the vote, *see* Security Through Regularized Immigration and a Vibrant Economy (STRIVE) Act of 2007, H.R. 1645, 110th Cong. (2007); 2007 STRIVE hearing, http://judiciary.house.gov.

38 *See* Charlie Savage, *Senate Confirms Sotomayor for the Supreme Court*, N.Y. Times, Aug. 7, 2009, at A1. Justice Sonia Sotomayor was confirmed to the US Supreme Court on August 6, 2009, with a 68–31 vote. Jess Bravin, *Senate Confirms Sotomayor in Largely Partisan 68–31 Vote*, Wall St. J., Aug. 7, 2009, at A3.

39 For a comprehensive study of how the political and media cycles of the US presidency have evolved, *see* Jeffrey E. Cohen, *The Presidency in the Era of 24-Hour News* (2008). For detailed studies of how immigration and DREAMers have employed social media, *see* Walter J. Nicholls, *The DREAMers: How the Undocumented Youth Movement Transformed the Immigrant Rights Debate* (Stanford Univ. Press 2013); Sasha Costanza-Chock, *Out of the Shadows, Into the Streets! Transmedia Organizing and the Immigrant Rights Movement* (MIT Press 2014).

40 Julia Preston, *Congress Quarrels on Covering Immigrants*, N.Y. Times, Nov. 4, 2009, at A14.

41 A week after he shouted out in the chambers, Rep. Wilson was admonished by the House by a vote of 240 to 179: "[The House d]eclares that the House of Representatives disapproves of the behavior of the Representative from South Carolina, Mr. Wilson, during the joint session of Congress held on September 9, 2009." H.R. Res. 744, 111th Cong. (2009) (as passed by Senate, Sept. 15, 2009). On the issue of immigrant health care, *see* Randy Capps, Marc R. Rosenblum & Michael Fix, Migration Pol'y Inst., *Immigrants and Health Care Reform, What's Really at Stake?* (2009); Kevin Sack, *Hospital Falters as Refuge for Illegal Immigrants*, N.Y. Times, Nov. 21, 2009, at A1.

42 There is a lifetime of reading on the subject of nativism, restrictionism, and the racist roots of immigration. *See generally* Mae Ngai, *The Strange Career of the Illegal Alien: Immigration Restriction and Deportation Policy in the United States, 1921–1965*, 21 Law & Hist. Rev. 69 (2003) (examining the immigration and deportation policy under the Immigration Act of 1924); Daniel J. Tichenor, *Dividing Lines: The Politics of Immigration Control in America* 242–88 (Princeton Univ. 2002); Kevin R. Johnson, *Opening the Floodgates: Why America Needs to Rethink Its Borders and Immigration Laws* (New York University Press 2007); David Bacon, *Illegal People: How Globalization Creates Migration and Criminalizes Immigrants* (Beacon Press 2008); Leo R. Chavez, *The Latino Threat: Constructing Immigrants, Citizens, and the Nation* (Stanford Univ. Press 2008); Laura E. Gomez, *What's Race Got to Do with It? Press Coverage of the Latino Electorate in the 2008 Presidential Primary Season*, 24 St. John's J. Legal Comment. 425 (2009); Alejandro Portes & Rubén G. Rumbaut, *Immigrant America: A Portrait* (Univ. Calif. Press 4th ed. 2014).

43 *See* Olivas, *IIRIRA*, at 456–57 (internal citations omitted): "While only a few states have changed their practice post-IIRIRA and enacted statutes to allow the undocumented to attend college as resident students, the major receiver states have done so, and it is likely that political pressure will continue to fill in the spots on the map, at least the spots where the undocumented are likely to enroll. In addition, the unlikely scenario of a major conservative Republican U.S. Senator from Utah (Sen. Orrin Hatch) taking on this issue after September 11 has rendered it more likely that federal action will occur, and not only accord these students federal protection, but a limited amnesty of one form or another."

44 Gary Reich & Alvar Ayala Mendoza, *"Educating Kids" Versus "Coddling Criminals": Framing the Debate over In-State Tuition for Undocumented Students in Kansas*, 8 State Pol. & Pol'y Q. 177, 192–94 (2008) (internal citations omitted); *see also* Gary Reich & Jay Barth, *Educating Citizens or Defying Federal Authority? A Comparative Study of In-State Tuition for Undocumented Students*, 38 Pol'y Stud. J. 419 (2010).

45 *See* Susan Simpson & Michael McNutt, *New Immigration Law Is Raising Questions for Many*, The Daily Oklahoman, May 10, 2007, at A1. For an excellent summary

of the various backstories on the enactment and partial repeal of the Oklahoma statute, *see* Elizabeth McCormick, *The Oklahoma Taxpayer and Citizenship Protection Act: Blowing Off Steam or Setting Wild-Fires?*, 23 Geo. Immigr. L.J. 293 (2009). A similar strategy has been employed by restrictionists in Texas and in Nebraska, though repeal efforts were undertaken in Texas. *See* Susan Carroll, *In-State Rates for Illegal Immigrants Attacked; Group Says Texas Violating Federal Law by Allowing Such Tuition Breaks; LAWSUIT: Texas Led the Way*, Hous. Chron., Dec. 16, 2009, at B1; Beck, *Lawsuit Targets Nebraska's Immigrant-Tuition Law---*; Shelly, *Kris Kobach's War*; Stoddard, *In-State Tuition Repeal Unlikely*.

46 David Montgomery, *No Turning Back, Rep. Luis Gutierrez Is Making Immigration Reform a Personal Cause*, Wash. Post, May 8, 2009, at C1.

47 *See* Hockstader, *Immigration Awaits Its Turn*, at A23; Muszaffar Chishti & Claire Bergeron, *New Immigration Bill Edges Comprehensive Reform Back on the Legislative Agenda*, Migration Policy Institute, Jan. 2010, www.migrationinformation.org; *see also* Kane & Murray, *Democrats Confused*, at A1; Hulse & Stolberg, *His Health Bill Stalled*, at A1; Chan, *Dodd Calls Obama Plan Too Grand*, at B1, B9 (discussing complexities of financial regulation).

48 Notwithstanding, the logjam broke in March 2010 as President Obama made his first formal announcement on immigration reform, linking it to the need for bipartisan support. Julia Preston, *Obama Links Immigration Overhaul in 2010 to G.O.P. Backing*, N.Y. Times, Mar. 12, 2010, at A12. By use of the reconciliation process, Congress gave final approval to health care legislation without a single Republican vote. Robert Pear & David M. Herszenhorn, *House Approves Health Overhaul, Sending Landmark Bill to Obama*, N.Y. Times, Mar. 22, 2010, at A1.

49 In the House, H.R. 1751, "To amend the Illegal Immigration Reform and Immigrant Responsibility Act of 1996 to permit States to determine State residency for higher education purposes and to authorize the cancellation of removal and adjustment of status of certain alien students who are long-term United States residents and who entered the United States as children, and for other purposes," sponsored by Rep. Howard L. Berman (D-Cal.), was introduced on March 26, 2009, with 102 cosponsors and referred to House Judiciary and House Education and Labor Committees; on May 14, 2009, referred to House subcommittee, and then to Subcommittee on Higher Education, Lifelong Learning, and Competitiveness.) In the U.S. Senate, S. 729, "A bill to amend the Illegal Immigration Reform and Immigrant Responsibility Act of 1996 to permit States to determine State residency for higher education purposes and to authorize the cancellation of removal and adjustment of status of certain alien students who are long-term United States residents and who entered the United States as children, and for other purposes," sponsored by Sen. Richard Durbin (D-Ill.), was introduced on March 26, 2009, with thirty-one cosponsors and referred to the Senate Judiciary Committee). *See* http://thomas.loc.gov. *See also* Carl Hulse & Adam Nagourney, *Obama's Afghanistan Decision Is Straining Ties with Democrats*, N.Y. Times, Dec. 4, 2009, at A20; John M. Broder & Elisabeth

Rosenthal, *Obama Has Goal to Wrest a Deal in Climate Talks*, N.Y. Times, Dec. 18, 2009, at A1.

50 Broder, *Social Causes Defined Kennedy*, at A1. *See also* Michael Cooper, *G.O.P. Surges to Senate Victory in Massachusetts*, N.Y. Times, Jan. 20, 2010, at A1 (GOP state senator wins Sen. Kennedy's seat).

51 Pear & Herszenhorn, *House Approves Health Overhaul*. The comprehensive federal ACA website is www.hhs.gov.

52 In the 111th Congress (2009–10), nearly a dozen DREAM Acts were introduced and consigned to House and Senate committees and subcommittees: H.R. 4986, National Defense Authorization Act for Fiscal Year 2008; S. 729, DREAM Act of 2009; H.R. 1751, DREAM Act of 2009; H.R. 5281, Removal Clarification Act of 2010; H.R. 6327, Citizenship and Service Act of 2010; H.R. 6497, DREAM Act of 2010; S. 3827, DREAM Act of 2010; S. 3932, Comprehensive Immigration Reform Act of 2010; S. 3962, DREAM Act of 2010; S. 3963, DREAM Act of 2010; S. 3992, DREAM Act of 2010. The comprehensive (and complicated) calendar is www.congress.gov.

53 H.R. 5281, Removal Clarification Act of 2010 (7/27/2010 Passed House; 12/03/2010 Passed Senate; Last action 12/08/2010 Resolving Differences), www.congress.gov (bill record); http://clerk.house.gov (roll call vote); www.congress.gov (Congressional Record, H8223–8226).

54 December 8, 2010: Resolving differences—House actions: On motion to agree to the Senate amendments numbered 1 and 2, and that the House agree to the Senate amendment numbered 3 with an amendment Agreed to by the Yeas and Nays: 216–198: http://clerk.house.gov (roll call vote); text as House agreed to certain Senate amendments with an amendment: www.congress.gov (Congressional Record, H8223–8226).

55 Cloture on the motion to agree to House amendment to Senate amendment numbered 3 not invoked in Senate by Yea-Nay Vote. 55–41: www.senate.gov (roll call vote); www.congress.gov (Congressional Record, S10665–10666).

56 On the day of the final cloture vote, Sen. Hatch issued a press release citing his objection to the lame-duck session vote and did not mention the merits of the DREAM Act bill itself. Press Release, *Hatch on Senate Consideration of Dream Act, Other Partisan Proposals, Utah Senator Says What We Need Is Real Action to Get Economy Moving, Get American People Back to Work*, Dec. 8, 2010, www.hatch.senate.gov.

CHAPTER 4. THE AFTERMATH OF THE DREAM ACT DEFEATS, STATE DEVELOPMENTS

1 As demonstrated in Chapter 3 (this volume), the DREAM Act had come tantalizingly close in 2007 with S. 2205, 110th Cong. (2007), and there followed many public stories about undocumented college students in the media. These continued through the 2010 lame duck session, where once again the votes were not there, for S. 3992, 111th Cong. (2010). *See generally* Benjamin Marquez & John F.

Witte, *Immigration Reform: Strategies for Legislative Action*, 7 The Forum 1 (2009); Michael A. Olivas, *The Political Economy of the DREAM Act and the Legislative Process: A Case Study of Comprehensive Immigration Reform*, 55 Wayne L. Rev. 1757 (2009); Julia Preston, *Political Battle on Immigration Shifts to States*, N.Y. Times, Jan. 1, 2011, at A1; Julia Preston, *Students Spell Out Messages on Their Immigration Frustration*, N.Y. Times, Sept. 21, 2010, at A14; *see also* Danielle Holley-Walker, *Searching for Equality: Equal Protection Clause Challenges to Bans on the Admission of Undocumented Immigrant Students to Public Universities*, Mich. St. L. Rev. 357 (2011); Gary Reich & Jay Barth, *Educating Citizens or Defying Federal Authority? A Comparative Study of In-State Tuition for Undocumented Students*, 38 Pol'y Stud. J. 419 (2010). There has been a surprisingly robust literature on the media savvy and organizing skills of the DREAMers both in comprehensive articles and also in full-length book treatments. *See, e.g.*, Lisa M. Martinez, *Dreams Deferred: The Impact of Legal Reforms on Undocumented Latina/o Youth*, 58 Am. Beh. Sci., 1873–90 (2014); Liana Gamber-Thompson & Arely M. Zimmerman, *DREAMing Citizenship: Undocumented Youth, Coming Out, and Pathways to Participation*, in *By Any Media Necessary: The New Youth Activism* 186–218 (Henry Jenkins, Sangita Shresthova, Liana Gamber-Thompson, Neta Kligler-Vilenchik & Arely M. Zimmerman eds., New York University Press 2016); Rene Galindo, *The Functions of Dreamer Civil Disobedience*, 24 Tex. Hisp. J.L. & Pol'y 41–60 (2017); Chris Zepeda-Millán, *Latino Mass Mobilization: Immigration, Racialization, and Activism* (Camb. Univ. Press 2017); Abigail Leslie Andrews, *Undocumented Politics: Place, Gender, and the Pathways of Mexican Migrants* (Univ. Calif. Press 2018); Deborah A. Boehm & Susan J. Terrio, eds., *Illegal Encounters: The Effect of Detention and Deportation on Young People* (New York University Press 2019).

2 Wis. Stat. Ann. § 36.27(2)(cr) (West 2010) (repealed 2011).

3 Md. Code Ann., Educ. § 15–106.8 (West 2011) (pending November 2012 repeal ballot referendum).

4 Gina Macris, *Panel: In-State Tuition Rates for Undocumented RI Students*, Providence J., Sept. 19, 2011, http://news.providencejournal.com; Latino Pol'y Inst., Roger Wms. U., *The Effects of In-State Tuition for Non-Citizens: A Systematic Review of the Evidence* (2011), www.rwu.edu.

5 110 Ill. Comp. Stat. Ann. 947/67 (West 2011); H.B. 60, 93d Gen. Assemb., Reg. Sess. (Ill. 2003).

6 A.B. 131, 2011 Leg., Reg. Sess. (Cal. 2011) (amending Section 68130.7 of and adding Sections 66021.6, 69508.5, and 76300.5 to the Education Code, relating to state financial aid); A.B. 844, 2011 Leg., Reg. Sess. (Cal. 2011) (amending Cal. Educ. Code § 72023.5 and adding Sections 66016.3 and 66016.4, relating to state financial aid to certain student leadership positions); A.B. 130, 2011 Leg., Reg. Sess. (Cal. 2011) (amending Cal. Educ. Code § 68130.7 and adding § 66021.7, relating to non–state-funded scholarships); A.B. 540, 2001 Leg., Reg. Sess. (Cal. 2001) (adding Cal. Educ. Code § 68130.5). *See* Nanette Asimov & Wyatt Buchanan, *Brown OKs Student Aid for Illegal Immigrants*, S.F. Chron., Oct. 8, 2011, at A1; Stephen Magagnini,

Dream Act Students Live in Limbo—Aid Doesn't Help Get Citizenship or Career, Sacr. Bee, Dec. 26, 2011, at A1; Patrick McGreevy & Anthony York, *Brown Signs California Dream Act Funding Bill,* L.A. Times, Oct. 9, 2011, at A1.

7 Conn. Gen. Stat. § 10a-29 (West 2011); H.B. 6390, 2011 Leg., Reg. Sess. (Conn. 2011).

8 Nicholas Riccardi, *Effort to Repeal California Dream Act Comes Up Short,* Political (Jan. 6, 2012), http://latimesblogs.latimes.com. *See* Asimov & Buchanan, *Brown OKs Student Aid,* at A1; McGreevy & York, *Brown Signs,* at A1; Rebecca R. Ruiz, *Dream Act Becomes Law in California,* N.Y. Times, Oct. 10, 2011, http://thechoice.blogs.nytimes.com. Maryland has an unusual process for challenging new statutes through the ballot measure. Md. Const. art. XVI, www.msa.md.gov; Md. Code Ann., Elec. Law, §§ 7-101-7-102 (2012). *See also* Aaron C. Davis, *Md. Tuition Law May Be Halted,* Wash. Post, June 29, 2011, at B1; *Maryland's "Dream Act" Suspended Amid Petition Drive for Referendum,* Fox News, July 1, 2011, www.foxnews.com.

9 Seth Hoy, *Colorado, Hawaii and Delaware Progress on Tuition Equity for Undocumented Students,* Immigr. Impact, Apr. 16, 2012, http://immigrationimpact.com. A careful study of state initiatives showed that many of the anti-immigrant bills, including those concerning K–12 and higher education, were being proposed by the Republican Party to try to embarrass Democrats or get them on the record when they control the legislative agenda. *See* Joshua N. Zingher, *The Ideological and Electoral Determinants of Laws Targeting Undocumented Migrants in the U.S. States,* 14 State Pol. & Pol'y Qtly 90–117 (2014) (arguing that the Republican Party has used restrictive immigration bills to divide the Democratic Party).

10 The Illegal Immigration Reform and Immigrant Responsibility Act of 1996 (IIRIRA) provides: "A State may provide that an alien who is not lawfully present in the United States is eligible for any State or local public benefit for which such alien would otherwise be ineligible under subsection (a) of this section only through the enactment of a State law after August 22, 1996, which affirmatively provides for such eligibility." 8 U.S.C. § 1621(c)(3)(d) (2006). Under this federal provision, a state such as Rhode Island, which apportions tuition-setting authority to its Board of Governors for Higher Education, would "enact a State law" by this administrative means. *See also* Gina Macris, *A Bid to Extend In-State Tuition,* Providence J., Sept. 20, 2011, at 1; Erika Niedowski, *RI Education Board OK's In-State Tuition for Undocumented Students,* Bos. Globe, Sept. 27, 2011, articles. boston.com.

11 *Martinez v. Regents of Univ. of Cal.,* 241 P.3d 855 (Cal. 2010) (upholding state statute, providing resident tuition to undocumented), *cert. denied,* 131 S. Ct. 2961 (2011); Josh Keller, *California Supreme Court Upholds Law Giving In-State Tuition to Illegal Immigrants,* Chron. Higher Educ., Nov. 15, 2010, chronicle.com.

12 *Mannschreck v. Clare,* CI10-8 (Neb. Dist. Ct. Aug. 19, 2010) (challenging the Nebraska residency statute, but dismissed in 2010 on standing). *See* Kevin Abourezk,

Judge Tosses Suit on Tuition to Illegal Immigrants; Plaintiffs Likely to Refile Suit, Lincoln J. Star, Dec. 18, 2010, at A1.

13 *Texas*, H.B. 1403, 77th Leg., Reg. Sess. (Tex. 2001) [amended by S.B. 1528, 79th Leg., Reg. Sess. (Tex. 2005), relating to student financial aid]; Tex. Educ. Code Ann. §§ 54.052 and 54.053. *Immigration Reform Coal. of Texas (IRCOT) v. Texas*, 706 F. Supp. 2d 760 (S.D. Tex. 2010) (removed to state court); IRCOT's Notice of Nonsuit, *Immigration Reform Coal. of Texas v. Hegar*, No. 2009-79110 (281st Dist. Ct., Harris County, Tex. Dec. 10, 2015) (dismissing original suit); refiled as *Lone Star Coll. Sys. v. Immigration Reform Coal. of Texas (IRCOT)*, 418 S.W.3d 263 (Tex. App.—Houston [14th Dist.] 2013) (standing and procedural issues); *Lone Star Coll. Sys. and Richard Carpenter v. Immigration Reform Coal. of Texas (IRCOT)*, No. 14-0031 (Tex. Oct. 24, 2014) (Supreme Court of Texas denied petition for review; motion to reurge intervention and motion to file brief dismissed as moot).

14 *New Jersey Denies College Financial Aid to U.S. Citizen Because Her Mother Is Undocumented*, Latino Fox News, June 14, 2011, http://latino.foxnews.com. *See A.Z. ex rel. B.Z. v. Higher Educ. Student Assistance Auth.*, 48 A.3d 1151 (N.J. Super. Ct. App. Div. 2012) (reversing the administrative agency's determination that a U.S. citizen student was ineligible for New Jersey state financial aid because her parents were undocumented); *see also Brief and Appendix of Appellant Arturo Cortes, Cortes v. Higher Educ. Student Assistance Auth.*, No. A-2142-11-T1 (N.J. Super. Ct. App. Div. Mar. 26, 2012) (appealing to reverse the action of the Higher Education Assistance Authority (HESAA), dated August 15, 2011, and reaffirmed after appeal on November 21, 2011, denying assistance under the Tuition Aid Grant and Educational Opportunity Fund (EOF) programs). *A.Z. ex rel. B.Z. v. Higher Educ. Student Assistance Auth.*, 48 A.3d 1151 (N.J. Super. Ct. App. Div. 2012) (N.J. financial aid case concerning USC children and undocumented parents); consolidated with *Cortes v. Higher Educ. Student Assistance Auth.*, No. A-2142-11-T1 (N.J. Super. Ct. App. Div. 2012).

15 Ray Downs, *U.S. Citizens in Fla. Charged Higher Tuition Rates Because of Parents' Immigration Status*, Christian Post, Oct. 31, 2011, http://global.christianpost.com; *Ruiz v. Robinson*, 892 F. Supp. 2d 1321 (S.D. Fla. 2012) (Fla. resident tuition case concerning USC children and undocumented parents).

16 Erin Cunningham, *Montgomery College Sued over Illegal Immigrant Policy*, Gazette.net, Jan. 21, 2011, www.gazette.net/stories/01212011/polinew205826_32538.php; Len Lazarick, *Montgomery College Sued for Giving In-County Tuition to Illegal Immigrants*, Marylandreporter.com, Jan. 21, 2011, http://marylandreporter.com; *Doe v. Maryland State Bd. of Elections*, No. 02-C11-163050 (Md. Cir. Ct. Feb. 17, 2012) (unsuccessful challenge to the state ballot measure "freezing" the 2011 Maryland Dream Act implementation), *aff'd on appeal, Doe v. Maryland State Bd. of Elections*, 53 A.3d 1111 (Md. 2012).

17 Lisa W. Foderaro, *In Suing SUNY, Out-of-State Students Seek In-State Tuition*, N.Y. Times, Feb. 6, 2011, at CT1 (describing a suit for N.Y. resident tuition by N.J. resi-

dents who had attended high school in New York). In New York, a settlement was reached in the residency case *Strum, et al. v. SUNY, et al.* (Index No. 2011/00064), www.suny.edu (regarding out-of-state students who attended high school in the state); the residency policy was amended accordingly: *Policy Title: Residency, Establishment of for [sic] Tuition Purposes* (III. Guidelines for Determining Residence/Eligibility for Resident Tuition, Sec. D: Emancipation of a Student) (Document Number: 7810; Effective Date: July 9, 2018), www.suny.edu.

18 *See, e.g.,* Michael A. Olivas, *IIRIRA, the DREAM Act, and Undocumented College Student Residency,* 30 J.C. & U.L. 435, 449–55 (2004) (providing a statutory analysis of sections 505, 1621, and 1623 of the IIRIRA). *See generally* Victor C. Romero, *Noncitizen Students and Immigration Policy Post-9/11,* 17 Geo. Immigr. L.J. 357 (2003); Victor C. Romero, *Postsecondary School Education Benefits for Undocumented Immigrants: Promises and Pitfalls,* 27 N.C. J. Int'l L. & Com. Reg. 393 (2002); Jessica Salsbury, Comment, *Evading "Residence": Undocumented Students, Higher Education, and the States,* 53 Am. U. L. Rev. 459 (2003); Michael A. Olivas, *Dreams Deferred: Deferred Action, Prosecutorial Discretion, and the Vexing Case(s) of DREAM Act Students,* 21 Wm. & Mary Bill Rts J. 463 (2012).

19 *See Hispanic Interest Coal. of Ala. v. Governor of Ala.,* Nos. 11-14535, 11-14675, 2012 WL 3553613 (11th Cir. Aug. 20, 2012); *see also* Michael A. Olivas, *Sweet Home Alabama?,* Inside Higher Ed, Oct. 13, 2011, www.insidehighered.com (reviewing federal litigation enjoining comprehensive Alabama restrictionist statute). *See generally* Alan Gomez, *Immigrants Return to Alabama; Scores Fled State After Illegal Immigration Law Went into Effect,* USA Today, Feb. 21, 2012, at 3A; Campbell Robertson, *Critics See "Chilling Effect" in Alabama Immigration Law,* N.Y. Times, Oct. 28, 2011, at A14; Campbell Robertson, *In Alabama, Calls for Revamping Immigration Law,* N.Y. Times, Nov. 17, 2011, at A15; *Hispanic Interest Coal. of Ala. v. Governor of Ala.,* 691 F.3d 1236 (11th Cir. 2012), *cert den. Alabama v. U.S.,* 133 S. Ct. 2022 (2013).

20 Tom LoBianco, *Immigrant Tuition Fight Derails Bill,* OnPolitix (Mar. 1, 2012), http://indiana.onpolitix.co.

21 In 2011, the Ohio legislature changed the policy concerning undocumented college students in the state who already had not previously been eligible for resident tuition. Ohio Rev. Code § 3333.31(D) (2011). The policy now states in relevant parts: "(1) The rules of the chancellor for determining student residency shall grant residency status to a person who, while a resident of this state for state subsidy and tuition surcharge purposes, graduated from a high school in this state . . . if the person enrolls in an institution of higher education and establishes domicile in this state, regardless of the student's residence prior to that enrollment. (2) The rules of the chancellor for determining student residency shall not grant residency status to an alien if the alien is not also an immigrant or a nonimmigrant." *See* Aaron Marshall & Reginald Fields, *Budget Bill Passed by Senate Does More Than Spend Money: Changes Are Coming to Communities, Consumers, Students,* Plain Dealer, June 13, 2011, at A1; Aaron Marshall, *Senate OKs Compromises in $112 Bil-*

lion State Budget: House to Vote Today on Range of Cuts, Tax, Breaks, Plain Dealer, June 29, 2011, at A1.

22 *Hispanic Interest Coal. of Ala. v. Bentley*, No. 5:11-CV-2484-SLB, 2011 WL 5516953 (N.D. Ala. Sept. 28, 2011), *vacated as moot*, Nos. 11-14535, 11-14675, 2012 WL 3553613 (11th Cir. Aug. 20, 2012) (enjoining the section 8 college provisions of the Beason-Hammon Alabama Taxpayer and Citizen Protection Act, H.B. 56).

23 *Hispanic Interest Coal. of Ala. v. Governor of Ala.*, Nos. 11-14535, 11-14675, 2012 WL3553613 (11th Cir. Aug. 20, 2012); *Hispanic Interest Coal. of Alabama v. Governor of Alabama*, 691 F.3d 1236 (11th Cir. 2012), *cert den. Alabama v. U.S.*, 133 S. Ct. 2022 (2013). *See* Jay Reeves, *Hispanic Children Bullied in Law's Wake*, Bos. Globe, Oct. 23, 2011, www.articles.boston.com/2011-10-23/news/303/3879_1_illegal-immigrants-new-law-justice-department-officials; Robertson, *Critics See "Chilling Effect,"* at A14.

24 *New Jersey Denies College Financial Aid*; *New Jersey*, S. 2479, 215th Leg., 1st Ann. Sess., N.J. Stat. Ann. § 18A:62-4.4 (West Supp. 2014); Erika J. Nava, *Tuition Equality Act Is a Half-Measure Without Access to Financial Aid* (New Jersey Policy Perspective report, Apr. 2015), www.njpp.org (study of the year-old law in New Jersey allowing certain undocumented students to pay in-state tuition). *See also* NJPP Press Release, www.njpp.org. *See also* Rodrigo Torrejon, *Financial Aid May Grow for Undocumented Students: These NJ Schools Enroll the Most*, NorthJersey. com, May 8, 2018, www.northjersey.com.

25 New Jersey eventually yielded on both financial aid and residency determination. *A.Z. ex rel. B.Z. v. Higher Educ. Student Assistance Auth.*, 48 A.3d 1151 (N.J. Super. Ct. App. Div. 2012) (N.J. financial aid case concerning USC children and undocumented parents); consolidated with *Cortes v. Higher Educ. Student Assistance Auth.*, No. A-2142-11-T1 (N.J. Super. Ct. App. Div. 2012). Amy L. Travis, *Note, New Jersey's Attack on Mixed-Status Families: The Unconstitutionality of New Jersey's Immigrant Eligibility Requirements for Foster Parents*, 67 Rutgers U. L. Rev. 441–68 (2015).

26 *See* Michael R. Vasquez, *U.S.-Citizen Children of Immigrants Protest Higher Tuition Rates*, Miami Herald, Oct. 24, 2011, at B1.

27 *Ruiz v. Robinson*, 892 F. Supp. 2d 1321 (S.D. Fla. 2012) (Fla. resident tuition case concerning USC children and undocumented parents). After losing the *Ruiz* case, Florida eventually also passed accommodationist residency tuition legislation in 2014. Fla. Stat. § 1009.26 (2014).

28 Maura Dolan & Larry Gordon, *In-State Tuition Benefit Upheld*, L.A. Times, Nov. 16, 2010, at A1.

29 Cal. Educ. Code § 68130.5 (2011); *Martinez v. Regents of Univ. of Cal.*, 241 P.3d 855 (Cal. 2010), *cert. denied*, 131 S. Ct. 2961 (2011). *See* Laurel Rosenhall, *California High Court Upholds College Tuition Break for Illegal Immigrants*, Sacr. Bee, Nov. 16, 2010, at 1A.

30 Hoy, *Colorado, Hawaii and Delaware Progress on Tuition Equity*. A careful study of state initiatives showed that many of the anti-immigrant bills, including those

concerning K–12 and higher education, were being proposed by the Republican Party to embarrass Democrats or get them on the record when they control the legislative agenda. *See* Zingher, *Ideological and Electoral Determinants* (arguing that the Republican Party has used restrictive immigration bills to divide the Democratic Party). *See also* Andrews, *Undocumented Politics*; Beth C. Caldwell, *Deported Americans: Life After Deportation to Mexico* (Duke Univ. Press 2019); Kevin R. Johnson, *Immigration and Civil Rights in an Era of Trump* (forthcoming, Valparaiso U. L. Rev., 2019).

31 Peter Catapano, *Opinionator: Battle of the Borders*, N.Y. Times, Oct. 21, 2011, http://opinionator.blogs.nytimes.com.

32 Trip Gabriel, *Stance on Immigration May Hurt Perry Early On*, N.Y. Times, Sept. 24, 2011, at A12. On the withdrawal of Gov. Perry, *see* Mimi Swartz, *Overmisunderestimating Rick Perry*, N.Y. Times, Jan. 20, 2012, http://campaignstops.blogs.nytimes.com. *See* Philip Rucker, *Romney Works to Round Up Key Support*, Wash. Post, Jan. 21, 2012, at A6.

33 Editorial, *Rick Perry's "Oops" Moment Isn't All*, L.A. Times, Nov. 11, 2011, http://articles.latimes.com. Ironically, Perry could not remember the name of one of the three federal agencies he was proposing to eliminate, and he was eventually appointed secretary of that department (energy) in the Trump administration in 2017. *See* James Conca, *Rick Perry Vows to Protect Dept of Energy; Al Franken Blushes*, Forbes.com, Jan. 19, 2017, www.forbes.com.

34 Jennifer Raab, *Rick Perry's Tuition Policy, Immigrants' Dream: Why Students Need a Path to Citizenship*, N.Y. Daily News, Sept. 30, 2011, http://articles.nydailynews.com.

35 *See* Gabriel, *Stance*.

36 Erika Bolstad, *Rivera Introduces a Military-Only Version of the DREAM Act*, Miami Herald, Jan. 26, 2012, www.miamiherald.typepad.com. Sen. Marco Rubio (R-Fla.) also had introduced a version of the DREAM Act—one that provided no pathway to citizenship. Lizette Alvarez, *With G.O.P.'s Ear, Rubio Pushes Dream Act Proposal*, N.Y. Times, Apr. 27, 2012, at A13; Mary Giovagnoli, *Rubio Proposal Overlooks Obstacles Ahead for DREAMers*, Immigr. Impact, May 4, 2012, http://immigrationimpact.com.

37 *See* Wendy Sefsaf, *22 Senators Demand President Obama Exercise Executive Action on Immigration*, Immigr. Impact, Apr. 14, 2011, http://immigrationimpact.com.

38 *Id.*

39 *See* Julia Preston, *Immigration Vote Leaves Policy in Disarray*, N.Y. Times, Dec. 19, 2010, at A35.

40 Elise Foley, *Senate Dems to Obama: Stop Deporting DREAM Act Students*, Huffington Post, June 14, 2011, www.huffingtonpost.com.

41 Elise Foley, *Officials Refuse to Budge on Deportation of Students, Families*, Huffington Post, June 1, 2011, www.huffingtonpost.com.

42 *Id. See also Memorandum from John Morton, Dir. U.S. Immigration and Customs Enforcement, to All Field Office Directors, All Special Agents in Charge & All Chief Counsel, on Exercising Prosecutorial Discretion Consistent with the Civil Immigra-*

tion Enforcement Priorities of the Agency for the Apprehension, Detention, and Removal of Aliens, June 17, 2011, www.ice.gov. A year earlier, Director Morton had begun to lay the groundwork for the 2011 initiative by estimating that ICE could afford under its current budget and personnel to remove approximately 400,000 noncitizens. *See Memorandum from John Morton, Dir. U.S. Immigration and Customs Enforcement, to All ICE Employees, on Civil Immigration Enforcement: Priorities for the Apprehension, Detention, and Removal of Aliens* (June 30, 2010), www.ice.gov.

43 *Id. Exercising Prosecutorial Discretion.*

44 Julia Preston, *U.S. to Review Cases Seeking Deportations*, N.Y. Times, Nov. 17, 2011, at A1.

45 Morton, *Prosecutorial Discretion with Civil Immigration*, at 4–5; *see* Preston, *U.S. to Review*, at A4. Thereafter, ICE and DHS released a number of memoranda outlining the many details regarding prosecutorial discretion. For a listing and review of these memoranda and other documents, *see* Shoba Sivaprasad Wadhia, *Prosecutorial Discretion in Immigration Agencies: A Year in Review*, LexisNexis 2012 Emerging Issues 6173 (Jan. 12, 2012). For the most authoritative treatment of prosecutorial discretion in the immigration context, *see* Shoba Sivaprasad Wadhia, *Beyond Deportation: The Role of Prosecutorial Discretion in Immigration Cases* (New York University Press 2017).

46 On the issue of the marches, which were attended by several hundreds of thousands of participants, *see* Alfonso Gonzales, *The 2006 Mega Marchas in Greater Los Angeles: Counter-Hegemonic Moment and the Future of El Migrante Struggle*, 7 Latino Stud. 30 (2009); Kevin R. Johnson & Bill Ong Hing, *The Immigrant Rights Marches of 2006 and the Prospects for a New Civil Rights Movement*, 42 Harv. C.R.–C.L. L. Rev. 99 (2007); Sylvia R. Lazos Vargas, *The Immigrant Rights Marches (Las Marchas): Did the "Gigante" (Giant) Wake Up or Does It Still Sleep Tonight?*, 7 Nev. L.J. 780 (2007); *see also* Caroline B. Brettell, *Immigrants as Netizens: Political Mobilization in Cyberspace*, in *Citizenship, Political Engagement, and Belonging* 226–43 (Deborah Reed-Danahay & Caroline B. Brettell eds., 2008); Roberto G. Gonzales & Leo R. Chavez, *"Awakening to a Nightmare": Abjectivity and Illegality in the Lives of Undocumented 1.5-Generation Latino Immigrants in the United States*, 53 Current Anthropology 255, 257–59 (2012).

47 *See* James Fallows, *Obama, Explained*, Atlantic Monthly, Mar. 2012, at 54, 69–70: "But part of political leadership is being able to project a positive idealism that you know is at odds with the real world. I am ready to believe that Obama adopted this faux-harmonious tone, apart from its being his natural register, as a way to win the election, and as a marker for what he hoped America could become, and—crucially—that once in office, he maintained it as a sound position for himself as he moved toward reelection. Late last year, he also applied it with chess-master skill against the congressional Republicans, in daring them to let the widely popular payroll-tax cut expire at the start of an election year. They backed off, and when the dust settled, the Republicans found themselves at an unaccus-

tomed political disadvantage. Having secured an agreement on government funding for the rest of the year, Obama had taken one of their favorite tools, the threat
of a government shutdown, out of their hands through the campaign season. And
after three years of seeming to shy from 'partisan' rhetoric, he began linking the
slate of GOP presidential contenders to the Tea Party–dominated Republican
Congress, whose approval ratings were far worse than his own." Ironically, it was
immigration in the form of the wall separating the U.S. southern border that
occasioned the longest government shutdown in history, prompted by President
Trump. Chapter 7 covers this ground in painful detail.

48 *Plyler v. Doe*, 457 U.S. 202 (1982). *See generally* Michael A. Olivas, *No Undocumented Child Left Behind: Plyler v. Doe and the Education of Undocumented
Children* (New York University Press 2012).

49 Helene Cooper & Tripp Gabriel, *Obama's Announcement Seizes Initiative and Puts
Pressure on Romney*, N.Y. Times, June 16, 2012, at A16; Teresa Watanabe & Es-
meralda Bermudez, *For Immigrants' Rights Activists, Battle Continues*, L.A. Times,
June 17, 2012, at A1; *Republican Immigration Platform Backs "Self-Deportation,"*
N.Y. Times, Aug. 23, 2012, http://thecaucus.blogs.nytimes.com.

CHAPTER 5. THE DREAM ACT AND PROSECUTORIAL DISCRETION

1 *Olivas Kicks Out the Jams: UHLC Professor Explores the Law and Business of Rock
and Roll*, U. Hous. L. Ctr. (Mar. 1, 2012), www.law.uh.edu (reporting on Continuing Legal Education workshop).

2 *See* Starr Nelson, Comment, *Rock and Roll Royalties, Copyrights and Contracts
of Adhesion: Why Musicians May Be Chasing Waterfalls*, 1 J. Marshall Rev. Intell.
Prop. L. 163 (2001).

3 *See, e.g., Fogerty v. Fantasy*, 510 U.S. 517 (1994) (regarding attorney's fees from a
copyright infringement claim that a jury trial found in favor of musician John
Fogerty); *Croce v. Kurnit*, 737 F.2d 229 (2d Cir. 1984) (affirming trial court decision
to award the surviving spouse of entertainer Jim Croce royalties for breach of
contract claim); *Elvin Assocs. v. Franklin*, 735 F. Supp. 1177 (S.D.N.Y. 1990) (finding
singer Aretha Franklin liable for failure to appear in musical production under
theory of promissory estoppel).

4 *See Olivas Kicks Out the Jams.*

5 The litigation in the John Lennon immigration matter included three interrelated
lawsuits and a Board of Immigration Appeals (BIA) petition for review. *See Lennon
v. INS*, 527 F.2d 187 (2d Cir. 1975) (vacating and remanding BIA decision that had
upheld his deportation); *Lennon v. United States*, 387 F. Supp. 561 (S.D.N.Y. 1975)
(seeking to enjoin deportation on grounds of political beliefs); *Lennon v. Richardson*, 378 F. Supp. 39 (S.D.N.Y. 1974) (suing under the Administrative Procedure Act,
5 U.S.C. § 522 (1966), to obtain Immigration Service records concerning nonpriority status); *Lennon v. Marks*, Civil No. 72-1784 (S.D.N.Y. filed May 1, 1972) (seeking
injunction compelling the INS to act upon Lennon's third preference petition; it
became moot when the petition was reviewed). After the remand, Immigration

Judge Fieldsteel granted relief to Lennon, allowing him to remain in the country. *See also* Leon Wildes, *The Nonpriority Program of the Immigration and Naturalization Service—a Measure of the Attorney General's Concern for Aliens* (Parts I & II), 53 Interp. Rel. 25, 33 (Jan. 26–30, 1976). *See generally* Leon Wildes, *The Nonpriority Program of the Immigration and Naturalization Service Goes Public: The Litigative Use of the Freedom of Information Act*, 14 San Diego L. Rev. 42, 43 n.4 (1976) (identifying the three district court actions and Petition for Review before the Second Circuit as a result of Lennon's difficulties with the INS). The court had held that Lennon's earlier 1968 guilty plea in London for cannabis possession had violated British drug laws and rendered him removable from the U.S. Leon Wildes, *All You Need Is Love—and a Good Jewish Lawyer*, N.J. Jewish Standard, Dec. 10, 2010, www.jstandard.com (providing a first-person account of the litigation in the Lennon immigration matter from the perspective of his attorney); *see also* Jon Wiener, *Come Together: John Lennon in His Time* 225–80 (1984); Jon Wiener, *Gimme Some Truth: The John Lennon FBI Files* (2000). For the details of the underlying child custody dispute and family court matter, much of which occurred in Houston, *see* Mark Davidson, *"I Really Want to See You": Cause No. 893,663; Anthony D. Cox v. Yoko Ono Lennon*, Hous. Law., Sept.–Oct. 2011, at 24, 25–26.

6 Wildes, *The Nonpriority Program of the Immigration and Naturalization Service Goes Public*, at 44–46 (footnotes omitted); *see also* Wildes, *Attorney General's Concern*; Leon Wildes, *The Operations Instructions of the Immigration Service: Internal Guides or Binding Rules?*, 17 San Diego L. Rev. 99, 102–06 (1979) (explaining circuit courts' use of the Nonpriority Operations Instruction during the 1970s).

7 Wildes, *The Nonpriority Program of the Immigration and Naturalization Service Goes Public*, at 42–43.

8 *Id.* at 46.

9 *See id.* at 46–47.

10 *See id.* at 43. A number of courts downplayed or minimized the role of OI as mere intra-agency guidance or informal procedural guidelines with no substantive weight or binding precedent. *See, e.g., Velasco-Gutierrez v. Crossland*, 732 F.2d 792, 798 (10th Cir. 1984).

11 Shoba Sivaprasad Wadhia, *The Role of Prosecutorial Discretion in Immigration Law*, 9 Conn. Pub. Int. L.J. 243, 251 (2010).

12 Of course, this happened most famously after *Lennon v. INS*, where the Second Circuit reversed the BIA decision that had upheld Lennon's deportation and remanded to the Immigration Court. 527 F.2d 187 (2d Cir. 1975). Then, Immigration Judge Fieldsteel granted relief to Lennon, allowing him to remain in the country. *See* Wildes, *The Nonpriority Program of the Immigration and Naturalization Service Goes Public*, at 43 n.4 (providing an overview of Lennon's five-year court battle and identifying that Lennon was granted residence after the July 27, 1976, Immigration Court hearing).

13 *See* Wadhia, *The Role of Prosecutorial Discretion*, at 252–53.

14 *See id.* at 246–65 (summarizing the complex trend of the discretionary status).

15 527 F.2d 187 (2d Cir. 1975).

16 Illegal Immigration Reform and Immigrant Responsibility Act of 1996 (IIRIRA), Pub. L. No. 104–208, 110 Stat. 3009.

17 Anti-Terrorism and Effective Death Penalty Act of 1996 (AEDPA), Pub. L. No. 104-132, 110 Stat. 1214.

18 Personal Responsibility and Work Opportunity Reconciliation Act of 1996 (PRWORA), Pub. L. No. 104-193, 110 Stat. 2105 (1996).

19 *See generally* Wadhia, *Role of Prosecutorial Discretion*, at 252–56.

20 *Id.*

21 Adam B. Cox & Cristina M. Rodriguez, *The President and Immigration Law*, 119 Yale L.J. 458, 517–18 (2009).

22 *Id.*; *see also* Mary Kenney, *Prosecutorial Discretion: How to Advocate for Your Client*, Am. Immigr. Council, June 24, 2011, www.aila.org.

23 *See* Wadhia, *Role of Prosecutorial Discretion*, at 256–59.

24 There are reams of materials on this important intersection of national security law and immigration in the border control and enforcement contexts. For two of the better articles linking and critiquing the two domains, *see* Jennifer M. Chacon, *Unsecured Borders: Immigration Restrictions, Crime Control and National Security*, 39 Conn. L. Rev. 1827 (2007); Kevin R. Johnson & Bernard Trujillo, *Immigration Reform, National Security After September 11, and the Future of North American Integration*, 91 Minn. L. Rev. 1369 (2007).

25 Cox & Rodriguez, *President and Immigration Law*, at 518–19.

26 *See* Suzy Khimm, *Obama DREAMs On: The DREAM Act Is Dead in Congress, but the White House Is Quietly Moving to Limit Deportations of Certain Undocumented Immigrants*, Mother Jones, June 27, 2011, www.motherjones.com.

27 *See id.* (explaining the president's use of executive power to drive immigration policy).

28 *See* Cox & Rodriguez, *President and Immigration Law*, at 460–63 (explaining the history of the allocation of powers between the president and Congress in the immigration context).

29 *See* Richard S. Beth, Cong. Research Serv., 98-628 Gov. *Private Bills: Procedure in the House* (2005); Kati L. Griffith, *Perfecting Public Immigration Legislation: Private Immigration Bills and Deportable Lawful Permanent Residents*, 18 Geo. Immigr. L.J. 273 (2004); Robert Hopper & Juan P. Osuna, *Remedies of Last Resort: Private Bills and Deferred Action Status*, 97–106 Immigr. Briefings, June 1997, at 2–9 (history and procedures for forms of private relief); Penn State Law Sch. et al., *Private Bills & Deferred Action Toolkit* (2011), http://law.psu.edu.

30 Margaret Mikyung Lee, Cong. Research Serv., RL33024, *Private Immigration Legislation* (2007). For a useful and comprehensive site where all such private immigration legislation is tracked, *see Search of Private Immigration Legislation*, Libr. Congress, www.loc.gov.

31 *See* Penn State Law Sch. et al., *Toolkit*, at 33–34.

32 Given the prominence of the Beatles' founder, including his early accomplishments and tragic death in 1980, there is literally a bookcase filled with full-length

books on his life and music. *See, e.g.*, Dennis R. Miller, *Imagine: 12 Great Books About John Lennon*, HuffPost, Dec. 6, 2017, www.huffingtonpost.com. I own seven of the books and have read them carefully, as well as many dozens of the articles on the author and his immigration history.

33 *See* Penn State Law Sch. et al., *Toolkit*, at 7–9.

34 *An Act for the Relief of Shigeru Yamada*, Priv. L. No. 111-1 (2010), www.gpo.gov; *Congress Passes Two Private Immigration Relief Bills*, 87 Interpreter Releases 2414 (2010) (explaining the case of Shigeru Yamada); *see also* Ruxandra Guidi, *Undocumented Immigrant Granted Rare Pathway to Legalization*, KPBS.org, Jan. 31, 2011,www.kpbs.org; Roxana Popescu, *Bob Filner Leads House in Sponsoring Private Bills*, Kpbs.org, Oct. 27, 2011, www.kpbs.org.

35 Ben Pershing, *Bill to Help Marine Widow Hotaru Ferschke Set to Become Law*, Wash. Post, Dec. 15, 2010, http://voices.washingtonpost.com.

36 *An Act for the Relief of Hotaru Nakama Ferschke*, Priv. L. No. 111-2 (2010), www. gpo.gov; *see also Congress Passes Two Private Immigration Relief Bills*, at 2414 (explaining the case of Hotaru Nakama Ferschke).

37 *See* Lee, *Private Immigration Legislation*, at 3–5.

38 Griffith, *Perfecting Public Immigration Legislation*, at 293 (quoting representative Barney Frank that these private bills should be reviewed case by case); *see also* Michael J. Wishnie, *Immigrants and the Right to Petition*, 78 N.Y.U. L. Rev. 667 (2003) (reviewing redress rights for noncitizens); Penn State Law Sch. et al., *Toolkit*, at 9 (suggesting a private bill as a remedy for only "extraordinary cases").

39 *See* Penn State Law Sch. et al., *Toolkit*, at 33 ("Deferred action is a limited remedy in that the [Department of Homeland Security] can alternatively choose to terminate at any time.").

40 Lidiane Carmo, *Sole Survivor of Family Killed in I-75 Crash, Won't Be Deported*, Huffington Post, Feb. 3, 2012, www.huffingtonpost.com.

41 *Id.*

42 The various and complicated provisions for "special immigrant juveniles" (SIJs) are found in section 203(b)(4) of the Immigration and Nationality Act (INA), 8 U.S.C. § 1153(b)(4) (2006), which sets aside immigrant visas for children considered "special immigrants" under section 101(a)(27). Immigration and Nationality Act § 101(a)(27), 8 U.S.C. § 1101(a)(27) (2006) (defining "special immigrant"). Section 113 of Public Law No. 105-119 amended the class to noncitizen juveniles deemed eligible for long-term foster care based on abuse, neglect, or abandonment and added other stringent requirements. Immigration and Nationality Act § 101(a)(27)(J), Pub. L. No. 105-119, 11 Stat. 2460 (1997). *See generally Interoffice Memorandum, U.S. Citizenship and Immigration Services*, www.uscis.gov (describing field guidance on Special Immigrant Juvenile Status Petitions).

43 *See* Penn State Law Sch. et al., *Toolkit*, at 37.

44 Wadhia, *Role of Prosecutorial Discretion*, at 250.

45 Leon Wildes, *The Deferred Action Program of the Bureau of Citizenship and Immigration Services: A Possible Remedy for Impossible Immigration Cases*, 41 San Diego

L. Rev. 819, 823 (2004) ("The [DA] status is granted for a temporary period and reviewed biennially.").

46 Wadhia, *Role of Prosecutorial Discretion*, at 246.

47 *See id.* at 248, 251–52 (detailing discretionary features in determining whether a case is eligible for deferred action). *See generally* Shoba Sivaprasad Wadhia, *The Policy and Politics of Immigrant Rights*, 16 Temp. Pol. & Civ. Rts. L. Rev. 387 (2007) (examining the impact of immigration policies on immigrant rights). Professor Stephen Lee, in his detailed article *Monitoring Immigration Enforcement*, noted that the grant of prosecutorial discretion was itself "a response to Congress's failure to pass the DREAM Act" but also, "[i]mportantly, those noncitizens who receive the benefit of this exercise of discretion become eligible for work authorization." Lee, *Monitoring Immigration Enforcement*, 53 Ariz. L. Rev. 1089, 1109 & n.72 (2011). However, his footnote to this assertion cites the second sentence of ICE FAQ memorandum: "[Q:] Will beneficiaries of an exercise of prosecutorial discretion automatically receive work authorization? [A:] No. Nothing about this process is automatic and nobody who goes through this process is automatically entitled to work authorization. Per longstanding federal law, individuals affected by an exercise of prosecutorial discretion will be able to request work authorization, including paying associated fees, and their requests will be separately considered by USCIS on a case-by-case basis." *Frequently Asked Questions on the Administration's Announcement Regarding a New Process to Further Focus Immigration Enforcement Resources on High Priority Cases*, U.S. Immigr. & Customs Enforcement, www.ice.gov. Some of the DREAM Act students and others with similar low-priority status are receiving some kind of response, and their removals have been stayed. *See, e.g.*, Mark Curnutte, *Pastor's Stay of Deportation Extended*, NKY.com, Dec. 19, 2011, http://nky.cincinnati.com(reporting ICE granting deferred action status to a church pastor); Michael A. Olivas, *Some DREAM Students Face Nightmare Scenarios, Obama Administration Must Honor Commitment*, Hous. Chron., Apr. 6, 2011, www.chron.com (reporting on a college student who was given a one-year stay by the intervention of Rep. Sheila Jackson Lee); *see also* Roberto G. Gonzales, *Learning to Be Illegal: Undocumented Youth and Shifting Legal Contexts in the Transition to Adulthood*, 76 Am. Soc. Rev. 602, 613–15 (2011) (following up with DREAM Act–eligible students after college graduation). At best, the hypothetical ICE answer to the FAQ is inconsistent and contradictory—it assumes *no* but says the noncitizen can apply. Importantly, emphasizing the second part of the FAQ answer rather than the first part leads to different conclusions, and even the grant of prosecutorial discretion has not always resolved or even frozen the case. Some noncitizens who would appear from the record to be eligible have found themselves deported or given brief reprieves but no reconstitution of their status. *See, e.g.*, Susan Carroll, *New Immigration Policy Too Late for Sick Teacher: Man Deported to Spain Despite Clean Record, Job*, Hous. Chron., Aug. 27, 2011, at A1 (reporting that a K–12 teacher with illness was removed); Daniel Gonzalez, *Deportee Struggles to Readjust*, Ariz. Rep., Jan. 23, 2012, at A1 (reporting

that a former Phoenix high school cross-country coach failed to gain discretionary relief and was deported to Mexico); *Montgomery County Student, Family Win Reprieve from Deportation*, Wash. Post, Mar. 14, 2012, www.washingtonpost.com (chronicling a DREAM Act student who won a one-year stay); Ruben Navarrette, *Quit Playing Favorites, Politics with Deportations*, Sacr. Bee, Mar. 14, 2012, www. sacbee.com (reporting on a high school valedictorian who was given a two-year stay); Michael Biesecker & Gosia Wozniacka, *NC Judge Could Terminate Parental Rights of Deported Worker, Put US-Born Sons up for Adoption*, Fox News, Mar. 9, 2012, http://us.foxnews.mobi/quickPage.html?page=26028&content=70199782& pageNum=-1 (reporting that a father was deported and U.S. citizen children were put up for adoption). A listing on the University of Houston's website includes over two hundred stories of DREAM Act students in various stages of their legal action. *See* IHELG, *DREAM Act Newspaper, Magazine, and Website Stories, 2002– 2012 (Partial Listing)*, U. Houston L. Center, www.law.uh.edu.

48 Deferred Enforced Departure (DED) grants certain qualified citizens and nationals of designated countries a temporary, discretionary, administrative protection from removal from the United States and eligibility for employment authorization for the period of time in which DED is authorized. The president determines which countries will be designated based on issues that may include, but are not limited to, ongoing civil strife, environmental disaster, or other extraordinary or temporary conditions. The decision to grant DED is issued as an executive order or presidential memorandum. U.S. Citizenship & Immigration Services, *Affirmative Asylum Procedures Manual* 56 (2010), www.uscis.gov. DED, which was designated Extended Voluntary Departure until 1990, is conferred upon nationals from countries (such as Liberia) deemed to require temporary protection. *See, e.g.*, Lynda J. Oswald, *Note, Extended Voluntary Departure: Limiting the Attorney General's Discretion in Immigration Matters*, 85 Mich. L. Rev. 152, 157 (1986) ("EVD is granted to aliens who are temporarily unable to return to their home country because of dangerous conditions there.").

49 Immigration and Nationality Act § 244(a), 8 U.S.C. § 1254(a) (2006).

50 *See How Do I Apply for Temporary Protected Status (TPS)?*, U.S. Citizenship & Immigr. Services, www.uscis.gov (explaining who is eligible for TPS and how to apply).

51 8 U.S.C. § 1254(a); U.S. Citizenship & Immigration Services, *Affirmative Asylum Procedures Manual*, at 71.

52 Press Release, U.S. Citizenship & Immigration Services, *USCIS Announces Interim Relief for Foreign Students Adversely Impacted by Hurricane Katrina* (Nov. 25, 2005), www.uscis.gov (outlining deferred action action available to F-1 students impacted by Hurricane Katrina college closures). Deferred action relief was not made available to M-1 or J-1 visa holders—even those whose situations in the hurricane were just as dire. *Id.*

53 *Short-Term Employment Authorization and Reduced Course Load for Certain F-1 Nonimmigrant Students Adversely Affected by Hurricane Katrina*, 70 Fed. Reg.

70992-96 (Nov. 25, 2005). *See generally* Brian Huddleston, *Legal Education Under Extreme Stress: A Semester in Exile: Experiences and Lessons Learned During Loyola University New Orleans School of Law's Fall 2005 Hurricane Katrina Relocation*, 57 J. Legal Educ. 319 (2007) (documenting a day-by-day analysis of Katrina and its aftermath on Loyola University New Orleans School of Law).

54 8 U.S.C. § 1101(a)(15)(U) (2006) (outlining the availability of a visa to those aliens who have "suffered substantial physical or mental abuse as a result of having been a victim of criminal activity"). In an April 6, 2007, "Recommendation from the CIS Ombudsman [Prakash Khatri] to the Director, USCIS [Emilio T. Gonzalez]," there was acknowledgment that U visa holders could receive deferred action, including work authorization and family beneficiary eligibility. *See* § 1101(a)(15)(U); *Memorandum from Prakash Khatri, CIS Ombudsman, to Emilio T. Gonzales, Dir. USCIS, on Recommendations to USCIS* (Apr. 6, 2007), www.dhs.gov. Gonzalez published his response to the ombudsman on August 7, 2007, agreeing on the need for data but stressing the infeasibility of doing so. *Memorandum from Emilio T. Gonzalez, Dir. USCIS, to Prakash Khatri, USCIS Ombudsman, Response to Recommendation #32, Deferred Action* (Aug. 7, 2007), www.dhs.gov. There are not many U visa holders, and the data had not yet been fully analyzed, but early reports included some problems with the use of the U visa because they were not made available for almost seven years and can require severe abuse and violence to be visited upon the victims and also because the normal rough-and-tumble of court cases involving victims can often revictimize the witnesses. *See* Jessica Farb, *The U Visa Unveiled: Immigrant Crime Victims Freed from Limbo*, 15 Hum. Rts. Brief 26, 26–27 (2007) (examining the delay in implementing the U visa); Micaela Schuneman, *Seven Years of Bad Luck: How the Government's Delay in Issuing U-Visa Regulations Further Victimized Immigrant Crime Victims*, 12 J. Gender Race & Just. 465 (2009) (analyzing delays and problems involved with using U visas).

55 *See* Refugee, Asylum and International Operations Directorate: Humanitarian Parole Program, U.S. Citizenship & Immigr. Services, www.uscis.gov (giving an overview of humanitarian parole).

56 8 C.F.R. § 274a.12(c)(14). *See generally* U.S. Naturalization and Immigration Service, *Inspector's Field Manual*, www.gani.com (including a memorandum canceling the OI).

57 Khatri, *Memorandum from Prakash Khatri*.

58 Hopper & Osuna, *Remedies*, at 10.

59 Wildes, *Deferred Action Program* (analyzing new deferred action files).

60 *Id.* at 826 (footnotes omitted).

61 Hopper & Osuna, *Remedies*, at 11.

62 *See* Julia Preston, *U.S. Says Fast Pace Continues*, N.Y. Times, Sept. 15, 2012, at A17 (reporting on data released by DHS on deferred action applications); *see also* Julia Preston, *Quick Start to Program Offering Immigrants a Reprieve*, N.Y. Times, Sept. 12, 2012, at A19 ("As the deferral program expands, resistance to it has grown

among Republicans in Congress, who say it is undermining the administration's broader enforcement against illegal immigration and making it difficult for immigration agents to do their jobs.").

63 *See* Preston, *Fast Pace.*

64 *See, e.g.,* Shoba Sivaprasad Wadhia, *Sharing Secrets: Examining Deferred Action and Transparency in Immigration Law,* 10 U.N.H. L. Rev. 1 (2012).

65 *Id.* at 42–43 (footnotes omitted). Remarkably, these data included more than one hundred emergency Haitian cases following the 2010 earthquake in that country. *Id.* at 40. Professor Wadhia indicated that the data were in very poor shape and drolly noted, "It is neither possible to conclude that the records I received were complete, nor is it possible to analyze the entirety of what I received, because there is great disparity between how the data on deferred action is collected and recorded by each office, if at all." *Id.* at 39. Her impressive forensic skills in gathering and analyzing the data were at the level of television's *CSI* quality and quite exceptional by immigration scholarship standards.

66 *Id.* at 22.

67 *See id.* From 2005–08, the last years of its eight years in office, the Bush administration averaged 771 deferred action grants per year and 301,418 deportations; the Obama administration averaged 661 deferred action grants annually and 391,348 deportations during 2009–10, its first two years in office. *Id.* (citing Dara Lind, *La Opinion: Obama Has Granted a Record Low Number of Deferred Actions to Immigrants,* America's Voice Online Blog (Apr. 28, 2011), http://americasvoiceonline.org; *see also* Julia Preston, *Deportation Program Sows Mistrust, U.S. Is Told,* N.Y. Times, Sept. 16, 2011, at A12; Julia Preston, *Federal Policy Resulting in Wave of Deportations Draws Protests,* N.Y. Times, Aug. 17, 2011, at A12; Julia Preston, *Latinos Said to Bear Weight of a Deportation Program,* N.Y. Times, Oct. 19, 2011, at A16; Julia Preston & Sarah Wheaton, *Meant to Ease Fears of Deportation Program, Federal Hearings Draw Anger,* N.Y. Times, Aug. 26, 2011, at A13.

68 *See* Liz Halloran, *Supporters Ponder Next Move as DREAM Act Fades,* NPR, Dec. 9, 2010, www.npr.org (reporting that the DREAM Act likely died because of lack of bipartisan support).

69 Sen. McCain's absence during DREAM Act deliberations was widely regarded as strategic because he was in the thick of the 2007–08 Republican primary fight. *See, e.g.,* Stephen Dinan, *McCain Caters to GOP Voters,* Wash. Times, Oct. 31, 2007, at A1 (stating that "Sen. John McCain has quietly been piling up flip-flops," citing previous DREAM Act support).

70 Carl Hulse, *John McCain, a Last Lion of the Senate,* N.Y. Times, Aug. 25, 2018, www.nytimes.com. As close as he had been to Sen. Kennedy, he never cottoned to Mr. Trump and made certain that the president was not invited to attend or speak at his funeral. Robert D. McFadden, *John McCain, 81, Battler in War and Politics,* N.Y. Times, Aug. 26, at A18.

71 *See, e.g.,* Morton, *Prosecutorial Discretion with Civil Immigration* (advising on how ICE agents should exercise prosecutorial discretion).

72 *See generally* Migration Policy Inst., *Migration and the Great Recession: The Transatlantic Experience* (Demetrios G. Papademetriou, Madeleine Sumption & Aaron Terrazas eds., 2011); William H. Frey, *Population Growth in Metro America Since 1980: Putting the Volatile 2000s in Perspective*, Brookings Inst. Metro. Pol'y Program (Mar. 2012), www.brookings.edu (revealing growth has slowed in metropolitan areas in the 2000s); Michael Hoefer, Nancy Rytina & Bryan C. Baker, *Estimates of the Unauthorized Immigrant Population Residing in the United States: January 2010*, DHS Office of Immigr. Statistics, Feb. 2011, www.dhs.gov (reviewing the declining number of unauthorized noncitizens in the United States).

73 *See generally* Jacqueline Stevens, *U.S. Government Unlawfully Detaining and Deporting U.S. Citizens as Aliens*, 18 Va. J. Soc. Pol'y & L. 606 (2011) (arguing Immigration and Customs Enforcement is detaining and deporting U.S. citizens without jurisdiction); Carola Suarez-Orozco, Hirokazu Yoshikawa, Robert T. Teranishi & Marcelo M. Suarez-Orozco, *Growing Up in the Shadows: The Developmental Implications of Unauthorized Status*, 81 Harv. Educ. Rev. 438 (2011) (outlining the developmental challenges children with undocumented parents face); Preston, *Bear Weight*, at A16; Julia Preston, *Risks Seen for Children of Illegal Immigrants*, N.Y. Times, Sept. 21, 2011, at A17 (reporting that children with such parents have negative effects on social development); Int'l Human Rights Law Clinic, Univ. of Cal., Berkeley, Sch. of Law et al., *In the Child's Best Interest? The Consequences of Losing a Lawful Immigrant Parent to Deportation* (2010), www.law.berkeley.edu (chronicling the effects on children of having a parent deported); *Shattered Families: The Perilous Intersection of Immigration Enforcement and the Child Welfare System*, Applied Research Ctr. (Nov. 2011), www.arc.org (investigating the lack of foster children reuniting with their deported families).

74 Julia Preston, *Deportation Halted for Some Students as Lawmakers Seek New Policy*, N.Y. Times, Apr. 27, 2011, at A20.

75 In a series of detailed articles, the *New York Times* reporter Julia Preston followed the complex issues involved in the deferred action policy and the resultant changes in immigrant communities. *See, e.g.*, Preston, *Deportation Halted*, at A20; Preston, *Sows Mistrust*, at A12; Preston, *Federal Policy*, at A12; Preston & Wheaton, *Meant to Ease Fears*, at A13; Julia Preston, *New Rules for Guest Workers Are Issued by the Labor Dept.*, N.Y. Times, Feb. 11, 2012, at A11; Julia Preston, *Obama Policy on Deporting Used Unevenly*, N.Y. Times, Nov. 13, 2011, A16.

76 *Oversight of the Department of Homeland Security: Hearing Before the S. Comm. on the Judiciary*, 112th Cong. 32–33 (2011) (statement of Janet Napolitano, Sec'y, U.S. Dep't of Homeland Security). In April 2011, lawyers who had served as INS general counsel and other immigration bar leaders issued a brief memo indicating the various administrative and discretionary means available to the several immigration authorities, none of which required congressional action. *See Memorandum from Jeanne Butterfield, Former Exec. Dir., Am. Immigration Lawyers Ass'n et al., to Interested Parties*, Apr. 29, 2011, www.immigrationpolicy.org; *see also* Julia

Preston, *Immigration Decreases, but Tensions Remain High*, N.Y. Times, Mar. 11, 2012, at A15.

77 *See* Julia Preston, *In Test of Deportation Policy, 1 in 6 Get a Fresh Look and a Reprieve*, N.Y. Times, Jan. 20, 2012, at A13 (noting the "huge backlogs [of immigration cases] swamping the immigration courts").

78 Using comprehensive FOIA-initiated data from the EOIR, the Syracuse University Transactional Records Access Clearinghouse (TRAC) has analyzed case-by-case data. *U.S. Deportation Proceedings in Immigration Courts*, TRAC Immigration, http://trac.syr.edu (reporting deportation proceedings by state, nationality, court, and city); *see also* Preston, *1 in 6*, at A13.

79 *See* Institute for Higher Education Law and Governance (IHELG), *Listing*, for a sample of the hundreds of news stories about undocumented college students, including those engaged in civil disobedience and self-identifying to make public points. *See, e.g.*, Susan Carroll, *Student's Hopes Ride on DREAM Act as He Faces Deportation*, Hous. Chron., Dec. 13, 2010, www.chron.com; Kevin Freking, *Immigrants Protest State Education Policy*, Waterloo Region Rec., June 29, 2011, at D11; Erin Kelly, *Successful Young Illegal Migrants Daring to Dream*, Ariz. Rep., June 29, 2011, at A1; Khimm, *Obama DREAMs On*; Rene Galindo, *Undocumented & Unafraid: The DREAM Act 5 and the Public Disclosure of Undocumented Status as a Political Act*, Univ. Hous. L. Ctr. (IHELG Research Monograph No. 11-02, 2011), www.law.uh.edu.

80 *See, e.g.*, Jason Buch, *Graduate's Deportation Case Dropped*, San Antonio Express-News, Nov. 3, 2011, at A1; Christopher Connell, *Keeping the Dream Alive*, Int'l Educator, Jan.–Feb. 2012, at 4, 5; Preston, *Unevenly*, at A16.

81 *See generally* Marisa Gerber, *Vaya Con Mom; After Their Mother Was Deported to Mexico, the Brito Children Embarked on a Two-Year Journey Trying to Navigate Life in the United States on Their Own*, OC Weekly, Oct. 20, 2011, at 10; Kimberly Hefling, *Duncan Praises Push to Help Immigrant Students: Education Secretary Arne Duncan Said Monday He's Encouraged That Some States Are Allowing the Children of Illegal Immigrants to Pay In-State Tuition at Public Colleges*, Seattle Times, Nov. 7, 2011, http://seattletimes.nwsource.com; Nathan Pippenger, *One Family in Limbo: What Obama's Immigration Policy Looks like in Practice*, New Republic, Sept. 16, 2011, www.tnr.com; Maria Sacchetti, *Two Reprieves Give Immigrants Cautious Hope; Advocates See Signs of Prioritizing Cases*, Bos. Globe, Nov. 26, 2011, at Metro-1; Ronald Trowbridge, *Educated Illegal Immigrants Bring Fiscal Gain*, InsideHigherEd.com, Nov. 17, 2011, www.insidehighered.com; *see also* Alvin Melathe & Suman Raghunathan, *Tuition Equity Bills Continue to Build Momentum in State Legislatures*, Immigr. Impact, Feb. 10, 2012, http://immigrationimpact.com; Leah Muse-Orlinoff, *Staying Put but Still in the Shadows: Undocumented Immigrants Remain in the Country Despite Strict Laws*, Center for Am. Progress, Feb. 22, 2012, www.americanprogress.org.

82 Morton, *Prosecutorial Discretion with Civil Immigration; Memorandum from John Morton, Dir. U.S. Immigration and Customs Enforcement, to All Field Office Direc-*

tors., *All Special Agents in Charge, and All Chief Counsel on Prosecutorial Discretion: Certain Victims, Witnesses, and Plaintiffs* (June 17, 2011), www.ice.gov.

83 Legal Action Ctr. & Alexsa Alonzo, *DHS Review of Low Priority Cases for Prosecutorial Discretion*, Am. Immigr. Council, Feb. 13, 2012, www.legalactioncenter.org; *see also Letter from Janet Napolitano, Secretary, Department of Homeland Security, to Senator Dick Durbin* (Aug. 18, 2011), http://durbin.senate.gov (identifying the establishment of the interagency working group and implementation of a "case by case" review process).

84 *See, e.g., Memorandum from Peter Vincent, Principal Legal Advisor, Immigration and Customs Enforcement, to All Chief Counsel, Office of the Principal Legal Advisor, on Case-by-Case Review of Incoming and Certain Pending Cases* (Nov. 17, 2011), www.ice.gov; *Guidance to ICE Attorneys Reviewing the CBP, USCIS, and ICE Cases Before the Executive Office for Immigration Review*, U.S. Immigr. & Customs Enforcement (2011), www.ice.gov; *Next Steps in the Implementation of the Prosecutorial Discretion Memorandum and the August 18th Announcement on Immigration Enforcement Priorities*, U.S. Immigr. & Customs Enforcement (2011), www.ice.gov.

85 Preston, *1 in 6*, at A13.

86 *See, e.g., Guidance to ICE Attorneys*, at 1–2.

87 *See, e.g.*, Julian Aguilar, *DHS Refutes Immigration "Stonewalling" Allegations*, Tex. Trib., Nov. 22, 2011, www.texastribune.org.

88 *See, e.g., House Judiciary Immigration Subcommittee Holds Hearing on OIG Adjudications Report*, AILA InfoNet Doc. No. 12021649, AILA InfoNet (Feb. 16, 2012), www.aila.org ("On February 15, 2012, the House Judiciary's Subcommittee on Immigration Policy and Enforcement held a hearing 'Safeguarding the Integrity of the Immigration Benefits Adjudication Process.'"); *see also* Susan Carroll, *Report: Feds Downplayed ICE Case Dismissals: Documents Show Agency Had Approval to Dismiss Some Deportation Cases*, Hous. Chron., June 27, 2011, www.chron.com (asserting that "Homeland Security officials misled the public and Congress last year in an effort to downplay a wave of immigration case dismissals in Houston and other cities amid accusations that they had created 'back-door amnesty.'"). The chair of the House Judiciary Committee, Rep. Lamar Smith (R-Tex.), has been a persistent critic of any deferred action initiatives. *See, e.g.*, Aguilar, *DHS Refutes* (reporting that Smith "threatened to hold the [DHS] in contempt for failing to provide immigration enforcement information" and "accused DHS of 'stonewalling'"); Lamar Smith, *SMITH: Obama Budget's Backdoor Amnesty: President's Spending Plan Weakens Immigration Enforcement*, Wash. Times, Feb. 23, 2012, www.washingtontimes.com. *But see* Editorial, *The Forgetful Mr. Smith*, N.Y. Times, July 13, 2011, at A26 (noting examples of Rep. Smith's support for similar discretion during President George W. Bush's administration). In Spring 2012, Rep. Smith memorably characterized the security accommodations for detainees as "Holiday on ICE." *See* Julia

Preston, *Union Chief Says New U.S. Rules for Immigration Detention Are Flawed*, N.Y. Times, Mar. 29, 2012, at A18.

89 This genre has wide and deep roots. *See, e.g.*, Editorial, *The Forgetful Mr. Smith*; Alana Goodman, *Feds Misled Public on "Backdoor Amnesty" Scandal*, Commentary, June 27, 2011, www.commentarymagazine.com; Hans von Spakovsky, *Backdoor Amnesty—Abusing the Constitution and Presidential Authority*, Heritage. org (Aug. 19, 2011), http://blog.heritage.org.

90 Editorial, *How a Democracy Works: President Obama Has the Authority to Start Fixing Immigration, If Only He Would Use It*, N.Y. Times, June 4, 2011, at A20; Julia Preston, *U.S. Pledges to Raise Deportation Threshold*, N.Y. Times, June 18, 2011, at A14 (describing a "groundswell of local resistance" to Secure Communities programs); Kristian Ramos, *The Problem with the GOP's Love Affair with "Backdoor Amnesty,"* Huffington Post, Sept. 2, 2011, www.huffingtonpost.com; Gary Endelman & Cyrus D. Mehta, *Keeping Hope Alive: President Obama Can Use His Executive Power Until Congress Passes the DREAM Act*, The Insightful Immigr. Blog—Commentaries on Immigr. Pol'y, Cases, and Trends (Dec. 18, 2010), http:// cyrusmehta.blogspot.com. As the war on terrorism has escalated, a number of initiatives have arisen. For a critical and comprehensive review of how immigration rhetoric has played out in strategic and terrorism terms, *see* Geoffrey A. Hoffman & Susham M. Modi, *The War on Terror as a Metaphor for Immigration Regulation: A Critical View of a Distorted Debate*, 15 J. Gender Race & Just. 449 (2012).

91 *See generally* Morton, *Prosecutorial Discretion: Certain Victims*.

92 *See, e.g.*, Morton, *Prosecutorial Discretion with Civil Immigration*; Morton, *Prosecutorial Discretion: Certain Victims*.

93 *Id.; see also* Maritza Reyes, *Constitutionalizing Immigration Law: The Vital Role of Judicial Discretion in the Removal of Lawful Permanent Residents*, 84 Temp. L. Rev. 637, 692 (2012) (identifying that the Morton Memo "provides guidance for ICE agents, officers, and attorneys to consider when deciding whether to exercise prosecutorial discretion"); Shoba Sivaprasad Wadhia, *The Morton Memo and Prosecutorial Discretion: An Overview*, Immigr. Pol'y Center, July 20, 2011, www. immigrationpolicy.org.

94 *Memorandum from John Morton, Assistant Sec'y, U.S. Immigration and Customs Enforcement, to Peter S. Vincent, Principal Legal Advisor, on Guidance Regarding the Handling of Removal Proceedings of Aliens with Pending or Approved Applications or Petitions* (Aug. 20, 2010), www.ice.gov.

95 John, Morton, Dir. U.S. Immigration and Customs Enforcement, to All ICE Employees, on *Civil Immigration Enforcement: Priorities for the Apprehension, Detention, and Removal of Aliens*, June 30, 2010. www.ice.gov. *See generally* Wadhia, *The Morton Memo*.

96 Morton, *Prosecutorial Discretion with Civil Immigration*.

97 Morton, *Prosecutorial Discretion: Certain Victims; see also* U.S. Immigration and Customs Enforcement, *Guidance to ICE Attorneys; Next Steps*.

98 Legal Action Ctr. & Alonzo, *DHS Review* (identifying DHS enforcement policies regarding cases of "particular care and concern" and those categories of individuals "who are to receive particular care and attention" pursuant to the Morton Memoranda). *See also* Wadhia, *The Morton Memo* (reviewing the pros and cons of the Morton Memoranda).

99 *See generally* Norman Abrams, *Internal Policy: Guiding the Exercise of Prosecutorial Discretion*, 19 UCLA L. Rev. 1 (1971).

100 Leon Wildes & Shoba Sivaprasad Wadhia, *Prosecutorial Discretion and the Legacy of John Lennon*, Immigr. Impact, July 20, 2011, http://immigrationimpact.com.

101 *See id.*

102 *Id.*

103 Michelle Malkin, *ICE Memos Open Another Door to Illegal Alien Amnesty-by-Fiat* (June 22, 2011), http://michellemalkin.com.

104 *Id.*

105 Walter Ewing, *Border Patrol to Roll Out New "Get Tough" Policy on Unauthorized Immigrants*, Immigr. Impact, Jan. 19, 2012, http://immigrationimpact.com; *see also Authority of U.S. Customs and Border Protection Agents: An Overview*, Immigr. Pol'y Center, Feb. 2012, http://immigrationpolicy.org.

106 Ewing, *Border Patrol to Roll Out.*

107 *Id.*

108 *Id.*

109 *Id.*

110 *Id.*

111 *Rising Immigration Backlog at All-Time High Yet Criminal, National Security, and Terrorism Cases Fall*, TRAC Immigration (Sept. 14, 2011), www.trac.syr.edu.

112 *Id.*

113 *Id.* Syracuse University's authoritative TRAC reported that immigration-related prosecutions referred by the DHS immigration enforcement agencies totaled 59 percent of all federal prosecutions in federal courts, including both Article III district courts (predominantly illegal reentry and drug-related offenses) and those of magistrate judges (mostly illegal reentry and illegal entry offenses). *Id.* Reporting October 2011 data, the study also found that the number of immigration-related prosecutions filed in that period were 119.5 percent greater than were such prosecutions filed in 2006. *Id.* The data are also reported by federal judicial districts by the largest number of prosecutions per capita for immigration matters during this period. *Id.* The report's Table 3 revealed that the highest concentration was the same five districts as five years before, although the order of the top five had shifted to California's Southern District, Arizona, Texas's Western District, New Mexico, and Texas's Southern District. *Id.*

114 *Secure Communities*, U.S. Immigr. & Customs Enforcement, www.ice.gov; *see Secure Communities: A Fact Sheet*, Immigr. Pol'y Center, www.immigrationpolicy.org.

115 Julia Preston, *States Resisting Program Central to Obama's Immigration Strategy*, N.Y. Times, May 6, 2011, at A18. *Id.*; *see also* Editorial, *Glad Gov. Cuomo's*

Withdrawal from Program to Catch Criminal Illegal Aliens Will Have Little Effect, N.Y. Daily News, June 4, 2011, http://articles.nydailynews.com; Dave Harmon, *Undocumented Immigrants in Jail: Who Gets Deported?*, Austin Am.-Statesman, Mar. 18, 2012, www.statesman.com (criticizing "Secure Communities" efforts in Austin as excessive, particularly with emphasis on misdemeanors); Preston, *Sows Mistrust*, at A12; Preston & Wheaton, *Meant to Ease Fears*, at A13; Kirk Semple, *Cuomo Ends State's Role in U.S. Immigrant Checks*, N.Y. Times, June 2, 2011, at A21.

116 Harmon, *Undocumented Immigrants in Jail.*

117 The ICE Union held a unanimous vote of no confidence in Assistant Secretary Morton and Executive Director Coven in June 2010. *See Am. Fed. Gov't Emp. Nat'l Council, Vote of No Confidence in ICE Director John Morton and ICE ODPP Assistant Director Phyllis Coven* (2010), www.iceunion.org; *see also* John W. Slagle, *Fraudulent Documents Puerto Rico/ICE Administration Policies*, St. Louis L. Enforcement Examiner, Jan. 16, 2012, www.examiner.com (recounting employee dissatisfaction and no-confidence votes).

118 Slagle, *Fraudulent Documents Puerto Rico* (defining the issue to be "amnesty through policy" because "[t]he majority of ICE ERO Officers are prohibited from making street arrests or enforcing United States immigration laws outside of the institutional (jail) setting").

119 *See id.* (noting that "[r]arely was any political appointee considered in a position of 'No Confidence' for leadership abilities dating from 1972").

120 *See id.*

121 *Fugitive Operations*, U.S. Immigr. & Customs Enforcement, www.ice.gov.

122 *Id.* The details of the program are maintained at the DHS website. *Id.* In 2007, an evaluation of the program and its growth was conducted by the DHS inspector general. *An Assessment of United States Immigration and Customs Enforcement's Fugitive Operations Teams OIG-07-34, Dep't of Homeland Sec. Office of the Inspector Gen.* (Mar. 2007), www.oig.dhs.gov.

123 *Southwest Border Security Operations*, Nat'l Immigr. Forum 7 (Dec. 2010), www.immigrationforum.org; *see also* U.S. Immigration and Naturalization Service, *Populating a Nation: A History of Immigration and Naturalization*, U.S. Customs and Border Protection, www.cbp.gov; U.S. Customs and Border Protection, *Snapshot: A Summary of CBP Facts and Figures* (Nov. 2019), www.cbp.gov/sites/default/files/assets/documents/2019-Nov/CBP-Snapshot-Nov-2019.pdf.

124 "A fiscal year 2013 budget brief released by Homeland Security today has some details on the Obama administration's immigration enforcement priorities, and one of the losers is the federal-local partnership known as 287(g). The administration is proposing a budget reduction of $17 million up front, and the document suggests a gradual phase-out in favor of Secure Communities, which is described as more consistent, efficient and cost effective.'" Leslie Berestein Rojas, *DHS Budget Proposes Discontinuing 287(g) in Some Jurisdictions*, S. Cal. Public Radio, Feb. 14, 2012, http://multiamerican.scpr.org.

125 Wadhia, *The Role of Prosecutorial Discretion*, at 293; *see also* Helen B. Marrow, *Immigrant Bureaucratic Incorporation: The Dual Roles of Professional Missions and Government Policies*, 74 Am. Soc. Rev. 756 (2009).

126 *See* Darren Bush, *Mission Creep: Antitrust Exemptions and Immunities as Applied to Deregulated Industries*, Utah L. Rev. 761 (2006) (discussing the "mission creep" phenomenon).

127 *See generally* Abrams, *Internal Policy* (discussing pre-Lennon administrative law prosecutorial discretion issues in U.S. Attorney offices); David H. E. Becker, *Judicial Review of INS Adjudication: When May the Agency Make Sudden Changes in Policy and Apply Its Decisions Retroactively?* 52 Admin. L. Rev. 219 (2000). A growing number of scholars also note the vertical problems of coordination across governmental jurisdiction in immigration enforcement in light of the fact that immigration is a federal domain with local coordination dimensions. *See, e.g.*, Mathew Coleman, *The "Local" Migration State: The Site-Specific Devolution of Immigration Enforcement in the U.S. South*, 34 Law & Pol'y 159 (2012); Michael A. Olivas, *Immigration-Related State and Local Ordinances: Preemption, Prejudice, and the Proper Role for Enforcement*, U. Chi. Legal F. 27 (2007); Monica Varsanyi, Paul G. Lewis, Doris Marie Provine & Scott Decker, *A Multilayered Jurisdictional Patchwork: Immigration Federalism in the United States*, 34 L. & Pol'y 138 (2012).

128 *See generally* Coleman, *"Local" Migration State.*

129 *Id.* at 164–66.

130 *See, e.g.*, Lee, *Monitoring Immigration Enforcement*, at 1096–1113 (detailing asymmetric enforcement authority issues between ICE and DOL); Hiroshi Motomura, *The Rights of Others: Legal Claims and Immigration Outside the Law*, 59 Duke L.J. 1723, 1746 (2010) (analyzing agency monitoring issues).

131 Kirk Semple, *U.S. to Pay Immigrants Over Raids*, N.Y. Times, Feb. 15, 2012, at A22.

132 *Id.*

133 Hilda Munoz et al., *11 New Haven Men Arrested in Immigration Raid Reach Landmark Settlement with U.S. Government*, Hartford Courant, Feb. 15, 2012, www.courant.com; Semple, *U.S. to Pay*, at A22.

134 *See, e.g.*, Wadhia, *Sharing Secrets*, at 52–60. She analyzes "the values of equal justice, accuracy, consistency, efficiency, and acceptability in the deferred action context." *Id.* at 52; *see also* Mary E. O'Leary, *Yale Law School Immigration Clinic Files Class Action Lawsuit Challenging Secure Communities Detainers*, New Haven Reg., Feb. 22, 2012, www.nhregister.com (detailing another suit filed in New Haven, Conn.).

135 *Next Steps.*

136 *Id.*; *see* Morton, *Prosecutorial Discretion: Certain Victims.*

137 Preston, *1 in 6*, at A13.

138 Julia Preston, *In Test of Deportation Policy, 1 in 6 Offered Reprieve*, Aretz & Heise Immigr. LLC (Jan. 20, 2012), www.immigrationdenver.com (reprinting an earlier version of Preston, *1 in 6*).

139 P. Solomon Banda, *Courts Suspend Hearings to Deport: US Reviews Illegal Immigrant Status*, Bos. Globe, Jan. 17, 2012, www.bostonglobe.com; Jeff Bliss, *U.S. Agency Said to Urge Closing 1,600 Deportation Cases*, Bloomberg.com, Jan. 19, 2012, www.bloomberg.com.

140 Preston, *1 in 6*, at A13; *see also* Nancy Lofholm, *Prosecutorial Review Puts Immigration Cases in Holding Pattern, Infuses a Sense of Hope*, Denv. Post, Dec. 21, 2011, www.denverpost.com.

141 Preston, *1 in 6*, at A13.

142 John Fritze, *Hundreds of Deportation Cases May Be Closed: Baltimore, Denver Pilot Cities for Expedited Review*, Balt. Sun, Jan. 19, 2012, http://articles.baltimoresun.com. In the technical argot of immigration, these were predominantly forms of administrative closure or termination. Such distinctions do not make a difference in my overall narrative, but God is in the details. Shoba Sivaprasad Wadhia has examined these details in very comprehensive fashion in her estimable *The Immigration Prosecutor and the Judge: Examining the Role of the Judiciary in Prosecutorial Discretion Decisions*, 10 U.N.H. L. Rev. 1 (2012).

143 *See* Preston, *1 in 6*, at A13.

144 *See* Muzaffar Chishti & Faye Hipsman, *Key Factors, Unresolved Issues in New Deferred Action Program for Immigrant Youth Will Determine Its Success*, Migration Pol'y Inst., Aug. 16, 2012, www.migrationinformation.org.

145 *See* Preston, *1 in 6*, at A13.

146 *See, e.g., Lafler v. Cooper*, 132 S. Ct. 1376, 1381 (2012) (noting the prevalence of plea bargains and prosecutorial discretion in the criminal justice system: "the reality [is] that criminal justice today is for the most part a system of pleas, not a system of trials").

147 *See* Christi & Hipsmun, *Key Factors*.

148 *Id.* (noting the difficulty of measuring effectiveness).

149 *See* Yasmin Amer, *Despite Immigration Reforms, Many Young Immigrants Still in Limbo*, CNN.com, Dec. 24, 2011, www.cnn.com.

150 Preston, *1 in 6*, at A13 (describing the situation as "indefinite limbo").

151 *Id.*

152 *See, e.g.,* Amer, *Despite Immigration Reforms* (staying removal but "without an exact timeline or a plan of action").

153 *See, e.g.,* Muzaffar Chishti & Claire Bergeron, *Questions Arise with Implementation of Obama Administration's New Prosecutorial Discretion Policy*, Migration Pol'y Inst., Feb. 29, 2012, www.migrationinformation.org. The policy's reach was still not entirely clear. For example, on February 6, 2012, the U.S. Court of Appeals for the Ninth Circuit demanded that DHS explain how it would apply the new prosecutorial discretion policy to noncitizens already ordered to be removed and who were in the appeals process if they qualified for such discretion—whether detained or released on bond. *Court Ruling Could Prompt More Deportation Reviews*, CBSNews.com, Feb. 11, 2012, www.cbsnews.com. In *Rodriguez v. Holder*, the

circuit court wrote, "In light of ICE Director John Morton's June 17, 2011 memo regarding prosecutorial discretion, and the November 17, 2011 follow-up memo providing guidance to ICE Attorneys, the government shall advise the court by March 19, 2012, whether the government intends to exercise prosecutorial discretion in this case and, if so, the effect, if any, of the exercise of such discretion on any action to be taken by this court with regard to Petitioner's pending petition for rehearing." 668 F.3d 670, 671 (9th Cir. 2012). Additional lower-court skepticism arose when a federal judge ordered clarification about U.S. removal policy and it was suggested that the U.S. Solicitor General may have misled SCOTUS on the policy. The judge noted, in tart language, "Trust everybody, but cut the cards," as the old saying goes. When the Solicitor General of the United States makes a representation to the Supreme Court, trustworthiness is presumed. Here, however, plaintiffs seek to determine whether one such representation was accurate or whether, as it seems, the government's lawyers were engaged in a bit of a shuffle. *Nat'l Immigration Project v. U.S. Dep't of Homeland Sec.*, 842 F. Supp. 2d 720, 722 (S.D.N.Y. 2012); *see also* Jess Bravin, *Judge Suggests U.S. Misled Court on Immigration Policy*, Wall St. J., Feb. 10, 2012, at A6; Joe Palazzolo, *Rakoff: SCOTUS May Have Been Misled in Immigration Case*, Wall St. J., Feb. 10, 2012, http://blogs.wsj.com. Adam Liptak reported that the DOJ apologized for its misrepresentation. Adam Liptak, *Justice Department Submits Correction Letter to Supreme Court*, N.Y. Times, Apr. 24, 2012, http://thecaucus.blogs.nytimes.com; *see also* Julian Aguilar, *Few Satisfied by Obama's Immigration Policies*, Tex. Trib., Sept. 22, 2011, www.texastribune.org. In addition, other politically sensitive issues, such as potential beneficiaries from gay and lesbian immigrant marriages, were also in play under the general review of case-by-case situations. Amer, *Despite Immigration Reforms*; Pamela Constable, *Montgomery County Student Wins Reprieve from Deportation*, Wash. Post, Mar. 14, 2012, www.washingtonpost.com (granting a one-year stay); Kirk Semple, *U.S. Drops Deportation Proceedings Against Immigrant in Same-Sex Marriage*, N.Y. Times, June 30, 2011, at A16. For a good summary of the highly technical details of administrative closure, EAD, and the like, *see* Legal Action Ctr. & Alonzo, *DHS Review* (noting "independent basis" issue and consequences for noncitizens).

154 *See generally* Morton, *Handling of Removal Proceedings.*

155 *See* Aguilar, *Few Satisfied* (describing widespread criticisms of new policy).

156 A Denver ICE prosecutor called the deferred cases "sleeping beaut[ies]," presumably awaiting the prince's kiss to dismiss them, while a Denver immigration lawyer characterized them as being consigned to "immigration purgatory." Preston, *1 in 6*, at A13.

157 *See generally* Olivas, *IIRIRA*; Romero, *Noncitizen Students.*

158 *See generally* Cecilia Menjivar, *Liminal Legality: Salvadoran and Guatemalan Immigrants' Lives in the United States*, 111 Am. J. Soc. 999 (2006).

159 *See, e.g.*, Patricia Zavella, *I'm Neither Here nor There* (Duke Univ. Press 2011); Graeme Boushey & Adam Luedtke, *Immigrants Across the U.S. Federal Labora-*

tory: Explaining State-Level Innovation in Immigration Policy, 11 St. Pol. & Pol'y Q. 390 (2011); Andrew Thangasamy, *State Policies for Undocumented Immigrants*, in *The New Americans* (Stephen J. Gold & Ruben G. Rumbaut eds., 2010).

160 *See* Preston, *1 in 6*, at A13.

161 *Id.*; *see also* Julian Aguilar, *Immigration Proposal Not Seen as Major Step*, Tex. Trib., Jan. 11, 2012, www.texastribune.org (noting mixed reactions to proposals by immigration attorneys); Jenna Greene, *Deportation Cases Get a Fresh Look; Feds Test Effort to Prioritize Most Serious Immigration Cases*, Nat'l L.J., Jan. 9, 2012, at 1 (describing options for clients as "the difference between the fifth and the eighth circles of Hell").

162 Ralph Adam Fine, *Plea-Bargaining: An Unnecessary Evil*, 70 Marq. L. Rev. 615, 616 (1987) (arguing against plea-bargaining in the criminal justice system because "leniency" operates as a "quid pro quo" for reduced transaction costs and conserved prosecutorial resources rather than as a reduced punishment reflecting less certainty of conviction or an offense of lesser severity). If Fine's reasoning applies to immigration proceedings as it does to criminal prosecutions—and there is little reason to think it should not—then prosecutors may trade "leniency" for "hardball" tactics for those who press for permanent relief rather than the "half-loaf" of deferred action. *See id.*

163 Preston, *1 in 6*, at A13; *see also* Mirela Iverac, *Seeking Deferred Action, Young Immigrants with Blemished Records Give Pause*, WNYC News, Aug. 29, 2012, www. wnyc.org ("'No one is going to want to be the guinea pig,' [an immigration lawyer] said. 'No one wants to bring a test case in a program like this that hasn't been implemented before.'").

164 *See, e.g.*, Immigration Litigation Reduction: Hearing Before the S. Comm. on the Judiciary, 109th Cong. 34 (2006) (statement of Sen. Jeff Sessions, member, S. Comm. on the Judiciary) (expressing surprise that an "illegal immigrant" might appeal the result of a BIA deportation hearing and "get to stay here [two] more years" as the appeals can take as long as twenty-seven months to reach the U.S. circuit courts of appeals).

165 *See generally* Wildes, *All You Need Is Love* (sharing stories about his client John Lennon).

166 Preston, *1 in 6*, at A13.

167 *See* Greene, *Fresh Look*, at 1; Jenna Greene, *Discretionary Program Draws Praise, Derision; Reaction to Pilot for Undocumented Immigrants Mixed*, Daily Bus. Rev., Jan. 11, 2012, at A3; David Leopold, *Why Morton's Memo Is the Best Road Map on Prosecutorial Discretion Yet*, Immigr. Impact, July 1, 2011, http://immigrationimpact.com. *But see* Angelo A. Paparelli & Ted J. Chiappari, *No More Waiting on Legal Immigration*, Seyfarth Shaw LLP, www.seyfarth.com ("[A]n assertive President Obama, with his eyes transfixed on the reelection prize, can do much more to improve our immigration regulations and agency practices, which the President oversees through the Departments of Homeland Security, State, Justice and Labor.").

168 *See* Press Release, N.Y. Immigration Coal., *On First Day of Historic Immigration Policy Change, over a Thousand DREAMers and Family Members Sought Application Assistance at the NYIC Legal Clinic So Far Today* (Aug. 15, 2012), www. thenyic.org.

169 *See* Greene, *Fresh Look* (describing how the trial runs apply only to a portion of pending cases). *See generally* Jeanne Batalova & Margie McHue, *DREAM vs. Reality: An Analysis of Potential DREAM Act Beneficiaries*, Migration Pol'y Inst., July 2010, www.migrationpolicy.org.

170 *See* Richard Herman, *If Immigration Is a Game, Let's Play to Win*, Huffington Post, Aug. 8, 2012, www.huffingtonpost.com ("The USCIS is ramping up for an avalanche of applications. Processing them in a fair and timely manner will be a herculean task.").

171 For people who doubt the general negative press surrounding immigrants, there is a strong counternarrative of careful, nuanced scholarship, often summarized in accessible formats, that reveals immigrants are a substantial net gain, with lower criminality rates and large economic advantages. *See, e.g.,* Anna Flagg, *The Myth of the Criminal Immigrant*, N.Y. Times, Mar. 30, 2018, www.nytimes.com (data show no relationship between crimes and immigration status); Walter Ewing, *Immigrants' Taxes Help Save the Social Security System*, ImmigrationImpact.com, Apr. 15, 2019, http://immigrationimpact.com (all working immigrants pay into Social Security system, but very few are eligible for its benefits).

CHAPTER 6. UNDOCUMENTED LAWYERS, DACA, AND OCCUPATIONAL LICENSING

1 *See* Andrew Bartmess, *3D Chess from Star Trek*, Chess Variants, www.chess-variants.com (demonstrating the unique design of the chessboard). Enter this universe at some risk.

2 *See* Jordan Fabian, *Sergio Garcia: USA's First Undocumented Lawyer*, Atlantic, Jan. 6, 2014, www.theatlantic.com [https://perma.cc/49P8-YZZ8] (providing a brief history of Garcia's case and final ruling).

3 *See In re Garcia*, 315 P.3d 117, 119, 123 (Cal. 2014) (recognizing the Department of Justice's amicus curiae brief opposing Garcia's motion for California bar admission). *See also* Maura Dolan, *Feds Deal a Blow to Would-Be Attorney*, L.A. Times, Aug. 13, 2012, at LAT Extra 1, https://perma.cc/BH93-BVKP (reporting the administration's failure to support Garcia's efforts to gain bar admission).

4 *See* Michael A. Olivas, *Dreams Deferred: Deferred Action, Prosecutorial Discretion, and the Vexing Case(s) of DREAM Act Students*, 21 Wm. & Mary Bill Rts. J. 463, 491, n.131 (2012) (detailing annual statistics regarding DACAmented youth).

5 *See, e.g.,* Ryan Schultheis & Ariel G. Ruiz Soto, *A Revolving Door No More? A Statistical Profile of Mexican Adults Repatriated from the United States* (2017), www. migrationpolicy.org [https://perma.cc/28ZU-FB26] (providing statistics from the Migration Policy Institute).

6 *See* Michael A. Olivas, *Within You Without You: Undocumented Lawyers, DACA, and Occupational Licensing*, 52 Valparaiso U. L. Rev. 65 (2017), Appendix I, at 108 (providing a state-by-state breakdown of Professional License Eligibility Requirements for physicians, nurses, attorneys, and educators).

7 *Id.* Appendix II, at 154 (detailing the differences between state occupational licensing laws that require varying statuses of citizenship).

8 *Id.* Appendix II, at 154 (noting the substantial differences entangled between state occupational licensing laws and citizenship status).

9 *Id.* (reporting differences between state occupational licensing and citizenship requirements for funeral directors, massage therapists, temporary agency workers, occupational therapists, optometrists, pharmacists, physical therapists, private investigators, and real estate agents and brokers).

10 *See* David K. Lynch, *Tectonics* (2010), www.sanandreasfault.org [https://perma.cc/BPG2-Y3DV] (describing how the lithosphere creates continental drifts).

11 Olivas, *Within You Without You*, Appendix II. I have been influenced by my deep reading of licensing literature that is critical of the status quo, although I have searched largely in vain to discover immigration-related scholarship. *See, e.g.*, David E. Bernstein, *Licensing Laws: A Historical Example of the Use of Government Regulatory Power Against African Americans*, S. D. L. Rev. 89 (1994).

12 *Id.* In this area, among my many influences was Morris M. Kleiner, Allison Marier, Kyoung Won Park & Coady Wing, *Relaxing Occupational Licensing Requirements: Analyzing Wages and Prices for a Medical Service*, 59 J. L. & Econ. 261 (2016).

13 *See, e.g.*, Neil Deochand & R. Wayne Fuqua, *BACB Certification Trends: State of the States (1999 to 2014)* 9 Beh. Anal. in Prac. 243 (2016) (interesting national survey of Behavior Analyst Certification Board [BACB] trends, finding geographic differences).

14 Of all the extensive reading I undertook for this chapter, the most useful as for style and approach was a study by Alexandra L. Klein, *The Freedom to Pursue a Common Calling: Applying Intermediate Scrutiny to Occupational Licensing Statutes*, 73 Wash. & Lee L. Rev. 411 (2016). Analyzing the large number of baked-in barriers to licensing in many fields and in many states, she noted, "The majority of individuals harmed by protectionist statutes are poor, uneducated, or minorities. Although plaintiffs challenging these statutes do not fall easily within a 'suspect' or 'quasi-suspect' classification, their lack of political and economic power makes applying intermediate scrutiny reasonable." *Id.* at 457 (citations and references omitted). Although she tiptoed up to the issue of immigration criteria, it's a pity she did not cross into it more deeply.

15 *See* Sela Cowger, Jessica Bolter & Sarah Pierce, *The First 100 Days: Summary of Major Immigration Actions Taken by the Trump Administration* (2017) (offering general policy background). *See also* Eleanor Acer & Olga Byrne, *How the Illegal Immigration Reform and Immigrant Responsibility Act of 1996 Has Undermined*

U.S. Refugee Protection Obligations and Wasted Government Resources, 5 J. Migration & Hum. Security 356, 356–57 (2017) www.migrationpolicy.org [https://perma.cc/HX37-NKKZ] (stating recent record highs in backlogged immigration cases and refugee numbers).

16 *See* Am. Immigr. Council, *How the United States Immigration System Works*, Aug. 12, 2016, www.americanimmigrationcouncil.org [https://perma.cc/ZL4K-P3PF] (teasing the U.S. immigration system into categories, including family-based and employment-based). *Compare* 8 U.S.C. § 1153(a) (2012) (describing "[p]reference allocation for family-sponsored immigrants") *with* 8 U.S.C. § 1153(b) (outlining "[p]reference allocation for employment-based immigrants").

17 *See* Am. Immigr. Council, *How the United States Immigration System Works* (detailing the family- and employment-based immigration regimes). *See, e.g.*, 8 U.S.C. § 1151(a)(1)–(2) (2012) (allowing similar numbers of immigrant visas for "family-sponsored immigrants" as visas issued to "employment-based immigrants"). *See also Manichean*, Vocabulary.com, www.vocabulary.com [https://perma.cc/S8EH-3ASP] ("If you believe in the Manichean idea of dualism, you tend to look at things as having two sides that are opposed. To Manicheans, life can be divided neatly between good or evil, light or dark, or love and hate. When you see *Manichean*, think 'two.'")

18 *See Regulations, Guidance & MOUs*, U.S. Equal Empl. Opportunity Commission (EEOC), www.eeoc.gov [https://perma.cc/M6S7-Y826] (detailing specific statutory rights granted to employees working in the United States).

19 *See* Press Release, U.S. Citizenship & Immigration Services, *USCIS Will Issue Redesigned Green Cards and Employment Authorization Documents* (Apr. 19, 2017), www.uscis.gov [https://perma.cc/6LWQ-W5LC] (abbreviating Employment Authorization Documents). *See also* Maria Linda Ontiveros, *Immigrant Workers and Workplace Discrimination: Overturning the Missed Opportunity of Title VII Under Espinoza v. Farah*, 39 Berk. J. Empl. & Labor L., 117 Univ. of San Francisco Law Research Paper No. 2017-11. *Available at* SSRN: https://ssrn.com (arguing case law should be overruled to be more useful for immigrant workers); *Immigrants' Employment Rights Under Federal Anti-Discrimination Laws*, U.S. Equal Emp. Opportunity Commission, www.eeoc.gov [https://perma.cc/SV26-C62N] (providing examples of prohibited discrimination).

20 *See, e.g., Bernal v. Fainter*, 467 U.S. 216, 220, 227–28 (1984) (Supreme Court decision striking down citizen requirements for public notaries); *C.D.R. Enters., Ltd. v. Bd. of Educ.*, 412 F. Supp. 1164, 1172–73 (E.D.N.Y. 1976) (benefits and occupational licensing), *aff'd sub nom. Lefkowitz v. C.D.R. Enters., Ltd.*, 429 U.S. 1031 (1977) (public work construction); *Examining Bd. of Eng'rs, Architects & Surveyors v. Flores de Otero*, 426 U.S. 572, 601–02, 604–05 (1976) (civil engineers); *Ind. Real Estate Comm'n v. Satoskar*, 417 U.S. 938 (1974) (real estate license); *Sugarman v. Dougall*, 413 U.S. 634, 642–43, 646–47 (1973) (various civil service positions); *In re Griffiths*, 413 U.S. 717, 726, 729 (1973) (law practice). *See generally* Jennesa Calvo-Friedman, Note, *The Uncertain Terrain of State Occupational Licensing Laws for*

Noncitizens: A Preemption Analysis, 102 Geo. L.J. 1597 (2014). *Compare Dan-damudi v. Tisch*, 686 F.3d 66, 72, 79–80 (2d Cir. 2012) (striking down various New York state laws requiring citizenship) *with LeClerc v. Webb*, 419 F.3d 405, 410–12, 415, 422–26 (5th Cir. 2005) (upholding a Louisiana Supreme Court ruling that limited membership to the bar to U.S. citizens or lawful permanent residents—not to nonimmigrants with H-1B or J-1 exchange student visas, even though one was a foreign lawyer and another had graduated from a law school in the state). *See also* U.S. Dep't of Defense, Defense Security Clearance, *Security Assurances for Cleared Individuals and Facilities*, www.dss.mil/isp/international/laa.html [https://perma.cc/P3KS-6PY9] (listing issues of citizenship requirements and exceptions for security-classified employment).

21 U.S. Dep't of Defense, Defense Security Clearance, *Security Assurances* (exceptions to the general rule that noncitizens cannot gain security clearance).

22 *See, e.g., Nyquist v. Mauclet*, 432 U.S. 1, 3–5, 11–12 (1977) (holding a New York statute unconstitutional for requiring state residents seeking financial aid benefits to be U.S. citizens or declare intent to become U.S. citizens because permanent noncitizen residents, inter alia, pay taxes on benefits and should not be required to become citizens even if eligible to do so).

23 *See id.* at 11–12 (finding a violation of constitutional rights of permanent New York residents denied financial aid for not declaring intent to become U.S. citizens by wishing to retain citizenship in foreign countries). The Department of Justice also polices inappropriate EAD practices, such as when employers require certain paperwork of LPRs but not citizens even though both are authorized for employment. *See also* Press Release, Dep't of Justice, *Justice Department Settles Immigration-Related Discrimination Claims Against 121 Residency Programs and American Association of Colleges of Podiatric Medicine* (June 20, 2016), www.justice.gov [https://perma.cc/X55A-VXJZ] (explaining settlement over podiatric residency policies). *See, e.g.,* Press Release, Dep't of Justice, *Justice Department Settles Immigration-Related Discrimination Claim Against Florida Roadside Assistance Services Company* (Apr. 6, 2017), www.justice.gov [https://perma.cc/2EQA-SKTQ] (highlighting discriminatory policies in the field of podiatry that occurred between 2013 and 2015).

24 *See Nyquist*, 432 U.S. at 12 (finding that a noncitizen may become a leader in the community without having any political involvement).

25 *See* Am. Immigr. Council, *How the United States Immigration System Works* (providing more information on numbers of recipients of LPR status, including family-based and employment-based statistics). *See, e.g.,* 8 U.S.C. § 1151(a)(1)–(2) (2012) (granting visas to immigrants or LPRs regardless of family or employment-based categories).

26 *See Nyquist*, 432 U.S. at 12 (reporting that LPRs may apply for virtually any position).

27 *See* Olivas, *Within You*, Appendix II, at 108–154 (listing state statutes that require varying levels of citizenship to obtain specific occupational licenses).

28 *Id.* (noting at least fourteen state statutes that specifically require nothing short of U.S. citizenship for at least one occupation).

29 *See id.* at 136 (finding that Pennsylvania statutes require applicants wishing to become practical nurses to merely declare intent to become U.S. citizens, whereas private detective applicants must already be U.S. citizens).

30 *See* U.S. Citizenship & Immigration Services, Temporary (Nonimmigrant) Workers (Sept. 7, 2011), www.uscis.gov [https://perma.cc/SUQ2-Y4SB] (describing the process for a temporary worker to enter the country).

31 *See* U.S. Citizenship & Immigration Services, I-9, Employment Eligibility Verification (Jan. 23, 2017), www.uscis.gov [https://perma.cc/HG4Y-PSGX] (outlining occupational authorization procedure and purposes).

32 *See generally* Dan H. Berger & Rita Sostrin, *Immigration Options for Academics and Researchers* (2d ed. 2011) (noting various retention options for university-affiliated immigrants). Notwithstanding the disruptions of student flows, the year 2017 revealed a very large number of international students enrolled in U.S. colleges and a substantial percentage of them using the provisions to remain in the country to work after the completion of their degrees. *See also* Neil G. Ruiz, *More Foreign Grads of U.S. Colleges Are Staying in the Country to Work*, Pew Res. (May 18, 2017), http://pewrsr.ch/2qAofoh [https://perma.cc/9H2B-SZWK] (showing methods for foreign graduates to remain in the country and recent statistics). President Trump's rhetoric and policies, especially the travel ban, threw these practices into disarray, leading to substantial delays in processing and few foreign student applications and enrollments. *See* Kit Johnson, *Opportunities & Anxieties: A Study of International Students in the Trump Era*, 22 Lew. & Clark L. Rev. 414 (2018).

33 *See* Chris Cooke, *U.S. Border Control Says Performance Visas Required Even for Free Shows*, CompleteMusicUpdate.com, Mar. 15, 2017, www.completemusicupdate.com [https://perma.cc/4DYG-LDTT] (describing different standards of entry for performers based on how they are paid).

34 *See* Yeganeh Torbati, *Number of U.S. Visas to Citizens of Trump Travel Ban Nations Drops*, Reuters (Apr. 27, 2017), www.reuters.com [https://perma.cc/5AVR-G4FU] (finding that travel visa numbers dropped by nearly half since 2015); Cooke, *U.S. Border Control Says* (illustrating how the ban affected the annual South by Southwest festival by tying up participants and exacting more immigration-related inspections); Alana Durkin Richer, *Q&A: Trump's New Travel Ban Faces Key Test in Appeals Court*, Associated Press, May 6, 2017, www.usnews.com [https://perma.cc/M9KJ-ML2Q] (explaining that the general travel ban(s) are under review by a variety of federal courts). A modified version of the travel ban was upheld by SCOTUS. *Trump v. Hawaii*, 585 U.S. (2018). *See* Adam Liptak & Michael D. Shear, *Justices Back Travel Ban, Yielding to Trump*, N.Y. Times, June 26, 2018, at A1.

35 *See, e.g.,* U.S. Citizenship & Immigration Services, Q Cultural Exchange (July 14, 2015), www.uscis.gov [https://perma.cc/3DED-4J2P]. As an example, dependents

of Q-1 visa holders (persons participating in an international cultural exchange program for the purpose of providing practical training and employment and sharing the history, culture, and traditions of the noncitizen's home country) are ineligible for derivative EAD. *Id.* The Immigration and Nationality Act does not provide any specific nonimmigrant classification for dependents of Q-1 nonimmigrants, but this does not preclude the spouse or child of a Q-1 person from entering the United States in another nonimmigrant classification based on their own unique and separate qualifications and eligibility. *Id.*

36 *See* U.S. Citizenship & Immigration Services, Temporary (Nonimmigrant) Workers (Sept. 7, 2011), www.uscis.gov [https://perma.cc/SUQ2-Y4SB] (describing the process for a temporary worker to enter the country).

37 *See* U.S. Citizenship & Immigration Services, R-1 Temporary Nonimmigrant Religious Workers (Sept. 11, 2015), www.uscis.gov [https://perma.cc/5UBJ-3GW7] ("The petitioner must notify USCIS within 14 days of any change in the nonimmigrant religious worker's employment. The petitioner must also notify USCIS when the employment is terminated.").

38 *See id.* (R-1 status can be granted initially for thirty months and then extended to sixty months).

39 *See* U.S. Customs & Immigration Services, Handbook for Employers: Guidance for Completing Form I-9 Employment Eligibility Verification Form, www.uscis. gov [https://perma.cc/DQ57-H9RF] (providing a helpful, detailed, and comprehensive handbook). This footnote could include volumes on each of the several overlapping jurisdictions. *See also* EEOC, *Employment Rights of Immigrants Under Federal Anti-Discrimination Laws*, www.eeoc.gov [https://perma.cc/H2A8-XCDA] [hereinafter *Employment Rights of Immigrants*] (explaining immigrant rights). Many instructional resources also exist covering this large terrain. *See, e.g.,* T. Alexander Aleinikoff et al., *Immigration and Citizenship: Process and Pol'y* 269–70, 380–81, 444–45 (8th ed. 2016) (providing detailed instruction on immigration generally).

40 Immigration and Nationality Act 8 U.S.C. § 1101(a)(15)(B) (2012) (referencing temporary business or pleasure visitors).

41 Dept. of the Treasury Off. of Econ. Pol'y, Couns. of Econ. Advisers & the Dept. of Lab., *Occupational Licensing: A Framework for Policymakers* (July 2015), https:// obamawhitehouse.archives.gov [https://perma.cc/55TG-S7RY] (explaining that occupational licensing "plays an important role in protecting consumers and ensuring quality").

42 *See* U.S. Citizenship & Immigration Services, Permanent Workers (July 15, 2015), www.uscis.gov [https://perma.cc/ZP5J-WL4T] (setting out the preference categories enabling noncitizens to obtain employment based visas).

43 Soc. Security Admin., Prog. Operations Manual System, Si 00501.420(B)(2)–(3), Permanent Residence Under Color of Law (Prucol) Pre-1996 Legislation (May 5, 2012), https://secure.ssa.gov [https://perma.cc/4CTM-PWXP] [hereinafter PRUCOL] (providing a full manual on PRUCOL and relevant legislation).

44 *See id.* at SI 00501.420(B)(2)(j) ("Aliens admitted to the United States pursuant to section 203(a)(7) of the Immigration and Nationality Act (INA) are treated as if they are 'conditional entrants,'" that is, in a liminal status of permanently residing under color of law. In 1980, "Section 203(a) (7) of the INA was made obsolete by the Refugee Act of 1980 (Public Law (P.L.) 96-212) and replaced by section 207 of the INA, effective April 1, 1980.").

45 *See id.* at SI 00501.420(D)(2) (stating that under PRUCOL noncitizens may temporarily remain and work in the United States).

46 *See id.* at SI 00501.420(A)(1). The Social Security Administration, for example, defines PRUCOL as those permanently residing under color of law. *Id.* PRUCOL is not a formal immigration status; it is a term used to define the eligibility of certain noncitizens for certain Federal benefits (i.e., SSI, AFDC, Medicaid, unemployment insurance). *Id.* It includes any noncitizen who is residing in the United States with the knowledge and permission of DHS and whose departure from the United States DHS does not contemplate enforcing. *Id.*

47 Olivas, *Dreams Deferred*, at 542; Rose Cuison Villazor, *The Undocumented Closet*, 92 N.C. L. Rev. 1, 47–48, 64–65 (2013) (finding that many consider college degrees out of reach). *See generally* Vasanthi Venkatesh, *Mobilizing Under "Illegality": The Arizona Immigrant Rights Movement's Engagement with the Law*, 19 Harv. Latino L. Rev., 165 (2016) (covering Arizona immigration movements); Atheendar S. Venkataramani et al., *Health Consequences of the U.S. Deferred Action for Childhood Arrivals (DACA) Immigration Programme: A Quasi-Experimental Study*, 2 Lancet Pub. Health e175 (Apr. 2017), www.thelancet.com [https://perma.cc/JWY2-DUAF] (issuing results of health consequences study).

48 *See Dream Act: Summary*, Nat'l Immigration L. Ctr. (May 2011), www.nilc.org [https://perma.cc/8DMS-QCC9] (outlining the paths to citizenship under proposed DREAM Act).

49 Olivas, *Dreams Deferred*, at 475–78 (role of *Lennon v. United States*); Leon Wildes, *All You Need Is Love—and a Good Jewish Lawyer*, N.J. Jewish Standard, Dec. 10, 2010, www.jstandard.com [https://perma.cc/RM3F-HUBB] (providing a first-person account of the litigation in the Lennon immigration matter from the perspective of his attorney). *See also* Jon Wiener, *Come Together: John Lennon in His Time* 225–80 (1984) (detailing more background on the Lennon immigration); Jon Wiener, *Gimme Some Truth: The John Lennon FBI Files* 107–09, 194–95 (2000) (providing documentation showing U.S. government involvement with Lennon's deportation). For the details of the underlying child custody dispute and family court matter, much of which occurred in Houston, *see* Mark Davidson, *I Really Want to See You!*, 49 Hous. Law., Oct. 2011, at 24, 25–26; *Cox v. Lennon*, 457 F.2d 1190, 1193–94, 1198 (3d Cir. 1972) (ordering custody to Ono); Shoba Sivaprasad Wadhia, *Beyond Deportation: The Role of Prosecutorial Discretion in Immigration Cases* (New York University Press 2017) (explaining President Obama's use of prosecutorial discretion and the precedents of prosecutorial discretion).

50 *See* FAQ: U.S. Citizenship & Immigration Services, Frequently Asked Questions (Apr. 25, 2017), www.uscis.gov [https://perma.cc/NL7R-4WWZ] (offering instructive guidance on DACA and answering various questions). USCIS maintained an excellent and helpful website with program information, application protocols, and an informative and updated FAQ. *Id.* For the several years of DACA's early existence, there was almost not a day when I did not either employ the FAQ and tabular data or recommend that some colleague or DREAMer do so.

51 *Id.*

52 *Id.*

53 *Id.*

54 *Id.* (emphasis added).

55 *See, e.g.*, 8 U.S.C. § 1621(d) ("A State may provide that an alien who is not lawfully present in the United States is eligible for any State or local public benefit for which such alien would otherwise be ineligible under subsection (a) of this section only through the enactment of a State law after August 22, 1996, which affirmatively provides for such eligibility."); Tex. Dep't of Public Safety, *U.S. Citizenship or Lawful Presence Requirement*, www.dps.texas.gov [https://perma.cc/JJ63-8YUV] (requiring "lawful presence" as a precondition for a Texas driver's license).

56 *See generally* U.S. Customs & Immigration Services, *Number of I-821D, Consideration of Deferred Action for Childhood Arrivals by Fiscal Year, Quarter, Intake, Biometrics and Case Status: 2012–2016* (Mar. 2016), www.uscis.gov [https://perma.cc/FX4U-5JWV] (archiving USCIS DACA data).

57 *See Crane v. Napolitano*, 920 F. Supp. 2d 724, 736, 738, 742–43, 745–46 (N.D. Tex. 2013) (dismissing challenge to DACA under Civil Service Reform Act (CSRA)), *aff'd*, 783 F.3d 244, 247, 252–53, 255 (5th Cir. 2015) (affirming the district court's dismissal of plaintiff's challenge to DACA under CSRA).

58 *See id.* (referencing all DACA cases then in progress).

59 *See Ariz. Dream Act Coalition v. Brewer*, 855 F.3d 957, 968 (9th Cir. 2017) (finding that DACA recipients are similar to those relying on EAD status). *See also* Tania P. Linares Garcia, Note, *Protecting a Dream: Analyzing the Level of Review Applicable to DACA Recipients in Equal Protection Cases*, 39 S. Ill. L.J. 105, 116 (2014) (discussing Arizona's disparate treatment of DACA recipients as EAD holders); *see Table* 3.1 (summary of DACA/DREAM Act litigation).

60 *See, e.g., Juarez v. Nw. Mut. Life Ins. Co.*, 14-CV-5107 KBF, 69 F. Supp. 3d 364, 365, 370–74 (S.D.N.Y. 2014), *appeal filed*, No. 15-790 (2d Cir. Mar. 17, 2015) (finding allegations of refusal to recognize EAD for hiring sufficient to state section 1981 claim).

61 Kelly Knaub, *Northwestern Escapes DACA Bias Class Action*, Law360 (May 27, 2015), www.law360.com [https://perma.cc/2C6E-EY8G] (detailing dismissal of the lawsuit); Mandate, *Juarez v. Northwestern Mutual Life Ins. Co.*, No. 1:14-cv-05107 (S.D.N.Y. June 24, 2015), ECF No. 70 (noting the parties settled and the case closed).

62 *See Juarez*, 69 F. Supp. 3d, at 368–69 (finding it discriminatory to not hire lawfully present aliens just because they do not have a green card). Some large companies did not take the lesson to heart and resisted even after the *Juarez* case had been resolved. When Procter & Gamble similarly refused to acknowledge that EAD is EAD, the litigation took on more traction when the MALDEF lawyers sought class certification in order not to be required to retry the same issue company by recalcitrant company. *See* Tiffany Hu, *Aspiring Interns Seek Class Cert. In P&G DACA Bias Suit*, Law360.com, Apr. 15, 2019, www.law360.com (company refused to hire DACA recipients).

63 *See generally* Am. Immigr. Council, *Defending DAPA and Expanded DACA Before the Supreme Court: A Guide to* United States v. Texas (Apr. 11, 2016), www.americanimmigrationcouncil.org [https://perma.cc/G3YS-N6MG] (providing thoughtful and detailed coverage of the volumes of DAPA—*United States v. Texas* issues); Patricia L. Bellia, *Faithful Execution and Enforcement Discretion*, 164 U. Penn. L. Rev. 1753, 1754–56 (2016) (explaining the policy's executive genesis and its transition into the judicial sentence); Marisa Bono, *When a Rose Is Not a Rose: DACA, the DREAM Act, and the Need for More Comprehensive Immigration Reform*, 40 T. Marshall L. Rev. 193, 194–96 (2015) (detailing the DACA controversy and critics).

64 *See Rivera Hernandez v. Alford*, No. 2016-CV-274418 (Ga. Super. Ct. Dec. 30, 2016) (issuing a final order); Charles Kuck, *When Can a DACA Student Pay In-State Tuition in Georgia? Now!*, Musings on Immigration (Jan. 2017), http://musingsonimmigration.blogspot.com [https://perma.cc/3MDA-JM2U] (allowing DACA students to obtain in-state tuition); *Arizona ex rel. Brnovich v. Maricopa Cty. Cmty. Coll. Dist. Bd.*, No. 2013-009093 (Ariz. Super. Ct. May 5, 2015), *rev'd*, 395 P.3d 714, 719–24, 728–29 (Ariz. App. Ct. June 20, 2017) (reversing superior court ruling on lack of congressional intent to support finding benefits applied).

65 *See* Bono, *When a Rose*, at 214–18 (covering state driver's licenses). *See also Ariz. Dream Act Coalition v. Brewer*, 757 F.3d 1053, 1067–69 (9th Cir. 2015), *cert. denied*, 135 S. Ct. 889 (Dec. 17, 2014) (holding that Arizona's policy of denying driver's licenses to DACA recipients violated the Equal Protection Clause).

66 *See* Josh Blackman, *Gridlock*, 130 Harv. L. Rev. 241, 278–304 (2016) (critiquing *United States v. Texas*, 136 S. Ct. 2271 (2016)). Although I disagree with virtually every point made by professor Josh Blackman in his *Gridlock* article, it is a good example of principled objections to DAPA and, to a lesser extent, DACA and its extension. Someone who writes that well should be on my side—that of the angels.

67 *See Arpaio v. Obama*, 27 F. Supp. 3d 185, 211 (D.D.C. 2014) (striking down an Arizona sheriff's nativist challenge to DACA), *aff'd* 797 F.3d 11, 25 (D.C. Cir. 2015); 136 S. Ct. 900 (2016) (denying certiorari).

68 *See Texas v. United States*, 86 F. Supp. 3d 591, 676 (S.D. Tex. 2015) (issuing preliminary injunction).

69 *See Arpaio v. Obama*, 136 S. Ct. 900 (2016) (denying certiorari).

70 *Texas*, 86 F. Supp. 3d, at 676 (issuing preliminary injunction).

71 *Texas v. United States*, 787 F.3d 733, 743 (5th Cir. 2015) (denying stay of injunction); *Texas v. United States*, 809 F.3d 134, 188 (5th Cir. 2015) (affirming preliminary injunction).

72 *Texas*, 787 F.3d, at 743 (denying stay of injunction); *Texas*, 809 F.3d, at 188 (affirming preliminary injunction). *See generally* Am. Immigr. Council, *Defending DAPA and Expanded DACA* (finding that Texas has standing to bring lawsuit and would "likely prevail" on APA claim).

73 *See United States v. Texas*, 136 S. Ct. 2271, 2272 (2016) (affirming the temporary enjoinment). An equally divided (4–4) Court affirmed, by per curiam opinion, the judgment of the appeals court below. The Fifth Circuit had temporarily enjoined DAPA and the extension of DACA, resulting in the remand back to the federal district court to determine whether the discretionary actions should be permanently enjoined.

74 *See* Dana Goodyear, *Defiance and Anxiety Among Undocumented Youth in Trump's America*, New Yorker, Nov. 11, 2016, www.newyorker.com [https://perma.cc/S9C6-BVN5] (discussing President Trump's campaign promise to eliminate DACA); Priscilla Alvarez, *Trump's Quiet Reversal on Deporting Young Undocumented Immigrants*, Atlantic, Apr. 2017, www.theatlantic.com [https://perma.cc/7R4K-GJBX] (examining DACA's bleak future under the Trump administration). The uncertainty of the administration's policy intentions added to the *in terrorem* effect on DACA recipients, especially when a handful were deported for confusing reasons. *See, e.g.*, Samantha Schmidt & Peter Holley, *A "Dreamer" Claims He Was Secretly Deported. The Government Claims It Never Happened*, Wash. Post, Apr. 19, 2017, http://wapo.st/2orwIdH?tid=ss_mail [https://perma.cc/QRE8-2J7T] (highlighting the secret deportation of a DACA recipient). This paranoia concerning DACA and the DREAMers' fate has only increased during the Trump administration. *See, e.g.*, Beth C. Caldwell, *Deported Americans: Life After Deportation to Mexico* (Duke Univ. Press 2019); Deborah A. Boehm & Susan J. Terrio, eds., *Illegal Encounters: The Effect of Detention and Deportation on Young People* (New York University Press 2019); Shoba Sivaprasad Wadhia, *Banned: Immigration Enforcement in the Time of Trump* (New York University Press 2019). In a singular spot on any immigration bookshelf belongs Jayashri Srikantiah & Shirin Sinnar, *White Nationalism as Immigration Policy*, Stan. L. Rev. Online, Mar. 2019, www.stanfordlawreview. org (reviewing various policies and public statements by President Trump that have racist underpinnings in white nationalism and racial identity). *See also* Asne Seierstad, *The Anatomy of White Terror*, N.Y. Times, Mar. 18, 2019, at A27 (study of recent white nationalist terrorist attacks: "The two men mix rage with self-pity. They see themselves as victims and use terms like 'invasion,' 'mass immigration' and 'white genocide' to describe what they regard as the destruction of Europe and the white race. Both the Australian and the Norwegian barely mention their own homelands and focus on Europe and the United States.").

75 The Trump administration's proposed travel ban officially expired on October 24, 2017, and the Supreme Court withdrew its grant of certiorari accordingly but then

heard the case on something of an expedited schedule. A modified version of the travel ban was upheld by SCOTUS in June 2018. *Trump v. Hawaii*, 138 S. Ct. 2392 (2018). *See* Liptak & D. Shear, *Justices Back Travel Ban*, at A1.

76 *See* Angela D. Adams, *Deferred Action for "Dreamers": Advising DACA Students About Affording College*, Nat'l Ass'n of Student Fin. Aid Admins. (Dec. 6, 2012), www.nasfaa.org [https://perma.cc/SR2N-8NP5] (discussing considerations for students right after the DACA program was instituted).

77 *Id.* (outlining the requirements for qualifying under DACA and the issues arising with DACA qualified students paying for school). *See also* Michael A. Olivas, *Undocumented College Students, Taxation, and Financial Aid: A Technical Note*, 32 Rev. Higher Educ. 407 (2009). Although this article was written before DACA's start in 2012, the issues remained current because of the ban on federal Title IV financial assistance for both undocumented and DACA recipients.

78 *See* FAQ: U.S. Customs & Immigration Services, Frequently Asked Questions, www.uscis.gov [https://perma.cc/NL7R-4WWZ] (discussing the benefits conferred by deferred action for DACA recipients).

79 *See id.* (explaining that, if deferred status is not conferred or is conferred and then removed for cause under DACA, then removal proceedings can be instituted).

80 Literally hundreds of stories in the various social media have addressed the fear and liminality of noncitizen students, whether undocumented, DACAmented, or enrolled as nonimmigrants in F-1 student status. *See generally* Katherine Mangan, *DACA Remains Intact for Now, but Students Without It Are More Fearful Than Ever*, Chron. Higher Educ., Mar. 1, 2017, www.chronicle.com [https://perma.cc/HL8K-RFJL] (discussing DACA recipients' fear of getting deported); Stephanie Saul, *Amid "Trump Effect" Fear, 40% of Colleges See Dip in Foreign Applicants*, N.Y. Times, Mar. 16, 2017, www.nytimes.com [https://perma.cc/K2QW-29RW] (demonstrating international students' persistence in college applications despite President Trump's immigration policies); Sameer M. Ashar et al., *Navigating Liminal Legalities Along Pathways to Citizenship: Immigrant Vulnerability and the Role of Mediating Institutions*, Legal Stud. Res. Paper Series No. 2016-05 (Feb. 17, 2016), https://papers.ssrn.com [https://perma.cc/43KK-8QVG] (exploring personal and legal barriers of gaining legal status in the United States); Leisy J. Abrego & Sarah M. Lakhani, *Incomplete Inclusion: Legal Violence and Immigrants in Liminal Legal Statuses*, 37 L. & Pol'y 265–93 (2015) (focusing on social problems encountered by immigrants with various forms of temporary legal status); Lisa M. Martinez, *Dreams Deferred: The Impact of Legal Reforms on Undocumented Latina/o Youth*, 58 Am. Beh. Sci., 1873 (2014) (reporting on anxieties and uncertainty among noncitizen students); Rene Galindo, *The Functions of Dreamer Civil Disobedience*, 24 Tex. Hisp. J.L. & Pol'y 41–60 (2017) (studies on political participation by DREAMers); NYCLU & NYIC, *Report: False "Gang Allegations" Deny NY Teens' Access to Immigration Status and Bond Services*, https://d1jiktx9ot87hr.cloudfront.net/323/wp-content/uploads/sites/2/2019/02/020819-NYCLU-NYIC-Report.pdf (false accusations of gang membership used to deny DACA renewals).

81 One of the many tragedies of the upheaval caused by nativist policies and stigma-
    tizing rhetoric is that the Trump administration, in a game of hide the ball, does
    not gather or disseminate data as regularly as did the Obama administration. As
    professor Wadhia's work with FOIA has shown, however, the previous adminis-
    tration was not as committed to open records as scholars would have liked. *See,
    e.g.,* Camille Fassett, *The Freedom of Information Act Is Getting Worse Under the
    Trump Administration*, Freedom.Press/news, Mar. 14, 2019, https://freedom.press/
    news/freedom-information-act-getting-worse-under-trump-administration
    (reporting for Freedom of the Press Foundation, which tracks government open-
    ness).

82 *See generally* Paul J. Larkin Jr., *Public Choice Theory and Occupational Licensing*,
    39 Harv. L.J. & Pub. Pol'y 209, 212–13 (2016) (discussing the history of occupa-
    tional licensing); Walter Gellhorn, *The Abuse of Occupational Licensing*, 44 U.
    Chi. L. Rev. 6, 6 (1976) (pointing out that the commonality in over hundreds of
    professions is requiring occupational licenses).

83 *See generally* Russell G. Pearce et al., *A Taxonomy of Lawyer Regulation: How Con-
    trasting Theories of Regulation Explain the Divergent Regulatory Regimes in Aus-
    tralia, England/Wales, and North America*, 16 Legal Ethics 258 (2013) (discussing
    the North American approach to legal services regulation); Nicola Persico, *The
    Political Economy of Occupational Licensing Associations*, 31 J. L. Econ. & Orgs. 213
    (2014) (examining the political economy of licensure expansion). *See also* Raquel
    Muñiz, Mara Zrzavy & Nicole Prchal Svajlenka, *DACAmented Law Students and
    Lawyers in the Trump Era* (Center for American Progress and the Center for Im-
    migrants' Rights Clinic, Penn State Law 2018), https://cdn.americanprogress.org.

84 *See* Pamela A. McManus, *Have Law License: Will Travel*, 15 Geo. J. Legal Ethics 527,
    528–30 (2002) (explaining complex issues related to law licensure). In this article,
    McManus explores the history of the state's power to regulate lawyers through li-
    censure and advocates for the need of a multijurisdictional law practice (MJPOL)
    that would allow lawyers to service clients in a state other than where the lawyer
    has been licensed. *Id. See also* Trippe S. Fried, *Licensing Lawyers in the Modern
    Economy*, 31 Campbell L. Rev. 51, 52–53 (2008) (outlining the need for businesses
    to hire multijurisdictional lawyers to negotiate business transactions).

85 *See generally* Nicholas Matich, *Patent Office Practice After the America Invents Act*,
    23 Fed. Cir. B.J. 225, 244 (2013); Ken Port et al., *Where Have All the Patent Lawyers
    Gone: Long Time Passing*, 97 J. Pat. & Trademark Off. Soc'y 193, 198 (2015).

86 *See* Cal. R. State Bar.

87 Cal. R. State Bar tit. 1 *et seq.*

88 Cal. Bus. & Prof. Code § 6000 (West, Westlaw through Ch. 248 of 2017 Reg.
    Sess.) (chapter on attorneys and "may be cited as the State Bar Act"). Chapter 4 of
    California's Business and Professions Code comprises sixteen articles that govern
    attorneys in the state. *Id.*

89 *See id.* § 6046 (West, Westlaw through Ch. 179 of 2017 Sess.) (powers of Califor-
    nia's examining committee).

90 Larry E. Ribstein, *Lawyers as Lawmakers: A Theory of Lawyer Licensing*, 69 Mo. L. Rev. 299, 303–04 (2004) (outlining the costs and risks of licensure for lawyers).

91 *See id.* at 301 ("[L]icensing of lawyers . . . accomplishes little other than keeping the price of legal services and lawyers' wages high by restricting entry into the profession.").

92 *See* Fabian, *Sergio Garcia* (discussing the case of Sergio Garcia, a noncitizen law school graduate who passed the bar exam but was denied admission to California's bar).

93 *See* Nat'l Bar Ass'n for Undocumented Laws. & L. Students, *Mission Statement*, Dream Bar Ass'n, https://dreambarassociation.wordpress.com [https://perma.cc/3SQG-J9YH] (setting out the membership and purpose of the Dream Bar Association).

94 *See In re Garcia*, 315 P.3d 117, 121 (Cal. 2014) (highlighting the details of Sergio Garcia coming to the United States from Mexico).

95 *See id.* (describing Garcia's residency history in the United States).

96 *See id.* at 121–22 (explaining the path to legal status for Sergio Garcia's father contrasted with Sergio's long wait for status adjustment).

97 *See id.* at 121 (acknowledging the backlog of visas available for similar Mexican immigrants).

98 *Id.* at 120–21.

99 *In re Garcia*, 315 P.3d, at 121.

100 *Id.*

101 *Id.* (granting Sergio Garcia admittance to the state bar of California).

102 Cal. Bus. & Prof. Code § 6064 (West, Westlaw through Ch. 179 of 2017 Reg. Sess.).

103 *Id.* § 6064 (West, Westlaw through Ch. 179 of 2017 Sess.); *In re Garcia*, 315 P.3d, at 121 (discussing the legislative enactment of Section 6064).

104 Andre Byik, *Formerly Undocumented Chico Lawyer Sergio Garcia Pays Taxes with a Smile*, Chico Enterp.-Rec., Feb. 23, 2016, www.chicoer.com [https://perma.cc/ER4K-EFKZ] (noting Sergio Garcia's admittance to the California state bar as an undocumented immigrant).

105 Florida's statute regarding requirements for bar admission states:

> Upon certification by the Florida Board of Bar Examiners that an applicant who is an unauthorized immigrant who was brought to the United States as a minor; has been present in the United States for more than 10 years; has received documented employment authorization from the United States Citizenship and Immigration Services (USCIS); has been issued a social security number; if a male, has registered with the Selective Service System if required to do so under the Military Selective Service Act, 50 U.S.C. App. 453; and has fulfilled all requirements for admission to practice law in this state, the Supreme Court of Florida may admit that applicant as an attorney at law authorized to practice in this state and may direct an order be entered upon the court's records to that effect.

Fla. Stat. Ann. § 454.021(3) (West 2014). *See generally* Marianela Toledo, *Illegal Immigrants Can Practice Law in Florida*, Human Events, May 22, 2014, http://

humanevents.com [https://perma.cc/2RWJ-WCQY] (highlighting the new Florida law allowing undocumented immigrants to practice law in the state). A fascinating case study of Jose Manuel Godinez Samperio's case has been published by his former Florida State University law professor. *See* Wendi Adelson, *Lawfully Present Lawyers*, 18 Chapman L. Rev. 387, 387–89 (2015) (recounting the experiences of an undocumented individual and the hurdles he faced trying to obtain a license to practice law). It also has a comprehensive review of lawyer licensing in its appendix at 400–418. *Id.*

106 Cesar Vargas entered the country from Mexico without authorization when he was five years old and has resided continuously since then. He was sworn into the New York State bar in 2016 at the age of thirty-two. He graduated from law school and passed the New York State bar exam in 2011. He applied for admission to the bar in 2012 but was denied by the Committee on Character and Fitness because he lacked legal status. While he received DACA in 2013, his case was referred to the Appellate Division of the State Supreme Court, which voted to admit him pending resolution of an ill-advised 2015 arrest record for political protest. After six months of probation, he was able to expunge his record, and his admission was granted. He was not the first lawyer in New York without legal status, but the bar had not inquired into immigration status before his case. *See* Kirk Semple, *Bar Exam Passed, Immigrant Still Can't Practice Law*, N.Y. Times, Dec. 3, 2013, at A30 (examining the denial of Cesar Vargas to the New York bar); Liz Robbins, *An Immigrant's Four-Year Fight to Become a Lawyer Ends in Celebrations*, N.Y. Times, Feb. 3, 2016, at A18 (outlining Cesar Vargas's recent win and admission to the New York bar).

107 Stephane Mahe, *American Bar Association to Allow Illegal Immigrants to Become Lawyers*, RT News, Aug. 15, 2017, www.rt.com [https://perma.cc/WP4J-25LU] (revealing that, prior to California, seven states were already allowing undocumented immigrants to become lawyers).

108 In Texas, for example, a 2016 news story revealed that only one public medical school admitted DACA students to study even though the state legislature has provisions for certain undocumented students to receive resident tuition and state financial assistance. *See, e.g.*, Reynaldo Leonos Jr., *Immigration Status Is Keeping Students Out of Medical School*, Tex. Standard, May 24, 2016, www.texasstandard.org [https://perma.cc/Y2VP-BA2D] (indicating that only the University of North Texas admits DACA recipients to its medical school). Given that the state provides resident tuition even for undocumented college students (without reference to undergraduate or graduate level), Texas is a ripe target for challenges to its medical and law licensing practices, especially when the attorney requirements appear to envision DACAmented applicants. Rule II provides that "applicants must (5) qualify under one of the following categories: (D) be otherwise authorized to work lawfully in the United States, including in a period of Optional Practical Training." Tex. B. Admissions Rule *II* (2014) (emphasis deleted); OPT is a benefit of holding a student F-1 visa, which allows only limited and circum-

scribed work authorization. *See generally* Jeremy Raff, *What Will Happen to Undocumented Doctors?*, Atlantic, Feb. 2, 2017, www.theatlantic.com [https://perma.cc/SYZ8-9653] (discussing the uncertain fate of undocumented physicians). A list of Admissions Policies of Medical Schools Open to Undocumented and DACA Applicants is maintained, but the number of undocumented and DACAmented medical students is apparently small. *See* www.pomona.edu [https://perma.cc/2XTZ-J87J]. *See also* Mina Kim, *UCSF's First Undocumented Medical Student Begins Training*, KQED State of Health (Sept. 8, 2014), ww2.kqed.org [https://perma.cc/T6Y4-D6LA] (highlighting the first known undocumented medical student at UCSF).

109 *See, e.g.*, Jennifer Medina, *Allowed to Join the Bar, but Not to Take a Job*, N.Y. Times, Jan. 3, 2014, at A1 (discussing that even after admission to the state bar, under federal law, such a person cannot be legally employed; hanging out a shingle is not "employment").

110 *See* U.S. Legal, Reciprocity, https://attorneys.uslegal.com [https://perma.cc/WT64-USQS] (containing reciprocity agreements for all the states). Reciprocity agreements are entered into, and the terms are decided, independently by the individual states. States could therefore require immigration status concurrent with their laws as a condition to reciprocity. *Id.*

111 *See, e.g.*, Medina, *Allowed to Join the Bar* (outlining Sergio Garcia's acceptance to the California bar and noting that his employment opportunities other than solo practice or a legal partnership are limited).

112 *See* Dan Cadman, *Illegal Aliens Practicing Law*, Ctr. For Immigration Studies, July 19, 2017, https://cis.org [https://perma.cc/4N96-SKBM] (noting that it would "defy logic" for federal immigration courts to give undocumented immigrants the ability to practice before the Executive Office for Immigration Review).

113 The DOJ brief argued that section 1621 preempted the California Supreme Court from adjudicating the matter and that anyone such as Garcia who was not authorized to work could not fully serve as a lawyer. *See* Brief for the United States, at 5–6 as Amicus Curiae Supporting Applicant, *In re Garcia*, 315 P.3d 117 (Cal. 2014) (No. S202512) (arguing that section 1621 preempted California law and prohibited the admission of Sergio Garcia to the California bar). The California Supreme Court eventually held for Garcia, but only after state law was enacted, giving him the option of practicing law. This mooted the 1621 problem, and he was too old to be eligible for DACA's age provisions.

114 8 U.S.C. § 1621 (1998). I have written about this provision in some detail in the context of state postsecondary residency requirements. *See, e.g.*, Michael A. Olivas, *IIRIRA, the DREAM Act, and Undocumented College Student Residency*, 30 J.C. & U.L. 435, 450–455 (2004).

115 8 U.S.C. § 1621(c) (2000).

116 This was essentially the position cited by DOJ in opposition to the Sergio Garcia California bar admission matter. *See* Brief for the United States, at 5–6.

117 *See* Tal Kopan, *States Try to Force Trump's Hand on DACA*, CNN, July 1, 2017, www.cnn.com [https://perma.cc/VRE6-LLLV] (detailing several states' threat to challenge DACA in court if President Trump refused to end the program). *See generally* Jennifer Chacon, *Who Is Responsible for U.S. Immigration Policy?*, Insights on L. & Soc'y (2014), www.americanbar.org [https://perma.cc/8VTV-ZM9Q] (discussing the interaction between the federal and state governments concerning immigration law).

118 *See* Olivas, *Within You*, Appendix I: Professional License Eligibility Requirements (Physicians, Nurses, Attorneys, Teachers/Educators), at 108 (illustrating that the high-caste occupational law licensing immigration criteria are unpredictable).

119 Ala. Code § 34-3-6(d) (2017).

120 Alaska St. B. Rule 44.1 (2014); Internal Revenue Serv., *Individual Taxpayer Identification Number*, www.irs.gov [https://perma.cc/L4RV-T4GU] (explaining the use of ITINs).

121 U.S. Dep't of State, Bureau of Consular Affairs, *Student Visa*, https://travel.state.gov [https://perma.cc/N3UV-553Z].

122 Ark. B. Rule 12 (2005). *See* U.S. Dep't of State, Bureau of Consular Affairs, *Student Visa*, https://travel.state.gov [https://perma.cc/N3UV-553Z].

123 *See generally* Olivas, *Within You*, Appendix II, at 154 (revealing the lack of uniformity in occupational licensing laws).

124 Ironically, after the trial and Garcia's bar admission drama were completed, his long time in the fourth-preference queue as his U.S. citizen father's dependent was rewarded, enabling him to move from undocumented PRUCOL-ish status to being an LPR. *See* Paul Elias, *Chico Lawyer Undocumented No More: Sergio Garcia Gets His Green Card*, Chico Enterp.-Rec., June 4, 2015, www.chicoer.com [https://perma.cc/D9X4-NFW5] (highlighting Sergio Garcia's visa eligibility).

125 *See* Ala. Code § 34-3-6(d) (2017) (recognizing that in Alabama it is unlikely that those that who are covered under DACA will become licensed attorneys within their state).

126 *See* Elise Foley, *Alabama Immigration Law Asks Doctors for Their Papers*, Huffington Post, May 18, 2013, www.huffingtonpost.com [https://perma.cc/HM57-ZNRJ]. Indeed, the state enacted a draconian measure that in effect required all licensed medical personnel to prove their citizenship status:

> Already-licensed physicians and physician assistants now have only two weeks to get their information to the Medical Licensure Commission. Those applying for a license for the first time will be required to either demonstrate they are in the country legally or sign a declaration of U.S. citizenship and give proof, according to the letter. If they don't provide the information, they will not be able to receive or renew their licenses. *Id.*

127 Internal Revenue Serv., *Individual Taxpayer Identification Number* (discussing the differences between ITINs and Social Security numbers).

128 *Id.* (noting purposes of ITINs).

129 *See* Francine J. Lipman, *The "Illegal" Tax*, 11 Conn. Pub. Int. L.J. 93, 97–98 (2011) (explaining ITINs and noncitizens' filing or reporting obligations). *See also* Francine J. Lipman, *I've Got ITINs on My Mind*, Surly Subgroup (Sept. 24, 2016), https://surlysubgroup.com [https://perma.cc/YC78-N3BQ] (discussing ITINs being issued).

130 *Id.* (ITINs do not authorize individuals to work in the United States, do not provide eligibility for Social Security, and do not qualify ITIN holders as dependents for Earned Income Tax Credit purposes).

131 *See id.* (illustrating the gap in ITINs for immigration licensing eligibility because holding an ITIN does not necessarily authorize the individual to work in the United States).

132 *See, e.g., What Education or Type of Degree Is Needed to Be a Lawyer*, Study.com, http://study.com [https://perma.cc/92AY-HSYR] (highlighting the educational and licensing requirements needed to become a lawyer).

133 Morris M. Kleiner, *Guild-Ridden Labor Markets: The Curious Case of Occupational Licensing*, Upjohn.org (2015), www.upjohn.org [https://perma.cc/V7MS-MCF7] (describing one of the more useful and detailed studies of labor markets and occupational licensing and certification issues, but which does not venture into citizenship criteria, in an otherwise comprehensive study). It is the immigration dog that does not bark even as he discusses comparative policies. *Id. See, e.g.,* Patricia Cohen, *Moving to Arizona Soon? You Might Need a License*, N.Y. Times, June 17, 2016, at B1 (noting that a variety of challenges to the world of occupational licensing has arisen, including an unusual alliance of libertarians who think the labor markets are too restrictive and progressives who feel they are too punitive, such as with rules against felons voting). Space limitations have precluded any detailed analysis of teacher certification, although I have reported the state requirements, which suffer from the same overinclusiveness and underinclusive issues as the other baccalaureate-requiring professions. Interestingly, virtually no scholar in the voluminous teacher and alternative certification field has noted these issues, providing yet another dog that has not barked. *Id. See, e.g.,* Klein, *The Freedom to Pursue a Common Calling* (applying the intermediate scrutiny test to occupational licensing statutes); Tim R. Sass, *Licensure and Worker Quality: A Comparison of Alternative Routes to Teaching*, 58 J.L. & Econ. 1, 10 (2015) (arguing the differences between the alternative routes needed to get a teaching license); E. Frank Stephenson & Erin E. Wendt, *Occupational Licensing: Scant Treatment in Labor Texts*, 6 Econ J. Watch 181, 186 (2009) (analyzing occupational licensing's scant treatment in labor texts). These are all excellent and detailed works, but they all share the same inattention to even mentioning immigration issues.

134 *See* Raff, *What Will Happen to Undocumented Doctors?* (analyzing the confusion around statutory M.D. eligibility and admissions criteria).

135 State of West Virginia, *Overview*, West Virginia Board of Medicine (2017), https://wvbom.wv.gov [https://perma.cc/YD8V-2NZA] (summarizing West Virginia Code § 30-3-10).

136 Wisconsin Department of Safety and Professional Services, Application for Dental Hygiene Certificate to Administer Local Anesthesia, Dentistry Examining Board (Dec. 2016), http://dsps.wi.gov [https://perma.cc/Z7CM-SLRY].

137 Wyo. Stat. Ann. § 31-1-114 (West, Westlaw through the end of the 2017 General Session of the Wyoming legislature).

138 D.C. Code § 3-1205.05 (2009) (illustrating that there is no specific required immigration status in order to get M.D. license in Washington, D.C.).

139 *See* Olivas, *Within You*, Appendix I, at 108 (illustrating the gaps and inconsistencies in administering lawyering and M.D. licensing).

140 *See* Lipman, The *"Illegal" Tax*, at 108 (discussing ITINs and noncitizens filing or reporting obligations).

141 *See id.* (outlining ITINs and filing or reporting obligations for noncitizens).

142 *See* Ala. Code § 31-13-7(b) (indicating that Alabama has among the strictest immigration criteria); *see also* Mississippi Nursing Act, 1991 Miss. Laws Ch. 465 (S.B. 2205), *codified as amended at* Miss. Code Ann. § 73-15-19(10), www.msbn.ms.gov [https://perma.cc/F3J8-J8P7] (stating that Mississippi requires applicant to have a Social Security number); Arkansas State Board of Nursing Rules (2014), Chapter 2, Section 1, www.sos.arkansas.gov [https://perma.cc/G7AB-TDQE] (recognizing that Arkansas has no immigration criteria whatsoever).

143 Ala. Code § 31-13-7(b) (West, Westlaw through the end of the 2017 regular session).

144 *See id.*; Ala. Code § 34-21-21(a) (West, Westlaw through the end of the 2017 regular session).

145 *See* Mississippi Nursing Act, 1991 Miss. Laws Ch. 465 (S.B. 2205), *codified as amended at* Miss. Code Ann. § 73-15-19(10), www.msbn.ms.gov [https://perma.cc/F3J8-J8P7] (discussing the requirement under the Mississippi Nursing Act). *See also* Arkansas State Board of Nursing Rules (2014), Chapter 2, Section 1 (analyzing the Arkansas State Board of Nursing Rules).

146 *Compare* Arkansas State Board of Nursing Rules (2014), Chapter 2, Section 1 (entrance to Arkansas nursing practice, at LPN and RN levels, does not require a valid SSN) *with* NCLEX Prep and Exam info, easynclex.com (2017), http://easynclex.com [https://perma.cc/CCM2-9ZAK] (explaining the Arkansas application process and requiring individuals applying to enter a valid SSN to continue with the uniform application process).

147 *See id.* (exemplifying the significant differences between the licensing language and the application of the licensing language).

148 *See* New York Office of Information Technology Services, New York Business Express, N.Y. St., https://its.ny.gov [https://perma.cc/X7UZ-WR3E] (illustrating the state's License Center Portal to be comprehensive and detailed).

149 *See* New York Business Express, *Professional Licenses*, https://tinyurl.com [https://perma.cc/G8VE-FSE4] (outlining the aggregate variety of the different professional licenses available through New York's online portal).

150 *Id.*

151 New York State Office of the Professions, *The Licensed Professions in New York State*, N.Y. State, www.op.nysed.gov [https://897perma.cc/D6PN-VGGW] (discussing that the State Education Department, under the regents' direction, administers professional regulation through its Office of the Professions in conjunction with the various state boards for the professions).

152 *Security Dealers, Brokers and Salesperson Designation—State Notice*, N.Y. Bus. Express, www.businessexpress.ny.gov [https://perma.cc/DQR5-RMXJ] (illustrating the issuing agencies in New York).

153 I selected several at random to show the extraordinary range of licenses, certificates, and permits: *See* N.Y. State, *Milk Dealer License—Distributor (DISPS-7)*, N.Y. Bus. Express, www.businessexpress.ny.gov [https://perma.cc/87QC-X5FP] (discussing license requirements for a milk dealer); N.Y. State, *Milk Dealer License—Milk Hauler (DISPS-7)*, N.Y. Bus. Express, https://tinyurl.com [https://perma.cc/C6XH-K524] (conveying license requirements for a milk hauler). *See also* N.Y. State, *Appearance Enhancement—Business License (DOS-0035-a)*, N.Y. Bus. Express, https://tinyurl.com [https://perma.cc/V54V-7WBN] (listing license requirements for appearance enhancement); N.Y. State, *Brewer Tasting (Annual) Permit*, N.Y. Bus. Express, https://tinyurl.com [https://perma.cc/NR4A-NZ8H] (describing license requirements for brewer tasting); N.Y. State, *Special Entertainer's Permit (Minor)*, N.Y. Bus. Express, https://tinyurl.com [https://perma.cc/CX22-AV7R] (outlining license requirements for special entertainer's permit for minors).

154 *See* New York State Education Department, *U.S. Court of Appeals Decision on Litigation Involving 13 Professions That Require U.S. Citizenship or Permanent Lawful Residence for Licensure*, www.op.nysed.gov [https://perma.cc/9XNX-2VAN] (last updated Mar. 24, 2017) (listing the professions that no longer require citizenship in New York, including dentistry, medicine, and professional engineering). I am indebted to the careful research and advocacy of professor Janet Calvo, who, with her law students, prepared many careful tables to assist the New York attorney general in addressing licensing issues. Janet M. Calvo, *Professional Licensing and Teacher Certification for Non-Citizens: Federalism, Equal Protection and a State's Socio-Economic Interests*, 8 Colum. J. Race & L. 33–121 (2017).

155 Janet Calvo, *Letter to Board of Regents on Behalf of Latino Justice*, Latino Justice (2017), http://latinojustice.org [https://perma.cc/R8S5-6WYB].

156 *See* Calvo, *Professional Licensing and Teacher Certification for Non-Citizens* (professor Calvo analyzing twenty-nine occupational and licensing agencies).

157 *See id.* (noting that there have been evident administrative regimes instilled in New York and that the state has one of the nation's largest immigration populations).

158 *See* Olivas, *Within You*, Appendix I, at 108 (illustrating the lack of cohesiveness between the technical details of implementation and the legal underpinnings of occupational licensing in New York).

159 Robbins, *An Immigrant's Four-Year Fight* (articulating that DACA bar admissions allowed Cesar Vargas to obtain a license to practice law in New York).

160 *Nyquist v. Mauclet*, 432 U.S. 1, 5 (1977) (striking down the New York State statute that barred permanent residents from receiving state college financial assistance).

161 *Dandamudi v. Tisch*, 686 F.3d 66, 69–70 (2d Cir. 2012) (striking down the requirement under New York Education Law § 6805 (1), (6) that only U.S. citizens or Lawful Permanent Residents are eligible to obtain a pharmacist's license); Calvo, *Professional Licensing and Teacher Certification for Non-Citizens* (emphasizing that the Second Circuit court held unconstitutional a New York education law requiring an applicant to be a citizen or a lawful permanent resident).

162 *See* Calvo, *Professional Licensing and Teacher Certification for Non-Citizens* (stating that there are nine professions that do not require any citizenship or immigration criteria under the New York Education Law).

163 *See* Calvo, *Professional Licensing and Teacher Certification for Non-Citizens* (stating that there are nine occupations under the New York Education Law that do not have any immigration category requirement).

164 *See Office of the Professions, Education Law*, NYSED.gov (Oct. 3, 2017), www.op.nysed.gov [https://perma.cc/ZS38-MX5N] (outlining the New York online licensing application website that requires some form of citizenship criteria even though the New York Education Law has nine occupations with no such requirement).

165 Calvo, *Professional Licensing and Teacher Certification for Non-Citizens* (identifying that for thirteen professional licenses there is a permanent residence requirement even though the court in the Second Circuit had held that it was unconstitutional to require a licensing applicant to be only either a citizen or a permanent resident).

166 Calvo, *Letter to Board of Regents*.

167 *See* Olivas, *Within You*, Appendix I, at 108 (illustrating the gaps and inconsistencies related to immigration eligibility across occupational licensing in many different fields). *See also id.* at 90–93 (sampling four states' licensing requirement for attorneys (Alabama, Alaska, Arizona, and Arkansas); *id.* at 93–97 (illustrating other state-specific occupational licensing requirements).

168 *See, e.g.*, Heidi Jauregui & Ann Morse, *Professional and Occupational Licenses for Immigrants*, Nat'l Conf. of St. Legislatures, www.ncsl.org [https://perma.cc/8CDL-W3WN] (recognizing the different admissions requirements for California, Florida, Illinois, Minnesota, Nebraska, Nevada, South Dakota, Utah, West Virginia, and Wyoming, thereby illustrating the difficulty in theorizing about these requirements because of the stark differences between those different states' requirements).

169 *See id.* (various requirements to be eligible for the profession of law).

170 *See* Michael A. Olivas, *Drafting Justice: Statutory Language, Public Policy, and Legislative Reform*, U. Hous. L. Cntr. (2014), www.law.uh.edu [https://perma.cc/GNR9-KKTR] (describing experience in residency issues).

171 *See* Olivas, *Within You*, Appendix I, at 108 (outlining national examples of occupational licensing laws across dozens of fields and states, thereby illustrating that

the formal requirements do not match up with the actual implementation of the laws).

172 *See* Ashar et al., *Navigating Liminal Legalities*, at 32–34 (exploring the personal and legal barriers of gaining legal status in the United States).

173 *See* Jenny Jarvie, *President Trump Signs an Executive Order in January on Border Security and Immigration Enforcement*, L.A. Times, Apr. 19, 2017, www.latimes. com [https://perma.cc/52SN-AK94] (discussing DACA recipients in removal proceedings); Allissa Wickham, *Well-Known DACA Recipient Sues over Revoked Status*, Law360, May 11, 2017, www.law360.com [https://perma.cc/JT5A-L68K]. *See also* Kate Morrissey, *ICE Will No Longer Delay Deportations for Those With "Private Bills" Pending*, San Diego Union-Trib., May 9, 2017, www.sandiegounion-tribune.com [https://perma.cc/ZQQ7-MN2J].

174 *See, e.g.,* Olivas, *Within You*, Appendix I, at 108 (illustrating the differences and instabilities in state professional license eligibility requirements for physicians, nurses, attorneys, and teachers), and Appendix II, at 154 (revealing the differences and instabilities in the examples of different state occupational licensing laws requiring certain immigration status).

175 *See* Olivas, *Within You*, at 93–97 (demonstrating inconsistent West Virginia, Wisconsin, Wyoming, and Washington, D.C., immigration categorizations for admissions to the medical field).

176 *See* Caitlin Dickerson, *Immigration Arrests Rise Sharply as Agents Carry out a Trump Mandate*, N.Y. Times, May 17, 2017, at A22 (reporting there are already about 250,000 individuals who have benefited from DACA and that, although Trump has illustrated that he wants to crack down on illegal immigration, he will not focus on DACA). She miscalled this situation. *See also* Miriam Jordan, *7 Years After and Outcry, Young Woman Again Faces Deportation*, N.Y. Times, May 11, 2017, at A10 (discussing a DACA recipient in removal proceedings); Marcela Valdes, *Staying Power*, N.Y. Times Mag., May 28, 2017, at MM50 (analyzing legal tactics to slow deportations and removals). *See also* Amanda E. Lopez, *Still Dreaming: The Plight of the Undocumented Immigrant Student in the Professional World*, 18 Scholar: St. Mary's L. Rev Race & Soc. J. 451, 453 (2016) (discussing that a good gauge of the punctuated pathways of state legislation is regularly made available); National Conference of State Legislators: *Professional Licenses for Immigrants* (Jan. 2017), www.ncsl.org [https://perma.cc/P7TU-VKCL] (discussing the year's change in the barriers for immigrants to obtain professional licenses).

177 *See Plyler v. Doe*, 457 U.S. 202, 253–54 (1982) (holding that states could not charge tuition for the education of schoolchildren of unauthorized immigrants).

178 *See* Olivas, *Within You*, Appendix I, at 108 (outlining the national examples of occupational licensing laws across several different states and fields).

179 *Id.* (presenting different occupational licensing laws across all different states and occupational fields).

180 *Id.* Appendix I, at 108 (providing a state-by-state breakdown of professional license eligibility requirements for physicians, nurses, attorneys, and educators,

thereby illustrating the discrepancies among the different professional license immigration requirements and the fact that these professions have not smoothed out these discrepancies).

181 *Id.* Appendix II, at 154 (detailing the differences among state occupational licensing laws that require varying statuses of citizenship and illustrating the gaps and ridges in employment and immigration law).

182 *See* Olivas, *Within You,* Appendix I, at 108 (illustrating that the earlier occupational licensing requirements relating to immigration is at the forefront of many statutes and thus that there is hope that the gaps and ridges in these requirements will continue to be addressed).

183 To give readers a sense of the nature of the pending cases, this footnote is of a journalistic nature, with stories and narratives on DACA and professions. *See* Erica L. Green, *Protected for Now, Teachers Await Fate,* N.Y. Times, Feb. 2, 2018, at A14 (uncertainty over teacher licensing); Maria Sacchetti, *With Three Months Left in Medical School, Her Career May Be Slipping Away,* Wash. Post, Feb. 22, 2018, http://wapo.st/2CBQuKR?tid=ss_mail&utm_term=.b2835e7fe5e9 [https://perma. cc/NTA6-PBNG] (immigration eligibility for medical doctors); Jan Hefler, *N.J.'s Gurbir Grewal, the Nation's First Sikh Attorney General, Says American Dream Is Alive and Well,* The Inquirer, Mar. 1, 2018, www.philly.com [https://perma.cc/ D829-VGNV] (New Jersey swears in DACAmented lawyer). Indiana also has broadened its eligibility for immigration criteria. *See, e.g.,* Kevin Penton, *New Indiana Law Allows Pro Licenses for Certain Immigrants,* Law360.com, Mar. 22, 2018, www.law360.com [https://perma.cc/C7TL-3EWH] (allowing DACAmented professionals to apply for Indiana licenses); *Senate Enrolled Act No. 419,* https:// iga.in.gov [https://perma.cc/N8ZW-GKUC] (providing statutory details). *See also* Jeff Proctor, *Proposal: Immigrants Can Work as Lawyers in New Mexico Regardless of Federal Status,* Las Cruces Sun-News, Nov. 28, 2018, www.lcsun-news.com (New Mexico considering changes). Notwithstanding these and many other hopeful stories, DACA itself is in peril even though federal judges in several states have extended its life for those already enrolled (as detailed in Chapter 7).

CHAPTER 7. THE 2016 ELECTION OF DONALD TRUMP, THE
RESCISSION OF DACA, AND ITS AFTERMATH

1 *Letter to President Obama, Executive Authority to Grant Administrative Relief for DREAM Act Beneficiaries* (May 28, 2012), https://perma.cc/3C6D-F6NY (archived copy of letter); Frank James, *With DREAM Order, Obama Did What Presidents Do: Act Without Congress,* NPR.org, June 15, 2012, www.npr.org (reasons why President Obama created DACA); Mark Noferi, *136 Law Professors Say President Has Legal Authority to Act on Immigration,* ImmigrationImpact.com, Sept. 3, 2014, http://immigrationimpact.com (history of DACA policy).

2 *Plyler v. Doe,* 457 U.S. 202 (1982) (states cannot prevent children of undocumented immigrants from attending public school, unless a substantial state interest is involved, on grounds of equal protection). *See* Michael A. Olivas, *No Undocumented*

Child Left Behind: Plyler v. Doe *and the Education of Undocumented Children* (New York University Press 2012).

3 *See, e.g.*, Roberto G. Gonzales & Leo R. Chavez, *"Awakening to a Nightmare"*: *Abjectivity and Illegality in the Lives of Undocumented 1.5-Generation Latino Immigrants in the United States*, 53 Current Anthropology, 255 (2012) (examining stress factors of undocumented college students). *See also* Beth C. Caldwell, *Deported Americans: Life After Deportation to Mexico* (Duke Univ. Press 2019); Deborah A. Boehm & Susan J. Terrio, eds., *Illegal Encounters: The Effect of Detention and Deportation on Young People* (New York University Press 2019).

4 *See* Shoba Sivaprasad Wadhia, *The President and Deportation: DACA, DAPA, and the Sources and Limits of Executive Authority—Response to Hiroshi Motomura*, 55 Washb. L. Rev. 189 (2015) (examining details of establishment of DACA and DAPA). A former U.S. attorney general coauthored an article suggesting the efficacy of another form rather than deferred action (as was the format for DACA); he suggested the attorney general's less well known Referral and Review Authority. *See* Alberto R. Gonzales & Patrick Glen, *Advancing Executive Branch Immigration Policy Through the Attorney General's Review Authority*, 101 Iowa L. Rev. 841 (2016).

5 *United States v. Texas*, 136 S. Ct. 2271 (2016) (per curiam). *See, e.g.*, Peter M. Shane, *The U.S. Supreme Court's Big Immigration Case Wasn't About Presidential Power*, The Atlantic, June 28, 2016 (4–4 vote, upholding Fifth Circuit appellate decision that had affirmed state challenges to the DACA extension and DAPA).

6 Adam Liptak & Matt Flegenheimer, *Court Nominee Is Confirmed After Bruising Yearlong Fight*, N.Y. Times, Apr. 7, 2017, at A1 (reporting history leading up to 54–45 confirmation).

7 A small sample of the likely reading from such an extensive library would include the following: Lisa M. Martinez, *Dreams Deferred: The Impact of Legal Reforms on Undocumented Latina/o Youth*, 58 Am. Beh. Sci., 1873 (2014); Rene Galindo, *The Functions of Dreamer Civil Disobedience*, 24 Tex. Hisp. J.L. & Pol'y 41–60 (2017); Chris Zepeda-Millán, *Latino Mass Mobilization: Immigration, Racialization, and Activism* (Camb. Univ. Press 2017); Abigail Leslie Andrews, *Undocumented Politics: Place, Gender, and the Pathways of Mexican Migrants* (Univ. Calif. Press 2018); Boehm & Terrio, *Illegal Encounters*; Caldwell, *Deported Americans*.

8 Donna M. Goldstein & Kira Hall, *Postelection Surrealism and Nostalgic Racism in the Hands of Donald Trump*, 7 HAU: J. of Ethnogr. Theor. 397 (2017); Jayashri Srikantiah & Shirin Sinnar, *White Nationalism as Immigration Policy*, Stan. L. Rev. Online, Mar. 2019, www.stanfordlawreview.org (reviewing various policies and public statements by President Trump that have racist underpinnings in white nationalism and racial identity). As one aside, it has been a testimony to how President Trump conducts himself that scholars publishing in so many traditional and scholarly journals and books have concluded he is a racist—one who is so blatant that his words and tweets are said to have given safe harbor to white nationalists and dangerous racists throughout the world. *See, e.g.*, Damien

Cave, *Mass Shootings, an American Export*, N.Y. Times, Mar. 23, 2019, at SR7; Nicholas Kristof, *"A Racist . . . a Con Man . . . a Cheat,"* N.Y. Times, Feb. 27, 2019 (citing President Trump's former lawyer, a convicted felon, in congressional testimony).

9 *Memorandum from Elaine C. Duke, Acting Secretary, U.S. Dept. of Homeland Security, to James W. McCament, Acting Director, U.S. Citizenship and Immigration Services, et al., re. Rescission of the June 15, 2012 Memorandum Entitled "Exercising Prosecutorial Discretion with Respect to Individuals Who Came to the United States as Children,"* Sept. 5, 2017, www.dhs.gov.

10 DHS, *Rescission of Memorandum Providing for Deferred Action for Parents of Americans and Lawful Permanent Residents ("DAPA")*, June 15, 2017, www.dhs.gov.

11 The cases are looked at in great detail throughout earlier chapters and Appendix 3. The litigation in California includes five cases that were consolidated before Judge William Alsup in the U.S. District Court for the Northern District of California: *Regents of Univ. of California, et al. v. Dep't of Homeland Sec., et al.*, No. 3:17-cv-05211; *State of California, et al. v. U.S. Dep't of Homeland Sec., et al.*, No. 3:17-cv-05235; *City of San Jose v. Donald J. Trump, et al.*, No. 3:17-cv-05380; *Garcia, et al. v. United States of America, et al.*, No. 3:17-cv-05380; *Cty. of Santa Clara, et al. v. Donald J. Trump, et al.*, No. 3:17-cv-05813. The preliminary injunction is a helpful finding tool maintained by the National Immigration Law Center (NILC): www.nilc.org. For more information on the litigation and the implications for DACA recipients, *see FAQ: USCIS Is Accepting DACA Renewal Applications*: www.nilc.org; *USCIS and DACA Renewal Applications: What You Need to Know*, www.nilc.org; and *Alert: Court Orders the Dept. of Homeland Security to Allow Individuals with DACA to Apply to Renew It*, www.nilc.org.

12 *See* Shoba Sivaprasad Wadhia, *Banned: Immigration Enforcement in the Time of Trump* (New York University Press 2019). *See also* USCIS, *Temporary Protected Status Designated Country: Honduras*, www.uscis.gov. *See, e.g.*, Miriam Jordan, *Protected Status Ends for Thousands of Immigrants from Honduras*, N.Y. Times, May 4, 2018 at A11; Peniel Ibe, *Trump's Attacks on the Legal Immigration System Explained*, Nov. 26, 2018, www.afsc.org (outlining administration immigration policies). *See also* Michael D. Shear, Abby Goodnough & Maggie Haberman, *In Retreat, Trump Halts Separating Migrant Families*, N.Y. Times, June 20, 2018, at A1. *See* White House, *Executive Orders: Affording Congress an Opportunity to Address Family Separation* (June 20, 2018), www.whitehouse.gov.

13 *See, e.g.*, Eugene Scott, *Before the Midterms, Trump Harped on the Migrant Caravan. Since Then, He Hasn't Brought It Up*, Wash. Post, Nov. 8, 2018, www.washingtonpost.com (indicating that the president's racialization and derogatory depiction of migrants was a campaign tactic aimed at the November 2018 midterm elections). For a view in Spanish-language media of his narrative, *see, e.g.*, Mónica Verea, *Anti-Immigrant and Anti-Mexican Attitudes and Policies During the First 18 Months of the Trump Administration[Transl]*, 13 Norteamérica, https://dialnet.unirioja.es/servlet/articulo?codigo=6824826.

14 Michael D. Shear, Ron Nixon & Katie Benner, *Migrants Order Tosses a Wrench Into the System*, N.Y. Times, June 22, 2018, at A1 (revealing chaos in immigration policies and messages from the administration).

15 *Id.* at A1. In 2018, observers could be forgiven if their heads were spinning; —the news stories across all media showed DACA's life, death, zombie life ("It's Undead"), and other sightings. For a rough outline of the goings-on during that year seen through the lens of one news source, *see, e.g.,* Nolan D. McCaskill & Heather Caygle, *Dems Threaten Revolt Over DACA Deal*, Politico.com, Jan. 11, 2018, www. politico.com; Eric Columbus, *DACA Isn't Dead. It's Undead. The Program Isn't Actually Weeks Away From Ending—It's Already Dead, and It's Very Much Alive*, Politico.com, Jan. 11, 2018, www.politico.com; Ted Hesson, *Flake's DACA Long Shot*, Politico.com, Feb. 21, 2018, www.politico.com; Nolan D. McCaskill, *DACA Deadline Gone*, Politico.com, Feb. 27, 2018, www.politico.com; Ted Hesson, *DACA's Legal Labyrinth*, Politico.com, May 25, 2018, www.politico.com; Ted Hesson, *House GOP Huddles on DACA*, Politico.com, May 25, 2018, www.politico. com; Ted Hesson, *Judge Orders Full Restart of DACA Program*, Politico.com, Aug. 30, 2018, www.politico.com.

16 Hesson, *DACA's Legal Labyrinth*, provides the best thumbnail sketch of the 2018 events:

> The 9th Circuit will hear oral arguments Tuesday over President Donald Trump's decision to end the DACA program, which offers work permits and deportation relief to undocumented immigrants brought to the United States as children. In January, a San Francisco-based district court judge forced the administration to resume accepting DACA renewal applications, which it had stopped doing in early October. The Justice Department then appealed that decision to the 9th Circuit.
>
> A pair of district court judges in Brooklyn and D.C. similarly blocked the Trump administration's planned phaseout of DACA, with the latter judge threatening to force the administration not only to renew old DACA applications but also to accept new ones if the Justice Department can't present by late July a better rationale for ending the program. But earlier this month attorneys general in Texas and six other states filed suit to end DACA on the grounds that it oversteps the authority of the executive branch—the same argument that many of the same states used successfully in 2016 to sink DAPA, a broader Obama-era deportation relief program for parents of U.S. citizens or lawful permanent residents.
>
> How will it all play out? Here are a few possibilities, based on conversations with court watchers:
>
> 1. The liberal 9th Circuit—urged by the Supreme Court to act "expeditiously" in the California cases—rules by the end of the summer to keep DACA alive, prompting the administration to petition the Supreme Court. Oral arguments are heard in early spring 2019, and a high court decision is handed down in June. That's a scenario described Stephen Yale-Loehr, a Cornell Law School

professor and immigration lawyer. (This timetable, he concedes, "is very speculative.")

2. There's also the Texas case, which is now before Brownsville-based U.S. District Court Judge Andrew Hanen, who blocked DAPA in February 2015. In that case, he issued swiftly a nationwide preliminary injunction. Were Hanen to act as speedily this time out, he could have blocked DACA as early as July. The administration (or an intervener) would then appeal to the conservative 5th Circuit. In the DAPA case, the Obama administration sought to stay the injunction, but Hanen and the appeals court both denied it. The 5th Circuit then took nine months to affirm the ruling against the program.

3. But wait, observes Josh Blackman, an associate professor at the South Texas College of Law–Houston. A 5th Circuit preliminary injunction *halting* DACA would conflict with the district court injunctions in San Francisco, Brooklyn and New York to *re-start* DACA. An injunction to halt DACA might even conflict with a 9th-Circuit decision to re-start DACA. What then? Well, Hanen could issue an injunction halting DACA but stay it until the other cases were resolved. Or Hanen could press ahead with his injunction and leave it to the Supreme Court to untangle what the Homeland Security Department should do while the high court prepares to hear all these cases and rule on the merits. Eventually, he chose the latter.

4. Or, Congress could step in to codify DACA and President Donald Trump could sign that bill into law, mooting all these lawsuits. This was the plan last fall, and it made a certain amount of sense, because congressional Democrats, congressional Republicans, and Trump all said they don't want DACA to end. But Trump subsequently attached various conditions to preserving DACA, including imposing new limitations on legal immigration, that the Democrats wouldn't accept. The odds were always heavily against a congressional deal on DACA because the midterms were less than six months away.

Notwithstanding the careful explanation of possible outcomes, none of the four actually took place. However, a version of item 3 occurred on May 1, 2018, when Texas and six other states filed a follow-up lawsuit in the U.S. District Court for the Southern District of Texas challenging the 2012 DACA program itself, in effect pressing for a final decision in *U.S. v. Texas*, which had been remanded by SCOTUS on the deadlocked 4–4 vote. Judge Andrew Hanen, the U.S. district court judge who tried the original case in Brownsville, had been reassigned to the Southern District's Houston office, and the case followed him. On May 2, the plaintiff states asked Judge Hanen (who had kept the case since the remand) to issue a preliminary injunction to enforce his earlier plan to end DACA and to actually do so now by letting DACA expire as each grant ended with no renewals. After a Houston hearing on August 8, 2018, Judge Hanen declined to do so, rather remarkably determining that too much had occurred in several courts across the country and that the Supreme Court or the political process would eventually have to settle this standoff.

This left the matter wending its various ways through courts in California, New York, Maryland, and the District of Columbia . Ironically, these other DACA cases were faring better in those courts than they had with Judge Hanen pursuant to his original rulings. This had the effect of allowing DACA recipients to continue to apply for their two-year renewals; during the pendency of the litigation many had done so several times, each time being glad for the opportunity of extending the program that had given them a small and imperfect taste of living in the country permanently.

17 *Trump v. Hawaii*, 138 S. Ct. 2392 (2018). *See also* Adam Liptak & Michael D. Shear, *Justices Back Travel Ban, Yielding to Trump*, N.Y. Times, June 26, 2018, at A1.

18 Sheryl Gay Stolberg, *Senate Votes 50–48 to Put Kavanaugh on Supreme Court*, N.Y. Times, Oct. 6, 2018, at A1. Fueled by an alleged sexual assault against a female during high school, as well as doubts about the veracity of his original testimony for confirmation to the D.C. Circuit court, Justice Brett Kavanaugh's hearings in the Senate for appointment to the Supreme Court were among the most contentious in history. *See generally* Julia Jacobs, *Was the Kavanaugh Hearing the Worst Supreme Court Fight? You Be the Judge*, N.Y. Times, Oct. 7, 2018, www.nytimes.com.

19 *See generally* Hesson, *DACA's Legal Labyrinth*.

20 *Id.*

21 NILC, *Status of Current DACA Litigation*, www.nilc.org (discussing *Regents of Univ. of California, et al. v. Dep't of Homeland Security, et al.*).

22 *Securities and Exchange Comm'n v. Chenery*, 318 U.S. 80 (1943) (*"Chenery I"*): "Plaintiffs are therefore likely to succeed on the merits of their claim that the rescission was based on a flawed legal premise and must be set aside as 'arbitrary, capricious, an abuse of discretion, or otherwise not in accordance with law.'" *Massachusetts*, 549 U.S. at 528; *Sec. & Exch. Comm'n v. Chenery Corp.*, 318 U.S. 80, 94. See www.nilc.org/wp-content/uploads/2018/01/Regents-v-DHS-preliminjunction-2018-01-09.pdf at page 38.

23 *Id.* at 32–33, 49.

24 *Id.* 86 F. Supp. 3d 591 (S.D. Tex. 2015) (issuing preliminary injunction).

25 The options in this area are very clandestine and resemble the old Russian samizdat, or narratives written furtively to communicate among disfavored gulag prisoners. Albert Parry, *Samizdat Is Russia's Underground Press*, N.Y. Times, Mar. 15, 1970, at 249. The Trump administration's decision to revoke the advance parole option undoubtedly made it more difficult to apply for lawful permanent status, but sometimes water finds its way through rock or wears rock down. *See, e.g.*, Kelly S. O'Reilly, *Alternative to DACA Advance Parole*, Sept. 22, 2017, www.wilneroreilly.com.

26 *See* Lomi Kriel, *Flight Attendant with DACA Released After Month in Detention for Mexico Flight*, Hous. Chron., Mar. 22, 2019, www.houstonchronicle.com (social media pressure gets DACA flight attendant released from detention after

international flight); Reis Thebault, *How a Flight Attendant from Texas Ended up in an ICE Detention Center for Six Weeks*, Wash. Post, Mar. 23, 2019, www. washingtonpost.com (flight attendant with DACA held in detention because she left country and reentered with advance parole). *See generally* Laura E. Enriquez, Martha Morales Hernandez, Daniel Millán & Daisy Vazquez Vera, *Mediating Illegality: Federal, State, and Institutional Policies in the Educational Experiences of Undocumented College Students*, 45 L. & Soc. Inq. 1 (2019) ("university policies are a key site for intervening in immigration policy and constructing immigrant illegality"); NAFSA: Association of International Educators, *DACA Resource Page: For International Student Advisers and Education Abroad Advisers* (Jan. 15, 2019), www.nafsa.org.

27 The federal rules for civil and appellate procedure render the litigation pathways very confusing, especially as the Trump administration sought to circumvent or expedite traditional appellate procedures. In its Petition for a Writ of Certiorari Before Judgment, the administration submitted over a dozen pages spelling out the procedural history of the case. *See* the Petition, www.supremecourt.gov.

28 The Supreme Court denied the expedited cert petition. The entire record to that point is www.supremecourt.gov (Case No. 17-1003).

29 *Batalla Vidal, et al. v. Nielsen, et al.*, 1:16-cv-04756 (E.D.N.Y.); *State of New York, et al. v. Trump, et al.*, 1:17-cv-05228 (E.D.N.Y.). A comprehensive list of the many motions in the cases is www.nilc.org.

30 *NAACP v. Trump, et al.*; *Trustees of Princeton Univ., et al. v. United States of America, et al.*, 298 F. Supp. 3d 209, 238 (2018). In a third case, brought in neighboring Maryland, *CASA de Maryland v. U.S. Dep't of Homeland Security*, 284 F. Supp. 3d 758 (D. Md. 2018), the DACAmented plaintiffs failed to persuade the trial judge that the administration's approach had failed to follow the Administrative Procedure Act claim, being persuaded that the long-ago abandoned DAPA program was an indication that DACA could have been illegal: "Regardless of the lawfulness of DACA, the appropriate inquiry is whether or not DHS made a reasoned decision to rescind DACA based on the Administrative Record. Given the fate of DAPA, the legal advice provided by the Attorney General, and the threat of imminent litigation, it was reasonable for DHS to have concluded—right or wrong—that DACA was unlawful and should be wound down in an orderly manner. Therefore, its decision to rescind DACA cannot be arbitrary and capricious." *Id.* at 767–68. *See* Alex Johnson & Pete Williams, *Third Federal Judge Issues Strongest Order Yet Backing DACA*, NBCNews.com, Apr. 25, 2018, www.nbcnews. com.

31 *Id.* at 239.

32 *See* Harold Hongju Koh, *The Trump Administration and International Law* (Oxford Univ. Press 2018) (criticizing President Trump's legal theories and policies leading to "systematic disengagement with nearly all institutions of global governance"). *See also* Stephen Lee & Sameer M. Ashar, *DACA, Government Lawyers, and the Public Interest*, 87 Fordh. L. Rev. 1879 (2019) (roles of government lawyers

in adjudication policies and practices); Fred Barbash & Deanna Paul, *The Real Reason the Trump Administration Is Constantly Losing in Court*, Wash. Post, Mar. 19, 2019, https://wapo.st/2Fnvego?tid=ss_mail&utm_term=.ceec670f7e36 ("[R]egardless of whether the administration ultimately prevails, the rulings so far paint a remarkable portrait of a government rushing to implement far-reaching changes in policy without regard for long-standing rules against arbitrary and capricious behavior.").

33 *Memorandum from Secretary Kirstjen M. Nielsen* (June 22, 2018), www.dhs.gov.

34 *Id.* at 3.

35 *Supplemental Brief for State Appellees*, at 2, *Batalla Vidal v. Nielsen*, No. 18-00485 (2d Cir. Sept. 20, 2018), 2018 WL 4677348.

36 *Id.* at 2–3.

37 Jonathan Blitzer, *Will Anyone in the Trump Administration Ever Be Held Accountable for the Zero-Tolerance Immigration Policy?*, New Yorker, Aug. 22, 2018, www.newyorker.com (the administration thought it could implement the policy without notice); Julie Hirschfeld Davis & Michael D. Shear, *Border Policy Had Been Seen as Inhumane*, N.Y. Times, June 16, 2018, at A1 ("zero tolerance policy" results in unlawful immigrants being taken into federal criminal custody, at which point their children are considered "unaccompanied alien minors" and taken away).

38 Miriam Jordan, *Torn Apart at the Border, Kept Apart by Red Tape*, N.Y. Times, June 24, 2018, at A14 (stories of children separated from parents); Miriam Jordan, *Many Families Split at Border Went Untallied*, N.Y. Times, Jan. 17, 2019, at A1. Flash-forward six months and even official federal reports were critical of the unhealthy and dangerous detention facilities. Zolan Kanno-Youngs, *Squalor Pervasive in Detention Centers*, N.Y. Times, July 2, 2019, at A1 (inspector general report includes extensive details on dangerous overcrowding and squalid conditions for immigrants, including babies and minors, held in detention).

39 Maria Sacchetti, *In Another Blow to Trump, Judge Rules in Favor of ACLU in Family Separations Case*, Wash. Post, Mar. 8, 2019, https://wapo.st/2TIeOHk?tid=ss_mail&utm_term=.ee0653da7b58 (details of ACLU suit to reunite immigrant children).

40 Tara Golshan & Dylan Scott, *The Many Tragedies of the 115th Congress. Six Times Senators Thought They Could Break Through Partisan Politics—and Failed*, Vox.com., Jan. 3, 2019, www.vox.com (two of the six worst "tragedies" included the failure of the Senate to enact the DREAM Act: one involved Sen. Flake, and another involved Sens. Graham and Durbin). See Table 3.1.

41 *See, e.g.*, CNN Library, *2018 in Review Fast Facts*, CNN.com, Dec. 31, 2018, www.cnn.com.

42 *See* Shoba Sivaprasad Wadhia, *Banned*.

43 Emily Cochrane & Jennifer Medina, *When Is a Fence a Wall? An End to the Shutdown May Ride on the Answer*, N.Y. Times, Dec. 26, 2018, at A12 (uncertainty about construction terminology regarding the wall along the southern border).

44 Amy Howe, *After Federal Government Filing, 9th Circuit Rules in DACA Dispute,* SCOTUS Blog, Nov. 8, 2018, www.scotusblog.com.

45 *Regents of Univ. of California v. U.S. Dep't of Homeland Sec.,* 908 F.3d 476, 512 (9th Cir. 2018).

46 *Id.* at 486 (9th Cir. 2018).

47 Michael D. Shear & Julie Hirschfeld Davis, *Trump Moves to End DACA and Calls on Congress to Act,* N.Y. Times, Sept. 5, 2017, at A1.

48 *Regents of Univ. of California v. U.S. Dep't of Homeland Sec.,* 908 F.3d 476, 510 (9th Cir. 2018).

49 *Nat'l Ass'n for the Advancement of Colored People v. Trump,* 315 F. Supp. 3d 457 (D.D.C. 2018).

50 *Regents of Univ. of California v. U.S. Dep't of Homeland Sec.,* 279 F. Supp. 3d 1011, 1018 (N.D. Cal.), *aff'd sub nom. Regents of Univ. of California v. U.S. Dep't of Homeland Sec.,* 908 F.3d 476 (9th Cir. 2018).

51 *Dep't of Homeland Sec. v. Regents of Univ. of California,* 138 S. Ct. 1182 (2018).

52 *Regents of Univ. of California v. U.S. Dep't of Homeland Sec.,* 908 F.3d 476, 510 (9th Cir. 2018).

53 The Trump administration's reason for discontinuing DACA was that President Obama did not have the legal authority to do what he had done in enacting the program, and Trump's DOJ lawyers were losing badly in the repeal of various Obama initiatives because of bad luck or a stubborn insistence that the administration did have such presidential authority. After one full year of litigation, the administration had lost twenty-eight of thirty major challenges on Administrative Procedure Act cases. *See, e.g.,* Margot Sanger-Katz, *For Trump Administration, It Has Been Hard to Follow the Rules on Rules,* N.Y. Times, Jan. 22, 2019, www.nytimes.com.

54 *Regents of Univ. of California v. U.S. Dep't of Homeland Sec.,* 908 F.3d 476, 486 (9th Cir. 2018).

55 *Texas v. United States,* 328 F. Supp. 3d 662, 742 (S.D. Tex. 2018).

56 *Id.* at 687.

57 Because Democrats had not held the top leadership positions in the House, Senate, or White House, and because the Supreme Court had been restocked with two reliably conservative justices, it is unrealistic to hold them fully responsible for the failure to score legislative wins in 2017 and 2018 (especially in regard to immigration reform of any sort). And yet there were a number of examples where the DREAMers were in the mix of agendas and proposals only for the ethereal moments to pass without success. The Senate still had never voted on any version of a DREAM Act or DACA-related bill, and those that arose from the Republicans were chimerical and offered no substantive improvements even over the wounded but surviving DACA program. All this was a result of the administration's feckless lack of leadership on the issue, the president's unpredictable and nativist path on immigration, and amazingly poor litigation tactics by the DOJ and DHS decision-makers and lawyers. *See* Srikantiah & Sinnar, *White National-*

ism as Immigration Policy; Wadhia, *Banned. See also* W. James Antle III, *To Fix DACA, Remember How the DREAM Act Died*, Wash. Examin., Sept. 7, 2017, www.washingtonexaminer.com; Lee & Ashar, *DACA, Government Lawyers, and the Public Interest.*

58 Erica Werner & Damian Paletta, *GOP Leaders Aim to Avert Shutdown over Wall Funding, but Trump Makes No Promises*, Wash. Post, Nov. 15, 2018, https://wapo.st/2qPSpIm?tid=ss_mail&utm_term=.0927befa7a40.

59 Tiffany Hu, *Koch Groups Push for "Dreamer" Protections in Spending Bill*, Law360.com, Nov. 15, 2018, www.law360.com.

60 Werner & Paletta, *GOP Leaders Aim.*

61 Jonathan Martin & Alexander Burns, *Democrats Secure Control of the House; Republicans Build on Majority in Senate*, N.Y. Times, Nov. 6, 2018, at A1.

62 Werner & Paletta, *GOP Leaders Aim.*

63 Hu, *Koch Groups Push.*

64 Jazmine Ulloa, *How Young Immigrant "Dreamers" Made Flipping Control of the House a Personal Quest*, L.A. Times, Jan. 1, 2019, www.latimes.com.

65 Jimmy Breslin, *The Gang That Couldn't Shoot Straight: A Novel* (Viking 1969).

66 *The Gang That Couldn't Shoot Straight* (1971), www.imdb.com/title/tt0067124.

67 *See* U.S. Department of Justice (DOJ), *Attorney General Jeff Sessions Issues Statement on DACA Court Order* (Aug. 6, 2018), www.justice.gov. *See also* U.S. DOJ, *Attorney General Sessions Delivers Remarks on DACA* (Sept. 5. 2019), www.justice.gov. *See, e.g.*, Elaine Kamarck & Christine Stenglein, Brookings Institution, *Can Immigration Reform Happen? A Look Back* (Feb. 11, 2019), www.brookings.edu.

68 *See, e.g.*, Nicole Narea, *Trump Sticks to Wall Demand, but Offers DACA, TPS Extension*, Law360.com, Jan. 19, 2019, www.law360.com (to end shutdown, president offers TPS and DACA extension without a path to citizenship); Jeremy Diamond, Manu Raju, Kaitlan Collins, Abby Phillip & Phil Mattingly, *Trump Expected to Propose Extending DACA, TPS Protections in Exchange for Wall Funding*, CNN News, Jan. 19, 2019, www.cnn.com.

69 Gregory Krieg, *Someone Please Remind Trump That He Ended DACA*, CNN.com, Mar. 5, 2018, www.cnn.com.

70 *See* Lucy Madison, *Romney on Immigration: I'm for "Self-Deportation,"* CBSNews.com, Jan. 24, 2012, www.cbsnews.com/news/romney-on-immigration-im-for-self-deportation; Rachel Weiner, *Trump: Mitt Romney's "Maniacal" Self-Deportation Policy Cost Him Minorities*, Wash. Post, Nov. 26, 2012, https://wapo.st (for readers with a cruel sense of irony).

71 *See* Sanger-Katz, *For Trump Administration* (Trump administration has lost twenty-eight of "30 big regulations" on APA grounds).

72 *See* Brett Samuels, *Trump Targets Dems Over DACA Amid Shutdown Talks*, TheHill.com, Jan. 13, 2019, https://thehill.com; Annie Karni & Sheryl Gay Stolberg, *President Offers Deal on "Dreamers" to Secure a Wall*, N.Y. Times, Jan. 19, 2019, at A1.

73 *See generally* Linda Qiu, *The Many Ways Trump Has Said Mexico Will Pay for the Wall,* N.Y. Times, Jan. 11, 2019, at A12 (cites president as promising Mexico would "make a one-time payment," that Mexico would reimburse the United States, and that costs could be covered by imposing fees on Mexican diplomats and workers—all untrue); David Nakamura, *"The Story Keeps Changing": Trump Falsely Asserts He Never Promised Mexico Would Directly Pay for the Border Wall,* Wash. Post, Jan. 10, 2019, https://wapo.st.

74 U.S. Const. art. I, § 7.

75 U.S. Const. art. I, § 9.

76 Karni & Stolberg, *President Offers Deal,* at A1.

77 *See* Nicholas Fandos, Sheryl Gay Stolberg & Peter Baker, *Shutdown Ends With No Funding for Wall,* N.Y. Times, Jan. 25, 2019, at A1 (interim funding plan signed with no wall funds); Peter Baker, *A Stinging Defeat for the President,* N.Y. Times, Jan. 25, 2019, at A1 (given all the attention he drew to the shutdown and wall, president had to take half a loaf when he didn't have the votes); Trip Gabriel, *Rancor on Wall Slips Out of Sync With Border Voters,* N.Y. Times, Jan. 25, 2019, at A10 (all nine House members from border states oppose wall).

78 *See* Alex Horton, *"He Lied About It": Ann Coulter Rips Trump for Failing to Secure Border Wall Funding,* Wash. Post, Jan. 26, 2019, www.washingtonpost.com (conservative pundit Ann Coulter fiercely criticizes president, saying "he lied about" the wall); Abby Ohlheiser, Eli Rosenberg & Michael Brice-Saddler, *"Trump Caves" or "Genius": Right Wing Splits After Trump Ends Shutdown With No Wall Funding,* Wash. Post, Jan. 25, 2019, www.washingtonpost.com (range of critical assessments by right-wing media).

79 *See* Peter Baker & Maggie Haberman, *His Wall, His Shutdown and His Side of the Story,* N.Y. Times, Jan. 4, 2019, at A10 (history of various wall funding assertions).

80 Fandos, Stolberg & Baker, *Shutdown Ends With No Funding for Wall*; Baker, *A Stinging Defeat for the President*; Gabriel, *Rancor on Wall.*

81 Marc Fisher, Ben Guarino & Katie Zezima, *How the Shutdown Ended: Americans Just Had It up to Here,* Wash. Post, Jan. 25, 2019, https://wapo.st/2FNSqWB?tid=ss_mail&utm_term=.b989df99e131 (The "government shutdown morphed into a downpour, a winter storm of disruption, dysfunction and desperation that shocked stubborn politicians into action."). *See also* Scott Clement & David Nakamura, *Post-ABC Poll: Trump Disapproval Swells as President, Republicans Face Lopsided Blame for Shutdown,* Wash. Post, Jan. 25, 2019, https://wapo.st/2FPJ3pt?tid=ss_mail&utm_term=.a2d19b6d56ec (public disapproval of President Trump at 58 percent).

82 *Id. See also* Philip Rucker, Josh Dawsey & Damian Paletta, *"Am I Out of Touch?": Trump Administration Struggles to Show Empathy for Workers,* Wash. Post, Jan. 24, 2019, https://wapo.st/2FM7oOu?tid=ss_mail&utm_term=.dc46676576d9 (Trump administration officials appear cavalier or clueless about economic hardship experienced by furloughed federal employees).

83 The news stories reveal a nation fascinated with the drama and concerned about the larger issues as they depicted regular persons a paycheck away from financial ruin and revealed a glimpse into the marginality of many U.S. workers. *See, e.g.,* Jim Tankersley, Matthew Goldstein & Glenn Thrush, *Impasse Starting to Leave a Mark on the Economy*, N.Y. Times, Jan. 7, 2019, at A1; Denise Lu & Anjali Singhvi, *See How the Effects of the Government Shutdown Are Piling Up*, N.Y. Times, Jan. 8, 2019, www.nytimes.com (details of various agency closures); Jack Healy, Kirk Johnson & Kate Taylor, *Payday for Many Federal Workers Comes and Goes Without a Paycheck*, N.Y. Times, Jan. 8, 2019 at A14; Michael Tackett & Julie Hirschfeld Davis, *White House Sees Storm Aid as Way to Pay for Wall*, N.Y. Times, Jan. 10, 2019, at A1 (Trump administration seeking various ways to fund wall construction); Nakamura, *"The Story Keeps Changing"*; Maegan Vazquez, *Trump Says You Can Call His Wall "Peaches" for All He Cares*, CNN.com, Jan. 11, 2019, www.cnn.com (analysis of wall nomenclature); Julie Hirschfeld Davis & Maggie Haberman, *President's Abrupt Shifts on Impasse Baffle Even Those Within His Party*, N.Y. Times, Jan. 11, 2019, at A11; Michael D. Shear, *Seeking Wall, Trump Builds Ill Will Instead*, N.Y. Times, Jan. 12, 2019, at A1; Robert Costa, Josh Dawsey, Philip Rucker & Seung Min Kim, *"In the White House Waiting": Inside Trump's Defiance on the Longest Shutdown Ever*, Wash. Post, Jan. 12, 2019, https://wapo.st/2FrckXt?tid=ss_mail&utm_term=.34426a110f07 (deal options include DACA legislation); Mike DeBonis, *"We Will Be Out for a Long Time" Unless Democrats Budge, Trump Says, as Shutdown Enters 4th Week*, Wash. Post, Jan. 12, 2019, https://wapo.st/2FpnZ8R?tid=ss_mail&utm_term=.4e7789fc7455 (President Trump attempts to shift closure blame onto Democrats); Shear, *Seeking Wall* (irreconcilable differences in wall debate strategy); Sheryl Gay Stolberg, *Trump Country Calls on Party Not to Give In*, N.Y. Times, Jan. 14, 2019, at A1; Felicia Sonmez & Cat Zakrzewski, *Pressure on Senate Republicans to Break Shutdown Impasse Grows*, Wash. Post, Jan. 14, 2019, https://wapo.st/2Foom3D?tid=ss_mail&utm_term=.1da8d9c47293; Stolberg, *Trump Country*, at A1; Matt Viser, *Democrats and Activists Punish Trump with a New Strategy: Ignoring Him*, Wash. Post, Jan. 17, 2019, https://wapo.st/2FGm2EG?tid=ss_mail&utm_term=.120865308c14 (strategic Democratic actions to ignore and draw attention away from President Trump); Mark Sherman, *Supreme Court Inaction Suggests DACA Safe for Another Year*, APNews.com, Jan. 18, 2019, https://apnews.com (traditional deadline for cert grants passed without SCOTUS agreeing to take DACA-related cases); Julie Hirschfeld Davis, *$1 Billion More as Democrats Shift on Border*, N.Y. Times, Jan. 18, 2019, at A1 (no progress on negotiations, but Democratss offering more nonwall resources); Jonathan Blitzer, *As the Shutdown Continues, Trump Offers a Deal That Democrats Are Sure to Reject*, New Yorker, Jan. 19, 2019, www.newyorker.com (president recycled old temporary DACA proposal to negotiate with Democrats); Dara Lind & Javier Zarracina, *The People Directly Harmed Can Be Counted. The Indirect Effects Can't Be*, Vox.com, Jan 19, 2019, www.vox.com; Karni & Stolberg, *President Offers Deal*, at A1; Julie Hirschfeld Davis, *Trump Goes Beyond His Base and No One Is Happy*,

N.Y. Times, Jan. 19, 2019, at A1; Narea, *Trump Sticks to Wall Demand*; Diamond
et al., *Trump Expected to Propose Extending DACA*; Sheryl Gay Stolberg, *Centrists
Aim to Make Mark as Democrats*, N.Y. Times, Jan. 19, 2019, at A1; Russ Buettner &
Maggie Haberman, *As Mogul and President, Consistent in Chaos*, N.Y. Times, Jan.
20, 2019, at A1 (Trump's use of unscrupulous deals, deceit, and unpredictability
in business and the White House); Carl Hulse & Emily Cochrane, *Impasse Drives
Pelosi and McConnell, Already at Odds, Further Apart*, N.Y. Times, Jan. 20, 2019,
at A11 (political difference between two congressional leaders of their parties);
Sheryl Gay Stolberg, *G.O.P.'s Tactics Seek to Corner the Democrats*, N.Y. Times,
Jan. 20, 2019, at A1 (GOP trying to blame Democrats as unreasonable for not
taking president's offer of short term DACA; polls blame president for shutdown);
Sheryl Gay Stolberg, *McConnell to Pair Bills to Reopen Government with Trump's
Immigration Plan*, N.Y. Times, Jan. 20, 2019, www.nytimes.com (Sen. McConnell's
first foray into the shutdown, including Bridge plan for DACA temporary relief);
Elizabeth Redden, *Trump Proposes DACA Deal for a Wall*, InsideHigherEd.com,
Jan. 21, 2019, www.insidehighered.com (Speaker Nancy Pelosi calls president's
DACA plan a "non-starter"); Amy Davidson Sorkin, *The Republican Test at the
Border*, New Yorker, Jan. 21, 2019, www.newyorker.com (failure to agree on border
security, GOP leaving DREAMers in the lurch); Greg Sargent, *Trump's Phony
"Compromise" Has Now Been Unmasked as a Total Sham*, Wash. Post, Jan. 22,
2019, www.washingtonpost.com; Sheryl Gay Stolberg & Julie Hirschfeld Davis,
Senate Will Hold Competing Votes to End Shutdown, N.Y. Times, Jan. 22, 2019, at
A1 (Democrats and Republicans will separately present bills, neither of which will
likely pass); Peter Baker, *No Progress on Wall, or on Anything Else Worth Talk-
ing About*, N.Y. Times, Jan. 22, 2019, at A15 (White House focusing only on wall
issues to the exclusion of all other policies); Stolberg & Davis, *Senate Will Hold
Competing Votes*; Sargent, *Trump's Phony "Compromise"*; Sean Sullivan, *Senators
Hope Defeat of Dueling Plans Produces a Solution to Shutdown*, Wash. Post, Jan.
23, 2019, https://wapo.st (issues following Senate bill defeats); Stuart Anderson,
Analysts Find Restrictive Measures in New Trump Immigration Bill, Forbes.com,
Jan. 23, 2019, www.forbes.com; Josh Dawsey & Robert Costa, *"Master Negotiator"
or "Nonentity"? Kushner Thrusts Himself into Middle of Shutdown Talks*, Wash.
Post, Jan. 23, 2019, https://wapo.st (role of president's son-in-law in negotiating
shutdown issues); Jordan Carney, *Senate Rejects Two Measures to End Shutdown*, TheHill.com, Jan. 24, 2019, https://thehill.com (failure to gain veto-proof
majority on either the Republican or the Democratic bill to end shutdown); Julie
Hirschfeld Davis, *Senate Bills Fail, Raising Urgency of Impasse Talks*, N.Y. Times,
Jan. 24, 3019, at A1 (frustration over failed negotiations).

84 See Clement & Nakamura, *Post-ABC Poll*; Rucker, Dawsey & Paletta, *"Am I Out of
Touch?"*; Sargent, *Trump's Phony "Compromise."*

85 *Id.*

86 See, e.g., Costa, Dawsey, Rucker & Kim, *"In the White House Waiting"*; DeBonis
"We Will Be Out for a Long Time" Unless Democrats Budge, Trump Says; Shear,

Seeking Wall; Lind & Zarracina, *People Directly Harmed*; Karni & Stolberg, *President Offers Deal*; Davis, *Trump Goes Beyond His Base*.

87 *See, e.g.*, Viser, *Democrats and Activists Punish Trump*; Davis, *$1 Billion More*; Jonathan Blitzer, *Shutdown Continues*; Stolberg, *Centrists Aim to Make Mark as Democrats*; Hulse & Cochrane, *Impasse*; Stolberg, *G.O.P.'s Tactics*; Karni & Stolberg, *President Offers Deal*; Narea, *Trump Sticks to Wall Demand*; Diamond et al., *Trump Expected to Propose Extending DACA*; Anderson, *Analysts Find Restrictive Measures*.

88 Nicole Narea, *Parties Duel over Rationale for Blocking DACA in Texas Suit*, Law360.com, Aug. 14, 2018, www.law360.com (GOP-led states argue DACA is illegal overreach).

89 *See, e.g.*, Horton, *"He Lied About It"*; Karni & Stolberg, *President Offers Deal*; Davis, *Trump Goes Beyond His Base*.

90 *See* Stolberg, *McConnell to Pair Bills*; Redden, *Trump Proposes DACA Deal*; Sorkin, *Republican Test*.

91 *Id.*

92 *See generally* Davis, *Trump Goes Beyond His Base*; Stolberg, *G.O.P.'s Tactics*.

93 *See* Baker & Haberman, *His Wall, His Shutdown*, at A10; Robert Costa, Juliet Eilperin, Damian Paletta & Nick Miroff, *As Shutdown Drags on, Trump Officials Make New Offer, Seek Novel Ways to Cope with Its Impacts*, Wash. Post, Jan. 6, 2019, https://wapo.st/2FbqsDM?tid=ss_mail&utm_term=.f725903e1b36.

94 *See* Baker & Haberman, *His Wall, His Shutdown*, at A10; Costa et al., *Shutdown Drags On*.

95 *See* Sheryl Gay Stolberg, *President Delays His State of Union Amid a Shutdown*, N.Y. Times, Jan. 24, 2019, at A1; Emily Cochrane & Catie Edmondson, *State of the Union Address Is a Must, but Time and Place Are Debatable*, N.Y. Times, Jan. 23, 2019, at A12; Sheryl Gay Stolberg, *Trump Accepts Offer to Give State of Union*, N.Y. Times, Jan, 28, 2019, at A14; Carl Hulse, *Address Let Democrats Put Defiance on Display*, N.Y. Times, Feb. 6, 2019, at A14.

96 *Id.*

97 The press and social media had a field day with the clashing narratives, the subtle and steamroller tactics, and the convergence of the several dramatic stories. *See, e.g.*, Glenn Thrush & Emily Cochrane, *Trump's Options for Wall Shrink as G.O.P. Wavers*, N.Y. Times, Feb. 4, 2019, at A1 (Republican Party has mixed feelings about declaring national emergency to build wall); Emily Birnbaum, *Civil Liberties Groups Ask Congress to Refuse Border Tech Funding in Any Shutdown Deal*, The Hill.com, Feb. 5, 2019, https://thehill.com; Emily Cochrane, *Pelosi Says She'll Back What Negotiators Come Up with on the Border*, N.Y. Times, Feb. 6, 2019, at A19 (signs from Democrats that they will not fund wall itself but will add additional border security funds); Dara Linddara, *Congress's Deal on Immigration Detention, Explained*, Vox.com, Feb. 12, 2019, www.vox.com (details on agreement); Peter Baker & Glenn Thrush, *G.O.P. Pressures Trump to Accept Deal on Border*, N.Y. Times, Feb. 12, 2019, at A1 (committee reaches deal with

several concessions by both sides and less money than earlier version); Erica
Werner, Damian Paletta & Sean Sullivan, *Lawmakers Say They Have Reached
an "Agreement in Principle" to Avoid Government Shutdown*, Wash. Post, Feb.
12, 2019, https://wapo.st/2MYbJgN?tid=ss_mail&utm_term=.7fa530deocc1
(splitting differences in scope and amount of money); Peter Baker & Maggie
Haberman, *Trump's Task: Saving Face at the Border*, N.Y. Times, Feb. 13, 2019, at
A1 (president spins his loss in budget fight by saying he won concessions); Emily
Cochrane & Catie Edmondson, *Nearing Deal, Trump Says Shutdown Would Be
"Terrible,"* N.Y. Times, Feb. 13, 2019, at A14 (insider maneuvering by both houses
of Congress to assure signing); Nicholas Fandos, *Back in Earnest, Congress
Pushes to Reset Agendas*, N.Y. Times, Jan. 27, 2019, at A1 (difficulties in negotiat-
ing with looming new shutdown deadline); Alan Rappeport, *Huge Backlog for
the I.R.S., Just in Time for Tax Season*, N.Y. Times, Jan. 25, 2019, at A12 (examples
of hardships facing furloughed federal workers); Patrick McGeehan, *Thousands
Inconvenienced Amid Shutdown-Related Flight Delays*, N.Y. Times, Jan. 25,
2019, at A1 (examples of furloughed airport workers with the Federal Aviation
Administration causing flight delays).

98 *Id. See also* T. Christian Miller, *If Trump's Border Wall Becomes Reality, Here's How
He Could Easily Get Private Land for It*, ProPublica.org, Mar. 25, 2019, www.pro-
publica.org. In fact, the president soon did exactly what was being predicted and
reprogrammed money already appropriated. Daniel Wilson, *DOD Awards $1B in
Border Wall Deals After Funding Shift*, Law360.com, Apr. 10, 2019, www.law360.
com (Department of Defense reprograms nearly $1 billion for the wall pursuant to
an emergency declaration).

99 *See, e.g.*, Thrush & Cochrane, *Trump's Options for Wall*; Birnbaum, *Civil Liberties
Groups*; Baker & Thrush, *G.O.P. Pressures Trump*.

100 Jeremy Diamond & Kevin Liptak, *Trump Calls Border Wall a "Medieval Solution"
That Works*, CNN.com, Jan. 9, 2019, www.cnn.com; Vazquez, *Trump Says You
Can Call His Wall "Peaches."*

101 *See, e.g.*, Mark Mazzetti, Maggie Haberman, Nicholas Fandos & Michael S.
Schmidt, *Inside Trump's Angry War on Inquiries Around Him*, N.Y. Times, Feb. 19,
2019, at A1.

102 *Id.* What a difference a month makes. *See* Mark Mazzetti & Katie Benner, *Mueller
Finds No Trump-Russia Conspiracy*, N.Y. Times, Mar. 24, 2019, at A1. *See also*
Laurence R. Jurdem, *How Richard Nixon Charted the Path for Donald Trump's
Reelection*, Wash. Post, Mar. 11, 2019, www.washingtonpost.com. Unsurprisingly,
the momentum switched again when the fuller-but-still-redacted version was
released, and it turns out that Attorney General Barr and the president had seized
early control of the narrative until a fuller version of the report was released and
examined. Mark Mazzetti, *Mueller Report Lays Out Russian Contacts and Trump's
Frantic Efforts to Foil Inquiry*, N.Y. Times, Apr. 18, 2019, at A1 (redacted Special
Counsel report raised many instances of obstruction behavior by the president as
well as the testimony of many aides who lied under oath).

103 H.J. Res. 31, Consolidated Appropriations Act, 2019: www.congress.gov. The
     president, as promised, vetoed the bill the next day, March 15, 2019. *See generally*
     Michael Tackett, *Trump Issues First Veto After Congress Blocks Border Wall Emer-*
     gency, N.Y. Times, Mar. 15, 2019, at A15 (president vetoes HJR on March 15, 2019);
     Andrew Rudalevige, *Why Congress's Rebuke of Trump's Emergency Declaration*
     Matters—Despite the President's Veto, Wash. Post, Mar. 15, 2019, www.washing-
     tonpost.com. The House did not find enough votes to reverse the veto. Emily
     Cochrane, *House Fails to Override Trump's Veto, Preserving National Emergency*
     Order, N.Y. Times, Mar. 26, 2019, at A15. Soon after, on the issue of the president's
     plans for Yemen, there was a second veto, which also was not overridden. Felicia
     Sonmez, Josh Dawsey & Karoun Demirjian, *Trump Vetoes Resolution to End U.S.*
     Participation in Yemen's Civil War, Wash. Post, Apr. 16, 2019, www.washington-
     post.com (president's second veto, on his Yemen policy; there are not enough
     votes to overturn result); Mark Landler & Peter Baker, *Trump Vetoes Resolution to*
     Pull U.S. Out of Yemen, N.Y. Times, Apr. 16, 2019, at A12.
104 *See, e.g.,* Erica Werner, Seung Min Kim & John Wagner, *Senate on Cusp of Passing*
     Rebuke to Trump on National Emergency Declaration, Wash. Post, Mar. 13, 2019,
     https://wapo.st/2Jb3a3W?tid=ss_mail&utm_term=.459bddodf88a (Senate votes
     against emergency powers); Carl Hulse, *G.O.P.'s Attempt to Avoid Showdown with*
     Trump Is Scuttled by Trump, N.Y. Times, Mar. 13, 2019, at A17 (alternative bill to
     avoid voting against emergency powers not supported by the president).
105 *Id.*
106 Ballotpedia, *Presidential Candidates, 2020,* https://ballotpedia.org.
107 *See generally* Werner, Kim & Wagner, *Senate on Cusp of Passing Rebuke to Trump;*
     Hulse, *G.O.P.'s Attempt to Avoid Showdown With Trump.*
108 *See generally* Emily Cochrane, *G.O.P. Leaders Rally Troops Ahead of Vote to*
     Block Trump's Emergency, N.Y. Times, Feb. 25, 2019, at A17 (Republican Party
     losing some members who do not want to vote for emergency); Erica Werner,
     Seung Min Kim, Paul Kane & John Wagner, *House Passes Resolution to Nullify*
     Trump's National Emergency Declaration, Wash. Post, Feb. 26, 2019, https://wapo.
     st/2IRbxSb?tid=ss_mail&utm_term=.35bf5adafbc8 (House vote on emergency
     declaration); Aaron Leibowitz, *No Evidence Trump's Wall Contract Exists, Gov't*
     Atty Says, Law360.com, Feb. 27, 2019, www.law360.com (despite claim there is a
     wall contract in existence, government lawyer concedes there is no such contract).
     See also Daniel Wilson, *DOD Awards $1B.*
109 Kate Smith, *Every Congressperson Along Southern Border Opposes Border Wall*
     Funding, CBSNews.com, Jan. 8, 2019, www.cbsnews.com.
110 *See generally* Thrush & Cochrane, *Trump's Options for Wall;* Baker & Thrush,
     G.O.P. Pressures Trump, at A1; Erica Werner, Paletta & Sullivan, *"Agreement in*
     Principle."
111 Emily Cochrane & Glenn Thrush, *12 G.O.P. Senators Defect to Block Emergency*
     Move, N.Y. Times, Mar. 14, 2019, at A1 (emergency decree joint resolution loses
     59–41, including a dozen Republican senators).

112 *Id.*

113 *Texas v. United States*, 86 F. Supp. 3d 591 (S.D. Tex. Feb. 16, 2015) (enjoining DHS from implementing DAPA), *emergency stay denied*, 2015 WL 1540022 (S.D. Tex. Apr. 7, 2015), *aff'd*, 787 F.3d 733 (5th Cir. May 26, 2015), *preliminary injunction aff'd*, 809 F.3d 134 (5th Cir. Nov. 9, 2015), *aff'd* 136 S. Ct. 2271 (June 23, 2016), *pet. for rehearing denied*, 137 S. Ct. 285 (Oct. 3, 2016), *dismissal order*, ECF no. 471 (Sept. 8, 2017). *See also Texas v. United States*, No. 18-cv-00068 (S.D. Tex. filed May 1, 2018), *motion for summary judgment pending*, ECF no. 356 (Feb. 4, 2019): "[D]espite the fact that this ruling may imply that the Court finds differing degrees of merit as to the remaining claims, it is specifically withholding a ruling upon those issues until there is further development of the record. As stated above, preliminary injunction requests are by necessity the product of a less formal and less complete presentation. This Court, given the importance of these issues to millions of individuals—indeed, in the abstract, to virtually every person in the United States—and given the serious constitutional issues at stake. Given the dearth of cases in which the Take Care Clause has been pursued as a cause of action rather than asserted as an affirmative defense (and indeed the dearth of cases discussing the Take Care Clause at all), a complete record would no doubt be valuable for this Court to decide these unique claims. It also believes that should the Government comply with the procedural aspects of the APA, that process may result in the availability of additional information for this Court to have in order for it to consider the substantive APA claim under 5 U.S.C. § 706 finds it to be in the interest of justice to rule after each side has had an opportunity to make a complete presentation." *Id.* at 122–23 (sources omitted). *See also Texas v. United States*, No. 18-cv-00068 (S.D. Tex. filed May 1, 2018), *motion for summary judgment pending*, ECF no. 356 (Feb. 4, 2019): www.txs.uscourts.gov; *U.S. v. Texas* (Memorandum Opinion and Order, Civil Action No. 1:18-CV-00068 (Aug. 31, 2018)), at 117/117 (denying request for preliminary injunctive relief). *See also* Lomi Kriel, *DACA's Fate in Court's Hands*, Hous. Chron., Apr. 16, 2016, www.houston-chronicle.com; Lomi Kriel & Kevin Diaz, *Dreamer Immigrants Caught in Middle of Debate over Reform*, Hous. Chron., Jan. 28, 2018, www.houstonchronicle.com.

114 The separate pieces of *U.S. v. Texas* remain unresolved. *See, e.g.*, Appendix 3. *See also* NILC, *DACA Litigation Timeline* (Feb. 11, 2019), www.nilc.org. I have not found any published writer who has noted just how important the 4–4 tie was to DACA and, conceivably, a version of the DREAM Act. Had Merrick Garland, President Obama's 2016 nominee to the Supreme Court, been confirmed, then in all likelihood he would have broken the tie and the Court would have overturned *U.S. v. Texas*. It is not clear what Judge Hanen might have done on a remand (had there been such a remand), but if the opinion had been strongly in favor of DACA (and DAPA) we would be living in a different world. (For want of a nail and so on.) As long as I am DREAMing, I would never have thought that the Trump administration would be so inept at and flummoxed by closing a discretionary program properly. To be sure, Obama's plans were too little too late, but at least he

had a detailed plan and executed it. Unfortunately, this came after the Democrats had lost the House and Senate. *See* Lee & Ashar, *DACA, Government Lawyers, and the Public Interest*; Barbash & Paul, *The Real Reason*; Koh, *The Trump Administration and International Law.*

115 *See, e.g.,* Kamarck & Stenglein, Brookings Institution, *Can Immigration Reform Happen?*; Tom Jawetz, *Center for American Progress, Immigration Reform and the Rule of Law*, Feb. 11, 2019, www.americanprogress.org.

116 See Table 3.1.

117 Tackett, *Trump Issues First Veto.*

118 Cochrane, *House Fails to Override*, at A15. *See also* Daniel Wilson, *DOD Awards $1B in Border Wall Deals After Funding Shift*, Law360.com, Apr. 10, 2019, www.law360.com (Department of Defense reprograms nearly $1 billion for a wall on the southern border under emergency declaration).

119 Gen. Michael Hayden & Matthew G. Olsen, *What Emergency? We Served at the Highest Levels of the U.S. National Security Community. We're Here to Tell You That the President's Claim of an Emergency Along the Border Is Bogus*, Politico.com, Mar. 13, 2019, www.politico.com.

120 Democrats even used the doomed TPS and DED protections as a vehicle for trying to restart DREAM Act discussions, and Rep. Lucille Roybal-Allard of California reintroduced the measure as the Dream and Promise Act of 2019. There was little progress on the bill and scant prospects, so it lay on the table like all the earlier efforts. *See, e.g.,* Lindsey McPherson, *Democrats to Reintroduce Dream Act on March 12 with TPS and DED Protections*, RollCall.com, Mar. 12, 2019, www.rollcall.com; Tiffany Hu, *Bill Roundup: Refugee Admissions, Dreamers on the Hill*, Law360.com, Apr. 11, 2019, www.law360.com (bill to allow DACA recipients to be employed on Capitol Hill). This volume analyzes subject matter—the DREAM Act and all its iterations—that spans more than a quarter of a century. While the text was being copyedited for final publication, the United States Supreme Court granted certiorari and consolidated the related casesfor adjudication during the term beginning October 7, 2019: *See* Case No. 18-589 *McAleenan v. Vidal*, www.supremecourt.gov. [*Batalla Vidal v. McAleenan*, 291 F. Supp. 3d 260 (E.D.N.Y. 2018) (motions to dismiss granted in part, denied in part), *cert. granted*, — S.Ct. ——, 2019 WL 2649838 (U.S. June 28, 2019) (consolidated with *Regents of Univ. of California* and *Nat'l Ass'n for the Advancement of Colored People v. Trump*).] The case was heard on September 11, 2019. *See* Dayna Zolle and Brianne Gorod, *Symposium: The DACA cases may be the next big test for the Roberts Court*, SCOTUS BLOG (Sept. 11, 2019, https:shares.es/aHOEUf).

CONCLUSION

1 Van Morrison, "Astral Weeks," from *Astral Weeks* (Warner Bros. Records, 1968). *See* Jon Michaud, *The Miracle of Van Morrison's "Astral Weeks,"* New Yorker, Mar. 7, 2018, www.newyorker.com: Ryan H. Walsh, *"Astral Weeks": A Secret History of 1968* (Penguin Press 2018).

2 The Everly Brothers, "All I Have to Do Is Dream" (Cadence, 1958).

3 Bruce Springsteen, "Dream Baby Dream" (Columbia Records, 2014).

4 Beyoncé, "Sweet Dreams" (Columbia Records, 2009).

5 John Lennon, "# 9 Dream" (Apple, 1974).

6 John Lennon, "Imagine" (Apple, 1971).

7 Shakespeare, *Hamlet* at Act 3, scene 1 (1602).

8 *La vida es sueño*, Pedro Calderón de la Barca Edición electrónica de Matthew D. Stroud basada en la edición electrónica de Vern Williamsen y J. T. Abraham disponible en la colección de la Association for Hispanic Classical Theater, Inc., www.comedias.org.

9 Langston Hughes, "Harlem, What happens to a dream deferred?" (1951), in Selected Poems of Langston Hughes (Random House Inc. 1990), www.poetryfoundation.org.

10 Michael A. Olivas, *Dreams Deferred: Deferred Action, Prosecutorial Discretion, and the Vexing Case(s) of DREAM Act Students*, 21 Wm. & Mary Bill Rts J. 463 (2012).

11 I wrote briefly of my earliest experience in immigrant advocacy while working to recruit migrant farmworkers to attend college. *See* Michael A. Olivas, *No Undocumented Child Left Behind:* Plyler v. Doe *and the Education of Undocumented Children*, 87–88 (New York University Press 2012).

12 Chris Hayes, *The Idea That the Moral Universe Inherently Bends Towards Justice Is Inspiring. It's Also Wrong*, NBCNews.com, Mar. 24, 2018, www.nbcnews.com (analyzing underpinnings of meaning in the iconic Martin Luther King Jr. iconic statement "the arc of the moral universe is long, but it bends towards justice").

13 Edna St. Vincent Millay, "Dirge Without Music" (1928), Poemhunter.com, www.poemhunter.com. *See generally* Mark Diotte, Edna St. Vincent Millay's *Dirge Without Music*, 72 The Explicator 29 (2014).

ACKNOWLEDGMENTS

1 *Plyler v. Doe*, 457 U.S. 202 (1982).

2 "Driver is not alone in this view. In 'No Undocumented Child Left Behind' (2012), the University of Houston law professor Michael A. Olivas called Plyler 'the apex of the Court's treatment of the undocumented.'" Jill Lepore, *Is Education a Fundamental Right? The History of an Obscure Supreme Court Ruling Sheds Light on the Ongoing Debate over Schooling and Immigration*, New Yorker, Sept. 10, 2018, www.newyorker.com.

3 *Id.*

4 Michael A. Olivas, "Plyler v. Doe, Toll v. Moreno, *and Postsecondary Education: Undocumented Adults and 'Enduring Disability,'*" 15 J.L. & Educ. 19 (1986).

5 Immigration Reform and Control Act, Pub. L. 99-603, 100 Stat. 3359 (Nov. 6, 1986).

6 *See generally* Kevin R. Johnson, *An Essay on Immigration Politics, Popular Democracy, and California's Proposition 187: The Political Relevance and Legal Irrelevance of Race*, 70 Wash. L. Rev. 629, 634 (1995).

7 Personal Responsibility and Work Opportunity Reconciliation Act of 1996 (PRWORA), Pub. L. No. 104-193, 110 Stat. 2105 (1996).
8 Illegal Immigration Reform and Immigrant Responsibility Act of 1996 (IIRIRA), Pub. L. No. 104-208, 110 Stat. 3009 (1996) (codified as amended in scattered sections of 8, 18 U.S.C.).
9 California's governor, Pete Wilson, announced an early candidacy for the Republican nomination as president but withdrew when it appeared that Sen. Robert Dole of Kansas would be selected. Dole lost to the incumbent, President Bill Clinton.
10 *See* Appendix 1, this volume.
11 *See generally* Chapter 6, this volume.
12 *See In re Garcia*, 315 P.3d 117, 121 (Cal. 2014) (highlighting the entrance of Sergio Garcia to the United States from Mexico).
13 According to Fla. Stat. Ann. § 454.021(3) (West 2014), Florida's statute regarding requirements for bar admission states:

> Upon certification by the Florida Board of Bar Examiners that an applicant who is an unauthorized immigrant who was brought to the United States as a minor; has been present in the United States for more than 10 years; has received documented employment authorization from the United States Citizenship and Immigration Services (USCIS); has been issued a social security number; if a male, has registered with the Selective Service System if required to do so under the Military Selective Service Act, 50 U.S.C. App. 453; and has fulfilled all requirements for admission to practice law in this state, the Supreme Court of Florida may admit that applicant as an attorney at law authorized to practice in this state and may direct an order be entered upon the court's records to that effect.

See generally Marianela Toledo, *Illegal Immigrants Can Practice Law in Florida*, Human Events, May 22, 2014, http://humanevents.com [https://perma.cc/2RWJ-WCQY] (highlighting the new Florida law allowing illegal immigrants to practice law in the state). A fascinating study focusing on Jose Manuel Godinez Samperio's case has been published by his law professor at Florida State University. *See* Wendi Adelson, *Lawfully Present Lawyers*, 18 Chapman L. Rev. 387, 387–89 (2015) (recounting the experiences of an undocumented individual and the hurdles he faced trying to obtain a license to practice law).
14 Cesar Vargas entered the country from Mexico without authorization when he was five years old and has resided in this country continuously since then. He was sworn into the New York State bar in 2016 at the age of thirty-two. He graduated from law school and passed the New York State bar exam in 2011. He applied for admission to the bar in 2012 but was denied by the Committee on Character and Fitness because he lacked legal status. While he received DACA in 2013, his case was referred to the Appellate Division of State Supreme Court, which voted to admit him pending resolution of an ill-advised 2015 arrest record for political protest. After six months of probation, he was able to expunge the record, and his

admission was granted. He was not the first lawyer in New York without legal status, but the bar had not inquired into immigration status before his case. *See* Kirk Semple, *Bar Exam Passed, Immigrant Still Can't Practice Law*, N.Y. Times, Dec. 3, 2013, www.nytimes.com [https://perma.cc/S6FD-V9HU] (examining the denial of Cesar Vargas to the New York bar); Liz Robbins, *An Immigrant's Four-Year Fight to Become a Lawyer Ends in Celebrations*, N.Y. Times, Feb. 3, 2016, www.nytimes. com [https://perma.cc/U7UB-BC3M] (outlining Cesar Vargas's recent win and admission to the New York bar).

15 Tiffany Hu, *Koch Groups Push for "Dreamer" Protections in Spending Bill*, Law360. com, Nov. 15, 2018, www.law360.com (advocacy groups backed by the conservative Koch brothers have urged bipartisan lawmakers to prioritize DACA recipients in a spending bill for the 2019 fiscal year that also proposes funding for border security).

16 See Tables 5.1 and 5.2.

17 Peter Baker, Katie Benner & Michael D. Shear, *Trump Replaces Sessions with a Loyalist; Vows "Warlike" Stance on House Inquiries*, N.Y. Times, Nov. 7, 2018, at A1.

18 Ted Mitchell, *Perspective: Congress Must End the Purgatory for "Dreamers,"* Wash. Post, Nov. 9, 2018, www.washingtonpost.com.

19 Erica Werner & Damian Paletta, *GOP Leaders Aim to Avert Shutdown Over Wall Funding, but Trump Makes No Promises*, Wash. Post, Nov. 15, 2018 (Republicans say they are open to such a deal now, but it appears they are unlikely to come together in the short time lawmakers have ahead of the Dec. 7 deadline).

20 *See generally* www.uhd.edu.

21 Patrick Svitek, *Abbott Vows to Cut Funding for "Sanctuary Campus" Schools*, Tex. Trib., Dec. 1, 2016, www.texastribune.org (although the definition of a "sanctuary campus" is murky, Gov. Greg Abbott made it clear they are not welcome).

22 Ed Rogers, *Democrats Won the House, but Trump Won the Election*, Wash. Post, Nov. 7, 2018, https://wapo.st/2yW8vEx?tid=ss_mail&utm_term=.d3ceea9cb585.

23 Eric Levitz, *Trump: The Dreamers Are My Hostages—but the Wall Is Not My Ransom*, N.Y. Mag., Nov. 28, 2018, http://nymag.com.

24 John Lennon, "Beautiful Boy (Darling Boy)" from *Double Fantasy* (1980).

25 Maya Averbuch & Elisabeth Malkin, *Migrants in Tijuana Rush Border but Retreat in Clouds of Tear Gas*, N.Y. Times, Nov. 25, 2018, at A1 (U.S. troops fire tear gas at immigrants).

BIBLIOGRAPHY

Abourezk, Kevin. "Judge Tosses Suit on Tuition to Illegal Immigrants; Plaintiffs Likely to Refile Suit." *Lincoln Journal Star*, December 18, 2010, A1.

Abraham, Yvonne. "Immigrant Tuition Bill Defeated." *Boston Globe*, January 12, 2006, A1.

Abrams, Norman. "Internal Policy: Guiding the Exercise of Prosecutorial Discretion." *UCLA Law Review* 19, no. 1 (October 1971): 1–58.

Abrego, Leisy J., and Sarah M. Lakhani. "Incomplete Inclusion: Legal Violence and Immigrants in Liminal Legal Statuses." *Law & Policy* 37, no. 4 (October 2015): 265–93.

Abriel, Evangeline G. "Rethinking Preemption for Purposes of Aliens and Public Benefits." *UCLA Law Review* 42, no. 6 (August 1995): 1597–1630.

Acer, Eleanor, and Olga Byrne. "How the Illegal Immigration Reform and Immigrant Responsibility Act of 1996 Has Undermined US Refugee Protection Obligations and Wasted Government Resources." *Journal on Migration and Human Security* 5, no. 2 (2017): 356–78.

Adams, Angela D. "Deferred Action for 'Dreamers': Advising DACA Students about Affording College." National Association of Student Financial Aid Administrators, December 6, 2012. www.nasfaa.org.

Adelson, Wendi. "Lawfully Present Lawyers." *Chapman Law Review* 18, no. 2 (Spring 2015): 387–418.

Aguilar, Julian. "Dan Patrick Again Targeting In-State Tuition for Undocumented Students." *Texas Tribune*, September 9, 2016. www.texastribune.org.

———. "DHS Refutes Immigration 'Stonewalling' Allegations." *Texas Tribune*, November 22, 2011. www.texastribune.org.

———. "Immigration Proposal Not Seen as Major Step." *Texas Tribune*, January 11, 2012. www.texastribune.org.

———. "Obama Immigration Policies Satisfy Neither Right Nor Left." *Texas Tribune*, September 22, 2011. www.texastribune.org.

Aldana, Raquel E. "Silent Victims No More?: Moral Indignation and the Potential for Latino Political Mobilization in Defense of Immigrants." *Immigration and Nationality Law Review* 29 (2008): 379–403.

Aleinikoff, T. Alexander. "Citizens, Aliens, Membership and the Constitution." *Constitutional Commentary* 7, no. 1 (Winter 1990): 9–34.

———. "Federal Regulation of Aliens and the Constitution." *American Journal of International Law* 83, no. 4 (1989): 862–71.

Aleinikoff, T. Alexander, David Martin, Hiroshi Motomura, Maryellen Fullerton, and Juliet Stumpf. *Immigration and Citizenship: Process and Policy.* 8th ed. St. Paul, MN: West Academic Publishing, 2016.

Allen, Matthew B. "The Unconstitutional Denial of a Texas Veterans Benefit." *Houston Law Review* 46, no. 5 (Winter 2010): 1607–40.

Alvarez, Lizette. "With G.O.P.'s Ear, Rubio Pushes Dream Act Proposal." *New York Times*, April 27, 2012, A13.

Alvarez, Priscilla. "Trump's Quiet Reversal on Deporting Young Undocumented Immigrants." *Atlantic*, April 27, 2017. www.theatlantic.com.

Amer, Yasmin. "Despite Immigration Reforms, Many Young Immigrants Still in Limbo." *CNN*, December 24, 2011. www.cnn.com.

Anderson, Stewart. "Analysts Find Restrictive Measures in New Trump Immigration Bill." *Forbes*, January 23, 2019. https://americasvoice.org.

Andrews, Abigail Leslie. *Undocumented Politics: Place, Gender, and the Pathways of Mexican Migrants.* Berkeley: University of California Press, 2018.

Andrews, Alice C., and James W. Fonseca. "Community Colleges in the United States: A Geographical Perspective." Washington, DC: Association of American Geographers, 1998.

Antle, W. James, III. "To Fix DACA, Remember How the DREAM Act Died." *Washington Examiner*, September 7, 2017. www.washingtonexaminer.com.

Arhancet, Maria. "Developments in the Legislative Branch: Platforms of Presidential Candidates Regarding Immigration Reform." *Georgetown Immigration Law Journal* 21, no. 4 (Summer 2007): 507–10.

"Arkansas Att. Gen. Opines that Undocumented Individuals May Enroll in States, Public Colleges and Universities." *Interpreter Releases* 85 (2008).

Ashar, Sameer M., Edelina Burciaga, Jennifer M. Chacón, Susan Bibler Coutin, Alma Garza, and Stephen Lee. "Navigating Liminal Legalities Along Pathways to Citizenship: Immigrant Vulnerability and the Role of Mediating Institutions." Legal Studies Research Paper Series No. 2016–05, University of California, Irvine, 2015. https://papers.ssrn.com.

Ashburn, Elyse. "Massachusetts Plan for Free Community Colleges Meets with Skepticism." *Chronicle of Higher Education*, June 15, 2007, A22.

Asimov, Nanette, and Wyatt Buchanan. "Brown Oks Student Aid for Illegal Immigrants." *San Francisco Chronicle*, October 8, 2011, A1.

Associated Press. "Immigrant Veterans Sue for Waivers on Tuition." *Houston Chronicle*, June 29, 2007, B4.

Avalos, Mariana Alvarado. "Law Shuts Out Some Students." *Arizona Daily Star*, August 10, 2008, B1.

Averbuch, Maya, and Elisabeth Malkin. "Migrants in Tijuana Rush Border but Retreat in Clouds of Tear Gas." *New York Times*, November 25, 2018, A1.

Bacon, David. *Illegal People: How Globalization Creates Migration and Criminalizes Immigrants.* Boston: Beacon Press, 2008.

Baird, Vanessa A. *Answering the Call of the Court: How Justices and Litigants Set the Supreme Court's Agenda.* Charlottesville: University of Virginia Press, 2007.

Baker, Peter, Katie Benner, and Michael D. Shear. "Trump Replaces Sessions with a Loyalist; Vows 'Warlike' Stance on House Inquiries." *New York Times*, November 7, 2018, A1.

Baker, Peter, and Glenn Thrush. "G.O.P. Pressures Trump to Accept Deal on Border." *New York Times*, February 12, 2019, A1.

Baker, Peter, and Maggie Haberman. "His Wall, His Shutdown and His Side of the Story." *New York Times*, January 4, 2019, A10.

Baker, Peter. "No Progress on Wall, or on Anything Else Worth Talking About." *New York Times*, January 22, 2019, A15.

———. "A Stinging Defeat for the President." *New York Times*, January 25, 2019, A1.

———. "Trump's Task: Saving Face at the Border." *New York Times*, February 13, 2019, A1.

Banda, P. Solomon. "Courts Suspend Hearings to Deport: US Reviews Illegal Immigrant Status." *Boston Globe*, January 17, 2012. www.bostonglobe.com.

Barbash, Fred, and Deanna Paul. "The Real Reason the Trump Administration Is Constantly Losing in Court." *Washington Post*, March 19, 2019.

Bartmess, Andrew. "3D Chess from *Star Trek*." *The Chess Variant Pages*. www.chess-variants.com.

Basken, Paul, Kelly Field, and Sara Hebel. "Bush's Legacy in Higher Education: A Matter of Debate." *Chronicle of Higher Education*, December 19, 2008, A14.

Batalova, Jeanne, and Michael Fix. "New Estimates of Unauthorized Youth Eligible for Legal Status Under the DREAM Act." Migration Policy Institute, October 2006. www.migrationpolicy.org.

Batalova, Jeanne, and B. Lindsay Lowell. "Immigrant Professionals in the United States." *Society* 44, no. 2 (January/February 2007): 26–31.

Batalova, Jeanne, and Margie McHue. "DREAM vs. Reality: An Analysis of Potential DREAM Act Beneficiaries." Migration Policy Institute, July 2010. www.migrationpolicy.org.

Bauder, Harald. "Domicile Citizenship, Human Mobility and Territoriality." *Progress in Human Geography* 38, no. 1 (February 2014): 91–106.

Baynes, Leonard M. "Racial Profiling, September 11, and the Media: A Critical Race Theory Analysis." *Virginia Sports and Entertainment Law Journal* 2, no. 1 (Winter 2002): 1–62.

Beck, Margery A. "Kris Kobach, Kansas Secretary of State Candidate, Sues Nebraska over Immigrant Tuition Law." *Kansas City Star*, January 26, 2010.

———. "Lawsuit Targets Nebraska's Immigrant-Tuition Law." *Lincoln Journal-Star*, January 25, 2010. www.journalstar.com.

Becker, David H.E. "Judicial Review of INS Adjudication: When May the Agency Make Sudden Changes in Policy and Apply Its Decisions Retroactively?" *Administrative Law Review* 52, no. 1 (Winter 2000): 219–51.

Bellia, Patricia L. "Faithful Execution and Enforcement Discretion." *University of Pennsylvania Law Review* 164, no. 7 (June 2016): 1753–1800.

Berger, Dan H., and Rita Sostrin. *Immigration Options for Academics and Researchers.* 2d ed. Washington, DC: American Immigration Lawyers Association, 2011.

Berger, Joseph. "Debates Persist Over Subsidies for Immigrant College Students." *New York Times*, December 12, 2007, B8.

Bernstein, David E. "Licensing Laws: A Historical Example of the Use of Government Regulatory Power against African Americans." San Diego Law Review 31, no. 1 (February/March 1994): 89–104.

Beth, Richard S. "Private Bills: Procedure in the House." Congressional Research Service, October 21, 2004. www.everycrsreport.com.

Beyoncé. "Sweet Dreams." Columbia Records, 2009. Compact disc.

Biesecker, Michael, and Gosia Wozniacka. "NC Judge Could Terminate Parental Rights of Deported Worker, Put US-Born Sons up for Adoption." *Fox News*, March 9, 2012. www.reformtalk.net.

Binker, Mark. "Illegal Immigrants' Tuition Pays Way." *News and Record*, March 20, 2009, B1.

Birnbaum, Emily. "Civil Liberties Groups Ask Congress to Refuse Border Tech Funding in Any Shutdown Deal." *The Hill*, February 5, 2019. https://thehill.com.

Blackman, Josh. "Gridlock." *Harvard Law Review* 130, no. 1 (November 2016): 241–305.

Blank, Chris. "Missouri Lawmakers Approve Crackdown on Illegal Immigrants." *Jefferson City News-Tribune*, May 16, 2008.

Bliss, Jeff. "U.S. Agency Said to Urge Closing 1,600 Deportation Cases." *Bloomberg*, January 19, 2012. www.bloomberg.com.

Blitzer, Jonathan. "As the Shutdown Continues, Trump Offers a Deal That Democrats Are Sure to Reject." *New Yorker*, January 19, 2019. www.newyorker.com.

———. "Will Anyone in the Trump Administration Ever Be Held Accountable for the Zero-Tolerance Immigration Policy?" *New Yorker*, August 22, 2018. www.newyorker.com.

Blum, Cynthia. "Rethinking Tax Compliance of Unauthorized Workers after Immigration Reform." *Georgetown Immigration Law Journal* 21, no. 4 (Summer 2007): 595–620.

Boehm, Deborah A., and Susan J. Terrio, eds. *Illegal Encounters: The Effect of Detention and Deportation on Young People.* New York: NYU Press, 2019.

Boehmke, Frederick J. "The Initiative Process and the Dynamics of State Interest Group Populations." *State Politics & Policy Quarterly* 8, no. 4 (December 2008): 362–383.

Boldt, Megan. "2008–09 Minnesota Budget—Reluctant Governor OKs School Spending: Bill Adds $794m over 2 years, Restores Aid for Special Education." *St. Paul Pioneer Press*, May 31, 2007, B1.

Bollhofer, Joseph A. "Disenfranchisement of the College Student Vote: When a Resident is Not a Resident." *Fordham Urban Law Journal* 11, no. 3 (1982–1983): 489–525.

Bolstad, Erika. "Rivera Introduces a Military-Only Version of the DREAM Act." *Miami Herald*, January 26, 2012. https://miamiherald.typepad.com.

Bono, Marisa. "When a Rose Is Not a Rose: DACA, the DREAM Act, and the Need for More Comprehensive Immigration Reform." *Thurgood Marshall Law Review* 40, no. 2 (Spring 2015): 193–222.

Boone, Dana. "Her College Dream Is Slipping Away." *Des Moines Register*, April 11, 2006, 1A.

Bosniak, Linda S. "Opposing Prop. 187: Undocumented Immigrants and the National Imagination." *Connecticut Law Review* 28, no. 3 (Spring 1996): 555–619.

Boswell, Richard A. "Restrictions on Non-Citizens' Access to Public Benefits: Flawed Premise, Unnecessary Response." *UCLA Law Review* 42, no. 6 (August 1995): 1475–1507.

Boushey, Graeme, and Adam Luedtke. "Immigrants Across the U.S. Federal Laboratory: Explaining State-Level Innovation in Immigration Policy." *State Politics & Policy Quarterly* 11, no. 4 (December 2011): 390–414.

Bravin, Jess. "Judge Suggests U.S. Misled Court on Immigration Policy." *Wall Street Journal*, February 10, 2012, A6.

———. "Senate Confirms Sotomayor in Largely Partisan 68–31 Vote." *Wall Street Journal*, August 7, 2009, A3.

Breslin, Jimmy. *The Gang That Couldn't Shoot Straight*. New York: Viking Press, 1969.

Brettell, Caroline B. "Immigrants as Netizens: Political Mobilization in Cyberspace." In *Citizenship, Political Engagement, and Belonging*, edited by Deborah Reed-Danahay & Caroline B. Brettell, 226–43. New Brunswick, NJ: Rutgers University Press, 2008.

Brickman, Jaclyn. "Educating Undocumented Children in the United States: Codification of *Plyler v. Doe* through Federal Legislation." *Georgetown Immigration Law Journal* 20, no. 3 (Spring 2006): 385–405.

Broder, John M. "Obama Hobbled in Fight Against Global Warming." *New York Times*, November 16, 2009, A1.

Broder, John M., and Elisabeth Rosenthal. "Obama Has Goal to Wrest a Deal in Climate Talks." *New York Times*, December 18, 2009, A1.

Broder, John N. "Social Causes Defined Kennedy, Even at the End of a 46-Year Career in the Senate." *New York Times*, August 26, 2009, A1.

Brummett, John. "Beebe Rallies, Falls Short on Tuition." *Arkansas News*, March 28, 2009.

———. "Shame, Shame." *Arkansas News*, March 26, 2009, A13.

Buch, Jason. "Graduate's Deportation Case Dropped." *San Antonio Express-News*, November 3, 2011, A1.

Buettner, Russ, and Maggie Haberman. "As Mogul and President, Consistent in Chaos." *New York Times*, January 20, 2019, A1.

Buckner Inniss, Lolita K. "California's Proposition 187—Does It Mean What It Says? Does It Say What It Means? A Textual and Constitutional Analysis." *Georgetown Immigration Law Journal* 10, no. 4 (Summer 1996): 577–622.

Bulkeley, Deborah, and Lisa Riley Roche. "Immigrant Tuition Repeal Removed from Bill." *Deseret Morning News*, February 13, 2008, B7.

Bulkeley, Deborah. "Efforts to Repeal Immigrant Tuition Law Hit Speed Bump." *Deseret Morning News*, February 7, 2008, A1.

———. "A Law Granting In-State Tuition to Undocumented Students Is Legally Sound." *Deseret News*, February 2, 2006, A1.

———. "Measure to Repeal Tuition Break for Illegals Is Back." *Deseret News*, February 9, 2007, B4.

Bush, Darren. "Mission Creep: Antitrust Exemptions and Immunities as Applied to Deregulated Industries." *Utah Law Review* 2006, no. 3 (2006): 761–810.

Byik, Andre. "Formerly Undocumented Chico Lawyer Sergio Garcia Pays Taxes with a Smile." *Chico Enterprise-Record*, February 23, 2016. www.chicoer.com.

Cadman, Dan. "Illegal Aliens Practicing Law." *Center for Immigration Studies*, July 19, 2017. https://cis.org.

Calabresi, Steven G., and Lena M. Barsky. "An Originalist Defense of *Plyler v. Doe*." *Brigham Young Law Review* 2017, no. 2 (2017): 225–329.

Calderón de la Barca, Pedro. *La Vida Es Sueño*. Digital text published by the Association for Hispanic Classical Theater. www.comedias.org.

Caldwell, Beth C. *Deported Americans: Life after Deportation to Mexico*. Durham, NC: Duke University Press, 2019.

California. Postsecondary Education Commission. *Student Profiled* (1994), Table 1–5. www.cpec.ca.gov.

Calvo, Janet M. "Alien Status Restrictions on Eligibility for Federally Funded Assistance Programs." *New York University Review of Law & Social Change* 16, no. 3 (1987–88): 395–432.

———. "Letter to Board of Regents on Behalf of Latino Justice." *Latino Justice*, 2017. http://latinojustice.org.

———. "Professional Licensing and Teacher Certification for Non-Citizens: Federalism, Equal Protection and a State's Socio-Economic Interests." *Columbia Journal of Race and Law* 8, no. 1 (2017): 33–121.

Calvo-Friedman, Jennesa. "The Uncertain Terrain of State Occupational Licensing Laws for Noncitizens: A Preemption Analysis." *Georgetown Law Journal* 102, no. 6 (August 2014): 1597–1645.

Campbell, Kristina M. "Local Illegal Immigration Reform Act Ordinances: A Legal, Policy, and Litigation Analysis." *Denver Law Review* 84, no. 4 (2007): 1041–60.

Carbone, Robert. *Alternative Tuition Systems*. Iowa City: American College Testing Program, 1974.

———. "Resident or Nonresident? Tuition Classification in Higher Education." Denver: Education Commission of the States, 1970.

———. *Students and State Borders*. Iowa City: American College Testing Program, 1973.

Cardenas, Jose A., and Albert Cortez. "The Impact of *Doe v. Plyler* upon Texas Public Schools." *Journal of Law & Education* 15, no. 1 (Winter 1986): 1–17.

Carney, Jordan. "Senate Rejects Two Measures to End Shutdown." *The Hill*, January 24, 2019. https://thehill.com.

Carroll, Susan. "Immigrant Spends Life Looking over Her Shoulder." *Houston Chronicle*, November 28, 2009, B1.

———. "In-State Rates for Illegal Immigrants Attacked." *Houston Chronicle*, December 16, 2009, B1.

———. "New Immigration Policy Too Late for Sick Teacher: Man Deported to Spain Despite Clean Record, Job." *Houston Chronicle*, August 27, 2011, A1.

———. "Report: Feds Downplayed ICE Case Dismissals." *Houston Chronicle*, June 27, 2011. www.chron.com.

———. "Student's Hopes Ride on DREAM Act as He Faces Deportation." *Houston Chronicle*, December 13, 2010. www.chron.com.

———. "Texas Lawmaker Challenges In-State Tuition Law." *Houston Chronicle*, October 30, 2008, B1.

Cassidy, John. *How Markets Fail: The Logic of Economic Calamities*. New York: Farrar, Straus and Giroux, 2009.

Castillo, Juan. "After Delay, Bill Challenging In-State Tuition Law All but Dead." *Austin American-Statesman*, May 10, 2007, B1.

Catapano, Peter. "Battle of the Borders." *New York Times*, October 21, 2011. https://opinionator.blogs.nytimes.com.

Cave, Damien. "Mass Shootings, an American Export." *New York Times*, March 23, 2019, SR7.

Chacon, Jennifer M. "Unsecured Borders: Immigration Restrictions, Crime Control and National Security." *Connecticut Law Review* 39, no. 5 (July 2007): 1827–91.

———. "Who Is Responsible for U.S. Immigration Policy?" *Insights on Law & Society* 14, no. 3 (Spring 2014): 20–24. www.americanbar.org.

Chan, Sewell. "Dodd Calls Obama Plan Too Grand." *New York Times*, February 3, 2010, B1.

Chavez, Jorge M., and Doris Marie Provine. "Race and the Response of State Legislatures to Unauthorized Immigrants." *Annals of The American Academy of Political and Social Science* 623 (May 2009): 78–92.

Chavez, Leo R. *The Latino Threat: Constructing Immigrants, Citizens, and the Nation*. Stanford, CA: Stanford University Press, 2008.

Chavez, Maria, Jessica L. Lavariega Monforti, and Melissa R. Michelson. *Living the Dream: New Immigration Policies and the Lives of Undocumented Latino Youth*. Boulder, CO: Paradigm Publishers, 2015.

Chishti, Muzaffar, and Claire Bergeron. "Questions Arise with Implementation of Obama Administration's New Prosecutorial Discretion Policy." *Migration Policy Institute*, February 29, 2012. www.migrationpolicy.org.

Chishti, Muzaffar, and Faye Hipsman. "Key Factors, Unresolved Issues in New Deferred Action Program for Immigrant Youth Will Determine Its Success." Migration Policy Institute, August 16, 2012. www.migrationinformation.org.

Clement, Scott, and David Nakamura. "Post-ABC Poll: Trump Disapproval Swells as President, Republicans Face Lopsided Blame for Shutdown." *Washington Post*, January 25, 2019. https://wapo.st.

CNN. "2018 in Review Fast Facts." Last modified December 31, 2018. www.cnn.com.

Cochrane, Emily, and Catie Edmondson. "Nearing Deal, Trump Says Shutdown Would Be 'Terrible.'" *New York Times*, February 13, 2019, A14.

Cochrane, Emily, and Catie Edmondson. "State of the Union Address Is a Must, but Time and Place Are Debatable." *New York Times*, January 23, 2019, A12.

Cochrane, Emily, and Glenn Thrush. "12 G.O.P. Senators Defect to Block Emergency Move." *New York Times*, March 14, 2019, A1.

Cochrane, Emily, and Jennifer Medina. "When Is a Fence a Wall? An End to the Shutdown May Ride on the Answer." *New York Times*, December 26, 2018, A12.

Cochrane, Emily. "G.O.P. Leaders Rally Troops Ahead of Vote to Block Trump's Emergency." *New York Times*, February 25, 2019, A17.

———. "House Fails to Override Trump's Veto, Preserving National Emergency Order." *New York Times*, March 26, 2019, A15.

———. "Pelosi Says She'll Back What Negotiators Come up With on the Border." *New York Times*, February 6, 2019, A19.

Cohen, Jeffrey E. *The Presidency in the Era Of 24-Hour News.* Princeton, NJ: Princeton University Press, 2008.

Cohen, Patricia. "Moving to Arizona Soon? You Might Need a License." *New York Times*, June 17, 2016, B1.

Coleman, Mathew. "The 'Local' Migration State: The Site-Specific Devolution of Immigration Enforcement in the U.S. South." *Law & Policy* 34, no. 2 (April 2012): 159–190.

Collins, Kristin. "Colleges Profit from Illegal Immigrants." *News and Observer*, March 25, 2009, B3.

———. "Feds: College: OK for Illegal Immigrants." *News and Observer*, May 10, 2008, A1.

———. "Illegals May Enjoy a Brief College Life." *News and Observer*, August 15, 2008, B3.

Columbus, Eric. "DACA Isn't Dead. It's Undead." *Politico*, January 22, 2018. www.politico.com.

Conca, James. "Rick Perry Vows to Protect Dept. of Energy; Al Franken Blushes." *Forbes*, January 19, 2017. www.forbes.com.

Connell, Christopher. "Keeping the Dream Alive." *International Educator* 21, no. 1 (January-February 2012): 4–9.

Constable, Pamela. "Montgomery County Student Wins Reprieve from Deportation." *Washington Post*, March 14, 2012. www.washingtonpost.com.

Cooke, Chris. "U.S. Border Control Says Performance Visas Required Even for Free Shows." *Complete Music Update*, March 15, 2017. https://completemusicupdate.com.

Cooper, Helene, and Tripp Gabriel. "Obama's Announcement Seizes Initiative and Puts Pressure on Romney." *New York Times*, June 16, 2012, A16.

Cooper, Jonathan J. "Undocumented Immigrants Spend Millions Extra on Tuition." *Diverse Education*, August 10, 2009. https://diverseeducation.com.

Cooper, Michael. "G.O.P. Surges to Senate Victory in Massachusetts." *New York Times*, January 20, 2010, A1.

Corson, Christopher T. "Reform of Domicile Law for Application to Transients, Temporary Residents and Multi-Based Persons." *Columbia Journal of Law and Social Problems* 16, no. 3 (1981): 327–364.

Cortez, Nathan G. "The Local Dilemma: Preemption and the Role of Federal Standards in State and Local Immigration Laws." *SMU Law Review* 61, no. 1 (Winter 2008): 47–66.

Costa, Robert, Juliet Eilperin, Damian Paletta, and Nick Miroff. "As Shutdown Drags on, Trump Officials Make New Offer, Seek Novel Ways to Cope With Its Impacts." *Washington Post*, January 6, 2019. www.washingtonpost.com.

Costa, Robert, Josh Dawsey, Philip Rucker, and Seung Min Kim. "'In the White House Waiting': Inside Trump's Defiance on the Longest Shutdown Ever." *Washington Post*, January 12, 2019. www.washingtonpost.com.

Costanza-Chock, Sasha. *Out of the Shadows, Into the Streets! Transmedia Organizing and the Immigrant Rights Movement*. Cambridge, MA: MIT Press, 2014.

"Court Ruling Could Prompt More Deportation Reviews." *Fox News*, February 10, 2012. www.foxnews.com.

Cowger, Sela, Jessica Bolter, and Sarah Pierce. "The First 100 Days: Summary of Major Immigration Actions Taken by the Trump Administration." Migration Policy Institute, April 2017. www.migrationpolicy.org.

Cox, Adam B., and Cristina M. Rodriguez. "The President and Immigration Law." *Yale Law Journal* 119, no. 3 (December 2009) 458–547.

Coyle, John. "The Legality of Banking the Undocumented." *Georgetown Immigration Law Journal* 22, no. 1 (Fall 2007): 21–55.

Craig, Tim. "Va. House Approves Bill on Illegal Immigration: Aim Is to Block Access to State, Local Funds." *Washington Post*, January 31, 2007, A1.

———. "Va. Republican Bill Would Bar Illegal Immigrants from College." *Washington Post*, August 30, 2007, A1.

Crawford, Emily R. "The Ethic of Community and Incorporating Undocumented Immigrant Concerns Into Ethical School Leadership." *Educational Administration Quarterly* 53, no. 2 (April 2017): 147–79.

Cullen, James. "Blame the Newcomers." *Texas Observer*, August 19, 1994, 2.

Cunningham, Erin. "Montgomery College Sued Over Illegal Immigrant Policy." *Gazette*, January 21, 2011. www.communitycollegejobs.com.

Curnutte, Mark. "Pastor's Stay of Deportation Extended." *Cincinnati Enquirer*, December 19, 2011, 43.

Davidson, Mark. "'I Really Want to See You': Cause No. 893,663; *Anthony D. Cox v. Yoko Ono Lennon.*" *Houston Lawyer*, September–October 2011.

Davis, Aaron C. "Md. Tuition Law May Be Halted." *Washington Post*, June 29, 2011, B1.

Davis, Julie Hirschfeld, and Maggie Haberman. "President's Abrupt Shifts on Impasse Baffle Even Those within His Party." *New York Times*, January 11, 2019, A11.

Davis, Julie Hirschfeld, and Michael D. Shear. "Border Policy Had Been Seen as Inhumane." *New York Times*, June 16, 2018, A1.

Davis, Julie Hirschfeld. "$1 Billion More as Democrats Shift on Border." *New York Times*, January 18, 2019, A1

———. "Senate Bills Fail, Raising Urgency of Impasse Talks." *New York Times*, January 24, 2019, A1.

———. "Trump Goes Beyond His Base and No One Is Happy." *New York Times*, January 19, 2019, A1.

Dawsey, Josh, and Robert Costa. "'Master Negotiator' or 'Nonentity'? Kushner Thrusts Himself into Middle of Shutdown Talks." *Washington Post*, January 23, 2019. https://wapo.st.

DeBonis, Mike "'We will be out for a long time' unless Democrats Budge, Trump Says, as Shutdown Enters 4th Week." *Washington Post*, January 12, 2019, https://wapo.st.

De León, Arnoldo. *They Called Them Greasers: Anglo Attitudes toward Mexicans in Texas, 1821–1900*. Austin: University of Texas Press, 1983.

"Defending DAPA and Expanded DACA before the Supreme Court: A Guide to *United States v. Texas*." *American Immigration Council*, April 11, 2016. www.americanimmigrationcouncil.org.

Dempsey, Matt. "Confusion for Prairie View A&M Students on the Last Day for Voter Registration." *Houston Chronicle*, October 9, 2018. www.houstonchronicle.com.

Deochand, Neil, and R. Wayne Fuqua. "BACB Certification Trends: State of the States (1999 to 2014)." *Behavior Analysis in Practice* 9 (2016): 243–252.

Diamant, Jeff. "In-State Tuition for Illegal Immigrants Fizzles." *Star Ledger*, January 12, 2010, NJ-16.

Diamond, Jeremy, and Kevin Liptak. "Trump Calls Border Wall a 'Medieval Solution' That Works." *CNN*, January 9, 2019. www.cnn.com.

Diamond, Jeremy, Manu Raju, Kaitlan Collins, Abby Phillip, and Phil Mattingly. "Trump Expected to Propose Extending DACA, TPS Protections in Exchange for Wall Funding." *CNN*, January 19, 2019. www.kjrh.com.

Dickerson, Caitlin. "Immigration Arrests Rise Sharply as Agents Carry Out a Trump Mandate." *New York Times*, May 17, 2017, A22.

Dinan, Stephen. "McCain Caters to GOP Voters." *Washington Times*, October 31, 2007, A1.

Diotte, Mark. "Edna St. Vincent Millay's 'Dirge without Music,'" *The Explicator* 72, no. 1 (2014): 28–31.

Dolan, Maura, and Larry Gordon. "In-State Tuition Benefit Upheld." *Los Angeles Times*, November 16, 2010, A1.

Dolan, Maura. "Feds Deal a Blow to Would-Be Attorney." *Los Angeles Times*, August 13, 2012. https://perma.cc/BH93-BVKP.

Dominguez case materials, 2008. www.maldef.org.

Downs, Ray. "U.S. Citizens in Fla. Charged Higher Tuition Rates Because of Parents' Immigration Status." *Christian Post*, October 31, 2011. www.christianpost.com.

Downes, Lawrence. "Self-Deportation." New York Times Editor's Blog, August 23, 2012. https://takingnote.blogs.nytimes.com.

Draper, Robert. "It's Just a Texas-Governor Thing." *New York Times Magazine*, December 6, 2009, 30–35.

"DREAM Act Newspaper, Magazine, and Website Stories, 2002–2012 (Partial Listing)." *University of Houston Law Center*. Accessed December 6, 2012. www.law.uh.edu.

Eckstein, Megan. "College Board Announces Support for Immigration Bill." *Chronicle of Higher Education*, April 22, 2009. www.chronicle.com.

———. "In-State Tuition for Undocumented Students: Not Quite Yet." *Chronicle of Higher Education*, May 8, 2009, A19.

Editorial. "Glad Gov. Cuomo's Withdrawal from Program to Catch Criminal Illegal Aliens Will Have Little Effect." *New York Daily News*, June 4, 2011. www.nydaily-news.com.

Editorial. "How a Democracy Works: President Obama Has the Authority to Start Fixing Immigration, if Only He Would Use It." *New York Times*, June 4, 2011, A20.

Editorial. "The Forgetful Mr. Smith." *New York Times*, July 13, 2011, A26.

Editorial. "Rick Perry's 'Oops' Moment Isn't All." *Los Angeles Times*, November 11, 2011. http://articles.latimes.com.

Eldridge, Ashley. "Array of Students Pay In-State Costs Under 2001 Bill." *Daily Texan*, Jul. 31, 2005, 1.

Elias, Paul. "Chico Lawyer Undocumented No More: Sergio Garcia Gets his Green Card." *Chico Enterprise-Record*, June 4, 2015. www.chicoer.com.

Endelman, Gary, and Cyrus D. Mehta. "Keeping Hope Alive: President Obama Can Use His Executive Power Until Congress Passes the DREAM Act." *The Insightful Immigration Blog*, December 18, 2010. http://cyrusmehta.blogspot.com.

Engle, Karen. "The Political Economy of State and Local Immigration Regulation: Comments on Olivas and Hollifield, Hunt & Tichenor." *SMU Law Review* 61, no. 1 (Winter 2008): 159–170.

Enriquez, Laura E., Martha Morales Hernandez, Daniel Millán, and Daisy Vazquez Vera. "Mediating Illegality: Federal, State, and Institutional Policies in the Educational Experiences of Undocumented College Students." 44 *Law & Social Inquiry* (2019). doi:10.1017/lsi.2018.16.

Everly Brothers, The. "All I Have to Do Is Dream." Cadence, 1958.

Ewing, Walter. "Border Patrol to Roll Out New 'Get Tough' Policy on Unauthorized Immigrants." *Immigration Impact*, January 19, 2012. http://immigrationimpact.com.

———. "Immigrants' Taxes Help Save the Social Security System." *Immigration Impact*, April 15, 2019. http://immigrationimpact.com.

Fabian, Jordan. "Sergio Garcia: USA's First Undocumented Lawyer." *Atlantic*, January 6, 2014. www.theatlantic.com.

Faherty, John, and Maxine Park. "ASU Ends Scholarships for Illegal Immigrants." *Arizona Republic*, February 16, 2008, A1.

Falkenberg, Lisa. "This Just In: AG Finds the Constitution." *Houston Chronicle*, January 16, 2008, B1.

Fallows, James. "Obama, Explained." *Atlantic*, March 2012, 54.

Fandos, Nicholas, Sheryl Gay Stolberg, and Peter Baker. "Back in Earnest, Congress Pushes to Reset Agendas." *New York Times*, January 27, 2019, A1.

———. "Shutdown Ends With No Funding for Wall." *New York Times*, January 25, 2019, A1.

Farb, Jessica. "The U Visa Unveiled: Immigrant Crime Victims Freed from Limbo" *Human Rights Brief* 15, no. 1 (Fall 2007): 26–29.

Fassett, Camille. "The Freedom of Information Act Is Getting Worse under the Trump Administration." *Freedom of the Press Foundation*, March 14, 2019. https://freedom.press.

Feagans, Brian, Mary Lou Pickel, and Anna Varela. "A Fierce Divide: Georgia's New Law on Illegal Immigrants Looks Strict, but Is It a Real Crackdown?" *Atlanta Journal-Constitution*, June 30, 2007, A1.

Feagans, Brian. "I Can't Do What I Really Want to Do." *Atlanta Journal-Constitution*, December 16, 2007, at D7.

———. "Illegals to Lose In-State Tuition." *Atlanta Journal-Constitution*, December 16, 2006, A1.

———. "Valedictorian in a Paradox." *Atlanta Journal-Constitution*, May 30, 2007, B1.

"Federal Student Aid: Highlights of a Study Group on Simplifying the Free Application for Federal Student Aid." *Government Accountability Office* (2009). www.gao.gov.

Federation for American Immigration Reform. "The 'DREAM Act': Hatch-ing Expensive New Amnesty for Illegal Aliens." News Release, October 23, 2003. Accessed June 20, 2019. www.fairus.org.

Field, Kelly. "Deal Is Reached on Immigration Bill Affecting Students, Says Senate Leader." *Chronicle of Higher Education*, November 24, 2008.

"Fight for Rights: Tens of Thousands March for Immigration Reform." *Chicago Tribune*, March 13, 2006, 8.

Fine, Ralph Adam. "Plea-Bargaining: An Unnecessary Evil." *Marquette Law Review* 70, no. 4 (Summer 1987): 615–32.

Fischer, Howard. "Arizona Ends Court Appeal, Will Issue Driver's Licenses to All Deferred-Action Recipients." *Capitol Media Services*, January 23, 2019. https://tucson.com.

Fisher, Louis. *The Constitution and 9/11: Recurring Threats to America's Freedoms*. Lawrence: University Press of Kansas, 2008.

Fisher, Marc, Ben Guarino, and Katie Zezima. "How the Shutdown Ended: Americans Just Had It up to Here." *Washington Post*, January 25, 2019. https://wapo.st.

FitzGerald, Eileen. "Group Works to Improve Undocumented Student Aid." *News-Times*, May 2, 2014. www.newstimes.com.

Flagg, Anna. "The Myth of the Criminal Immigrant." *New York Times*, March 30, 2018. www.nytimes.com.

Fleisher, Lisa, and Trish G. Graber. "Right to In-State Tuition for Illegals Advances." *Star Ledger*, January 5, 2010, News-22.

Flores, Stella M. "State Dream Acts: The Effect of In-State Resident Tuition Policies and Undocumented Latino Students." *Review of Higher Education* 33, no. 2 (Winter 2010): 239–83.

Florida, Richard. "How the Crash Will Reshape America." *Atlantic*, March 2009, 44.

Foderaro, Lisa W. "In Suing SUNY, Out-of-State Students Seek In-State Tuition." *New York Times*, February 6, 2011, CT1.

———. "Two-Year Colleges, Swamped, No Longer Welcome All." *New York Times*, November 11, 2009, A17.

Foley, Elise. "Alabama Immigration Law Asks Doctors for Their Papers." *Huffington Post*, May 18, 2013. www.huffingtonpost.com.

———. "Officials Refuse to Budge on Deportation of Students, Families." *Huffington Post*, June 1, 2011. www.huffingtonpost.com.

———. "Senate Dems to Obama: Stop Deporting DREAM Act Students." *Huffington Post*, last updated June 14, 2011. www.huffpost.com.

Freedberg, Louis. "Gardner Leaves UC with Plan to Close Huge Budget Gap." *San Francisco Chronicle*, September 19, 1992, A1.

———. "How UC Regents Tried to Downplay the Gardner Deal." *San Francisco Chronicle*, April 16, 1992, A1.

———. "UC Retirement Deal for Gardner Assailed." *San Francisco Chronicle*, April 3, 1992, A1.

Fried, Trippe S. "Licensing Lawyers in the Modern Economy." *Campbell Law Review* 31, no. 1 (Fall 2008): 51–66.

Freking, Kevin. "Immigrants Protest State Education Policy." *Waterloo Region Record*, June 29, 2011, D11.

Frey, William H. "Population Growth in Metro America Since 1980: Putting the Volatile 2000s in Perspective." *Brookings Institute Metropolitan Policy Program*, March 2012. www.brookings.edu.

Fritze, John. "Hundreds of Deportation Cases May Be Closed: Baltimore, Denver Pilot Cities for Expedited Review." *Baltimore Sun*, January 19, 2012. http://articles.baltimoresun.com.

Gabriel, Trip. "Rancor on Wall Slips Out of Sync with Border Voters." *New York Times*, January 25, 2019, A10.

———. "Stance on Immigration May Hurt Perry Early On." *New York Times*, September 24, 2011, A12.

Galindo, René. "The Functions of Dreamer Civil Disobedience." *Texas Hispanic Journal of Law and Policy* 24 (Fall 2017): 41–60.

———. "Undocumented & Unafraid: The DREAM Act 5 and the Public Disclosure of Undocumented Status as a Political Act." University of Houston Law Center—Institute for Higher Education Law and Governance, 2011. www.law.uh.edu.

Gamber-Thompson, Liana, and Arely M. Zimmerman. "DREAMing Citizenship: Undocumented Youth, Coming Out, and Pathways to Participation." In *By Any Media Necessary: The New Youth Activism*, edited by Henry Jenkins, Sangita Shresthova, Liana Gamber-Thompson, Neta Kligler-Vilenchik, and Arely M. Zimmerman, 186–218. New York: New York University Press, 2016.

Garcia y Griego, Manuel. "The Rights of Undocumented Mexicans in the United States after *Plyler v. Doe*: A Sketch of Moral and Legal Issues." *Journal of Law & Education* 15, no. 1 (Winter 1986): 57–82.

Garcia, Ruben J. "Critical Race Theory and Proposition 187: The Racial Politics of Immigration Law." *Chicano Latino Law Review* 17 (1995): 118–54.

Garcia, Tania P. Linares. "Protecting a Dream: Analyzing the Level of Review Applicable to DACA Recipients in Equal Protection Cases." *Southern Illinois Law Journal* 39, no. 1 (Fall 2014): 105–24.

Gellhorn, Walter. "The Abuse of Occupational Licensing." *University of Chicago Law Review* 44, no. 1 (Fall 1976): 6–27.

Gerber, Marisa. "Vaya Con Mom." *OC Weekly*, October 20, 2011. https://ocweekly.com/vaya-con-mom-6419607/.

Giovagnoli, Mary. "Rubio Proposal Overlooks Obstacles Ahead for DREAMers." *Immigration Impact*, May 4, 2012. http://immigrationimpact.com.

Goldstein, Donna M., and Kira Hall. "Postelection Surrealism and Nostalgic Racism in the Hands of Donald Trump." *HAU: Journal of Ethnographic Theory* 7, no. 1 (Spring 2017): 397–406.

Golshan, Tara, and Dylan Scott. "The Many Tragedies of the 115th Congress. Six." *Vox*, January 3, 2019. www.vox.com.

Gomez, Alan. "Immigrants Return to Alabama; Scores Fled State after Illegal Immigration Law Went into Effect." *USA Today*, February 21, 2012, 3A.

Gomez, Laura E. "What's Race Got to Do with It? Press Coverage of the Latino Electorate in the 2008 Presidential Primary Season." *St. John's Journal of Legal Commentary* 24, no. 2 (Fall 2009): 425–59.

Gonzales, Alberto R., and Patrick Glen. "Advancing Executive Branch Immigration Policy through the Attorney General's Review Authority." *Iowa Law Review* 101, no. 3 (March 2016): 841–921.

Gonzales, Alfonso. "The 2006 *Mega Marchas* in Greater Los Angeles: Counter-Hegemonic Moment and the Future of *El Migrante* Struggle." *Latino Studies* 7, no. 1 (Spring 2009): 30–59.

Gonzales, Roberto G. "Learning to Be Illegal: Undocumented Youth and Shifting Legal Contexts in the Transition to Adulthood." *American Sociological Review* 76, no. 4 (August 2011): 602–19.

Gonzales, Roberto G., and Leo R. Chavez. "'Awakening to a Nightmare': Abjectivity and Illegality in the Lives of Undocumented 1.5-Generation Latino Immigrants in the United States." *Current Anthropology* 53, no. 3 (June 2012): 255–81.

Gonzalez, Daniel. "Deportee Struggles to Readjust." *Arizona Republic*, January 23, 2012, A1.

Gonzalez, Jennifer. "North Carolina Community Colleges to Resume Enrolling Illegal Immigrants." *Chronicle of Higher Education*, September 18, 2009. www.chronicle.com/article/North-Carolina-Community/48518.

———. "State Directors of Community Colleges See Bleak Financial Times Ahead." *Chronicle of Higher Education*, September 24, 2009, A20.

Goodman, Alana. "Feds Misled Public on 'Backdoor Amnesty' Scandal." *Commentary*, June 27, 2011. www.commentarymagazine.com.

Goodnough, Abby. "New Meaning for Night Class at 2-Year Colleges." *New York Times*, October 27, 2009, A1.

Goodyear, Dana. "Defiance and Anxiety among Undocumented Youth in Trump's America." *New Yorker*, November 11, 2016. www.newyorker.com.

Gordon, Larry. "Immigrants Face Cal State Fee Hike." *Los Angeles Times*, September 9, 1992, A3.

Governor Bill Richardson Website. "Gov. Richardson Signs Bill Prohibiting Discrimination in Admission and Tuition Policy of New Mexico Post Secondary Educational Institutions Based on Student's Immigration Status." Press Release, April 8, 2005. Archived. https://web.archive.org.

Green, Erica L. "Protected for Now, Teachers Await Fate." New York Times, February 2, 2018, A14.

Greene, Jenna. "Deportation Cases Get a Fresh Look; Feds Test Effort to Prioritize Most Serious Immigration Cases." National Law Journal, January 9, 2012, 1.

———. "Discretionary Program Draws Praise, Derision; Reaction to Pilot for Undocumented Immigrants Mixed." Daily Business Review, January 11, 2012, A3.

Goldbaum, Christina. "Legislature Passes Bill Giving College Aid to Undocumented Students." New York Times, January 23, 2019, A19.

Griffith, Kati L. "Perfecting Public Immigration Legislation: Private Immigration Bills and Deportable Lawful Permanent Residents." Georgetown Immigration Law Journal 18, no. 2 (Winter 2004): 273–304.

Guendelsberger, John W. "Equal Protection and Resident Alien Access to Public Benefits in France and the United States." Tulane Law Review 67, no. 3 (February 1993): 669–731.

Guidi, Ruxandra. "Undocumented Immigrant Granted Rare Pathway to Legalization." KPBS, January 31, 2011. www.kpbs.org.

Guy, Andrew. "Big Man on Campus: Law Professor Fights for Issues Dear to His Heart." Houston Chronicle, June 4, 2001, A1.

Halloran, Liz. "Supporters Ponder Next Move as DREAM Act Fades." National Public Radio, December 9, 2010. www.npr.org.

Harmon, Dave. "Undocumented Immigrants in Jail: Who Gets Deported?" Austin American-Statesman, last updated September 26, 2018. www.statesman.com.

Hayden, Michael, and Matthew G. Olsen. "What Emergency?" Politico, March 13, 2019. www.politico.com.

Hayes, Chris. "The Idea That the Moral Universe Inherently Bends toward Justice Is Inspiring. It's Also Wrong." NBC News, March 24, 2018. www.nbcnews.com.

Healy, Jack, Kirk Johnson, and Kate Taylor. "Payday for Many Federal Workers Comes and Goes Without a Paycheck." New York Times, January 8, 2019, A14.

Hebel, Sara. "Arizona's Colleges Are in the Crosshairs of Efforts to Curb Illegal Immigration." Chronicle of Higher Education, November 2, 2007, A15.

———. "Candidates Grapple With How to Expand Access to College." Chronicle of Higher Education, September 14, 2007, A17.

———. "States Take Diverging Approaches on Tuition Rates for Illegal Immigrants." Chronicle of Higher Education, November 30, 2001, A22.

Hefler, Jan. "N.J.'s Gurbir Grewal, The Nation's First Sikh Attorney General, Says American Dream Is Alive and Well." The Inquirer, March 1, 2018. www.philly.com.

Hefling, Kimberly. "Duncan Praises Push to Help Immigrant Students." Community College Week, Vol. 24, No. 8, November 28, 2011, 29. http://ccweek.com.

Henderson, J. Youngblood. "The Question of Nonresident Tuition for Tribal Citizens." *American Indian Law Review* 4, no. 1 (1976): 47–70.

Herman, Richard. "If Immigration Is a Game, Let's Play to Win." *Huffington Post*, August 8, 2012. www.huffingtonpost.com.

Herszenhorn, David M., and Robert Pear. "Democrats Put Lower Priority on Health Bill." *New York Times*, January 27, 2010, A27.

Hesson, Ted. "DACA's Legal Labyrinth." *Politico*, May 14, 2018. www.politico.com.

———. "Flake's DACA Long Shot." *Politico*, February 21, 2018. www.politico.com.

———. "House GOP Huddles on DACA." *Politico*, May 24, 2018. www.politico.com.

———. "Judge Orders Full Restart of DACA Program." *Politico*, August 30, 2018. www. politico.com.

Highton, Benjamin. "Voter Identification Laws and Turnout in the United States." *Annual Review of Political Science* 20 (2017): 149–67.

Hing, Bill Ong, and Kevin R. Johnson. "The Immigrant Rights Marches of 2006 and the Prospects for a New Civil Rights Movement." *Harvard Civil Rights-Civil Liberties Law Review* 42, no. 1 (Winter 2007): 99–138.

Hockstader, Lee. "Immigration Awaits Its Turn." *Washington Post*, September 13, 2009, A23.

Hoefer, Michael, Nancy Rytina, and Bryan C. Baker. "Estimates of the Unauthorized Immigrant Population Residing in the United States: January 2010." DHS Office of Immigration Statistics, February 2011. www.dhs.gov.

Hoffman, Geoffrey A., and Susham M. Modi. "The War on Terror as a Metaphor for Immigration Regulation: A Critical View of a Distorted Debate." *Journal of Gender, Race & Justice* 15, no. 3 (Spring 2012): 449–502.

Holley-Walker, Danielle. "Searching for Equality: Equal Protection Clause Challenges to Bans on the Admission of Undocumented Immigrant Students to Public Universities." *Michigan State Law Review* 2011, no. 2 (2011): 357–64.

Hopfensperger. Jean. "Immigration Proposals Clash: The Governor and DFL Lawmakers Offered Differing Views on Issues Involving the State's Immigrants." *Minneapolis Star Tribune*, February 15, 2007, 5B.

Hopper, Robert, and Juan P. Osuna. "Remedies of Last Resort: Private Bills and Deferred Action Status." *Immigration Briefings* 97–106 (June 1997): 2–9.

Horton, Alex. "'He lied about it': Ann Coulter Rips Trump for Failing to Secure Border Wall Funding." *Washington Post*, January 26, 2019. www.washingtonpost.com.

Horton, Renee Schafer. "119 UA Students Reclassified as Out-of-State." *Tucson Citizen*, January 1, 2008, A1.

"How the United States Immigration System Works." *American Immigration Council*, August 12, 2016. www.americanimmigrationcouncil.org.

Howe, Amy. "After Federal Government Filing, 9th Circuit Rules in DACA Dispute." *SCOTUS Blog*, November 8, 2018. www.scotusblog.com.

Hoy, Seth. "Colorado, Hawaii and Delaware Progress on Tuition Equity for Undocumented Students." *Immigration Impact*, April 16, 2012. http://immigrationimpact.com.

Hsu, Spencer S. "Obama Presses Congress to Rework Immigration Laws." *Washington Post*, November 14, 2009, A16.

Hu, Tiffany. "Aspiring Interns Seek Class Cert. in P&G DACA Bias Suit." *Law360*, April 15, 2019. www.law360.com.

———. "Bill Roundup: Refugee Admissions, Dreamers on the Hill." *Law360*, April 11, 2019. www.law360.com.

———. "Koch Groups Push for 'Dreamer' Protections in Spending Bill." *Law360*, November 15, 2018. www.law360.com.

Huddleston, Brian. "A Semester in Exile: Experiences and Lessons Learned During Loyola University New Orleans School of Law's Fall 2005 Hurricane Katrina Relocation." *Journal of Legal Education* 57, no. 3 (2007): 319–48.

Hughes, Langston. "Harlem." In *Selected Poems of Langston Hughes*. New York: Random House, 1990. www.poetryfoundation.org.

Hulse, Carl, and Emily Cochrane. "Impasse Drives Pelosi and McConnell, Already at Odds, Further Apart." *New York Times*, Jan. 20, 2019, A11.

Hulse, Carl, and Adam Nagourney. "Obama's Afghanistan Decision Is Straining Ties with Democrats." *New York Times*, December 4, 2009, A20.

Hulse, Carl, and Sheryl Gay Stolberg. "His Health Bill Stalled, Obama Juggles an Altered Agenda." *New York Times*, January 29, 2010, A1.

Hulse, Carl. "Address Let Democrats Put Defiance on Display." *New York Times*, February 6, 2019, A14.

———. "Democrats Gain as Stevens Loses His Senate Race." *New York Times*, November 19, 2008, A1.

———. "G.O.P.'s Attempt to Avoid Showdown with Trump Is Scuttled by Trump." *New York Times*, March 13, 2019, A17.

———. "John McCain, a Last Lion of the Senate." *New York Times*, August 25, 2018. www.nytimes.com.

———. "Specter Switches Parties." *New York Times*, April 28, 2009, A1.

Hunker, Paul B., III. "Cancellation of Removal or Cancellation of Relief?—The 1996 IIRIRA Amendments: A Review and Critique of Section 240A(a) of the Immigration and Nationality Act." *Georgetown Immigration Law Journal* 15, no. 1 (Fall 2000): 1–46.

Hunter, Desiree. "Board Bars Illegal Immigrants from Junior Colleges." *Press Register*, September 26, 2008, B2.

Hutchinson, Todd. "Texas AG Hits San Antonio with Anti-Sanctuary Cities Lawsuit." *Law360*, November 30, 2018. www.law360.com.

Ibe, Peniel. "Trump's Attacks on the Legal Immigration System Explained." *American Friends Service Committee*, March 22, 2019. www.afsc.org.

"INS Issues Guidelines on School Approval Petitions." *Interpreter Releases* 70, no. 10 (March 14, 1994): 347–8.

"In-State Tuition; Don't Kick Around Children of Immigrants." *Sacramento Bee*, December 26, 2005, B4.

Iverac, Mirela. "Seeking Deferred Action, Young Immigrants with Blemished Records Give Pause." *WNYC News*, August 29, 2012. www.wnyc.org.

Jacobs, Jennifer. "Iowans Learn to Deal with Immigration." *Des Moines Register*, December 7, 2006, 1A.

Jacobs, Julia. "Was the Kavanaugh Hearing the Worst Supreme Court Fight? You Be the Judge." *New York Times*, October 7, 2018. www.nytimes.com.

Jacobson, Robin Dale. *The New Nativism: Proposition 187 and the Debate over Immigration.* Minneapolis: University of Minnesota Press, 2008.

James, Frank. "With DREAM Order, Obama Did What Presidents Do: Act Without Congress." *National Public Radio*, June 15, 2012. www.npr.org.

Jarvie, Jenny. "Deportations of 'Dreamers' Who've Lost Protected Status Have Surged under Trump." *Los Angeles Times*, April 19, 2017. www.latimes.com.

Jaschik, Scott. "New Twist on Immigrant Students in NC." *Inside Higher Ed*, July 28, 2008. http://insidehighered.com.

———. "Post-DREAM Strategies." *Inside Higher Ed*, October 29, 2007. www.insidehighered.com.

Jauregui, Heidi, and Ann Morse. "Professional and Occupational Licenses for Immigrants." *National Conference of State Legislatures*, January 17, 2017. www.ncsl.org.

Jawetz, Tom. "Immigration Reform and the Rule of Law." Center for American Progress, February 15, 2019. www.americanprogress.org.

Jenkins, Nate. "Activists Blast Governor's Immigration Bill as Bigoted." *Journal Star*, January 23, 2008, B1.

Jobe, Valerie. "Immigration Reform Would Affect OCCC." *Oklahoma City Community College Pioneer*, April 2, 2007, 1.

Johnson, Alex, and Pete Williams. "Third Federal Judge Issues Strongest Order yet Backing DACA." *NBC News*, April 25, 2018. www.nbcnews.com.

Johnson, Kevin R. "An Essay on Immigration Politics, Popular Democracy, and California's Proposition 187: The Political Relevance and Legal Irrelevance of Race." *Washington Law Review* 70, no. 3 (July 1995) 629–73.

———. "Immigration and Civil Rights in an Era of Trump." *Valparaiso University Law Review*, forthcoming 2019.

———. *Opening the Floodgates: Why America Needs to Rethink Its Borders and Immigration Laws.* New York: NYU Press, 2007.

———. "Public Benefits and Immigration: The Intersection of Immigration Status, Ethnicity, Gender, and Class." *UCLA Law Review* 42, no. 6 (August 1995): 1509–75.

———. "September 11 and Mexican Immigrants: Collateral Damage Comes Home." *DePaul Law Review* 52, no. 3 (Spring 2003): 849–70.

Johnson, Kevin R., and Bernard Trujillo. "Immigration Reform, National Security after September 11, and the Future of North American Integration." *Minnesota Law Review* 91, no. 5 (May 2007): 1369–1406.

Johnson, Kevin R., and Bill Ong Hing. "The Immigrant Rights Marches of 2006 and the Prospects for a New Civil Rights Movement." *Harvard Civil Rights-Civil Liberties Law Review* 42, no. 1 (Winter 2007): 99–138.

Johnson, Kit. "Opportunities & Anxieties: A Study of International Students in the Trump Era." *Lewis & Clark Law Review* 22, no. 2 (2018): 413–440.

Johnson, Tory. "The State Immigration Laws You Should Know About." *Immigration Impact*, January 24, 2018. http://immigrationimpact.com.

———. "Tuition Equity Policies for Immigrant Students Continue to Advance at the State Level." *Immigration Impact*, April 22, 2019. http://immigrationimpact.com.

Jones, Andrea, and James Salzer. "Student Residency Mistakes Cost State." *Atlanta Journal-Constitution*, December 14, 2007, E1.

Jordan, Miriam. "7 Years after Arrest and Outcry, Young Woman Again Faces Deportation." *New York Times*, May 11, 2017, A10.

———. "Illegal at Princeton." *Wall Street Journal*, April 15, 2006, A1.

———. "Many Families Split at Border Went Untallied." *New York Times*, January 17, 2019, A1.

———. "Protected Status Ends for Thousands of Immigrants from Honduras." *New York Times*, May 4, 2018, A11.

———. "Torn Apart at the Border, Kept Apart by Red Tape." *New York Times*, June 24, 2018, A14.

Josephs, Gary S. "A Checklist for Determining Domicile." *Practical Lawyer* 27, no. 5 (July 15, 1981): 55–64.

Jurdem, Laurence R. "How Richard Nixon Charted the Path for Donald Trump's Re-election." *Washington Post*, March 11, 2019. www.washingtonpost.com.

Kamarck, Elaine, and Christine Stenglein. "Can Immigration Reform Happen? A Look Back." *Brookings*, February 11, 2019. www.brookings.edu.

Kane, Paul, and Shailagh Murray. "Democrats Confused about Road Forward." *Washington Post*, January 29, 2010, A1.

Karni, Annie, and Sheryl Gay Stolberg. "President Offers Deal on 'Dreamers' to Secure a Wall." *New York Times*, January 19, 2019, A1.

Kasarda, Ralph W. "Affirmative Action Gone Haywire: Why State Laws Granting College Tuition Preferences to Illegal Aliens Are Preempted by Federal Law." *Brigham Young University Education and Law Journal* 2009, no. 2 (2009): 197–244.

Kaushal, Neeraj "In-State Tuition for the Undocumented: Education Effects on Mexican Young Adults." *Journal of Policy Analysis and Management* 27, no. 4 (Autumn 2008): 771–92.

Keaton, Elise A. *Tuition Equity Legislation: Investing in Colorado High School Graduates through Equal Opportunity to Postsecondary Education.* Center for Policy and Entrepreneurship, 2008.

Kelderman, Eric. "At the U. of Arizona, Goals Collide with Reality." *Chronicle of Higher Education*, March 27, 2009, A1.

Kellams, Laura. "State's Colleges Warned about In-State Tuition." *Arkansas Democrat-Gazette*, May 23, 2008, A1.

Keller, Josh. "California Supreme Court Upholds Law Giving In-State Tuition to Illegal Immigrants." *Chronicle of Higher Education*, November 15, 2010. http://chronicle.com.

———. "State Legislatures Debate Tuition for Illegal Immigrants." *Chronicle of Higher Education*, April 13, 2007, A28.

———. "U.S. Citizens Reap Unintended Benefit from California's Immigrant-Tuition Law." *Chronicle of Higher Education*, December 6, 2009, A1.

Kelly, Erin. "Successful Young Illegal Migrants Daring to Dream." *Arizona Republic*, June 29, 2011, A1.

Kenney, Mary. "Prosecutorial Discretion: How to Advocate for Your Client." *American Immigration Council*, last updated March 18, 2015. www.americanimmigrationcouncil.org.

Kerwin, Donald, Roberto Suro, Tess Thorman, and Daniela Alulema. "The DACA Era and the Continuous Legalization Work of the US Immigrant-Serving Community." *Center for Migration Studies*, 2017. http://cmsny.org.

Khatcheressian, Laura. "FERPA and the Immigration and Naturalization Services: A Guide for University Counsel on Federal Rules for Collecting, Maintaining and Releasing Information about Foreign Students." *Journal of College & University Law* 29, no. 2 (2003): 457–84.

Khimm, Suzy. "Obama DREAMs On." *Mother Jones*, June 27, 2011. http://motherjones.com.

Kim, Keun Dong. "Current Development in the Legislative Branch: Comprehensive Immigration Reform Nixed." *Georgetown Immigration Law Journal* 21, no. 4 (Summer 2007): 685–7.

Kim, Mina. "UCSF's First Undocumented Medical Student Begins Training." *KQED State of Health*, September 8, 2014. http://ww2.kqed.org.

Kinzie, Susan. "The University of Uncertainty: Va. Children of Illegal Immigrants Lack In-State Status." *Washington Post*, March 14, 2008, B1.

———. "U-VA Accepts Residency Claim." *Washington Post*, March 24, 2008, B5.

Klein, Alexandra L. "The Freedom to Pursue a Common Calling: Applying Intermediate Scrutiny to Occupational Licensing Statutes." *Washington and Lee Law Review* 73, no. 1 (Winter 2016): 411–66.

Kleiner, Morris M. *Guild-Ridden Labor Markets: The Curious Case of Occupational Licensing*. Kalamazoo, MI: W.E. Upjohn Institute for Employment Research, 2015. www.upjohn.org.

Kleiner, Morris M., Allison Marier, Kyoung Won Park, and Coady Wing. "Relaxing Occupational Licensing Requirements: Analyzing Wages and Prices for a Medical Service." *Journal of Law and Economics* 59, no. 2 (May 2016): 261–92.

Knaub, Kelly. "Northwestern Escapes DACA Bias Class Action." *Law360*, May 27, 2015. www.law360.com.

Kobach, Kris W. "Immigration Nullification: In-State Tuition and Lawmakers Who Disregard the Law." *New York University Journal of Legislation and Public Policy* 10, no. 3 (2007): 473–523.

Koger, Gregory. "Making Change: A Six-Month Review." *The Forum* 7, no. 3 (2009). https://doi.org.

Koh, Harold Hongju. *The Trump Administration and International Law*. New York: Oxford University Press, 2018.

Konet, Dawn. "Unauthorized Youths and Higher Education: The Ongoing Debate." *Migration Policy Institute*, September 11, 2007. www.migrationinformation.org.

Konnath, Hailey. "Tech Co. VMware Denied Job to DACA Recipient, Suit Says." *Law360*, April 23, 2019. www.law360.com.

Kopan, Tal. "States Try to Force Trump's Hand on DACA." *CNN*, July 1, 2017. www.cnn.com.

Krieg, Gregory. "Someone Please Remind Trump That He Ended DACA." *CNN*, March 5, 2018. www.cnn.com.

Kriel, Lomi, and Kevin Diaz. "Dreamer Immigrants Caught in Middle of Debate Over Reform." *Houston Chronicle*, January 28, 2018. www.houstonchronicle.com.

Kriel, Lomi. "DACA's Fate in Court's Hands." *Houston Chronicle*, April 16, 2016. www.houstonchronicle.com.

———. "Flight Attendant with DACA Released after Month in Detention for Mexico Flight." *Houston Chronicle*, March 22, 2019. www.houstonchronicle.com.

Kristof, Nicholas. "He Is a Racist. He Is a Con Man. He Is a Cheat." *New York Times*, February 27, 2019. www.nytimes.com.

Kuck, Charles. "When Can a DACA Student Pay In-State Tuition in Georgia? Now!" *Musings on Immigration*, January 2017. http://musingsonimmigration.blogspot.com.

Lacey, Hank. "Legal Experts Dispute King's, GOP Certainty That Immigrant Bill Violates Federal Law." *Denver Statehouse Examiner*, March 12, 2009.

Landler, Mark, and Peter Baker. "Trump Vetoes Resolution to Pull U.S. out of Yemen." *New York Times*, April 16, 2019, A12.

Larkin, Paul J, Jr. "Public Choice Theory and Occupational Licensing." *Harvard Journal of Law & Public Policy* 39, no. 1 (Winter 2016): 209–331.

Lazarick, Len. "Montgomery College Sued for Giving In-County Tuition to Illegal Immigrants." *Maryland Reporter*, January 21, 2011. http://marylandreporter.com.

Lee, Margaret Mikyung. "Private Immigration Legislation." Congressional Research Service, 2007. www.everycrsreport.com.

Lee, Stephen, and Sameer M. Ashar. "DACA, Government Lawyers, and the Public Interest." *Fordham Law Review* 87, no. 5 (April 2019): 1879–1912.

Lee, Stephen. "Monitoring Immigration Enforcement." *Arizona Law Review* 53, no. 4 (2011): 1089–1136.

Legal Action Center and Alexsa Alonzo. "DHS Review of Low Priority Cases for Prosecutorial Discretion." American Immigration Council, February 13, 2012. www.slideshare.net.

Legomsky, Stephen H. "Fear and Loathing in Congress and the Courts: Immigration and Judicial Review." *Texas Law Review* 78, no. 7 (June 2000): 1615–32.

———. "Immigration, Federalism, and the Welfare State." *UCLA Law Review* 42, no. 6 (August 1995): 1453–74.

Leibowitz, Aaron. "No Evidence Trump's Wall Contract Exists, Gov't Atty Says." *Law360*, February 27, 2019. www.law360.com.

Leingang, Rachel. "Big Drop in 'Dreamers' Enrolled at Maricopa Community Colleges after Tuition Ruling." *Arizona Republic*, September 24, 2018. www.azcentral.com.

Lennon, John. "#9 Dream." Apple, 1974. Compact disc.

———. "Beautiful Boy (Darling Boy)." *Double Fantasy*. Geffen, 1980. Compact disc.

———. "Imagine." Apple, 1971. Compact disc.

Leonos, Reynaldo, Jr. "Immigration Status Is Keeping Students out of Medical School." *Texas Standard*, May 24, 2016. www.texasstandard.org.

Leopold, David. "Why Morton's Memo Is the Best Road Map on Prosecutorial Discretion Yet." *Immigration Impact*, July 1, 2011. http://immigrationimpact.com.

Lepore, Jill. "Is Education a Fundamental Right?" *New Yorker*, September 10, 2018. www.newyorker.com.

Levitz, Eric. "Trump: The Dreamers Are My Hostages—But the Wall Is Not My Ransom." *New York Magazine*, November 28, 2018. http://nymag.com.

Lewis, Raphael. "In-State Tuition Not a Draw for Many Immigrants." *Boston Globe*, November 9, 2005, A1.

Libman, Gary. "Losing Out on a Dream? Education: Tuition Changes Cloud Future for Illegal Immigrants Who Had Hopes of Attending UC Schools, Other State Colleges." *Los Angeles Times*, January 23, 1992, E3.

"Lidiane Carmo, Sole Survivor of Family Killed in I-75 Crash, Won't Be Deported." *Huffington Post*, February 3, 2012. www.huffingtonpost.com.

Lieb, David A. "Missouri Lawmakers Have Big Issues Left on Last Day." *Jefferson City News-Tribune*, May 16, 2008.

Lind, Dara. "Congress's Deal on Immigration Detention, Explained." *Vox*, February 12, 2019. www.vox.com.

———. "Obama Has Granted a Record Low Number of Deferred Actions to Immigrants." *America's Voice*, April 28, 2011. https://americasvoice.org.

Lind, Dara, and Javier Zarracina. "By the Numbers: How 2 Years of Trump's Policies Have Affected Immigrants." *Vox*, January 19, 2019. www.vox.com.

Lines, Patricia M. "Tuition Discrimination: Valid and Invalid Uses of Tuition Differentials." *Journal of College & University Law* 9, no. 3 (1982–83): 241–61.

Lipman, Francine J. "The 'Illegal' Tax." *Connecticut Public Interest Law Journal* 11, no. 1 (Fall-Winter 2011): 93–131.

———. "I've Got ITINs on My Mind." *Surly Subgroup*, September 24, 2016. https://surlysubgroup.com.

———. "The Taxation of Undocumented Immigrants: Separate, Unequal, and Without Representation." *Harvard Latino Law Review* 9 (2006): 1–58.

Liptak, Adam, and Matt Flegenheimer. "Court Nominee Is Confirmed after Bruising Yearlong Fight." *New York Times*, April 7, 2017, A1.

Liptak, Adam. "Justice Department Submits Correction Letter to Supreme Court." *New York Times*, April 24, 2012. http://thecaucus.blogs.nytimes.com.

Liptak, Adam, and Michael D. Shear. "Justices Back Travel Ban, Yielding to Trump." *New York Times*, June 26, 2018, A1.

Little, Theresa Lyon, and Donald Mitchell, Jr. "A Qualitative Analysis of Undocumented Latino College Students' Movement towards Developing Purpose." *Review of Higher Education* 42, no. 1 (Fall 2018): 137–72.

LoBianco, Tom. "Fight Over Tuition for Immigrants Derails Bill." *Clark County News and Tribune,* March 1, 2012. www.newsandtribune.com.

Lofholm, Nancy. "Prosecutorial Review Puts Immigration Cases in Holding Pattern, Infuses a Sense of Hope." *Denver Post,* December 21, 2011. www.denverpost.com.

Lopez, Amanda E. "Still Dreaming: The Plight of the Undocumented Immigrant Student in the Professional World." *Scholar: St. Mary's Law Review on Race & Social Justice* 18, no. 3 (2016): 451–75.

Lu, Adrienne. "N.J. Bill on In-State Tuition for Illegal Immigrants Advances." *Philadelphia Inquirer,* January 5, 2010.

Lu, Denise, and Anjali Singhvi. "See How the Effects of the Government Shutdown Are Piling Up." *New York Times,* January 8, 2019. www.nytimes.com.

Luo, Michael. "Romney's Words Testify to Threat from Huckabee." *New York Times,* December 2, 2007.

Lynch, David K. *Tectonics.* SanAndreasFault.org: 2010. www.sanandreasfault.org.

Macris, Gina. "A Bid to Extend In-State Tuition." *Providence Journal,* September 20, 2011.

———. "Panel: In-State Tuition Rates for Undocumented RI Students." *Providence Journal,* September 19, 2011.

Madison, Lucy. "Romney on Immigration: I'm for 'Self-Deportation.'" *CBS News,* January 24, 2012. www.cbsnews.com.

Magagnini, Stephen. "Dream Act Students Live in Limbo—Aid Doesn't Help Get Citizenship or Career." *Sacramento Bee,* December 26, 2011.

Mahe, Stephane. "American Bar Association to Allow Illegal Immigrants to Become Lawyers." *RT News,* August 15, 2017. www.rt.com.

Majors, Stephen. "Immigrant Tuition Bill Fails Again." *Bradenton Herald,* April 21, 2006.

Malkin, Michelle. "Document Drop: ICE Memos Open Another Door to Illegal Alien Amnesty-by-Fiat." *MichelleMalkin.com,* June 22, 2011, http://michellemalkin.com.

Mangan, Katherine. "Alabama Board Bars Illegal Immigrants from State's 2-Year Colleges." *Chronicle of Higher Education,* September 25, 2008. www.chronicle.com.

———. "Arizona State U. Reclassifies 207 Students as out of State." *Chronicle of Higher Education,* January 8, 2008. www.chronicle.com.

———. "Community Colleges in North Carolina Close Doors to Illegal Immigrants." *Chronicle of Higher Education,* August 18, 2008. www.chronicle.com.

———. "DACA Remains Intact for Now, but Students Without It Are More Fearful Than Ever." *Chronicle of Higher Education,* March 1, 2017. www.chronicle.com.

———. "Most Colleges Knowingly Admit Illegal Immigrants as Students, Survey Finds." *Chronicle of Higher Education,* March 17, 2009. www.chronicle.com.

———. "Thousands of Arizona College Students Denied In-State Tuition." *Chronicle of Higher Education,* January 9, 2008. www.chronicle.com.

Manuel, K. M. *Unlawfully Present Aliens, Higher Education, In-State Tuition, and Financial Aid: Legal Analysis.* Washington, DC: Congressional Research Service, March 28, 2014.

Marcus, Ruth. "Immigration's Scrambled Politics." *Washington Post*, April 4, 2006.

Sherman, Mark. "Supreme Court Inaction Suggests DACA Safe for Another Year." *Associated Press*, January 18, 2019, https://apnews.com.

Marklein, Mary Beth. "Illegal Immigrants Face Threat of No College." *USA Today*, July 6, 2008.

Marquez, Benjamin, and John F. Witte. "Immigration Reform: Strategies for Legislative Action." *The Forum* 7 (2009).

Marrow, Helen B. "Immigrant Bureaucratic Incorporation: The Dual Roles of Professional Missions and Government Policies." *American Sociological Review* 74, no. 5 (2009): 756–76.

Marshall, Aaron, and Reginald Fields. "Budget Bill Passed by Senate Does More Than Spend Money: Changes Are Coming to Communities, Consumers, Students." *Plain Dealer*, June 13, 2011.

Marshall, Aaron. "Senate OKs Compromises in $112 Billion State Budget: House to Vote Today on Range of Cuts, Tax Breaks." *Plain Dealer*, June 29, 2011.

Martin, Jonathan, and Alexander Burns. "Democrats Secure Control of the House; Republicans Build on Majority in Senate." *New York Times*, November 6, 2018.

Martinez, Lisa M. "Dreams Deferred: The Impact of Legal Reforms on Undocumented Latina/o Youth." *American Behavioral Scientist* 58, no. 14 (2014): 1873–90, https://journals.sagepub.com.

"Maryland's 'Dream Act' Suspended Amid Petition Drive for Referendum." *Fox News*, July 1, 2011. www.foxnews.com.

Matich, Nicholas. "Patent Office Practice after the America Invents Act." *Federal Circuit Bar Journal* 23, no. 2 (2013): 225–44.

Maxwell, Janette Fenn. Comment. "An Alien's Constitutional Right to Loan, Scholarships and Tuition Benefits at State Supported Colleges and Universities." *California Western Law Review* 14, no. 3 (1979): 514–62.

Mazzetti, Mark, and Katie Benner. "Mueller Finds No Trump-Russia Conspiracy." *New York Times*, March 24, 2019.

Mazzetti, Mark, Maggie Haberman, Nicholas Fandos, and Michael S. Schmidt. "Inside Trump's Angry War on Inquiries Around Him." *New York Times*, February 19, 2019.

Mazzetti, Mark. "Mueller Report Lays Out Russian Contacts and Trump's Frantic Efforts to Foil Inquiry." *New York Times*, April 18, 2019.

McCann, Hannah. "Privileged for Being Stationary: Why the Practice of Differentiating between In-State and Out-of-State Tuition Rates Is Unconstitutional." *Belmont Law Review* 4, no. 1 (2017): 279–309.

McCaskill, Nolan D. "DACA Deadline Gone." *Politico*, February 27, 2018. www.politico.com.

McCaskill, Nolan D., and Heather Caygle. "Dems Threaten Revolt Over DACA Deal." *Politico*, January 11, 2018. www.politico.com.

McCormack, Eugene. "Missouri." *Chronicle of Higher Education*, August 31, 2007.

McCormick, Elizabeth. "The Oklahoma Taxpayer and Citizenship Protection Act: Blowing Off Steam or Setting Wild-Fires?" *Georgetown Immigration Law Journal* 23, no. 2 (2009): 293–363.

McDonnell, Patrick J. "Davis Won't Appeal Prop. 187 Ruling, Ending Court Battles." *Los Angeles Times*, July 29, 1999.

———. "Prop. 187 Talks Offered Davis Few Choices." *Los Angeles Times*, July 30, 1999.

McFadden, Robert D. "John McCain, 81, Battler in War and Politics." *New York Times*, August 26.

McGee, Patrick. "Colleges See Rise in Illegal Aliens." *Fort Worth Star Telegram*, July 21, 2005.

McGeehan, Patrick. "Thousands Inconvenienced Amid Shutdown-Related Flight Delays." *New York Times*, January 25, 2019.

McGraw, Carol. "UC Worker Who Quit Over Fees Policy Loses Bid to Get Job Back." *Los Angeles Times*, August 29, 1990.

McGreevy, Patrick, and Anthony York. "Brown Signs California Dream Act Funding Bill." *Los Angeles Times*, October 9, 2011.

McKinley Jr., James C. "Texas Senator Now a Challenger Lagging in Polls." *New York Times*, February 21, 2010.

McKinley, Jr., James C. "Governor's Race Exposes Republican Rift in Texas." *New York Times*, August 14, 2009.

McKinley, Jr., James C., and Clifford Krauss. "'Yes' for Texas Governor Is 'No' to Washington." *New York Times*, March 3, 2010.

McKinley, Jesse. "Arizona Law Takes a Toll on Nonresident Students." *New York Times*, January 27, 2008.

McLendon, Michael K, James C. Hearn, and Christine G. Mokher. "Partisans, Professionals, and Power: The Role of Political Factors in State Higher Education Funding." *Journal of Higher Education* 80, no. 6 (2009): 686–713.

McManus, Pamela A. "Have Law License: Will Travel." *Georgetown Journal of Legal Ethics*, 15 (2002): 527–54.

McPherson, Lindsey. "Democrats to Reintroduce Dream Act on March 12 with TPS and DED Protections." *RollCall.com*, March 12, 2019. www.rollcall.com.

Medina, Jennifer. "Allowed to Join the Bar, but Not to Take a Job." *New York Times*, January 3, 2014.

Melathe, Alvin, and Suman Raghunathan. "Tuition Equity Bills Continue to Build Momentum in State Legislatures." *Immigration Impact*, February 10, 2012, http://immigrationimpact.com.

Melear, Kerry Brian. "Undocumented Immigrant Access to Public Higher Education: The Virginia Response." *West Education Law Reporter* 194 (2005): 27–41.

Memorandum from Ronald C. Forehand, Senior Assistant Att'y General, Chief, Education Section to Lee Andes, State Council of Higher Educ. for Va., March 6, 2008.

Menjivar, Cecilia. "Liminal Legality: Salvadoran and Guatemalan Immigrants' Lives in the United States." *American Journal of Sociology* 111 (2006): 999–1037.

Meola, Olympia. "Colleges' Admittance of Illegals Opposed." *Richmond Times-Dispatch*, January 18, 2008.

Michaud, Jon. "The Miracle of Van Morrison's 'Astral Weeks." *New Yorker*, March 7, 2018. www.newyorker.com.

Millay, Edna St. Vincent. *"Dirge Without Music."* www.poemhunter.com.

Miller, Dennis R. "Imagine: 12 Great Books about John Lennon." *Huffington Post*, December 6, 2017. www.huffingtonpost.com.

Miller, Kristen, and Celina Moreno. "Martinez v. Regents: Mis-step or wave of the future?" IHELG Monograph 08–07. *Houston: Institute of Higher Education Law and Governance, University of Houston Law Center*, 2008. www.law.uh.edu.

Miller, T. Christian. "If Trump's Border Wall Becomes Reality, Here's How He Could Easily Get Private Land for It." *ProPublica*, March 25, 2019. www.propublica.org.

Mitchell, Ted. "Perspective: Congress Must End the Purgatory for 'Dreamers,'" *Washington Post*, November 9, 2018. www.washingtonpost.com.

"Montgomery County Student, Family Win Reprieve from Deportation." *Washington Post*, March 14, 2012. www.washingtonpost.com.

Montgomery, David. "No Turning Back, Rep. Luis Gutierrez Is Making Immigration Reform a Personal Cause." *Washington Post*, May 8, 2009.

Moon, Chris. "Immigrant Tuition Vote Typifies Fragile Statehouse Ties." *Topeka Capital-Journal*, February 17, 2006.

Morgan, James N. "Tuition Policy and the Interstate Migration of College Students." *Research on Higher Education* 19 (1983): 183–95.

Morrissey, Kate. "ICE Will No Longer Delay Deportations for Those with 'Private Bills' Pending." *San Diego Union-Tribune*, May 9, 2017. www.sandiegouniontribune.com.

Motomura, Hiroshi. "Immigration and Alienage, Federalism and Proposition 187." *Virginia Journal of International Law* 35 (1994): 201–16.

———. "The Rights of Others: Legal Claims and Immigration Outside the Law." *Duke Law Journal* 59, no. 8 (2010): 1723–86.

Muñiz, Raquel, Mara Zrzavy, and Nicole Prchal Svajlenka. "DACAmented Law Students and Lawyers in the Trump Era" *Center for American Progress*, June 7, 2018. https://cdn.americanprogress.org.

Muñoz, Hilda, Samaia Hernandez, and Ayana Harry. "11 New Haven Men Arrested in Immigration Raid Reach Landmark Settlement With U.S. Government." *Hartford Courant*, February 15, 2012. www.courant.com.

Muse-Orlinoff, Leah. "Staying Put but Still in the Shadows: Undocumented Immigrants Remain in the Country Despite Strict Laws." Center for American Progress, February 22, 2012. www.americanprogress.org.

Nakamura, David. "'The story keeps changing': Trump Falsely Asserts He Never Promised Mexico Would Directly Pay for the Border Wall." *Washington Post*, January 10, 2019, https://wapo.st.

Napolitano, Janet. Secretary of Homeland Security, Remarks, Center for American Progress, November 13, 2009. www.americanprogress.org.

Narea, Nicole. "Parties Duel Over Rationale for Blocking DACA in Texas Suit." *Law360*, August 14, 2018. www.law360.com.

———. "Trump Sticks to Wall Demand, but Offers DACA, TPS Extension." *Law360*, January 19, 2019. www.law360.com.

Nava, Erika J. "Tuition Equality Act Is a Half-Measure Without Access to Financial Aid." *New Jersey Policy Perspective*, April 2015. www.njpp.org.

Navarrette, Ruben. "Quit Playing Favorites, Politics with Deportations." *Sacramento Bee*, March 14, 2012.

Neary, Ben. "Governor Signs Key Bills." *Caster Star Tribune*, March 11, 2006.

Nelson, Starr. "Comment: Rock and Roll Royalties, Copyrights and Contracts of Adhesion: Why Musicians May Be Chasing Waterfalls." *The John Marshall Review of Intellectual Property Law* 1 (2001): 163–78.

Nelson, Taylor. "PSD Says Program That Helps Undocumented Students Is Legal." *Fort Collins Coloradan*, August 16, 2007.

Neuman, Gerald L. "Aliens as Outlaws: Government Services, Proposition 187, and the Structure of Equal Protection Doctrine." *UCLA Law Review* 42, no. 6 (1995): 1425–52.

———. "Jurisdiction and the Rule of Law after the 1996 Immigration Act." *Harvard Law Review* 113, no. 8 (2000): 1963–98.

"New Jersey Denies College Financial Aid to U.S. Citizen Because Her Mother Is Undocumented." *Latino Fox News*, June 14, 2011. www.foxnews.com.

Ngai, Mae. "The Strange Career of the Illegal Alien: Immigration Restriction and Deportation Policy in the United States, 1921–1965." *Law and History Review* 21, no. 1 (2003): 69–107.

Nicholls, Walter J. *The DREAMers: How the Undocumented Youth Movement Transformed the Immigrant Rights Debate*. Stanford: Stanford University Press, 2013.

Niedowski, Erika. "RI Education Board OK's In-State Tuition for Undocumented Students." *Boston Globe*, September 27, 2011, http://archive.boston.com.

Noferi, Mark. "136 Law Professors Say President Has Legal Authority to Act on Immigration." *Immigration Impact*, September 3, 2014, http://immigrationimpact.com.

Nolan, Jim "Va. Senate Backs Bill to Restrict Tuition Benefits for Illegal Immigrants." *Richmond Times-Dispatch*, January 27, 2009.

O'Leary, Mary E. "Yale Law School Immigration Clinic Files Class Action Lawsuit Challenging Secure Communities Detainers." *New Haven Register*, February 22, 2012. www.nhregister.com.

O'Reilly, Kelly S. "Alternative to DACA Advance Parole." *Wilneroreilly.com*, September 22, 2017. www.wilneroreilly.com.

Ohlheiser, Abby, Eli Rosenberg, and Michael Brice-Saddler. "'Trump caves' or 'Genius': Right Wing Splits after Trump Ends Shutdown with No Wall Funding." *Washington Post*, January 25, 2019. www.washingtonpost.com.

"Olivas Kicks out the Jams: UHLC Professor Explores the Law and Business of Rock and Roll." University of Houston Law Center, March 1, 2012. www.law.uh.edu.

Olivas, Michael A. "Administering Intentions: Law, Theory, and Practice in Postsecondary Residency Requirements." *Journal of Higher Education* 59, no. 3 (1988): 263–90.

———. "Colleges Should Think Twice about Exporting Their Programs." *Chronicle of Higher Education*, November 7, 2008.

———. *Drafting Justice: Statutory Language, Public Policy, and Legislative Reform*. University of Houston Law Center, 2014. www.law.uh.edu.

———. "Dreams Deferred: Deferred Action, Discretion, and the Vexing Case(s) of DREAM Act Students." *William & Mary Bill of Rights Journal* 21, no. 2 (2012): 463–547.

———. "IIRIRA, the DREAM Act, and Undocumented College Student Residency." *Journal of College & University Law* 30, no. 2 (2004): 435–64.

———. "Immigration Related State and Local Ordinances: Preemption, Prejudice, and the Proper Role for Enforcement." *University of Chicago Legal Forum* 27 (2007).

———. "Immigration-Related State Statutes and Local Ordinances: Preemption, Prejudice, and the Proper Role for Enforcement." *University of Chicago Legal Forum*, University of Chicago Legal Forum: 2007, https://chicagounbound. uchicago.edu.

———. "Lawmakers Gone Wild? College Residency and the Response to Professor Kobach." *SMU Law Review* 61, no. 1 (2008): 99–132.

———. *No Undocumented Child Left Behind*: Plyler v. Doe *and the Education of Undocumented Children*. New York: New York University Press (2012).

———. "*Plyler v. Doe, Toll v. Moreno*, and Postsecondary Education: Undocumented Adults and 'Enduring Disability.'" *Journal of Law & Education* 15, no. 1 (1986): 19–55.

———. "*Plyler*'s Political Efficacy." *UC-Davis Law Review* 45, no. 1 (2011): 1–26.

———. "The Political Economy of Immigration, Intellectual Property, and Racial Harassment: Case Studies of the Implementation of Legal Change on Campus." *Journal of Higher Education* 63, no. 5 (1992): 570–98.

———. "The Political Economy of the DREAM Act and the Legislative Process: A Case Study of Comprehensive Immigration Reform." *Wayne Law Review* 55, no. 4 (2010): 1757–1810.

———. "Postsecondary Residency Requirements: Empowering Statutes, Governing Types, and Exemptions." *College Law Digest* 16, no. 1 (1986): 268–99.

———. "Preempting Preemption: Foreign Affairs, State Rights, and Alienage Classifications." *Virginia Journal of International Law* 35, no. 1 (1994): 217–36.

———. "The Rise of Nonlegal Legal Influences." In *Governing Academia*, edited by Ronald G. Ehrenberg. Ithaca: Cornell University Press, 2004.

———. "Some DREAM Students Face Nightmare Scenarios, Obama Administration Must Honor Commitment." *Houston Chronicle*, April 6, 2011. www.chron.com.

———. "Storytelling Out of School: Undocumented College Residency, Race, and Reaction." *Hastings Constitutional Law Quarterly* 22, no. 4 (1995): 1019–86.

———. "Sweet Home Alabama?" *Inside Higher Ed*, October 13, 2011. www.insidehighered.com.

———. "Undocumented College Students, Taxation, and Financial Aid: A Technical Note." *Review of Higher Education* 32, no. 3 (2009): 407–16.

———. "What the 'War on Terror' Has Meant for U.S. Colleges and Universities." In *Doctoral Education and the Faculty of the Future*, edited by. Ronald G. Ehrenberg and Charlotte V. Kuh. Ithaca: Cornell University Press, 2009.

———. "Within You Without You: Undocumented Lawyers, DACA, and Occupational Licensing." *Valparaiso University Law Review* 52, no. 1 (2017): 65–164.

Olivas, Michael A., and Kristi L. Bowman. "*Plyler*'s Legacy: Immigration and Higher Education in the 21st Century." *Michigan State Law Review* 2011, no. 2 (2011): 261–73.

Ontiveros, Maria Linda. "Immigrant Workers and Workplace Discrimination: Overturning the Missed Opportunity of Title VII Under *Espinoza v. Farah*." *Berkeley Journal of Employment & Labor Law*, 39, no. 1 (2018): 117–145. https://doi.org.

Orozco, Cynthia F. *No Mexicans, Women, or Dogs Allowed: The Rise of the Mexican American Civil Rights Movement*. Austin: University of Texas Press, 2009.

Oswald, Lynda J. "Extended Voluntary Departure: Limiting the Attorney General's Discretion in Immigration Matters." *Michigan Law Review*, 85, no. 1 (October 1986): 152–190. https://doi.org/10.2307/1288886.

Pabón López, Maria. "Reflections on Educating Latino and Latina Undocumented Children: Beyond *Plyler v. Doe*." *Seton Hall Law Review*, 35 (2005): 1373–1406.

Pabst, Georgia. "Some Illegal Immigrants Will Be Able to Get In-State Tuition." *Journal Sentinel*, June 29, 2009. http://archive.jsonline.com.

Palazzolo, Joe. "Rakoff: SCOTUS May Have Been Misled in Immigration Case." *Wall Street Journal*, February 10, 2012. https://blogs.wsj.com.

Palley, David. "Resolving the Nonresident Student Problem: Two Federal Proposals." *Journal of Higher Education*, 47, no. 1 (January-February 1976): 1–31.

Paparelli, Angelo A., and Ted J. Chiappari. "No More Waiting on Legal Immigration." *New York Law Journal*, February 22, 2012. www.seyfarth.com.

Parry, Albert. "Samizdat Is Russia's Underground Press." *New York Times*, March 15, 1970. www.nytimes.com.

Patler, Caitlin. "Citizen Advantage, Undocumented Disadvantage, or Both? The Comparative Educational Outcomes of Second and 1.5-Generation Latino Young Adults." *International Migration Review*, 53, no. 3 (Fall 2017) 1:31.

Patler, Caitlin. "To Reveal or Conceal: How Diverse Undocumented Youth Navigate Legal Status Disclosure." *Sociological Perspectives*, 61, no. 6 (December 2018) 857–873.

Pear, Robert, and David M. Herszenhorn. "Obama Hails Vote on Health Care as Answering 'The Call of History.'" *New York Times*, March 21, 2010. www.nytimes.com.

Penton, Kevin. "New Indiana Law Allows Pro Licenses for Certain Immigrants." *Law360*, March 22, 2018. www.law360.com/immigration.

Perez, William. *We Are Americans: Undocumented Students Pursuing the American Dream*. Herndon: Stylus Publishing, 2009.

Pershing, Ben. "Bill to Help Marine Widow Hotaru Ferschke Set to Become Law." *Washington Post*, December 15, 2010. http://voices.washingtonpost.com.

Perrefort, Dirk. "Filibuster Blocks Tuition Bill." *News-Times*, March 16, 2007, A1.

Persico, Nicola. "The Political Economy of Occupational Licensing Associations." *Journal of Law, Economics & Organization*, 31, no. 2 (2015): 213–241.

Pew Research Center. *A Portrait of Unauthorized Immigrants in the United States*, by Jeffrey S. Passel and D'Vera Cohn. Washington, DC, 2009. www.pewresearch.org.

Pippenger, Nathan. "One Family in Limbo: What Obama's Immigration Policy Looks Like in Practice." *New Republic*, September 16, 2011. https://newrepublic.com.

Popescu, Roxana. "Bob Filner Leads House in Sponsoring Private Bills." *KPBS*, October 27, 2011. www.kpbs.org.

Port, Kenneth, Lucas Hjelle, and Molly Littman. "Where Have All the Patent Lawyers Gone? Long Time Passing . . ." *Journal of the Patent and Trademark Office Society* 97, no. 2 (2015): 193–213.

Portes, Alejandro, and Rubén G. Rumbaut. *Immigrant America: A Portrait*. 4th ed. Berkeley: University of California Press, 2014.

Poulin, Jeffrey N. "Development in the Legislative Branch: The Piecemeal Approach Falls Short of Achieving the DREAM of Immigration Reform." *Georgetown Immigration Law Journal* 22, no. 2 (2008): 353–356.

"Presidential Candidates 2020." *Ballotpedia*, accessed June 20, 2019. https://ballotpedia.org.

Preston, Julia. "Bill for Immigrant Students Fails Test Vote in Senate." *New York Times*, October 24, 2007. www.nytimes.com.

———. "Deportation of Illegal Immigrants Under Review." *New York Times*, April 26, 2011. www.nytimes.com.

———. "Deportation Program Sows Mistrust, U.S. Is Told." *New York Times*, September 15, 2011. www.nytimes.com.

———. "Deportations Under New U.S. Policy Are Inconsistent." *New York Times*, November 12, 2011. www.nytimes.com.

———. "Federal Policy Resulting in Wave of Deportations Draws Protests." *New York Times*, August 16, 2011. www.nytimes.com.

———. "Health Care Debate Focuses on Legal Immigrants." *New York Times*, November 4, 2009. www.nytimes.com.

———. "Immigration Decreases, But Tensions Remain High." *New York Times*, March 10, 2012. www.nytimes.com.

———. "Immigration Vote Leaves Policy in Disarray." *New York Times*, December 18, 2010. www.nytimes.com.

———. "In Deportation Policy Test, 1 in 6 Offered Reprieve." *New York Times*, January 19, 2012. www.nytimes.com.

———. "In Increments, Senate Revisits Immigrant Bill." *New York Times*, August 3, 2007. www.nytimes.com.

———. "Labor Dept. Issues New Rules for Guest Workers." *New York Times*, February 10, 2012. www.nytimes.com.

———. "Latinos Said to Bear Weight of a Deportation Program." *New York Times*, October 18, 2011. www.nytimes.com.

———. "Lawyer Leads Local Fight Against Illegal Immigration." *New York Times*, July 20, 2009. www.nytimes.com.

———. "Measure Would Offer Legal Status to Illegal Immigrant Students." *New York Times*, September 20, 2007. www.nytimes.com.

———. "Obama Links Immigration Overhaul in 2010 to G.O.P. Backing." *New York Times*, March 11, 2010. www.nytimes.com.

———. "Political Battle on Illegal Immigration Shifts to States." *New York Times*, December 31, 2010. www.nytimes.com.

———. "Quick Start to Program Offering Immigrants a Reprieve." *New York Times*, September 11, 2012. www.nytimes.com.

———. "Risks Seen for Children of Illegal Immigrants." *New York Times*, September 20, 2011. www.nytimes.com.

———. "States Resisting Program Central to Obama's Immigration Strategy." *New York Times*, May 5, 2011. www.nytimes.com.

———. "Students Spell Out Messages on Their Immigration Frustration." *New York Times*, September 20, 2010. www.nytimes.com.

———. "Union Chief Says New U.S. Rules for Immigration Detention Are Flawed." *New York Times*, March 28, 2012. www.nytimes.com.

———. "U.S. Pledges to Raise Deportation Threshold." *New York Times*, June 17, 2011. www.nytimes.com.

———. "U.S. to Review Cases Seeking Deportations." *New York Times*, November 17, 2011. www.nytimes.com.

———. "U.S. Says Fast Pace Continues on Reprieves for Young Immigrants." *New York Times*, September 14, 2012. www.nytimes.com.

———. "White House Plan on Immigration Includes Legal Status." *New York Times*, November 13, 2009. www.nytimes.com.

Preston, Julia, and Sarah Wheaton. "Meant to Ease Fears of Deportation Program, Federal Hearings Draw Anger." *New York Times*, August 25, 2011. www.nytimes.com.

Qiu, Linda. "The Many Ways Trump Has Said Mexico Will Pay for the Wall." *New York Times*, January 11, 2019. www.nytimes.com.

Raab, Jennifer. "Rick Perry's Tuition Policy, Immigrants' Dream: Why Students Need a Path to Citizenship." *Daily News*, September 30, 2011. http://articles.nydailynews.com.

Raff, Jeremy. "What Will Happen to Undocumented Doctors?" *Atlantic* video, 9:57, February 2, 2017. www.theatlantic.com.

Ramírez, Eddy. "Should Colleges Enroll Illegal Immigrants?" *U.S. News & World Report*, August 7, 2008. www.usnews.com.

Ramos, Kristian. "The Problem with the GOP's Love Affair with 'Backdoor Amnesty.'" *Huffington Post*, September 2, 2011. www.huffpost.com.

Rappeport, Alan. "Many I.R.S. Workers Ignored Recall, Potentially Throwing Tax Season Into Chaos." *New York Times*, January 25, 2019. www.nytimes.com.

Redden, Elizabeth. "A Message to Prospective Undocumented Students." *Inside Higher Ed*, October 16, 2008. www.insidehighered.com.

Redden, Elizabeth. "Data on the Undocumented." *Inside Higher Ed*, March 17, 2009. www.insidehighered.com.

Redden, Elizabeth. "DREAM Act Vote on Tap." *Inside Higher Ed*, October 24, 2007. www.insidehighered.com.

Redden, Elizabeth. "For the Undocumented: To Admit or Not to Admit." *Inside Higher Ed*, August 18, 2008. www.insidehighered.com.

Redden, Elizabeth. "Success Obscured by Controversy." *Inside Higher Ed*, April 24, 2009. www.insidehighered.com.

Redden, Elizabeth. "Trump Proposes DACA Deal for a Wall." *Inside Higher Ed*, January 21, 2019. www.insidehighered.com.

Reeves, Jay. "Hispanic Children Bullied in Law's Wake." *Boston Globe*, October 23, 2011. www.articles.boston.com.

Reich, Gary, and Alvar Ayala Mendoza. "'Educating Kids' Versus 'Coddling Criminals': Framing the Debate over In-State Tuition for Undocumented Students in Kansas." *State Politics & Policy Quarterly* 8, No. 2 (June 2008): 177–197.

Reich, Gary, and Jay Barth. "Educating Citizens or Defying Federal Authority? A Comparative Study of In-State Tuition for Undocumented Students." *Policy Studies Journal* 38, no. 3 (August 2010): 419–445.

Reich, Peter L. "Environmental Metaphor in the Alien Benefits Debate." *UCLA Law Review* 42 (August 1995):1577–1596.

———. "Public Benefits for Undocumented Aliens: State Law into the Breach Once More." *New Mexico Law Review* 21, no. 2 (Spring 1991): 219–249.

Reyes, Maritza I. "Constitutionalizing Immigration Law: The Vital Role of Judicial Discretion in the Removal of Lawful Permanent Residents." *Temple Law Review* 84, no 3. (Spring 2012): 637–700.

Ribstein, Larry E. "Lawyers as Lawmakers: A Theory of Lawyer Licensing." *Missouri Law Review* 69, no. 2 (Spring 2004): 299–364.

Ricard, Michael. "Undocumented Students Stage Mock Graduation Ceremony in Support of Dream Act." *Washington Post*, June 24, 2009. www.washingtonpost.com.

Riccardi, Nicholas. "Effort To Repeal California Dream Act Comes up Short." *Los Angeles Times*, January 6, 2012. http://latimesblogs.latimes.com.

Richer, Alana Durkin. "Q&A: Trump's New Travel Ban Faces Key Test in Appeals Court." *Associated Press*, May 6, 2017. www.usnews.com.

Riley, Kate. "Harvesting a DREAM. (Opinion)." *Seattle Times*, June 5, 2009. NewsBank.

Riley, Lisa. "Hatch Skips DREAM Act Vote He Calls 'Cynical Exercise.'" *Deseret News*, December 20, 2010. www.deseretnews.com (discussing re-election political pressure causing Hatch to dodge vote).

Rincon, Alejandra. *Undocumented Immigrants and Higher Education: Si Se Puede!* New York: LFB Scholarly Publishing LLC, 2008.

Rivera, Carla. "Budget Cuts Hit Broad Swath of Cal State." *Los Angeles Times*, November 29, 2009. www.latimes.com.

Robbins, Liz. "An Immigrant's Four-Year Fight to Become a Lawyer Ends in Celebrations." *New York Times*, February 3, 2016. www.nytimes.com.

Robertson, Campbell. "Critics See 'Chilling Effect' in Alabama Immigration Law." *New York Times*, October 27, 2011. www.nytimes.com.

Robertson, Campbell "In Alabama, Calls for Revamping Immigration Law." *New York Times*, November 16, 2011. www.nytimes.com.

Robison, Clay, and R.G. Radcliffe. "Perry Defends Illegal-Immigrant Tuition." *Houston Chronicle*, January 12, 2007. www.chron.com.

Robison, Clay. "Budget Hits Include Judges' Pay Hike." *Houston Chronicle*, June 18, 2001. *NewsBank*. https://infoweb-newsbank.com.

Rogers, Ed. "Democrats Won the House, but Trump Won the Election." *Washington Post*, November 7, 2018. www.washingtonpost.com.

Rojas, Leslie Berestein. "DHS Budget Proposes Discontinuing 287(g) in Some Jurisdictions." *Southern California Public Radio*, February 14, 2012. www.scpr.org.

Romero, Victor C. "Noncitizen Students and Immigration Policy Post-9/11." *Georgetown Immigration Law Journal* 17 (2003): 357–707.

———. "Postsecondary School Education Benefits for Undocumented Immigrants: Promises and Pitfalls." *North Carolina Journal of International Law and Commercial Regulation* 27, no. 3 (Spring 2002): 393–418.

Rosberg, Gerald M. "The Protection of Aliens from Discriminatory Treatment by the National Government." *The Supreme Court Review* 1977 (January 1, 1977): 275–339.

Rosenhall, Laurel. "California High Court Upholds College Tuition Break for Illegal Immigrants." *Sacramento Bee*, November 16, 2010, A1. www.sacbee.com.

Rozemberg, Hernan. "Texas Vets Get Tuition Back." *San Antonio Express-News*, January 16, 2008, at 1B.

Rubin, Robert. "Walking a Gray Line: The Color of Law Test Governing Noncitizen Eligibility for Public Benefits." *San Diego Law Review* 24 (1987): 411–448.

Rubenstein, David S. "Taking Care of the Rule of Law." *George Washington Law Review* 86 (2018): 168–230.

Rucker, Philip, Josh Dawsey, and Damian Paletta. "'Am I out of touch?': Trump Administration Struggles to Show Empathy for Workers." *Washington Post*, January 24, 2019, https://wapo.st.

Rucker, Philip. "Romney Works to Round up Key Support." *Washington Post*, January 21, 2012, A6.

Rudalevige, Andrew. "Why Congress's Rebuke of Trump's Emergency Declaration Matters—despite the President's Veto." *Washington Post*, March 15, 2019. www.washingtonpost.com.

Ruiz, Neil G. "More Foreign Grads of U.S. Colleges Are Staying in the Country to Work." *Pew Research Center*, May 18, 2017, http://pewrsr.ch.

Ruiz, Rebecca R. "Dream Act Becomes Law in California." *New York Times*, October 10, 2011, http://thechoice.blogs.nytimes.com.

Ruiz, Rosanna. "Veterans Fight for Tuition Money From State." *Houston Chronicle*, June 30, 2007, B7.

Rutherford, Emelie. "House Scraps Tuition Deal for Illegal Immigrants' Kids." *Boston Herald*, January 12, 2006, A15.

Schultheis, Ryan, and Ariel G. Ruiz Soto. *A Revolving Door No More? A Statistical Profile of Mexican Adults Repatriated from the United States*, May 2017. www.migrationpolicy.org.

Ryman, Anne, and Lesley Wright. "ASU Plans to Lay Off Faculty to Save Cash." *Arizona Republic*, October 28, 2008, A1.

Ryman, Anne. "Community Colleges Don't Plan to Appeal Ruling Denying In-state Tuition to DACA Students." *Arizona Republic*, May 22, 2018. www.azcentral.com.

Sacchetti, Maria "In Another Blow to Trump, Judge Rules in Favor of ACLU in Family Separations Case." *Washington Post*, March 8, 2019, https://wapo.st.

———. "Tuition Aid to Illegal Immigrants Falters: Patrick Declines to Act on Behalf of Graduates." *Boston Globe*, May 22, 2008, B1.

———. "Two Reprieves Give Immigrants Cautious Hope; Advocates See Signs of Prioritizing Cases." *Boston Globe*, November 26, 2011, at Metro-1.

———. "With Three Months Left in Medical School, Her Career May Be Slipping Away." *Washington Post*, February 22, 2018, http://wapo.st.

Sack, Kevin. "Hospital Falters as Refuge for Illegal Immigrants." *New York Times*, November 21, 2009, A1.

Salinas, Vicky J. "You Can Be Whatever You Want to Be When You Grow up, Unless Your Parents Brought You to This Country Illegally: The Struggle to Grant In-State Tuition to Undocumented Immigrant Students." *Houston Law. Review* 43 (2006): 847–878.

Salsbury, Jessica. "Evading Residence: Undocumented Students, Higher Education, and the States." *American University Law Review* 53 (2003): 459–490.

Samuels, Brett. "Trump Targets Dems over DACA amid Shutdown Talks." *The Hill*, January 13, 2019, https://thehill.com.

San Miguel, Guadalupe. *"Let Them All Take Heed": Mexican Americans and the Campaign for Educational Equality in Texas, 1910–1981* (Austin: University of Texas Press, 1987).

Sanger-Katz, Margot. "For Trump Administration, It Has Been Hard to Follow the Rules on Rules." *New York Times*, January 22, 2019. www.nytimes.com.

Sargent, Greg. "Trump's Phony 'Compromise' Has Now Been Unmasked as a Total Sham." *Washington Post*, January 22, 2019. www.washingtonpost.com.

Sass, Tim R. "Licensure and Worker Quality: A Comparison of Alternative Routes to Teaching." *Journal of Law & Economics* 58 (2015): 1–45 (arguing the differences between the alternative routes needed to get a teaching license).

Saul, Stephanie. "Amid 'Trump Effect' Fear, 40% of Colleges See Dip in Foreign Applicants." *New York Times*, March 16, 2017. www.nytimes.com.

Saunders, Debra. "Fat Left to Trim on Wilson's Plate." *San Francisco Chronicle*, November 2, 1992, A14.

Savage, Charlie. "Senate Confirms Sotomayor for the Supreme Court." *New York Times*, August 7, 2009, A1.

Schiff, Adam B. "State Discriminatory Action Against Nonresidents: Using the Original Position Theory as a Framework for Analysis." *Harvard Journal on Legislation* 22 (1985): 583–608.

Schmidt, Samantha, and Peter Holley. "A 'Dreamer' Claims He Was Secretly Deported. The Government Claims It Never Happened." *Washington Post*, April 19, 2017, http://wapo.st.

Schrag, Philip G. *A Well-Founded Fear; The Congressional Battle to Save Political Asylum in America*. New York: Routledge, 2000.

Schuck, Peter H. "The Message of Proposition 187." *Pacific Law Journal* 26 (1994): 989–1000.

———. "The Transformation of Immigration Law." *Columbia Law Review* 84 (1984): 1–90.

Schuneman, Micaela. "Seven Years of Bad Luck: How the Government's Delay in Issuing U-Visa Regulations Further Victimized Immigrant Crime Victims." *Journal of Gender, Race & Justice* 12 (2009) 465–491.

Scott, Eugene. "Before the Midterms, Trump Harped on the Migrant Caravan. Since Then, He Hasn't Brought It Up." *Washington Post*, November 8, 2018. www.washingtonpost.com.

Seelye, Katharine Q. "Specter Feels Squeeze From New Friends and Old." *New York Times*, January 27, 2010, A12.

Sefsaf, Wendy. "22 Senators Demand President Obama Exercise Executive Action on Immigration." *Immigration Impact*, April 14, 2011, http://immigrationimpact.com.

Seierstad, Asne. "The Anatomy of White Terror." *New York Times*, March 18, 2019, A27.

Semple, Kirk. "Bar Exam Passed, Immigrant Still Can't Practice Law." *New York Times*, December 3, 2013, A30.

———. "Cuomo Ends State's Role in U.S. Immigrant Checks." *New York Times*, June 2, 2011, A21.

———. "In New Jersey, Bills Offering In-State Tuition to Illegal Immigrants Face a Fight." *New York Times*, April 20, 2009, A20.

———. "U.S. Drops Deportation Proceedings Against Immigrant in Same-Sex Marriage." *New York Times*, June 30, 2011, A16.

———. "U.S. to Pay Immigrants Over Raids." *New York Times*, February 15, 2012, A22.

Semple, Noel, Russell G. Pearce, and Renee Newman Knake. "A Taxonomy of Lawyer Regulation: How Contrasting Theories of Regulation Explain the Divergent Regulatory Regimes in Australia, England/Wales, and North America." *Legal Ethics* 16 (2013): 258–283.

Shakespeare, William. *Hamlet*, Act 3, scene 1.

Shane, Peter M. "The U.S. Supreme Court's Big Immigration Case Wasn't about Presidential Power." *The Atlantic*, June 28, 2016. www.theatlantic.com.

Shear, Michael D., and Julie Hirschfeld Davis. "Trump Moves to End DACA and Calls on Congress to Act." *New York Times*, September 5, 2017, A1.

Shear, Michael D., Abby Goodnough, and Maggie Haberman. "In Retreat, Trump Halts Separating Migrant Families." *New York Times*, June 20, 2018, A1.

Shear, Michael D. "Seeking Wall, Trump Builds Ill Will Instead." *New York Times*, January 12, 2019, A1.

Shear, Michael D., Ron Nixon, and Katie Benner. "Migrants Order Tosses a Wrench Into the System." *New York Times*, June 22, 2018, A1.

Shelly, Barb. "Kris Kobach's War on Undocumented College Students." *Kansas City Star*, January 26, 2010.

Sherry, Allison. "Tuition Tussle Takes Shape." *Denver Post*, August 15, 2007, A1.

Sikes, Chole, and Angela Valenzuela. "Texas Dream Act [House Bill 1403]." *Texas State Historical Association*. Updated August 23, 2016. https://tshaonline.org.

Simpson, Susan, and Michael McNutt. "New Immigration Law Is Raising Questions for Many." *The Daily Oklahoman*, May 10, 2007, A1.

Singer, Paula N., and Linda Dodd-Major. "Identification Numbers and U.S. Government Compliance Initiatives." *Tax Notes* 1429 (Sept. 20, 2004).

Slagle, John W. "Fraudulent Documents Puerto Rico/ICE Administration Policies." *St. Louis Law Enforcement Examiner*, January 16, 2012. www.examiner.com.

Smith, Ashely A. "No Bottom Yet in 2-Year College Enrollments." *Inside Higher Ed*, June 21, 2018. www.insidehighered.com.

Smith, Kate. *Every Congressperson along Southern Border Opposes Border Wall Funding*. CBSNews, January 8, 2019. www.cbsnews.com.

Smith, Lamar. "Obama Budget's Backdoor Amnesty: President's Spending Plan Weakens Immigration Enforcement." *Washington Times*, February 23, 2012. at www.washingtontimes.com.

Smithson, J. Austen. "Educate then Exile: Creating a Double Standard in Education for Plyler Students Who Want to Sit for the Bar Exam." *Scholar: St. Mary's Law Review on Minority Issues* 11, no. 1 (Fall 2008): 87–126.

Sonmez, Felicia, Josh Dawsey, and Karoun Demirjian. "Trump Vetoes Resolution to End U.S. Participation in Yemen's Civil War." *Washington Post*, April 16, 2019. www.washingtonpost.com.

Sonmez, Felicia, and Cat Zakrzewski. "Pressure on Senate Republicans to Break Shutdown Impasse Grows." *Washington Post*, January 14, 2019. https://wapo.st.

Sorkin, Andrew Ross. *Too Big to Fail: The Inside Story of How Wall Street and Washington Fought to Save The Financial System From Crisis—And Themselves*. New York: Penguin Press, 2009.

Sorkin, Amy Davidson. "The Republican Test at the Border." *New Yorker*, January 13, 2019. www.newyorker.com.

Spiro, Peter J. "The States and Immigration in an Era of Demi-Sovereignties." *Virginia Journal of International Law* 35, no. 1 (Fall 1994): 121–178.

Springsteen, Bruce. "Dream Baby Dream." Columbia Records, 2014. Compact disc.

Srikantiah, Jayashri, and Shirin Sinnar. "White Nationalism as Immigration Policy." *Stanford Law Review Online*, March 2019. www.stanfordlawreview.org.

Staff of Joint Commission on Taxation. "Present Law and Background Relating to Individual Taxpayer Identification Numbers." March 5, 2004. www.jct.gov.

State of Florida, Sec. 529 Plans. Available at "Florida Prepaid Savings Plan," www.myfloridaprepaid.com/savings-plan.

Stephenson, E. Frank, and Erin E. Wendt. "Occupational Licensing: Scant Treatment in Labor Texts." *Econ. Journal Watch* 6 (2009) 181–194.

Sterngold, James. "500,000 Throng L.A. to Protest Immigrant Legislation." *San Francisco Chronicle*, March 26, 2006, A1.

Stevens, Jacqueline. "U.S. Government Unlawfully Detaining and Deporting U.S. Citizens as Aliens." *Virginia Journal of Social Policy and Law* 18, no. 3 (Fall 2011) 606–720.

Stoddard, Martha. "In-State Tuition Repeal Unlikely." *Omaha World-Herald*, February 2, 2010. www.omaha.com.

———. "Legislators Split on Immigrant Tuition." *Omaha World-Herald*, December 29, 2005, A1.

———. "A Tougher Proposal on Immigration; Gov. Dave Heineman and a State Senator Want State and Local Law Enforcement Agencies to Aid Homeland Security." *Omaha World-Herald*, January 22, 2008, A1.

Stolberg, Cheryl Gay. "Centrists Aim to Make Mark as Democrats." *New York Times*, January 19, 2019, A1.

———. "G.O.P.'s Tactics Seek to Corner the Democrats." *New York Times*, January 20, 2019, A1.

———. "McConnell to Pair Bills to Reopen Government With Trump's Immigration Plan." *New York Times*, January 20, 2019. www.nytimes.com.

———. "President Delays His State of Union Amid a Shutdown." *New York Times*, January 23, 2019, A1.

———. "Senate Votes 50–48 to Put Kavanaugh on Supreme Court." *New York Times*, October 7, 2018, A1.

———. "Trump Accepts Offer to Give State of Union." *New York Times*, January 28, 2019, A14.

———. "Trump Country Calls on Party Not to Give In." *New York Times*, January 14, 2019, A1.

Stolberg, Sheryl Gay, and Julie Hirschfeld Davis. "Senate Will Hold Competing Votes to End Shutdown." *New York Times*, January 22, 2019, A1.

Stowe, Stacey "Bill Giving Illegal Residents Connecticut Tuition Rates Is Vetoed by the Governor." *New York Times*, June 27, 2007, C14.

"Strong Illegal Immigration Bill Biggest Legislative Achievement." *Post & Courier* (Charleston, S.C.), June 7, 2008, A10.

Suárez-Orozco, Carola, Hirokazu Yoshikawa, Robert Teranishi, and Marcelo Suárez-Orozco. "Growing up in the Shadows: The Developmental Implications of Unauthorized Status." *Harvard Educational Review* 81, no. 3 (2011): 438–473.

Sullivan, Sean "Senators Hope Defeat of Dueling Plans Produces a Solution to Shutdown." *Washington Post*, January 23, 2019, https://wapo.st.

Svitek, Patrick. "Abbott Vows to Cut Funding for 'Sanctuary Campus' Schools." *Texas Tribune*, December 1, 2016. www.texastribune.org.

Swanson, Perry. "Suthers: Kids of Illegal Immigrants Can Be Eligible for In-State Tuition" *Colorado Springs Gazette*, August 15, 2007. https://gazette.com.

Swartz, Mimi. "Overmisunderestimating Rick Perry." *New York Times*, January 20, 2012. http://campaignstops.blogs.nytimes.com.

Taboada, Melissa B. "Should Illegal Immigrants Receive In-State Tuition?" *Austin American-Statesman*, July 25, 2009, B1.

Tackett, Michael, and Julie Hirschfeld Davis. "White House Sees Storm Aid as Way to Pay for Wall." *New York Times*, January 10, 2019, A1.

Tackett, Michael. "Trump Issues First Veto after Congress Blocks Border Wall Emergency." *New York Times*, March 15, 2019. A15.

Tamari, Jonathan. "N.J. Legislature Denies In-State Tuition for Illegal Immigrants." *Philadelphia Inquirer*, January 12, 2010, B1.

Tang, Didi. "Colleges to Start Checking Legal Residency." *Springfield News-Leader,* November 3, 2008, 1A.

Tankersley, Jim, Matthew Goldstein, and Glenn Thrush. "Impasse Starting to Leave a Mark on the Economy." *New York Times*, January 7, 2019, A1.

"Texas Attorney General Considers Payment of In-State Tuition by Undocumented Immigrants." 86 *Interpreter Releases* 2029 (2009).

Texas Higher Education Coordinating Board. "An Evaluation of Exemption and Waiver Programs in Texas." (October 2006).

Thangasamy, Andrew. "State Policies for Undocumented Immigrants." *The New Americans: Recent Immigration and American Society*, ed. Stephen J. Gold & Ruben G. Rumbaut. LFB Scholarly Publishing, 2010.

The Gang That Couldn't Shoot Straight. Directed by James Gladstone. Metro-Goldwyn-Mayer (MGM), 1971.

Thebault, Reis. "How a Flight Attendant from Texas Ended up in an ICE Detention Center for Six Weeks." *Washington Post*, March 23, 2019. www.washingtonpost.com.

Thompson, Doug. "Bill for In-State Tuition for Undocumented Students Falters in Committee." *Morning News* (Little Rock, AR), March 23, 2009.

Thrush, Glenn, and Emily Cochrane. "Trump's Options for Wall Shrink as G.O.P. Wavers." *New York Times*, February 4, 2019, A1.

Tichenor, Daniel J. *Dividing Lines: The Politics of Immigration Control in America*. Princeton: Princeton University Press, 2002.

———. "Navigating an American Minefield: The Politics of Illegal Immigration." *The Forum*, Vol. 7: Iss. 3, Article 1 (2009).

Toledo, Marianela. "Illegal Immigrants Can Practice Law in Florida." *Human Events*, May 22, 2014. http://humanevents.com.

Torbati, Yeganeh. "Number of U.S. Visas to Citizens of Trump Travel Ban Nations Drops." *Reuters*, April 27, 2017. www.reuters.com.

Torrejon, Rodrigo. "Financial Aid May Grow for Undocumented Students: These NJ Schools Enroll the Most." *NorthJersey.com*, May 8, 2018. www.northjersey.com.

Travis, Amy L. "New Jersey's Attack on Mixed-Status Families: The Unconstitutionality of New Jersey's Immigrant Eligibility for Foster Parents." *Rutgers University Law Review* 67, no. 2 (Spring 2015): 441–468.

Tresaugue, Matthew, and R.G. Radcliffe. "The Legislature: Illegal Immigrants May See Tuition Hike." *Houston Chronicle*, January 11, 2007, B1.

Trowbridge, Ronald. "Educated Illegal Immigrants Bring Fiscal Gain." *Inside Higher Ed*, November 17, 2011. www.insidehighered.com.

Turnbull, Lornet. "Scramble to Help UW Graduate Who's an Illegal Immigrant." *Seattle Times*, September 30, 2009, B1.

Ulloa, Jazmine. "How Young Immigrant 'Dreamers' Made Flipping Control of the House a Personal Quest." *Los Angeles Times*, January 1, 2019. www.latimes.com.

"Undocumented Students Face Barriers to Higher Education." *Phys.org*, April 21, 2009. https://phys.org.

Valdes, Marcela. "Staying Power." *New York Times Magazine*, May 28, 2017, at MM50.

Varat, Johnathan D. "State Citizenship and Interstate Equality." *University of Chicago Law Review* 48, no. 3 (Summer 1981): 487–572.

Vargas, Edward D. "In-State Tuition Policies for Undocumented Youth." *Harvard Journal of Hispanic Politics* 23 (2010–2011): 43–58. http://hdl.handle.net/10919/84004.

Vargas, Sylvia R. Lazos. "The Immigrant Rights Marches (Las Marchas): Did the Gigante (Giant) Wake Up or Does It Still Sleep Tonight." *Nevada Law Journal* 7, no. 3 (Summer 2007): 780–825.

Varsanyi, Monica, Paul G. Lewis, Doris Marie Provine, and Scott Decker. "A Multilayered Jurisdictional Patchwork: Immigration Federalism in the United States." *Law and Policy* 34, no. 2 (2012): 138–158.

Vasquez, Michael R. "U.S.-Citizen Children of Immigrants Protest Higher Tuition Rates." *Miami Herald*, October 24, 2011, B1.

Vazquez, Maegan. "Trump Says You Can Call His Wall 'Peaches' for All He Cares." *CNN*, January 11, 2019. www.cnn.com.

Venkataramani, Atheendar S., Sachin J. Shah, Rourke O'Brien, Ichiro Kawachi, and Alexander C. Tsai. "Health Consequences of the US Deferred Action for Childhood Arrivals (DACA) Immigration Programme: A Quasi-experimental Study." *The Lancet Public Health* 2, no. 4 (2017): e175–e181.

Venkatesh, Vasanthi. "Mobilizing Under Illegality: The Arizona Immigrant Rights Movement's Engagement with the Law." *Harvard Latino Law Review* 19 (2016): 165–202.

Verea, Mónica. "Anti-Immigrant and Anti-Mexican Attitudes and Policies during the First 18 Months of the Trump Administration [transl]." 13 *Norteamérica*, https://dialnet.unirioja.es.

Villazor, Rose Cuison. "The Undocumented Closet." *North Carolina Law Review* 92, no. 1 (December 2013): 1–74.

Viser, Matt. "Democrats and Activists Punish Trump with a New Strategy: Ignoring Him." *Washington Post*, January 17, 2019. https://wapo.st.

Viser, Matt, and Maria Sacchetti. "Patrick Mulls New tack on Immigrant Tuition: May Try to Bypass Wary Legislature." *Boston Globe*, January 11, 2008, B1.

Vocabulary.com Dictionary. "Manichean." *Vocabulary.com*. www.vocabulary.com.

Vogel, Chris. "The DREAM Act Might Be Dead, But These Kids' Hopes Are Not." *Houston Press*, June 17, 2008.

von Spakovsky, Hans. "Backdoor Amnesty-Abusing the Constitution and Presidential Authority." *Heritage.org*, August 19, 2011. http://blog.heritage.org.

Wadhia, Shoba Sivaprasad. *Banned: Immigration Enforcement in the Time of Trump* (NY Univ. Press 2019).

———. *Beyond Deportation: The Role of Prosecutorial Discretion in Immigration Cases* (NY Univ. Press, 2017).

———. "Immigration Enforcement and the Future of Discretion." *Roger Williams University Law Review* 23 (2018): 353–368.

———. "The Immigration Prosecutor and the Judge: Examining the Role of the Judiciary in Prosecutorial Discretion Decisions." *Harvard Latino Law Review* 16 (2013): 39–78.

———. "The Morton Memo and Prosecutorial Discretion: An Overview." *Immigr. Pol'y Center* (July 20, 2011). www.immigrationpolicy.org.

———. "The Policy and Politics of Immigrant Rights." *Temple Political & Civil Rights Law Review* 16, no. 2 (Spring 2007): 387–422.

———. "The President and Deportation: DACA, DAPA, and the Sources and Limits of Executive Authority: Response to Hiroshi Motomura." *Washburn Law Journal* 55, no. 1 (Fall 2015): 189–196.

———. *Prosecutorial Discretion in Immigration Agencies: A Year in Review*, LexisNexis 2012 Emerging Issues 6173 (January 12, 2012).

———. "The Role of Prosecutorial Discretion in Immigration Law." *Connecticut Public Interest Law Journal* 9, no. 2 (Spring 2010): 243–300.

———. "Sharing Secrets: Examining Deferred Action and Transparency in Immigration Law." *University of New Hampshire Law Review* 10, no. 1 (March 2012): 1–68.

Wagner, John. "Session Winds Up, Bringing Benefits for Working Class." *Washington Post*, April 12, 2007, GZ-1.

Walsh, Ryan H. *"Astral Weeks": A Secret History of 1968* (Penguin Press, 2018).

"Washington Extends Resident Student Tuition Rate to Certain Nonimmigrants." *Interpreter Releases* 86 (2009).

Watanabe, Teresa, and Esmeralda Bermudez. "For Immigrants' Rights Activists, Battle Continues." *Los Angeles Times*, June 17, 2012, A1.

Weiner, Rachel. "Trump: Mitt Romney's 'Maniacal' Self-deportation Policy Cost Him Minorities." *Washington Post*, November 26, 2012. https://wapo.st.

Wenger, Yvonne. "Sanford Signs Broad Illegal Immigration Law." *Post & Courier* (Charleston, SC), June 5, 2008, A1.

Werner, Erica, and Damian Paletta. "GOP Leaders Aim to Avert Shutdown Over Wall Funding, but Trump Makes No Promises." *Washington Post*, November 15, 2018. https://wapo.st.

Werner, Erica, Damian Paletta, and Sean Sullivan. "Lawmakers Say They Have Reached an 'Agreement in Principle' to Avoid Government Shutdown." *Washington Post*, February 12, 2019. https://wapo.st.

Werner, Erica, Seung Min Kim, Paul Kane, and John Wagner. "House Passes Resolution to Nullify Trump's National Emergency Declaration." *Washington Post*, February 26, 2019. https://wapo.st.

Werner, Erica, Seung Min Kim, and John Wagner. "Senate on Cusp of Passing Rebuke to Trump on National Emergency Declaration." *Washington Post*, March 13, 2019. https://wapo.st.

"What Education or Type of Degree Is Needed to Be a Lawyer." *Study.com*. http://study.com.

"What's Happening at the Legislature?" *Richmond Times-Dispatch*, January 28, 2009, A6.

Wickham, Allissa. "Well-Known DACA Recipient Sues Over Revoked Status." *Law360.com* May 11, 2017. www.law360.com.

Wiener, Jon. *Come Together: John Lennon in His Time* (Random House, 1984).

———. *Gimme Some Truth: The John Lennon FBI Files* (University of California Press, 2000).

Wiggins, Ovetta. "Immigrant Tuition Bill Falters in Md. Senate." *Washington Post*, April 7, 2007, B1.

Wildes, Leon. "All You Need Is Love-and a Good Jewish Lawyer." *Jewish Standard*, December 10, 2010. https://jewishstandard.timesofisrael.com.

———. "The Deferred Action Program of the Bureau of Citizenship and Immigration Services: A Possible Remedy for Impossible Immigration Cases." *San Diego Law Review* 41, no. 2 (May-June 2004): 819–838.

———. "The Nonpriority Program of the Immigration and Naturalization Service—A Measure of the Attorney General's Concern for Aliens (Parts I & II)." *Interpreter Releases* 53 (January 26–30, 1976).

———. "The Nonpriority Program of the Immigration and Naturalization Service Goes Public: The Litigative Use of the Freedom of Information Act." *San Diego Law Review* 14, no. 1 (December 1976): 42–75.

———. "Operations Instructions of the Immigration Service: Internal Guides Or Binding Rules." *San Diego Law Review* 17, no. 1 (December 1979): 99–120.

Wildes, Leon, and Shoba Sivaprasad Wadhia. "Prosecutorial Discretion and the Legacy of John Lennon." *Immigration Impact*, July 20, 2011. http://immigrationimpact.com.

Wilson, Daniel. "DOD Awards $1B in Border Wall Deals after Funding Shift." *Law360.com*, April 10, 2019. www.law360.com.

Wingett, Yvonne, and Richard Ruelas. "ASU Helps Migrants Find Tuition." *Arizona Republic*, September 8, 2007, A1.

Wingett, Yvonne, and Matthew Benson. "Migrant Law Blocks Benefits to Thousands." *Arizona Republic*, August 2, 2007, A1.

Wingett, Yvonne. "Arizona's Colleges Struggle to Enforce New Tuition Statute." *Arizona Republic*, January 3, 2007, A1.

Wishnie, Michael J. "Immigrants and the Right to Petition." *New York University Law Review* 78, no. 2 (May 2003): 667–748.

Wolf, Jeffery. "Colo. Senate Rejects Illegal Immigrant Tuition." *Denver Post*, March 4, 2009, B10.

Young, JoAnne. "Senators Hear Arguments on Repealing Nebraska Dream Act." *Lincoln Journal-Star*, February 2, 2010. https://journalstar.com.

Zakaria, Fareed. *The Post-American World* (W. W. Norton & Co., 2008).

Zavella, Patricia. *I'm Neither Here nor There: Mexicans' Quotidian Struggles with Migration and Poverty* (Duke University Press, 2011).

Zepeda-Millán, Chris. *Latino Mass Mobilization: Immigration, Racialization, and Activism* (Cambridge University Press, 2017).

Zingher, Joshua N. "The Ideological and Electoral Determinants of Laws Targeting Undocumented Migrants in the US States." *State Politics & Policy Quarterly* 14, no. 1 (2014): 90–117.

Zong, Jie, and Jeanne Batalova. *How Many Unauthorized Immigrants Graduate from U.S. High Schools Annually?* Washington, DC: Migration Policy Institute, 2019. www.migrationpolicy.org.

GOVERNMENT AND INSTITUTIONAL DOCUMENTS AND REPORTS

AACRAO, Undocumented Students in the U.S.: Admission And Verification (2009). www.aacrao.org.

Am. Fed. Gov't Emp. Nat'l Council. *Vote of No Confidence in ICE Director John Morton and ICE ODPP Assistant Director Phyllis Coven*, 2010. www.iceunion.org.

American Immigration Lawyers Association. *House Judiciary Immigration Subcommittee Hearing on OIG Adjudications Report*, AILA InfoNet Doc. No. 12021649, February 16, 2012. www.aila.org.

Applied Research Center. *Shattered Families: The Perilous Intersection of Immigration Enforcement and the Child Welfare System*, November 2011. www.arc.org.

Bruno, Andorra. Cong. Research Serv., *Unauthorized Alien Students: Issues and "Dream Act" Legislation*, 2007. http://trac.syr.edu.

Butterfield, Jeanne, Former Exec. Dir., Am. Immigration Lawyers Ass'n et al., to Interested Parties. *Re: Executive Branch Authority Regarding Implementation of Immigration Laws and Policies*, April 29, 2011. www.immigrationpolicy.org.

Capps, Randy, Marc R. Rosenblum, and Michael Fix. Migration Policy Institute. *Immigrants and Health Care Reform, What's Really at Stake?* (2009). www.migrationpolicy.org.

Chisi, Muszaffar, and Clare Bergeron. *New Immigration Bill Edges Comprehensive Reform Back on the Legislative* Agenda, January 2010. www.migrationpolicy.org.

Dodd, Chris. "Dodd to Sponsor Rare Private Bill Preventing Haitian Girl's Deportation" (July 16, 2004). S.2683—A bill for the relief of Majan Jean (2004). www.congress.gov.

Duke, Elaine C., Acting Secretary, U.S. Dept. of Homeland Security, to James W. McCament, Acting Director, U.S. Citizenship and Immigration Services et al. *Re.*

Rescission of the June 15, 2012 Memorandum Entitled "Exercising Prosecutorial Discretion with Respect to Individuals Who Came to the United States as Children." Sep. 5, 2017. www.dhs.gov.

Executive Order 13841 of June 20, 2018. "Affording Congress an Opportunity to Address Family Separation." *Code of Federal Regulations*, title 3 (2018): 29435–29436. www.federalregister.gov.

Feder, Jody. Congressional Research Service. *Unauthorized Alien Students, Higher Education, and In-State Tuition Rates: A Legal Analysis* (2008). www.digitalcommons. ilr.cornell.edu.

Gonzalez, Emilio T., Dir. USCIS, to Prakash Khatri, USCIS Ombudsman. *Response to Recommendation #32, Deferred Action*, August 7, 2007 www.dhs.gov.

Gonzalez, Roberto G., College Board Advocacy. *Young Lives on Hold: The College Dreams of Undocumented Students*, 2009. https://secure-media.collegeboard.org.

Griswold, Daniel. Cato Institute. *Comprehensive Immigration Reform: Finally Getting It Right* (2007). www.cato.org.

Immigration Policy Center. *Authority of U.S. Customs and Border Protection Agents: An Overview*, February 23, 2012. www.americanimmigrationcouncil.org.

Immigration Policy Center, *Secure Communities: A Fact Sheet*. www.immigrationpolicy.org.

Indiana State Senate. *Senate Enrolled Act No. 419*, Second Regular Session, 120th General Assembly (2018), https://iga.in.gov.

Internal Revenue Service. *Individual Taxpayer Identification Number*. www.irs.gov.

International Human Rights Law Clinic. *In the Child's Best Interest? The Consequences of Losing a Lawful Immigrant Parent to Deportation*, 2010. www.law.berkeley.edu.

Khatri, Prakash, CIS Ombudsman, to Emilio T. Gonzales, Dir. USCIS. *Recommendations to USCIS*, April 6, 2007. www.dhs.gov.

Kobach, Kris W. The Heritage Foundation. *The Senate Immigration Bill: A National Security Nightmare*, Webmemo No. 1513, 2007. www.heritage.org.

Kobach, Kris W. The Heritage Foundation. *The Senate Immigration Bill Rewards Lawbreaking: Why the DREAM Act Is a Nightmare*, Heritage Foundation Backgrounder No. 1960 (2006). https://papers.ssrn.com.

Latino Policy Institute, Roger Williams University. *The Effects of In-State Tuition for Non-Citizens: A Systematic Review of the Evidence* (2011). www.rwu.edu.

Law Professors, to President Obama. Executive Authority to Grant Administrative Relief for DREAM Act Beneficiaries, May 28, 2012. https://perma.cc/A48V-TWCB (archived copy of letter).

Library of Congress, Search of Private Immigration Legislation. www.loc.gov.

Mann, Anastasia R. *Garden State Dreams: In-State Tuition for Undocumented*. New Jersey Policy Perspective Report, 2010. www.njpp.org.

Maryland General Assembly. *Fiscal and Policy Note*, Senate Bill 41, 2009 Session. www. mlis.state.md.us.

Migration Policy Institute. *Migration and the Great Recession: The Transatlantic Experience*, eds. Demetrios G. Papademetriou, Madeleine Sumption, and Aaron Terrazas, 2011.

Morton, John, Assistant Sec'y, U.S. Immigration and Customs Enforcement, to Peter S. Vincent, Principal Legal Advisor, on *Guidance Regarding the Handling of Removal Proceedings of Aliens with Pending or Approved Applications or Petitions*, August 20, 2010. www.ice.gov.

———. Dir. U.S. Immigration and Customs Enforcement, to All Field Office Directors, All Special Agents in Charge & All Chief Counsel, on *Exercising Prosecutorial Discretion Consistent with the Civil Immigration Enforcement Priorities of the Agency for the Apprehension, Detention, and Removal of Aliens*, June 17, 2011. www.ice.gov.

———. Dir. U.S. Immigration and Customs Enforcement, to All ICE Employees, on *Civil Immigration Enforcement: Priorities for the Apprehension, Detention, and Removal of Aliens*, June 30, 2010. www.ice.gov.

———. Dir. U.S. Immigration and Customs Enforcement, to All Field Office Directors., All Special Agents in Charge, and All Chief Counsel on *Prosecutorial Discretion: Certain Victims, Witnesses, and Plaintiffs*, June 17, 2011. www.ice.gov.

NAFSA, *DACA Resource Page: For International Student Advisers and Education Abroad Advisers*, January 15, 2019. www.nafsa.org.

Napolitano, Janet, Secretary, Department of Homeland Security, to Senator Dick Durbin, August 18, 2011. www.shusterman.com.

National Bar Association for Undocumented Lawyers & Law Students. *Mission Statement, Dream Bar Association*, https://dreambarassociation.wordpress.com.

National Conference of State Legislators. *Professional Licenses for Immigrants*, January 2017. www.ncsl.org.

———. *Immigration Reform—Official Policy*, 2009. www.ncsl.org.

———. *State Laws Related to Immigrants and Immigration*, June 30, 2009. www.ncsl.org.

National Immigration Forum. *The Border Security Buildup: True Border Security Requires Reforming Our Broken Immigration Laws*, May 4, 2010. https://immigrationforum.org.

National Immigration Law Center. *Alert: Court Orders the Dept. of Homeland Security to Allow Individuals with DACA to Apply to Renew It*, 2018. www.nilc.org.

———. *Basic Facts about In-State Tuition for Undocumented Immigrant Students* (2009).

———. *DACA Litigation Timeline*, February 11, 2019. www.nilc.org.

———. *Dream Act Summary*, May 2011. www.nilc.org.

———. *FAQ: USCIS Is Accepting DACA Renewal Applications*, August 2018. www.nilc.org.

———. *Status of Current DACA Litigation*, June 7, 2019. www.nilc.org.

———. *USCIS and DACA Renewal Applications: What You Need to Know*, January 29, 2018. www.nilc.org.

"NCLEX Prep and Exam info." easynclex.com, 2017. http://easynclex.com.

New Jersey Policy Perspective. *It's Time to Follow Through on the True Promise of the Tuition Equality Act*, April 8, 2015. www.njpp.org.

New York Business Express. *Professional Licenses*. www.op.nysed.gov/prof (outlining the aggregate variety of the different Professional Licenses available through New York's online portal).

———. *Security Dealers, Brokers and Salesperson Designation—State Notice*. www. businessexpress.ny.gov.

New York Civil Liberties Union and New York Immigration Coalition. *New Report: False "Gang Allegations" Deny NY Teens' Access to Immigration Status and Bond Services*, 2019. https://d1jiktx90t87hr.cloudfront.net.

New York State Education Department. *U.S. Court of Appeals Decision on Litigation Involving 13 Professions that Require U.S. Citizenship or Permanent Lawful Residence for Licensure*. www.op.nysed.gov.

New York Immigration Coalition. *On First Day of Historic Immigration Policy Change, Over a Thousand DREAMers and Family Members Sought Application Assistance at the NYIC Legal Clinic ao Far Today*, August 16, 2012. http://muslimcommunityreport.com.

New York State Office of Information Technology Services. *New York Business Express*, https://its.ny.gov/nys-license-center-business-wizard [https://perma.cc] (illustrating the NYS License Center Portal to be comprehensive and detailed).

New York State Office of the Professions. *Education Law*, October 3, 2017. www. op.nysed.gov.

———. *The Licensed Professions in New York State*. www.op.nysed.gov/ [https://897perma.cc].

New York State. *Appearance Enhancement—Business License (DOS-0035-a)*. N.Y. Bus. Express. www.dos.ny.gov/forms/licensing/en/0035-f-a.pdf.

———. *Brewer Tasting (Annual) Permit*, N.Y. Bus. Express, https://sla.ny.gov/ permits-available-online.

———. Department of State Division of Licensing Services. *Index of Licensees and Registrants*, https://appext20.dos.ny.gov [https://perma.cc].

———. *Milk Dealer License—Distributor (DISPS-7)*. N.Y. Bus. Express. www.businessexpress.ny.gov/app/answers/cms/a_id/2499/kw/milk%20dealer.

———. *Milk Dealer License—Milk Hauler (DISPS-7)*. N.Y. Bus. Express. www.businessexpress.ny.gov/app/answers/cms/a_id/2502.

———. *Special Entertainer's Permit (Minor)*. N.Y. Bus. Express. www.businessexpress.ny.gov.

Pendergraph, Jim. Executive Director, Office of State and Local Coordination, U.S. Immigration and Customs Enforcement, to Thomas J. Ziko, Special Deputy Attorney General, N.C. Dep't of Justice, July 28, 2008. www.nacua.org.

———. Executive Director, Office of State and Local Coordination, U.S. Immigration and Customs Enforcement, to Thomas J. Ziko, Special Deputy Attorney General, North Carolina Department of Justice, July 9, 2008.

Penn State Law School et al. *Private Bills & Deferred Action Toolkit*, 2017. www.informedimmigrant.com.

Popeo, Daniel, Chairman and General Counsel, Washington Legal Foundation and Richard A. Samp, Chief Counsel, Washington Legal Foundation, to Daniel Sutherland, Officer for Civil Rights and Civil Liberties, Dep't of Homeland Sec., August 9, 2005. www.wlf.org.

Reid, Harry. Remarks made at NLEO, a national Latino organization in 2008: https://dreamact.info.

Schumer, Chuck. *Keynote Speaker at the Immigration Law and Policy Conference*, Migration Policy Institute, June 24, 2009. www.migrationpolicy.org.

"Short-Term Employment Authorization and Reduced Course Load for Certain F-1 Nonimmigrant Students Adversely Affected by Hurricane Katrina." 70 Code of Federal Regulations, 70992–96, November 25, 2005. www.federalregister.gov.

South Carolina Commission on Higher Education, *Issuance of Transcripts to Non-Verified Students*, January 16, 2009, at 2.

Spalding, Matthew. "Getting Reform Right: The White House's Immigration Initiative" *Heritage Foundation*, August 10, 2007. www.heritage.org.

State of Connecticut. "Governor Rell Vetoes Bill to Provide In-State Tuition to Illegal Aliens." June 26, 2007. www.ct.gov.

State of West Virginia. *Overview, West Virginia Board of Medicine*, 2017. https://wvbom.wv.gov.

State University of New York. *Residency, Establishment of for [sic] Tuition Purposes* (III. Guidelines for Determining Residence/Eligibility for Resident Tuition, Sec. D: Emancipation of a Student), Document Number: 7810; Effective Date: July 9, 2018. www.suny.edu.

Statement of Sen. Sessions. 152 CONG. REC. S4847, S4918 (daily ed. May 22, 2006).

Texas Department of Public Safety. *U.S. Citizenship or Lawful Presence Requirement*. www.dps.texas.gov.

Texas Higher Education Coordinating Board. *Residency and In-State Tuition*, 2018. www.thecb.state.tx.us.

TRAC Immigration. *New Deportation Proceedings Filed in Immigration Courts*, May 2019, http://trac.syr.edu.

———. *Rising Immigration Backlog All-Time High Yet Criminal, National Security, and Terrorism Cases Fall*, September 14, 2011. https://trac.syr.edu.

U.S. Citizenship and Immigration Services. *Affirmative Asylum Procedures Manual* 56, 2013. www.uscis.gov.

———. *Handbook for Employers: Guidance for Completing Form I-9 Employment Eligibility Verification Form*, July 2017. www.uscis.gov.

———. "How Do I Apply for Temporary Protected Status (TPS)?" https://my.uscis.gov.

———. *I-9, Employment Eligibility Verification*, January 23, 2017. www.uscis.gov [https://perma].

———. *Interoffice Memorandum from William R. Yates, Assoc. Dir. for Operations, to Reg. Dirs. & Dist. Dirs.* (May 27, 2004). www.uscis.gov.

———. *Permanent Workers*, July 15, 2015. www.uscis.gov (setting out the preference categories enabling non-citizens to obtain employment based visas).

———. *Q Cultural Exchange*, July 14, 2015. www.uscis.gov.

———. *R-1 Temporary Nonimmigrant Religious Workers*, September 11, 2015. www.uscis.gov.

———. *Refugee, Asylum, and International Operations Directorate.* www.uscis.gov.

———. *Special Immigrant Juveniles (SIJ) Status.* www.uscis.gov (setting out the SIJ criteria and policies).

———. "Temporary (Nonimmigrant) Workers," September 7, 2011. www.uscis.gov.

———. *Temporary Protected Status Designated Country: Honduras.* www.uscis.gov.

———. *USCIS Announces Interim Relief for Foreign Students Adversely Impacted by Hurricane Katrina*, November 25, 2005. www.uscis.gov/sites/default/files/files/pressrelease/F1Student_11_25_05_PR.pdf.

———. "USCIS Will Issue Redesigned Green Cards and Employment Authorization Documents." News Release, April 19, 2017. www.uscis.gov.

U.S. Congress, House, House Subcommittee on Immigration, Citizenship, Refugees, Border Security, and International Law. *The Future of Undocumented Immigrant Students: Hearing on Comprehensive Immigration Reform*, 110th Cong., May 2007. https://catalog.loc.gov.

U.S. Congress, Senate, Senate Committee on the Judiciary. *Oversight of the Department of Homeland Security*, 112th Cong. 32–33 (2011).

U.S. Customs and Border Protection. *Border Patrol History.* www.cbp.gov.

U.S. Customs and Immigration Services. *Frequently Asked Questions*, April 25, 2017. www.uscis.gov.

———. *Number of I-821D, Consideration of Deferred Action for Childhood Arrivals by Fiscal Year, Quarter, Intake, Biometrics and Case Status: 2012–2016* March 2016. www.uscis.gov.

U.S. Department of Defense, Defense Security Service. *Security Assurances for Cleared Individuals and Facilities.* www.dss.mil.

U.S. Department of Homeland Security, Office of the Inspector General. *An Assessment of United States Immigration and Customs Enforcement's Fugitive Operations Teams*, OIG-07-34, March 2007. www.oig.dhs.gov.

———. Secretary Kirstjen M. Nielsen. *Memorandum*, June 22, 2018. www.dhs.gov.

———. *Rescission of Memorandum Providing for Deferred Action for Parents of Americans and Lawful Permanent Residents ("DAPA")*, June 15, 2017. www.dhs.gov.

U.S. Department of Justice. *Attorney General Jeff Sessions Issues Statement on DACA Court Order*, August 6, 2018. www.justice.gov.

———. *Attorney General Sessions Delivers Remarks on DACA*, September 5, 2019. www.justice.gov.

———. *Justice Department Settles Immigration-Related Discrimination Claims Against 121 Residency Programs and American Association of Colleges of Podiatric Medicine*, June 20, 2016. www.justice.gov.

———. *Justice Department Settles Immigration-Related Discrimination Claim Against Florida Roadside Assistance Services Company*, April 6, 2017. www.justice.gov.

U.S. Department of State, Bureau of Consular Affairs. *Student Visa*, https://travel.state. gov.

U.S. Department of the Treasury Office of Economic Policy, the Council of Economic Advisers, and the Department of Labor. *Occupational Licensing: A Framework for Policymakers*, July 2015. https://obamawhitehouse.archives.gov.

U.S. Equal Employment Opportunity Commission. "Immigrants' Employment Rights Under Federal Anti-Discrimination Laws." Accessed June 27, 2019. www.eeoc.gov.

———. "Workplace Law Not Enforced by EEOC." Accessed June 24, 2019. www.eeoc. gov.

U.S. Federal Student Aid. *Eligibility for Title IV Program Assistance for Victims of Human Trafficking*, May 11, 2006. http://ifap.ed.gov.

U.S. Immigration and Customs Enforcement. *Frequently Asked Questions on the Administration's Announcement Regarding a New Process to Further Focus Immigration Enforcement Resources on High Priority Cases*. www.uscis.gov [Archived FAQ materials].

———. *Fugitive Operations* (2012). www.ice.gov.

———. *Guidance to ICE Attorneys Reviewing the CBP, USCIS, and ICE Cases Before the Executive Office for Immigration Review* (2011). www.ice.gov.

———. *Next Steps in the Implementation of the Prosecutorial Discretion Memorandum and the August 18th Announcement on Immigration Enforcement Priorities* (2011). www.ice.gov.

———. *Secure Communities*. www.ice.gov.

U.S. Immigration and Naturalization Service. *Inspector's Field Manual*. www.gani.com.

US Legal. *Reciprocity*. https://attorneys.uslegal.com.

U.S. Office of Management and Budget, *Statement of Administrative Policy: S. 2205—Development, Relief, and Education for Alien Minors Act of 2007*, 2007. www. whitehouse.gov.

U.S. Social Security Administration, Program Operations Manual System. SI 00501.420(B)(2)–(3), Permanent Residence under Color of Law (PRUCOL) Pre-1996 Legislation, May 5, 2012. https://secure.ssa.gov.

Vincent, Peter, Principal Legal Advisor, Immigration and Customs Enforcement, to All Chief Counsel, Office of the Principal Legal Advisor, on *Case-by-Case Review of Incoming and Certain Pending Cases*, November 17, 2011. www.ice.gov.

Wisconsin Department of Safety and Professional Services, Dentistry Examining Board. "Application for Dental Hygiene Certificate to Administer Local Anesthesia." December 2016. http://dsps.wi.gov.

INDEX

AAW. See *American Association of Women v. California State University*

AB 540, California, 29, 36, 145

Administrative Procedure Act (APA), 114–16, 157, 265n113

advance parole, 111–13, 124, 254n25

Alabama, 56; *Hispanic Interest Coal. of Alabama v. Governor of Alabama*, 154; lawyers, licensing of, in, 99–100; medical licensing in, 243n126; nurses, licensing of, in, 103; residency requirements, college, in, 100; restrictionist legislation in, 149

Alaska, 99

Alexander, Lamar, 128–29

"All I Have to Do Is Dream" (song), 133

American Association of Women v. California State University (*AAW*): *Bradford* and, 17–20; *Leticia "A"* and, 17–18, 171n123

American Dream Act, *48*, 176n1

American Dream and Promise Act of 2019, *51*

American Immigration Lawyers Association, 80

APA. *See* Administrative Procedure Act

Arizona, 188n94; Arpaio in, 92–93, 153; Border Patrol enforcement in, 74; driver's license ban in, 156; lawyers, licensing of, in, 99–100; residency requirements, college, in, 148–49, 155; restrictionist legislation in, 34, 149; restrictionist policies in, 74, 156

Arizona v. Maricopa Cnty. Cmty. Coll. Dist. Bd., 155

Arkansas, 100, 103

Arpaio, Joseph, 92–93, 153

Arpaio v. Obama, 153

"Astral Weeks" (song), 133

Ayala Mendoza, Alvar, 46–47

A. Z. ex rel. B. Z. v. Higher Educ. Student Assistance Auth., 154

bar admission. *See* lawyers

Batalla Vidal v. Baran, 157

Batalla Vidal v. Nielsen, 157

Berman, Howard L., 52

Beyoncé, 133

Blackman, Josh, 236n66, 252n16

Board of Regents of Univ. of Cal. v. Superior Ct. (Bradford II), 170n104

Border Patrol, United States, 73–74

Border Security, Economic Opportunity, and Immigration Modernization Act, *50*

border wall: DACA and funding for, 120–22, 124–26, 130; emergency powers invoked for, 124–30; government shutdown over, 125–30, 260n83, 262n97

Bradford v. Board of Regents of the University of California (Bradford), 170n104; *AAW* and, 17–20; IRCA and, 21–22; *Leticia "A"* and, 15–18, 21, 172n125; population impacted by, California, 175n164, 179n11; on residency requirements, college, 15–22, 172n125, 175n164, 179n11

DACA and, 241n108; undocumented student population in, 36, 192n114

Texas v. United States: DAPA, DACA in, 92–93, 108–11, 117, 119, 124, 129, 153, 236n66, 237n73, 252n16, 265nn113–14; SCOTUS and, 93, 108–10, 117, 153, 237n73, 265nn113–14

Toll v. Moreno, 21, 167n42, 168n77; Brennan in, 10–12, 167n62; dissent in, 12–13; *Elkins v. Moreno*, 172n141; equal protection in, 11; G-4 visa holders and, 10–13, 165n31, 172n141; on nonimmigrants, 10, 12–14, 19; *Plyler v. Doe* and, 13, 15; Supremacy Clause in, 10–11

TPS. *See* Temporary Protected Status

Transactional Records Access Clearinghouse, 74, 222n113

travel ban, under Trump, 89, 110, 117, 232n32, 232n34, 237n75

Trump, Donald, 63, 168n71, 217n70; border wall under, 120–22, 124–30, 260n83, 262n97; DAPA under, 111, 117, 119, 153, 237n73, 252n16, 265nn113–14; data gathering, dissemination under, 239n81; Democrats and, 119–23, 125–29, 257n57, 266n120; DREAM Act, possibilities for, under, 110, 113, 115, 120–22, 129, 257n57, 266n120; emergency powers invoked by, 124–30; Gorsuch appointed by, 108; government shutdown under, 125–30, 260n83, 262n97; Mueller and, 127, 263n102; nativism and, 109–10, 116, 125, 250n8; occupational licensing uncertainty under, 106; racism of, 250n8; Republicans and shutdown of, 127–29; travel ban of, 89, 110, 117, 232n32, 232n34, 237n75; zero tolerance border policy under, 109–10, 115, 256n38

Trump, Donald, DACA under, 106–7, 237n74, 252n15; advance parole and, 111–13, 124, 254n25; border wall funding and, 120–22, 124–26, 130; DHS and, 111–

15, 255n30, 257n53; legal challenges on, 109–19, 121, 123–24, 126, 129, 131, 157–58, 251n11, 252n16, 255n30, 255nn27–28, 257n53, 265nn113–14, 266n120; rescission approach, flawed, of, 122–24, 126, 130, 257n53, 265n114; rescission of, 81, 93, 109–19, 121, 129, 131, 157–58, 251n11, 252n16, 255n30, 266n120

Trump v. Hawaii, 117

tuition, resident. *See* residency requirements, college

two-year colleges, 32

UC. *See* University of California

UCLA. *See* University of California, Los Angeles

United States Court of Appeals for the Ninth Circuit. *See* Ninth Circuit court, federal

United States v. Juarez-Escobar, 153

United States v. Texas. See Texas v. United States

University of California (UC): AB 540 and, 29; *Bradford* case of, 15–22, 170n104, 172n125, 175n164, 179n11; *Leticia "A"* on, 13–18, 20–21, 135, 169n82, 169n90, 170n100, 170n102, 171n121, 171n123, 171nn118–19, 172n125; *Martinez v. Regents of the University of California*, 28–30, 35, 155; *Regents of Univ. of California v. United States Dep't of Homeland Sec.*, 157; undocumented student population in, 16

University of California, Los Angeles (UCLA), 15–17, 170n107

University of Michigan, 148

University of North Carolina, 151–52

US Citizenship and Immigration Services (USCIS), 65–67, 235n50

Utah: Hatch of, 46, 54, 184n61, 200n43, 202n56; residency requirements, college, in, 31, 35, 145

U visas, 65, 71, 216n54

ABOUT THE AUTHOR

Michael A. Olivas is the William B. Bates Distinguished Chair in Law at the University of Houston. In 2016–17, he was Interim President of the UH Downtown. He is the author of sixteen books and has a regular NPR show, "The Law of Rock and Roll," where he reviews legal developments in entertainment law.

Printed in the USA
CPSIA information can be obtained
at www.ICGtesting.com
JSHW081039040524
62494JS00001B/1

9 781479 830992